T Kuehn

# VIOLENCE IN
# MEDIEVAL EUROPE

The Medieval World

Series editor: Julia Smith, University of Glasgow

# VIOLENCE IN MEDIEVAL EUROPE

WARREN C. BROWN

**Longman**
**is an imprint of**

Harlow, England • London • New York • Boston • San Francisco • Toronto
Sydney • Tokyo • Singapore • Hong Kong • Seoul • Taipei • New Delhi
Cape Town • Madrid • Mexico City • Amsterdam • Munich • Paris • Milan

**PEARSON EDUCATION LIMITED**

Edinburgh Gate
Harlow CM20 2JE
Tel: +44 (0)1279 623623
Fax: +44 (0)1279 431059
Website: www.pearsoned.co.uk

First published in Great Britain in 2011

Pearson Education is not responsible for the content of third party internet sites.

ISBN: 978-1-4058-1164-4

*British Library Cataloguing-in-Publication Data*
A catalogue record for this book is available from the British Library

*Library of Congress Cataloging-in-Publication Data*
Brown, Warren C.
Violence in medieval Europe / Warren C. Brown.
p. cm. – (The medieval world)
Includes bibliographical references and index.
ISBN 978-1-4058-1164-4 (pbk.)
1. Violence–Europe–History–To 1500.   2. Violent crimes–Europe–History–
To 1500.   3. Civilization, Medieval.   4. Europe–History–476-1492.   I. Title.
HN380.Z9V525 2010
303.6094′0902–dc22
2010013483

10  9  8  7  6  5  4  3  2  1
14  13  12  11  10

Typeset in 10.5/13pt Galliard by 35
Printed and bound in Malaysia (CTP-VP)

# CONTENTS

CONTENTS

# SERIES EDITOR'S PREFACE

Violence troubles us. It raises acute moral issues. It may invoke potent religious sanctions. It poses challenges to ideas about the proper boundaries between the "public" and "private", between the individual and the wider community and thus may call into question the nature of the "state". And the control of all forms of violence is deeply embedded in common notions of human progress towards a better society. But is it correct simply to dismiss the Middle Ages as violent and therefore somehow backward? We are all in Warren Brown's debt for his refutation of this popular stereotype in this splendid new addition to Longmans Medieval World. In this book, he argues forcefully that to dismiss the Middle Ages as somehow "more violent" than the modern western world is fundamentally to misunderstand that era as well as our own. Instead, he explores a medieval world of differences: different forms of violence, justifications for it, and arguments about it. Above all, he presents the Middle Ages as a world of competing norms of behaviour that cannot be reduced to a simple, linear story. The implications for the ways in which we understand the contemporary world around us are immense.

In this lucid and exceptionally wide-ranging study Brown covers the whole span of the Middle Ages from Merovingian Gaul to the Hundred Years War. In so doing, he helps us to rethink conventional wisdom about the development of royal power and authority, the role of Christianity in social action, the rise of justice, and even the nature of the "self". He is exceptionally well-qualified to guide his readers through this sensitive and fascinating material. An expert on conflict and disputing in the Middle Ages, he brings historical, anthropological and sociological insights to bear on the question of how people in the Middle Ages conceptualized, justified, and deployed violence, in which circumstances, and to what purposes. By refusing to let modern pre-conceptions cloud his judgement, he makes sense of how and why people acted and re-acted as they did. By situating violence within wider competitions for power and legitimacy, he shows how the norms which regulated it shifted over time and thus enables his readers to appreciate the interplay between the normative and the subjective experience of violence.

I welcome this addition to Longmans Medieval World for its breadth of vision, deep humanity and engagement with pressing concerns.

Julia M.H. Smith

# PREFACE AND AUTHOR ACKNOWLEDGEMENTS

This book looks in two directions. On the one hand, it makes a set of arguments about violence in medieval Europe, arguments that concern in particular the ways that medieval Europeans understood violence and how their attitudes towards violence developed over time. It draws, therefore, on the primary sources in Latin, and on the secondary works in German, French, and Italian as well as English that are necessary to support the arguments and to enable my colleagues in the field and their graduate students to properly evaluate them.

On the other hand, and in keeping with the goals of the Medieval World series, the book is designed to serve as a gateway to one of the most vibrant areas of current research in medieval studies, that is, into conflict, power, and political order. In this regard, it is aimed at undergraduate students, scholars in other fields, and those outside academia who are interested in these subjects or in learning about what goes on inside the ivory tower. The book is based, therefore, on primary sources that are readily available in English translation so that these readers too, in the classroom or on their own, can explore what the sources say and decide for themselves what to make of my arguments. Doing so has been made easier not only by the great number of medieval source translations that have been published in recent years, but also by those that have been posted on the World Wide Web. Such online source translations have been matched, as we will see in one important case, by outstanding digitized facsimiles of medieval manuscripts. One can only express profound gratitude for the professionalism of those who put long and intense labor into these facsimiles and then made them freely available to everyone on the Web.

Neither of this book's two faces has required any sacrifice from the other. As it happens, the most important primary sources for the study of medieval violence are also among those that are most important for studying the Middle Ages in general. Most of them have, therefore, been translated. In order to meet the needs of different audiences, I have cited both the original texts and the English translations, including WWW addresses whenever possible. I have also taken advantage of the burgeoning amount of secondary scholarship available on the Web, at sites such as the Internet Medieval Sourcebook (**http://www.fordham.edu/halsall/ sbook.html**) or the Online Reference Book for Medieval Studies (**http:// www.the-orb.net**). I have likewise made use of online language diction- aries, such as the online edition of the *Oxford English Dictionary*, with its extensive entries on etymology (**http://dictionary.oed.com**), the online edition of Lewis and Short's Latin dictionary (**http://www.perseus. tufts.edu/hopper/**), or the Germanic Lexicon Project (**http://lexicon. ff.cuni.cz**), which includes dictionaries of everything from Gothic to Old Saxon.

To write a book of this nature required the help of a number of people. To begin with the colleagues who read and commented on early drafts of parts or the whole: Courtney Booker (as well as the students in his advanced undergraduate seminar at UBC in Vancouver in the fall of 2007), Jennifer R. Davis, and Jason Glenn (as well as the talented and refreshingly direct members of his graduate seminar at USC in the fall of 2007). Piotr Górecki has earned my particular gratitude for his exceptionally close and helpful reading of the manuscript's early chapters. Thanks also go to John Hudson, Paul Hyams, and the graduate students of the seminar "Conflict and the Law in Medieval Europe" held at the Central European University in Budapest, Hungary, in July of 2005, who helped me think through the sources underlying Chapters 3 and 6. Chapters 6 and 9 also benefited a great deal from conversations with Thomas N. Bisson and John Gillingham at a meeting in Kraków, Poland, in April 2007. The Division of Humanities and Social Sciences at Caltech provided me with research leave during the academic year 2006–2007, part of which I spent in Vienna as a guest of the University of Vienna's Institute for Austrian Historical Research, and the Austrian Academy of Sciences' Institute for Medieval Research, studying the German-language scholarship on violence; I thank the directors of these two institutions, Karl Brunner and Walter Pohl. Finally, I tip my hat to the Caltech undergraduates who took my advanced seminar "Violence in Medieval Europe" in the spring of 2008, in which I laid out the sources for the book in sequence to see what real-live undergraduates would make of them. The enthusiasm with which they took up the subject, and the lively and intelligent discussions in which we engaged, gave me confidence and helped me shape my arguments.

I am grateful to the editor for the Medieval World series, Julia Smith, for inviting me to write this book in the first place. Both she and Longman's Mari Shullaw helped me hammer down what was a project of challenging scope into a readable book; I appreciate their help and the time they graciously allowed me. The anonymous reader of the manuscript likewise helped me see where I was succeeding and where

I was not, and saved me from some potentially embarrassing mistakes. Finally, I want to express my gratitude to my wife Louise, and to my sons Christopher, Peter, and Michael, for putting up with the long hours I spend locked away in my study and my occasional crankiness when facing deadlines (though they did get a trip to Vienna out of it). To them the book is dedicated.

# PUBLISHER'S ACKNOWLEDGEMENTS

*We are grateful to the following for permission to reproduce copyright material:*

**Maps**
Map 1 from *Gregory of Tours: The Merovingians*, Broadview (ed. and trans. Alexander C. Murray 2006) p. 271 © University of Toronto Press, Inc. Reprinted with permission of the publisher; Maps 2 and 8 from *A Short History of the Middle Ages*, Broadview (Rosenwein, B.H. 2004) pp. 109 and 293, © University of Toronto Press, Inc. Reprinted with permission of the publisher; Map 6 from *King John*, Longman (Turner, R.V. 1994), with permission of Ralph V. Turner, Professor Emeritus, Florida State University; Map 7 from *Frederick II: A Medieval Emperor*, Penguin (Abulafia, D. 1988), with permission of the Glenfield Trust.

**Text**
Extracts on pages 1 and 22–3 from CHRONICLES by Froissart, translated by Geoffrey Brereton (Penguin Classics 1968, Revised 1978). Translation copyright © Geoffrey Brereton, 1968. Reproduced by permission of Penguin Books Ltd; Poetry on page 11 from *The Song of Roland*, Penguin Classics (trans. Dorothy L. Sayers 1957) p. 62 with permission of David Higham Associates Limited; Extract on page 15 from THE HISTORY OF THE FRANKS by Gregory of Tours, translated with an introduction by Lewis Thorpe (Penguin Classics, 1974). Copyright © Lewis Thorpe, 1974. Reproduced by permission of Penguin Books Ltd; Extracts on pages 15, 150 and 154 from *Ottonian Germany: The Chronicon of Thietmar of Merseburg*, Manchester University Press (trans. David A. Warner 2001) pp. 230–1, 342, 275.

**Plates**
Plates 1–6 courtesy of Herzog August Bibliothek Wolfenbüettel:

Plate 1, page 229: Herzog August Bibliothek Wolfenbüettel: Cod. Guelf. 3.1 Aug. 2°, fol. 1r
Plate 2, page 233: Herzog August Bibliothek Wolfenbüettel: Cod. Guelf. 3.1 Aug. 2°, fol. 19v

PUBLISHER'S ACKNOWLEDGEMENTS

Plate 3, page 234: Herzog August Bibliothek Wolfenbüettel: Cod.
Guelf. 3.1 Aug. 2°, fol. 9v
Plate 4, page 237: Herzog August Bibliothek Wolfenbüettel: Cod.
Guelf. 3.1 Aug. 2°, fol. 42r
Plate 5, page 240: Herzog August Bibliothek Wolfenbüettel: Cod.
Guelf. 3.1 Aug. 2°, fol. 29v
Plate 6, page 242: Herzog August Bibliothek Wolfenbüettel: Cod.
Guelf. 3.1 Aug. 2°, fol. 27r

In some instances we have been unable to trace the owners of copyright
material, and we would appreciate any information that would enable us
to do so.

# ABBREVIATIONS

| | |
|---|---|
| Bosworth and Toller | Joseph Bosworth and T. Northcote Toller, *An Anglo-Saxon Dictionary* (Oxford: Oxford University Press, 1882–98 and Clarendon Press, 1921), online as part of the Germanic Lexicon Project at **http://lexicon.ff.cuni.cz/texts/oe_bosworthtoller_about.html** |
| DRW | *Deutsches Rechtswörterbuch*, online edition, **http://www.rzuser.uni-heidelberg.de/~cd2/drw/** |
| LDM | Robert Auty *et al.*, eds., *Lexikon des Mittelalters* (Munich: Artemis & Winkler Verlag, 1977–98) |
| Lewis and Short | Charleton T. Lewis and Charles Short, eds., *A Latin Dictionary. Founded on Andrews' edition of Freund's Latin dictionary* (Oxford: Clarendon Press, 1879), online at the Perseus Digital Library, **http://www.perseus.tufts.edu/hopper/** |
| Linc. | Doris M. Stenton, ed., *The Earliest Lincolnshire Assize Rolls, A.D. 1202–1209* (Lincoln: Lincoln Record Society, 1926) |
| Mansi | Joannes Dominicus Mansi *et al.*, eds., *Sacrorum conciliorum nova et amplissima collectio*, 53 vols. (H. Welter, 1900–1927) |
| MGH | *Monumenta Germaniae Historica* Capit. = Capitularia regum Francorum Epist. = Epistolae LL = Leges SSRM = Scriptores rerum Merovingicarum |
| MHW | *Mittelhochdeutsches Wörterbuch. Mit Benutzung des Nachlasses von Georg Friedrich Benecke ausgearbeitet von Wilhelm Müller und Friedrich Zarncke.* 4 vols. (Stuttgart: S. Hirzel, 1990; reprint of the original, Leipzig 1854–66), **http://germazope.uni-trier.de/Projects/WBB/woerterbuecher/** |
| MSF | *Liber Miraculorum Sancte Fidis*, ed. Luca Robertini (Spoleto: Centro Italiano di studi sull'alto medioevo, 1994) |

NCMH — *The New Cambridge Medieval History*, 7 vols. (Cambridge: Cambridge University Press, 1995–2005)

Niermeyer — Jan Frederick Niermeyer, *Mediae latinitatis lexicon minus*, 2nd rev. ed., 2 vols. (Leiden: Brill, 2002)

OED — *Oxford English Dictionary*, online edition: **http://dictionary.oed.com**

ORB — *The Online Reference Book for Medieval Studies*, **http://www.the-orb.net**

SM — A. Richard, ed., *Chartes et documents pour servir a l'histoire de l'abbaye de Saint-Maixent*, vol. 1 (Poitiers: Oudin, 1887)

WGS — A. Fick *et al.*, *Wörterbuch der indogermanischen Sprachen: Dritter Teil: Wortschatz der Germanischen Spracheinheit* (Göttingen: Vandenhoeck and Ruprecht: 1909); revised by Alf Torp and placed online as part of the Germanic Lexicon Project, **http://lexicon.ff.cuni.cz/**

## chapter one

# VIOLENCE AND THE MEDIEVAL HISTORIAN

The English knight hit Sir Regnault de Roye very hard near the top of his helm, but did no other damage to him; Sir Regnault hit him on the shield with such a firm, powerful thrust, delivered with so strong an arm – for he was one of the strongest and toughest jousters in France at that time and also he was truly in love with a gay and beautiful young lady, and this contributed greatly to his success in all his undertakings – that his lance pierced the left-hand side of the English knight's shield and went straight into his arm. As it did so, the lance broke, the longer part falling to the ground and the shorter part remaining in the shield with the steel point in the arm.

*Jean Froissart (c. 1337–c. 1410),* Chronicles, *IV, on the tournament held at Saint-Inglevert in 1390.*[1]

Medieval violence seems to exercise a certain fascination for a great many people, as witnessed by the violent tenor of movies or books set in the Middle Ages and of the ever more popular fantasy role-playing games set in medieval-like worlds. The appeal perhaps lies in the fact that violence in the Middle Ages was personal, direct, and visceral; it involved not guns or bombs but swords, knives, and lances, wooden staffs, clubs, and fists. According to the texts that describe it, it was often motivated by equally visceral feelings: anger, shame, and the craving for revenge, but also love, pride, and the desire for justice and glory. Medieval texts make no effort to hide the effects of violence. They tell us quite openly of torn or burnt flesh, spurting blood, the noise of metal striking metal, and the suffering of victims. It is possibly because of these qualities that medieval violence can be compellingly interesting, particularly to undergraduate students; the courses I have taught on violence in the Middle Ages, or on its purveyors such as knights, have consistently been the most well-attended of my offerings.

I too am drawn to medieval violence, not simply because it fascinates me as it does my students, but also because it opens up a route into the medieval worldview. From a modern perspective, medieval accounts of violence can seem contradictory. They can present violence as lawless and anarchic, as a force for evil that disrupts the right order of the world. They can also present it as a tool of right and justice, as a weapon for the protection of the poor and helpless, and even as God's way of aiding his faithful. Violence lays waste to villages and towns; it offers its disciples glory, power, and lasting fame. Violence desecrates churches and monasteries; it is also the means by which God and his followers protect the faithful and their interests and avenge wrong. One gets the sense in fact that violence was not considered intrinsically bad. It could rather be good or bad depending on who was using it against whom and for what purpose. More puzzling to modern western sensibilities, it seems that anyone could wield violence. Though bearers of constituted authority, such as counts or kings, did use violence against wrongdoers or those that harmed their interests, so did many other people, often with the applause of their fellows.

Medieval violence presents us, therefore, with attitudes towards violence and its legitimate use, but more fundamentally towards right, wrong, power, and the proper ordering of human society, which differ profoundly from those that dominate modern western societies. We live at the dawn of the twenty-first century in a world in which the dominant idea of order claims a monopoly on the legitimate use of violence for the state. At the same time, our world is riven by violence, much of which is very difficult to understand when seen through the lens of western ideas about order. Societies that appear to be more violent than our own, or acts of violence that seem particularly incomprehensible – i.e., cruel, unjustified, wanton, irrational, or driven by religious beliefs – are often called "medieval".[2] Those who do so apparently see the Middle Ages as having been similarly violent and/or disordered.

Yet the societies of the modern West are direct heirs to those of medieval Europe. Studying medieval violence thus gives us an opportunity to explore attitudes towards violence and order that are at once foreign and yet ancestors to our own. If we try to understand how medieval people thought about such things as justice and injustice, power and responsibility, and political order, we might get a sense for how some of our own attitudes towards violence evolved. We come away from the effort being able to see – without necessarily validating – violence in our own world that we do not understand not inevitably as irrational but rather driven possibly by worldviews and ideas of order that are different from our own.

> So violent and motley was life, that it bore the mixed smell of blood and roses.
> *Johan Huizinga,* The Waning of the Middle Ages *(1921).*[3]

Were medieval societies more violent than those of the modern West? Much of the past scholarship on the Middle Ages certainly thought so.[4] Two decades after the Dutch historian Johan Huizinga published his famous work on the end of the Middle Ages, the French medievalist Marc Bloch in his *Feudal Society* (1939–40) declared that "violence was . . . deep-rooted in the social structure and in the mentality of the age".[5] Bloch's countryman Georges Duby connected violence particularly with knights; "the brutality of these men," he commented in *The History of French Civilization* (1958), "accustomed as they are to fighting wild animals, and incapable of checking their anger. The battlefields described in the *chansons de geste* are strewn with severed heads and scattered brains."[6]

Statements such as this reflect the impression created by all kinds of medieval sources, ranging from histories and literary works to hagiography and charters.[7] These sources were, however, as interested in recording the spectacular, the dramatic, the entertaining, the shocking, the legally important, or the polemically useful as are the stories, journalism, records, and blogs of our own day. It is hard to say for certain, therefore, how well they represent the experience of most medieval people.

One might look for safety in statistics. Though the difficulties are profound, efforts have indeed been made to quantify levels of violence in parts of medieval Europe and to compare them to those in modern societies. One of the best remains James B. Given's 1977 discussion of homicide rates in thirteenth-century England.[8] Given chose homicide as a relatively clear and measurable index of violence (though more on this below), and looked for incidents recorded in royal circuit court, or eyre court, records from individual English counties, or shires. He chose as his measure one that is still in use, namely the number of homicides per 100,000 of population per year. Using his own estimates of the population in his target counties, Given found the highest homicide rate in Warwickshire in 1232, namely 64 homicides per 100,000 per year. The lowest was in the county of Bristol in 1227 and again in 1248, at 4/100,000/year. Over time, Given found that the homicide rate remained highest in Warwickshire, at c. 47/100,000/year over 25 years, while the lowest was in the county of Norfolk, at c. 9/100,000/year over 23 years.

Population estimates for medieval Europe, however, come with a very large margin of error; even the relatively dense documentation of thirteenth-century England permits at best only an educated guess about the number of people living in a given area. So Given redid his calculations using two other population estimates, one done by J.C. Russell for England in 1377 and one produced for the British parliament in 1801.[9] The first of these calculations produced a high of 30/100,000/year (likewise Warwickshire in 1232) and a low of 11/100,000/year (county of

Norfolk, 1250); the second produced a high of 18.9/100,000/year (Bedfordshire, 1276) and a low of 6.8/100,000/year (Kent, 1227).

Given then noted that the United Kingdom as a whole from 1930 onwards had a more or less stable homicide rate of c. 0.4/100,000/year; the United States in 1974 had a homicide rate of 9.7/100,000/year. Within the United States, figures for major cities in the mid-twentieth century ranged from 5.7/100,000/year for Philadelphia to 15.1/100,000/year for Miami. Since Given wrote, various national and international agencies have continued to compile homicide statistics. The UK Home Office, for example, has issued a set of international comparisons of homicide rates for the years 1999–2001.[10] The lowest rates were found in the European Union as a whole, which boasted a homicide rate of 1.6/100,000/year for the period. The highest individual rates within the EU were in Finland at 2.9, Northern Ireland at 2.7, and Scotland at 2.2/100,000/year. The Home Office report found higher rates of homicide outside the EU. Lithuania and Estonia, for example, each had 10.6/100,000/year, while Russia had an eye-catching homicide rate of 22.1/100,000/year. The United States in the same period had a rate of 5.6/100,000/year,[11] but interesting peaks and valleys appear in the numbers for individual cities. The report found 8.1/100,000/year in San Francisco and 8.7/100,000/year in New York City, as compared to a modest 2.6/100,000/year in London (for which the 1244 eyre court session had produced a figure of 8, and the 1276 session a figure of 15/100,000/year). Washington DC was, however, in a different league, at 42.9/100,000/year.

When stacked up against Given's for thirteenth-century England, these figures would seem to indicate clearly that life in high medieval England was more violent than life in the modern developed world. Modern homicide rates are for the most part lower, even much lower than Given's, the range of Given's population estimates notwithstanding. And yet, it is hard to make this claim absolutely. Given's estimate for Bristol in 1227, 4/100,000/year, while higher than the 1999–2001 EU numbers produced by the UK Home Office, is lower than the US average. The picture gets more difficult to assess when we break apart the Home Office's aggregate figures. With Estonia and Lithuania we start to approach the low end of Given's range for Warwick (11/100,000/year); with Russia we enter into it. With Washington DC we are comfortably above the middle.

To make matters worse, homicide itself as a measure can be misleading. As Given himself points out, thirteenth-century England did not possess the level of weapons technology available to modern killers. In 1970, he notes, guns were estimated in Chicago to be five times as likely to kill as knives.[12] Medieval homicide rates may not, therefore, include the number of times someone tried to kill someone else but failed. By the same token, the modern west possesses medical technology vastly superior to that of medieval England. An assault that would in the latter have resulted in death may well be survivable today and thus not show up in the records as a homicide.[13]

It is possible, therefore – counterintuitive as it might seem – that thirteenth-century England as a whole was not significantly more violent than the US or EU around the turn of the twenty-first century. Warwick may have been thirteenth-century England's Washington DC, while Bristol suffered homicide rates only slightly higher than many places in the modern EU. All of this is to say that while much of the US or EU experiences far less violence than much of thirteenth-century England, some city dwellers in the United States and some inhabitants of Russia endure about the same level. And some parts of thirteenth-century England experienced levels of violence little different from those found in much of the west today.

What is certain, however, is that medieval societies were *differently* violent. As I noted above, violence played a different and in many cases more central role in many medieval societies than it does in modern western ones; it shows up in medieval sources in contexts that are often unimaginable today. This feature of medieval violence, in fact, may well be responsible for the Middle Ages' reputation as a violent epoch; a different range of people used violence in situations, in ways, and according to norms different from those we have been conditioned by our own experience to expect.

In recent years, a number of scholars have investigated medieval violence from this perspective; that is, they have asked not how violent were the Middle Ages but rather: how were the Middle Ages violent? They have approached this vast subject either by focusing on a particular part of the Middle Ages,[14] a particular place,[15] on a particular class of sources (such as literature or charters),[16] on particular social groups within medieval society (such as knights or peasants),[17] on a particular kind of violence (such as vengeance killings),[18] or on particular methodological approaches to violence (such as those informed by anthropology or literary theory).[19]

With the help of some of these studies, I would like to explore the variety of ways that medieval people used violence and understood its use, and the range of norms according to which they legitimated or criticized it. I will offer a series of case studies covering the full range of the Middle Ages in time, and much of medieval Europe in space. These case studies will focus on times and places, as well as on sources, that I think are particularly accessible and illuminating and/or that have drawn significant scholarly attention or provoked particularly intense debate. At the end, I will sketch a picture of how medieval norms of violence developed over time and space.

> At that time, sinners were rising up like stalks of wheat. Evil people wasted the vineyard of the Lord just as briars and thorns choke the harvest of the land. Therefore it pleased bishops, abbots, and other religious men that a council be held at which the taking of booty would be prohibited and the property of the saints, which had been unjustly stolen, would be restored. Other evils that fouled the fair countenance of the holy church of God were also struck down by the sharp points of anathemas.
>
> *Letaldus of Micy,* The Journey of the Body of St Junianus to the Council of Charroux *(989; text composed c. mid 990s?).*[20]

To begin with, we have to be clear about what exactly we mean by "violence", and what exactly we mean by "norms". The *Oxford English Dictionary* offers the following definition of violence: "the exercise of physical force so as to inflict injury on, or cause damage to, persons or property; action or conduct characterized by this; treatment or usage tending to cause bodily injury or forcibly interfering with personal freedom".[21] This definition probably captures the gut sense for what "violence" means that many if not most people share. Violence is the application of physical force in a way that hurts someone or something or that aims to hurt someone or something, such as people, animals, buildings, or other property. Violence causes pain and injury. The pain and injury do not have to be immediately visible. They can be internal, such as the concussion injuries Flemish townspeople in the fourteenth century inflicted when they struck knights wearing plate armor with spears sporting heavy metal cudgels.[22] Or they can be mental or emotional, such as the anguish and mental trauma caused by seeing one's relatives killed or one's house or farm destroyed. Violence is much easier to grasp, however, when the pain and injury are visible, that is, when one sees flowing blood, broken bodies, and shattered buildings. Violence crosses boundaries. It is physical contact without permission (hence the corresponding verb, "to violate"); the quintessential example of this aspect of violence is, of course, rape. Violence also restricts one's freedom; one cannot protect or control one's body or property as one would wish.

Because the OED definition is so straightforward, it is tempting to think that violence as a category of action or event is timeless or independent of differences in human culture or experience. Unfortunately (especially for historians of violence) this is not true. Violence is not a static, transcultural concept, nor is it an absolute that always transcends differences in perspective.[23] To begin with the word violence itself: the English word, as a catch-all term for the kinds of actions described above, does appear in the Middle Ages, but only from the end of the thirteenth century.[24] As it is used today, the word encompasses acts that for most of the Middle Ages would have been described in Latin and with different words. Violence derives from the Latin *violentia*, which originally denoted a particular quality of behavior, namely vehemence, impetuosity, or ferocity.[25] To capture the sorts of phenomena covered by the modern word violence, medieval sources in general tend to use words more specific to what was happening, such as *occidere* or *interficere* (to kill), *vulnere* (to wound), *pugnare* (to fight), *percutere* (to strike), *perdere* (to destroy), *rapere* (to seize, plunder, or rape), *incendere* (to burn) or *per vim* (with force).[26]

When we use the word violence to capture such phenomena as described in Latin texts, therefore, we are uniting them under our own heuristic umbrella. We are perfectly entitled to do so; the OED definition of violence does map onto something real and observable in medieval sources. Medieval people hurt or killed other people; they forcibly seized people or property; they burned, destroyed, or pillaged buildings; they caused emotional injury or trauma. What is not always easy to see, however, is when they did so and, if they did, whether everyone involved would have agreed on whether a given act of violence was legitimate or illegitimate.

In a seminal essay on violence, William Ian Miller has identified three figures whose perspectives we have to understand in order to decide whether an act was violent and, if so, whether it was legitimate or not: the victim, the victimizer (or perpetrator), and the observer.[27] The victim experiences the violence, the victimizer/perpetrator carries it out, and the observer witnesses and interprets it (either directly or after the fact through someone else's report). The victim might most easily draw our sympathy, especially if there is blood involved, that is, physical evidence that the victim had experienced terror, pain, and loss of limb or life. Correspondingly, it might seem natural to condemn the perpetrator; he or she caused the terror, pain, and loss of limb or life. But how an observer evaluates what happened really depends on whom he or she asks. In modern accounts of police activity, for example, some victims complain that they were subjected to unjustified violence. The police sometimes respond that they had simply restrained someone who posed a threat to society.[28] It is also not as easy as we might like to identify the figures in Miller's triad. As Miller himself pointed out, the lines between the figures can become very blurred.[29] The victim can become, after the fact, the observer or reporter; so can the perpetrator. A third-party observer can, depending on his or her own worldview and position with respect to the victim or perpetrator, easily identify with one or the other.

Regardless of his or her position in the triad, everyone involved in an act of violence interprets and legitimates what he or she has experienced, done, or seen according to the social norms to which he or she gives priority. In other words, the observer or reporter's position, whether he or she is the victim, perpetrator, or a third party, is embedded in the norms about what constitutes violence and about when violence is justified that he or she believes to apply, believes ought to apply, or has an interest in applying. When faced with a case of possible police brutality, for example, one person might say that the victim had experienced illegitimate violence. Another might argue that the victim was a criminal trying to escape the consequences of his actions who had forced the police to subdue him. One could easily imagine which position might be taken by a politician campaigning on a platform of law and order as opposed to a social worker fighting for the rights of the disadvantaged. It is entirely possible, therefore, that an account of violence might not really tell us much at all about what happened. It might say more about the reporter's attitude towards the other figures and the preconceptions he or she brings to the situation.

Violence lends itself to rhetorical use because it is often so messy, painful, and sympathy evoking. The words and adjectives associated by a culture with illegitimate violence in particular (such as "horrific", "raging", or "bloody") trigger very strong emotions. They are, therefore, very good for making those that hear or read them think badly of their target. In short, even while violence might seem to be a fairly straightforward phenomenon, we have to be constantly aware that in any given case violence might simply be something of which we accuse someone when we do not like them or their actions, or when we are contesting interests with them and are trying to gain someone else's sympathy.[30]

Nevertheless, rhetorical charges of violence can still be quite fruitful for our purposes, because to succeed they have to connect with society's ideas of what constitutes violence and what the differences are between good violence and bad violence. The norms from which observers or reporters can choose in order to identify, evaluate, and judge an act of violence are limited by the pool of norms that are available in their cultural environment. We can therefore say something about that pool of norms by sifting through what they say.

And if anyone from among our sworn followers wishes to engage in a fight or in some struggle against his enemies, and he calls to himself someone from among his peers so that he might render aid to him, and he [the one called] does not wish to and then remains indifferent, let the benefice which he has held be taken away from him and be give to him who has remained firm in his steadfastness and fidelity.

*Charlemagne, Capitulary of Aachen (801–813), c. 20.*[31]

I define norms as models, standards, or patterns of social behavior that are accepted or expected by members of a group.[32] They are patterns of conduct, reflecting a shared or common sense of "the right thing to do". Such patterned behavior creates what Neil MacCormick has called "normative order". To paraphrase MacCormick, whenever people con-⎤ duct themselves in relation to others on the basis of an opinion about the right thing to do which they suppose to be mutual, there is order, provided that there is sufficient overlap in people's opinions about what the right thing to do is (there can hardly be order when each member of a group holds a different opinion about what is right and what is wrong).⎦

Norms can be stated explicitly in some form. If they are not, we can infer them by watching how people behave; that is, we can look at the behavior of a given group, identify patterns of behavior, and try to articulate the norm or framework of norms that the members of the group seem to be following. Granted, the actual people involved might not have been consciously thinking in terms of the norm or norms we have derived from their behavior, or, if they were, they might not formulate it in the way that we have. Moreover, if we were able to ask them, different people might express the norms differently, or even disagree with each other about what the norms were. They might tell us that they were following one norm while in reality following another,[33] or that their behavior violated their own norms, but that circumstances forced them to act as they did.[34] Nevertheless, if the evidence suggests strongly enough that people are acting in patterned ways that can be explained by norms, we are justified – particularly in historical cases where we cannot inquire – in articulating those norms to the best of our ability.

Explicitly expressed norms are easier to grasp. They might show up in our sources in a couple of ways. An author, in order to legitimate behavior of which he approves, or delegitimize behavior of which he does not approve, might write a story about it and express an opinion about how things were done or ought to have been done. No matter how strongly our source expresses his norm, it need not be a norm agreed with by any of the people whose actions he is describing, or by anyone else for that matter; simply because a given writer or text declares a norm does not mean that anyone else in his society agreed or paid attention. Unless our source is a complete outsider to the society he is writing about, however, we can assume that the norm is one that is at least comprehensible in his world.

Another possibility is that someone claiming or recognized as having authority over others explicitly formulates a norm, either by oral declaration (recorded by someone else) or in the form of a normative text. We can call such an explicit norm backed by authority a rule.[35] A rule might express a consensus among members of the group it is targeted at. Or it might not; it might reflect an attempt to impose a new normative order, or to modify an existing one, or to get a subgroup that disagrees with the dominant idea of order to go along with it. The latter seems to be the case with the chapter from Charlemagne's capitulary of Aachen quoted above. In the early ninth century, followers of the king were supposed to respond when their fellows asked for help in fighting their enemies. Some followers apparently preferred when such situations arose not to get involved, prompting Charlemagne to remind them pointedly what they were supposed to do.

It is when a person or a group of persons with authority over an entire society promulgates rules and tries to enforce them over a long span of time that we reach the arena of law.[36] Rule making and rule enforcing become institutionalized. It is dangerous to apply this definition of law to the Middle Ages, however, because we cannot assume that this is what medieval texts meant when they used words that we might translate as "law". Law is in fact very difficult to grasp for much of the period. The Latin term for law, *lex*, originally meant more or less the same thing as law in the modern sense: a binding norm (*ius*) that had been committed to writing in an authoritative form (thus becoming *lex*).[37] By the early Middle Ages, however, what *lex* meant is much harder to understand. The word overlaps, and sometimes appears to be almost interchangeable with, related Latin words such as *ius* or *usus*, which strictly translate as "right" and "custom" respectively.[38]

In France and England after the turn of the first millenium, *lex* (*laga* or *lei* in Old English or Old French respectively) could refer either to written law, ranging from the law of the Old Testament to a new law issued by a king, or to all binding norms written or unwritten. It could refer simply to what was considered correct or just in a given situation. It could be contrasted with agreement or settlement, but it could also refer to the terms of an agreement or settlement. Law differed from violent self-help, but some violent self-help was lawful. It is also sometimes difficult to distinguish *lex/laga/lei* from *ius/riht/dreit* = "right", as in "this property belonged to him by right".[39] Moreover, *lex* did not necessarily stem from one particular authority. Christian bishops, for example, could issue *leges* for the members of their own households.[40]

From the later eleventh and twelfth centuries, the medieval idea of law gradually came to focus on what we can call "learned law", that is, written, codified, and rationally organized bodies of norms that were studied and taught in law schools by legal scholars and that came to possess their own logic, rules, and vocabulary. One such law (Roman law), however, transcended actual governments and existed seemingly of its own right in its own legal space (though another such law, canon law, was firmly anchored in the government of the Roman Church, and a third, the English Common Law, in the authority of the English kings).[41]

Along our journey, we will look at how law related to and affected the use of violence in several different contexts. We will do so, however, with the constant awareness that the English word law has associations that might not apply to the world of our sources.

> [Ganelon] says to Roland: "Fool! What has made thee mad?
> I am thy step-sire, and all these know I am,
> And me thou namest to seek Marsilion's camp!
> If God but grant I ever thence come back
> I'll wreak on thee such ruin and such wrack
> That thy life long my vengeance shall not slack."
> Roland replies: "This is all boast and brag!"
>        The Song of Roland *(c. 1100), v. 20, ll. 286–92.*[42]

As noted above, different people could observe, experience, or participate in the same act of violence at the same time but understand it in different ways depending on their circumstances, perspectives, and purposes. Some medieval authors understood this perfectly well. Such a clash of norms, for example, forms the central conflict in the early French vernacular poem *The Song of Roland*. Written down sometime around 1100, *Roland* tells the mythologized story of a historical figure, Roland, who served Charlemagne in the late eighth century. Nevertheless, the poem puts its characters squarely in the world of the late eleventh and early twelfth centuries, that is, of knights fighting on horseback with lances and swords, of "sweet France", and of a campaign against Muslims that evokes the First Crusade. As the poem opens, Charlemagne and his Franks have been campaigning against the Muslims in Spain for seven long years. Tired and eager to return home, they are willing to accept a peace-offer from their foes, an offer that included a wagonload of treasure and a promise from the Muslim king to accept Christian baptism. All of Charlemagne's barons urge him to agree, save Roland, who is Charlemagne's nephew and best knight, and one of the Twelve Peers of France. Roland urges Charlemagne not to trust the Muslims, but instead to finish the job they had started.

Nevertheless persuaded to accept the Muslim offer, Charlemagne asks for volunteers to lead the embassy. Roland and others of the Peers step forward, but Charlemagne refuses them. His Peers are too important and the mission is very dangerous; the last Frankish envoys to the Muslim king were decapitated. Roland then suggests his stepfather, Ganelon, and Charlemagne agrees. Ganelon is outraged. Not only has he been insulted – he is obviously less important than Roland – but he has been ordered to face his possible death at the urging of his own stepson. Roland has thus betrayed the loyalty due to kin. Ganelon therefore (in the passage quoted above) declares his intent to take vengeance on Roland.

Ganelon achieves his revenge by betraying the Frankish army. He suggests to the Muslim king that his forces ambush the Frankish rear-guard as it moves through a narrow pass in the Pyrenees mountains. Commanding the rear-guard would be Roland. The ambush succeeds. Despite a heroic resistance by Roland, his companions Oliver and Archbishop Turpin, and the rest of his troops, the rear-guard is killed to the last man. Only a despairing signal from Roland on his mighty war-horn alerts Charlemagne, who comes thundering back to exact his own vengeance on the treacherous foe.

Ganelon is captured, and taken back to Charlemagne's palace in France for a trial.[43] There the clash of norms involved in Roland's death is laid bare. Ganelon argues that he had a valid grievance; he had been insulted and betrayed by his own kin. He had moreover publicly declared his intent to claim revenge and had done so. He was, therefore, perfectly within his rights to arrange for Roland's death. His argument gains some sympathy among the gathered Frankish magnates. Thirty of his kinsmen agree to support him with their lives, and some of Charlemagne's advisors urge the emperor to forgive Ganelon and receive him back into his service. Only one man, Thierry, argues to the contrary. Ganelon has committed treason, Thierry declares; though Roland had injured him, Roland's service to Charlemagne should have guaranteed his safety. Thierry's position ultimately triumphs because it has the support of God. A judicial duel is held between Thierry and one of Ganelon's kinsmen. Thierry prevails with God's help. Ganelon and his entire group of kin and followers are executed.

These two norms – one legitimating a violent response to personal injury or insult and one subordinating the use of violence to the needs and interests of the ruler – are two of the most important norms of violence visible in medieval sources. Medieval people appealed to these norms, but to others as well, according to their needs, their interests, and their particular situations. The story of violence in the Middle Ages, therefore, can be told as the story of the norms that people invoked as they sought to justify the use of violence by themselves or their allies, or to criticize the use of violence by others.

Violence . . . was as normal and enduring as the public order it afflicted. That it was dis-order, no one who placed their hope in legitimate authority doubted.

*Thomas N. Bisson, "The Feudal Revolution" (1994), 13.*[44]

At this point it needs to be asked: does violence have to be governed by norms at all? For example, what about pathological violence, i.e. violence that results from mental disorder? Unfortunately, it is very difficult to pin down what different societies regard as pathological. As Michel Foucault and others have made clear, pathology lies very much in the eye of the beholder, who is in turn shaped by his own culture and context.[45] One time and place's pathology might be another's valid and normal behavior. Feeding Christians to lions, for example, was regarded by many good, upstanding Romans of the first and second centuries as perfectly understandable, and even necessary for the moral health of society. To many of us, this kind of public execution might seem to reflect a disordered community blood lust.[46]

What about violence provoked by strong emotions?[47] Violence is intimately linked with emotions, especially fear and anger, but also in some cases (as we will see) with passions such as joy and love. It is tempting to assume that emotions are the antithesis of order, that when people are confronted with a situation that provokes a strong emotion such as anger, fear, or disgust, they sometimes simply act in response to that emotion, without spending any time thinking about the norms that according to their society ought to apply. A flagrant injury provokes outrage; the injured party immediately responds with violence.

There is considerable evidence that emotions are hard-wired into the human organism and that physiological responses to emotions are similar across human cultures. There is also considerable evidence, however, that the experiences that trigger a given emotion, and the ways that people react to that emotion, are socially constructed.[48] What makes someone angry in one society may not be the same as what makes someone angry in another; what one does when angry may not be the same either. Moreover, a person who acted violently out of anger, when asked after the fact, will usually explain his or her behavior in terms of some normative framework, even if it is as simple as "he made me angry by doing/saying X and therefore I killed him". Since norms play an essential role in triggering emotions and in channeling responses, it seems unlikely that emotion-driven violence can be normless – though such violence may well violate a community's idea of which norms should be followed. A written account of emotion-driven violence may, therefore, tell us about the social norms and beliefs that provoke strong emotions and about the responses that these emotions trigger. It may also, however, do no such thing. As we will see, one popular tactic for blackening an opponent is to accuse him or her of having been violent without cause or reason, or of having been driven by wild and senseless emotion. Such an accusation will, however, tell us a great deal about the norms that the author thinks were being violated or ought to have been upheld.

What about violence driven by greed, ambition, or the desire for power, and carried out simply because one can? If one were to try to articulate a norm behind such violence, it might be: "you have something I need or want, therefore I am entitled to take it because I can and because you cannot stop me". This sort of violence certainly takes place in all societies, and it is disruptive in all sorts of ways. People forcibly steal and rape, and injure and kill, because they have the power, because they want to, and because they want the fruits; such violent acts quite obviously have threatened and continue to threaten or collapse political orders. However, they do not have to; this kind of violence does not by definition mean that normative order has failed.

If the sort of violence described above is going to be more than a short-term activity, it runs into some natural limits. Supposing one steals for profit and kills those who resist. The first time or two will be successful. Sooner or later, however, one's target, be it an individual, a farm, or a town, will either be dead, have run out of things to steal, or have become good enough at defending itself that the potential cost of stealing becomes too high. Our perpetrator will have to move on to fresher and less prepared targets, that is, become what Mancur Olson has called a "roaming bandit".[49] Unless one is prepared to move over a very wide range, however, this well too will eventually run dry after all targets have become exhausted or too costly to hit (unless one is in a situation like a small-time criminal in a large modern city, where the scale of violence is small and the supply of potentially lucrative targets is virtually inexhaustible). Over the long term, it is much more profitable to work out an arrangement with one's target, or with a limited and coherent group of targets, whereby one guarantees it the stability necessary to continue to generate wealth that one can take in exchange for a promise to protect it from other bandits and to leave it enough income to make generating wealth worthwhile. In other words, one becomes a "stationary bandit" running what amounts to a protection racket. At this stage, the bandit and the target by necessity become bound up over time in a set of norms about what level of extortion is permissible, what levels of violence are necessary to maintain the arrangement, what sorts of threats obligate the bandit to defend those whom he is claiming to protect, etc.[50] Olson has gone so far as to suggest that all human government, with its taxation, police forces, armies, and laws, originated in some fashion from stationary banditry.

An altercation now arose between certain Franks in Tournai. The immediate cause was that the son of one of them angrily and repeatedly rebuked the son of another, who had married his sister, for neglecting his wife and going after loose women. The young man at fault took no notice. The ill-feeling reached such a pitch that the girl's brother attacked his brother-in-law and killed him, with some of his relations. Then the brother in his turn was killed by those who had supported his brother-in-law. In the end not a single member of either family remained alive, except one survivor for whom there was no opponent left.

> *Gregory, Bishop of Tours (c. 539–594)*, Ten Books of Histories, *X/27*.[51]

Then, [the king] sent Bishop Henry of Würzburg and Erkanbald, abbot of Fulda, to burn and destroy the burg Schweinfurt. When they arrived, Margrave Henry's illustrious mother, Eila, received and greeted them, as was proper for such persons. As soon as she understood the nature of the king's orders, she became agitated and hurried to the church, declaring that she would rather die in the flames than cooperate in the burning of this building by departing alive. Hence, the previously mentioned lords, putting aside secular concerns in favor of the love of Christ, modified the punishment and merely pulled down the walls and outbuildings. They also mollified the sorrowful woman with the promise that they would themselves restore everything, whenever the king's favor permitted.

> *Thietmar of Merseburg*, Chronicon, *V.38 (1003)*.[52]

As noted above, people can be violent in response to entirely different needs or desires, that is, those prompted by emotion, by honor and insult, by wrongs that demand to be made right. When violence erupts in such contexts, it can be very disruptive and touch off what is frequently called a "feud".[53]

Feud is one of those terms that historians like to argue about. The argument rests on the quite reasonable point that for scholars to communicate successfully, they need to agree on what their terms mean. Is any act of personal violence in retaliation for a perceived wrong, that is, for the sake of vengeance, by definition a feud? Or does a violent conflict only reach the level of feud when one such attack follows another in a tit-for-tat chain? Violence for the sake of vengeance shows up quite frequently in medieval sources, often in a tantalizing but ambiguous connection with words such as *faidus* that evoke, but may not necessarily have meant the same thing, as our modern word feud. It should come as no surprise, therefore, that medievalists have argued about how to label it. Some use the term feud for any act of violence carried out for the sake of vengeance. Others restrict the term to series of tit-for-tat actions that demonstrate a lasting enmity transcending its immediate cause. Others restrict it to hostility between kin-groups, while still others, faced with sources that do not allow one to put a particular quarrel clearly in one box or another, opt for terms such as "feud-like" behavior.[54]

Since feud has been understood in so many different ways by so many different people, I am reluctant to use it as a category of analysis, and I will therefore avoid the term wherever possible. I think it is much more helpful and illuminating to talk about acts of violence in the terms used by the sources themselves, which usually have to do with things like right or wrong, vengeance, etc. Otherwise we risk imposing artificial distinctions on our sources and thus limiting our inquiry in an artificial way.

As suggested by the quotation above from Gregory of Tours, vengeance attacks can destroy the parties involved and potentially the society around them as well. So is this kind of violence the enemy of normative order? How do societies that admit (not to mention glorify) vengeance survive? This question was tackled in the latter half of the twentieth century by social and legal anthropologists, who turned it on non-western societies that appeared to function stably despite the absence of the laws, judicial systems, etc. that in modern western societies limit violent self-help. An important result of this work is the idea of the so-called "peace in the feud" advanced by Max Gluckman and since elaborated on by others.[55] According to this model, violent vengeance can itself serve as the basis for a functioning social order, especially in smaller scale, relatively egalitarian societies in which people are more likely to know or at least have some sort of connection to each other. Should someone do some sort of wrong to another, he faces the threat of violent vengeance. This threat, however, also affects others. These others can include the victim's kin, who might be obligated to support one of their own in a vengeance attack, or the perpetrator's kin, who could expect to have to defend the perpetrator, whether or not they were directly involved in or agreed with his actions. They could also include third parties who might enjoy kinship, friendship, or economic connections with both sides and who see their interests threatened by an outbreak of violence. Whatever the case, those whose interests might be harmed by an outbreak of violence deploy peer pressure, usually with the help of third parties with ties to both sides, to induce (or force) the perpetrator to pay an acceptable compensation of some sort to the victim or his family. This compensation would satisfy the victim group's need for redress, both materially but especially emotionally; the perpetrator would have acknowledged publicly that he had wronged them. Should one or the other party refuse to give or accept compensation, however, that party ran the risk of losing the support of everyone who felt threatened by the prospect of further violence, including perhaps their own kin. This is a very dangerous situation in which to be, because without support one has to face the vengeance of one's probably very angry opponents alone.

Peer pressure and negotiation of this kind require norms, for example governing what level of compensation is appropriate for what level of wrong, whom parties in conflict will accept as third-party mediators, etc. As several scholars have demonstrated in different contexts, these norms can form the basis for a stable social system.[56] Violence has tacitly acknowledged limits; someone with a grievance makes a display of violence to signal his (or her) anger and intent (and ability) to seek violent satisfaction. This sets in motion a dance of counter-threat, of negotiation and mediation, and ultimately compensation and settlement. Quite detailed norms can also govern breaches of the limits that would cause someone to lose all support and be expelled from the community or left open to real retributive violence. For in order for such a system to work, it has to be based ultimately on the threat of real violence. Ritual or token displays of violence have to evoke actual and dangerous violence in order to compel people to follow the rules. They cannot be simple posturing, or no one would pay attention. If one side in a dispute refuses to play ball, so to speak, then the other side has to be prepared to escalate the threat or risk losing its credibility.[57]

The "peace in the feud" model, as I have described it here, poses some problems for medieval historians. To begin with, it tends to reduce human beings to cogs in a theoretical machine. It leaves out all of the individual variations in human temperament and motivation that can produce a thousand variations in behavior in a thousand different cases, and that can explain why in particular contexts some people might be afraid to breach social norms while others roll right over them. Moreover, the model presupposes a closed, small-scale, and egalitarian society in which everybody has more or less the same ability to wield violence and the same access to support from their fellows or to potential mediators.[58] Medieval societies were indeed smaller in scale than our own. Furthermore, they were usually made up of different social groups, each of which in isolation could be said to have the characteristics necessary for "peace in the feud" to work. However, medieval societies were also strongly hierarchical, with marked differences between social groups not only in status but also in access to power. The social norms that applied among the members of the aristocracy, say, who could (with variations in scale, of course) muster at least comparable levels of violence and support from their fellows, rarely applied when it came to conflicts of interest between aristocrats and commoners, and not at all between aristocrats and the unfree laborers known as serfs.

What the "peace in the feud" model does do is give us a set of ideas about how people might behave, ideas that we can test against medieval sources in order to see whether they help us understand how the sources say medieval people did behave. It also, like Olson's bandit model, makes at least plausible the proposition that the kinds of violence that might seem most corrosive to normative order can themselves be the basis for a stable order.

> At that very moment his muscles lost their ability to move and stiffened completely; the wretch lay paralyzed on the ground, his arms and legs drawn up to his body. In addition, his mouth was stretched back to his ears and gaped obscenely, and the filth that streamed foully from his entrails manifestly revealed how harshly and distressingly he had been afflicted.
>
> *Bernard of Angers*, Book of the Miracles of Sainte Foy *(c. 1013–1020)*,
> *1. 6, on the fate of a man who attempted to seize wine belonging*
> *to the monastery of St. Foy at Conques.*[59]

Medieval society was not static. Norms of violence will seem to appear and disappear from our sources, and along our way we will see norms emerge that we have not seen before. In order to understand medieval violence, we will need to have some idea about why norms change. Some recent work on norms, both in and outside the field of medieval studies, suggests some possible reasons that have to do with how people in general use and respond to norms.[60]

What makes someone choose to invoke one norm over another? Self-interest is one answer; I decide which norm from among those available will help me best persuade others that I am right, that my actions were legitimate, and that I therefore deserve community support or should not draw community sanction. To suggest that people act in such a goal-oriented way is not to reduce human behavior to a set of rational calculations or choices made simply to maximize some set of assumed material benefits.[61] The community I need to persuade can, for example, include the supernatural. In a world dominated by Christianity, as was medieval Europe, even if my appeal to norms does not satisfy my neighbors or a judge, it may well satisfy God and His saints and therefore increase my chances of salvation. Even without God, I may decide that my sense of what is right and my need to live accordingly override my material well being and thus demand self-sacrifice. My interests may also be emotional. As discussed above, I can choose (or feel driven) to commit an act of violence, or sanction someone else's act of violence, out of anger and outrage or out of love for some member of my community whom I believe I need to support. I may likewise decide to act, or not, out of fear. A given norm might be supported by my community, and I might fear the sanctions that the community can impose if I do not follow it. Or the norm might be backed by a powerful person who likewise has painful sanctions at his disposal. Such a person might be a king enforcing his law. It might also be God; as the above passage from the *Miracles of Sainte Foy* illustrates, God may act directly to punish me for behavior that He considers wrong.

There would seem to be little point, however, in invoking or acting according to the norms advocated by a segment of one's society if that segment has no power to help one or harm one's opponent. Similarly, it makes little sense to invoke norms backed by a human or divine authority figure, or both, if neither has the power to reward or punish. From this perspective, then, the key to which norms appear to win out in a particular conflict would seem to be the relative amount of power or support each of the parties involved can command. Of course, glaring differences in power remove all ability to negotiate, and therefore make any appeal to norms irrelevant; the more powerful simply act while the less powerful are forced simply to accede.[62] But things get more complicated when the interest groups involved wield comparable levels of power. In this case, the strongest party cannot unilaterally control the outcome of a conflict. Resistance, or the threat of resistance, may force it to acknowledge norms less favorable to itself and its interests than it would have otherwise. Put simply, the more powerful may have to compromise with the less powerful. In such a compromise, the more powerful may be able to win the publicity contest; it may have its norms publicly affirmed. But the less powerful party may be able to win tacit acceptance of some of its claims as the price of settlement.

If the context of a given dispute and in particular the power relationships among the disputants affect the norms that come into play and how they are treated, it follows that changes in that context, i.e., changes in the relative power or even the identity of the interest groups involved, can change the normative system or systems that show up in reports of violent conflicts. In other words, when the relative power among interest groups changes, the weight within the available pool of norms will shift from one norm to another that better serves the newly powerful group. Fredric Cheyette has expressed this idea in the language of genetics. Out of a sea of genetic possibilities, the environmental context determines that a few will become dominant. Should the context change, other genetic traits will prove to be more successful, and the dominant genes will change; so too with norms.[63] The norm or norms around which a new order coalesces can be pre-existing and latent. Or they can be new ones, generated out of conflict as new interest groups assert themselves or imported from the outside and seized upon by those whose interests they serve.

The shift from one normative framework to another does not have to be quick and clean; in fact, it is generally not. Various actors and interest groups within a given society can have conflicting preferences among the normative alternatives available. As we will see, the period of competition among them can be quite long.

> Before either Hugh or his men did any harm, the men of the count seized a benefice from Hugh's men in the name of war (guerra).
> *Agreements between Count William of the Aquitanians*
> *and Hugh of Lusignan (1028).*[64]

Norms of violence do not just depend on context or on the landscape of power; they also depend on culturally constructed boundaries that separate social groups from each other. The norms that people apply to conflicts can vary a great deal depending on whether the people involved are considered to be "inside" or "outside" a certain culturally drawn circle. To cite an example offered by William Miller: Vikings in tenth- and eleventh-century Europe behaved quite differently to their targets than they did to each other. They were quite tender and nurturing to their own children, but apparently thought nothing of taking small French children in a village raid, throwing them in the air, and impaling them on their spears as they fell.[65] In the modern West, we tend to apply quite different norms to the behavior of people living within nations than we do to the behavior of nations towards each other. The former is (at least ideally) structured by the rule of law and the authority of government. The latter, however, generally follows rules based more on friendship and enmity, face-saving and shame than on the developing norms of international law.[66]

When violence erupts in the context of international relations (i.e., war), it is currently wielded, at least in theory, according to different rules than those that apply to internal violence; people in uniform fighting an enemy nation can be violent in ways that are not legitimate at home (though the boundaries can sometimes swim, as in the case of civil wars, or the "war on terror"). Inside their borders, nation states tend to draw boundaries around violence based on a distinction between "public", i.e. the sphere of government, and "private", that is, interactions among citizens in which the government has no interest. The state may wield violence in the public interest, that is, to maintain order and protect its authority; private citizens may not wield violence in their interests, save in exceptional cases such as self-defense. Acts of violence committed by private citizens outside of these exceptions are considered to be serious crimes, or felonies, that merit punishment in order to make it clear how wrong they were and to deter others from doing the same.[67]

Where do we draw the lines of "inside" and "outside" for medieval Europe? Trying to locate national boundaries is difficult. Nation states as we understand them simply did not exist; they only started to emerge at the very end of the Middle Ages. Neither were distinctions between language and culture groups in Europe so starkly drawn as to make it easy to say when one society, like the "French", was "at war" with another society, like the "Germans". There are of course clear examples of what we would call war, both external and civil. Among them one could count the civil war among the grandsons of Charlemagne that led to the tragic battle at Fontenoy in 843 or the war between King John of England and his ally, the emperor Otto IV, and Philip Augustus of France that culminated in the great battle of Bouvines in 1214. But these were wars between rulers, not nations. Moreover, it is hard to say for much of the period to what degree Europeans may have conceptually distinguished warfare from other kinds of violence. The Romans had used the Latin word *bellum* to denote public war, while using more specific words such as *pugna*, meaning a fight or combat, to describe other kinds of violent quarrels.[68] Some early medieval authors followed suit.[69] A distinction between warfare and other group violence is also visible in accounts of the often stylized way that early medieval armies were raised and campaigns conducted.[70]

However, as one moves towards the high Middle Ages, the sources tend to use *bellum* and words such as *werra/guerra* (a word of Germanic origin meaning violent strife or quarrel) almost interchangeably, in a way that blurs or eliminates distinctions between royal wars against foreign enemies, rebellions or violent competition between political rivals, attacks to settle personal grievances, or violence employed simply for personal gain. A violent conflict between neighboring knights could be a *werra*, but so could one between neighboring kings; at the same time, a judicial duel could be a *bellum*.[71] In addition, as we will see, kings and their followers often engaged in violence in the same ways and for the same reasons as people farther down the political and social scale. It is often up to the observer, therefore, based on descriptions of particular acts of violence, to decide whether warfare in the modern sense is a useful way to understand them. It is only at the end of our period that royal war begins consistently to be claimed by kings as violence between powers that, when formally declared, changed the rules of the game in a way that delegitimized violence carried out by others.[72]

Inside a given sphere of authority (such as the realm governed by a king), it is also very hard for much of our period to draw a line between "public" and "private". Many of the people who wrote our sources did have an idea, inherited from Roman tradition, of a community interest or common weal (*res publica*). Nevertheless, if one tries to understand medieval sources according to the modern notion of a public sphere of interests, regulated by a government's public power, that is separate from a private sphere, one quickly runs into confusion. One finds oneself faced with what we would call private action backed by royal authority, with kings or other officials blending "public" and "private" interests in a way that we would call corrupt but that they regarded as perfectly normal and even necessary, etc. Similarly, the distinction between a civil wrong as a private matter and a criminal wrong as an injury to the public weal, though it had existed in Roman law, is equally elusive. We cannot really talk about violent "crime" until "crime" as a legal category in the modern sense begins to emerge in the twelfth century.[73] It will in fact be a major part of our purpose in this book to follow how the ideas even developed that there was such a thing as an injury to a king as the embodiment of a people, that a king and his government had qualitatively different rights to use violence than did other people, and ultimately that the government might enjoy something like a monopoly over the legitimate use of violent force.

The clearest lines between "inside" and "outside" in the Middle Ages were based not on political divisions, or on a division between public and private power, but rather on social and economic status. The norms of violence that applied among the aristocracy did not apply when it came to conflicts between the aristocracy and the peasantry, no matter what country one came from or to which king one owed allegiance. Peasants simply did not deserve the same treatment as a fellow aristocrat. One of the starkest examples of this difference in outlook can be found in the *Chronicles* of Jean Froissart, written in the late fourteenth century. Froissart describes the peasants' revolt, or Jacquerie, that broke out in 1358 in France following a series of devastating defeats of the French by the English in what would later be called the Hundred Years War. He tells in particular of a group of knights, some owing allegiance to the English king and some to the French, who had taken advantage of a truce to go campaigning together in Prussia. On their way home they heard of a group of aristocratic ladies who were trapped by a peasant army in the town of Meaux and hurried to their rescue. The peasants appear in Froissart's account almost as if they were a different and sub-human race:

> The Count of Foix and the Captal de Buch and their men, who were ready armed, formed up in the market-place [where the ladies were lodged] and then moved to the gates of the market and flung them open. There they faced the villeins, small and dark and very poorly armed, confronting them with the banners of the Count of Foix and the Duke of Orléans and the pennon

of the Captal de Buch, and holding lances and swords in their hand, fully prepared to defend themselves and to protect the market place.[74]

It is across divisions like these, but also divisions such as those between aristocrats and townspeople, or between lay people and churchmen, that we will be looking for differences in attitudes towards violence.

It is time to set out on our journey, a journey that will take us from the dawn of the Middle Ages in the sixth century to its twilight in the fourteenth. We will be spending most of our time on the continent of Europe, both east and west of its major dividing line, the Rhine River. Nevertheless, we will occasionally venture west across the English Channel to see what is going on in England. We will pause in particular periods in particular places that I think are representative, or for which the sources are especially good, to look at the available norms governing the use of violence by individuals and small groups in the course of ongoing social and political interactions. We will also explore how violence fitted in, or did not fit in, to their bag of tools for advancing their own interests and the interests of their allies, and for resisting the interests of their opponents and competitors. Along the way we will explore debates among scholars as they apply to these issues in particular times and places. What we find will help us understand medieval political orders and the degree to which violence, or the absence of violence, supported or undermined those orders. At the end we will also have something to say about broad changes over time in medieval attitudes towards violence.

Exploring medieval violence in this fashion strikes me as an interesting way to explore how violence fitted in to medieval worldviews; moreover, it lends itself to covering a great deal of time and space in a single volume. Taking this route, however, means that we will not take others. I will not be able to talk, for example, about such obvious manifestations of medieval violence as the Vikings or the Crusades. Though there is a great deal to learn about medieval attitudes towards violence from Crusade polemic or from descriptions of Viking raids, these represented incursions by, or campaigns against, cultures outside those I have targeted. Nor will I be able to devote much time to other subjects with which we will cross paths (many of which have in fact already earned their own books), such as sexual violence, violence and gender, violence against minority groups, violence and religion, or violence as depicted in literature. I will address these subjects as they apply to our search for medieval norms of violence, but I cannot in the confines of this book give them all the attention they deserve.

Much, if not most, of the violence that we will see falls into the broad area of the obvious. Blood, terror, broken bodies, burned and wasted buildings and crops, injury and death, will make it clear that it is violence with which we are dealing. At several crucial points in our story, however, we will be forced out into that penumbra where violence is hard to pin down, where one man's violence is another's right order, and where being violent is something you accuse someone else of when you do not like them.

Since we will be looking at how violence fitted into the more or less normal interactions of people within a society, we will spend much of our time looking at the local or small-scale, that is, at violence carried out by individuals or armed bands rather than armies, operating in their own localities or regions rather than in someone else's. I will avoid large-scale military actions aimed at other polities, as well as violence carried out in extraordinary circumstances that even contemporaries would have described as "public war". Nevertheless, I will not avoid large-scale acts of violence altogether. As discussed above, kings and armies in the early Middle Ages in particular often carried out violence within their own realms in the same ways and for the same reasons as smaller groups or individuals.

In a couple of situations, I will look on purpose at situations that were quite extraordinary. In the chapters on twelfth-century Flanders (Chapter 6) and fourteenth-century France (Chapter 9) I have chosen to study societies under the stress of civil war, or political collapse as a result of declared war between kings. I do so not only because the sources for each offer extraordinarily rich descriptions of violence. Both sources, as they describe the behavior and claims of competing groups struggling for power, and as their authors filter what they describe through their own attitudes and purposes, highlight competing norms of violence that were there to be worked with in their worlds. In addition, the chapter on fourteenth-century France illuminates a world in which warfare has been more clearly and legally defined as the business of rulers, and thus more clearly distinguished in practice as well as in theory from other kinds of violence. The norms surrounding war in this period had an impact on other norms of violence, that is, on how, why, and when people used violence and how they justified it. The particular conditions we will explore in the chapter will, therefore, help us see some basic attitudes towards violence held by different groups within late medieval French society.

The norms of violence projected by the different sources we will be examining reflect the kinds of sources they are, their purposes, and in particular the often quite pronounced perspectives and agendas of their authors. Medieval writers were not terribly interested in providing future readers with objective historical information. They were instead unapologetically biased; they were out to make their heroes look good and tar their opponents with the brush of pure evil. They also assumed that the supernatural took an active and interested part in human affairs, an assumption that can baffle us moderns.

However, these characteristics of medieval sources are very helpful for our purposes. Medieval authors constructed images and arguments in terms of norms; they advanced norms that served their purposes, and criticized, or tried to hide, norms that got in the way. They even presented the supernatural as acting in terms of their norms. As a result, we can, by looking at the norms that they advance and trying to uncover those they try to hide, get a good idea of the norms that were present in their society to be played with. So as I tell my story of violence in medieval Europe, I will be doing both some history, some anthropology, some cultural studies, and some literary criticism; I will try to untangle the norms that dictated what each source said and how it said it, as well as to look through the source as best as possible to get at other norms of violence that might have been present in the same society at the same time. In each time and place I will look at the normative worlds projected by different kinds of sources and stand them up next to each other, to see what they have in common and how they differ. My goal is to get a sense for the different ways of thinking about violence that were possible, and how these ways of thinking evolved as the Middle Ages progressed.

## Notes

1. Jean Froissart, *Chronicles*, trans. Geoffrey Brereton (New York: Penguin Books, 1968), 376–7.
2. For example, during the trial at the Hague of Slobodan Milošević for war crimes in 2002, the chief prosecutor, Carla del Ponte, accused the former Yugoslav president of "medieval savagery"; see Sean McGlynn, "Violence and the Law in Medieval England", *History Today*, April 2008, 53–9.
3. Johan Huizinga, *The Waning of the Middle Ages: A Study of the Forms of Life, Thought and Art in France and the Netherlands in the XIVth and XVth Centuries*, trans. F. Hopman (London: Edward Arnold, 1924 – translated from *Herfsttij der Middeleeuwen*, 2nd edn, 1921), 18.
4. James B. Given, *Society and Homicide in Thirteenth Century England* (Stanford: Stanford University Press, 1977), 33–4.
5. Marc Bloch, *Feudal Society*, trans. L.A. Manyon (London: Routledge & Kegan Paul, 1961 – translation of *La société féodale*, Paris: A. Michel, 1939–40), 411.
6. Georges Duby, *A History of French Civilization*, trans. James Blakely Atkinson (New York: Random House, 1964 – translation of original *Histoire de la civilisation française*, 1958), 45.

7. Cf. Guy Halsall, "Violence and Society in the Early Medieval West: An Introductory Survey", in *Violence and Society in the Early Medieval West*, ed. Guy Halsall (Woodbridge, Suffolk: Boydell Press, 1998), 1–45 @2–4.

8. Given, *Society and Homicide*, 35–40.

9. See ibid., 36, table 2.

10. Gordon Barclay and Cynthia Tavares *et al.*, "International Comparisons of Criminal Justice Statistics 2001", *Home Office Statistical Bulletin*, 24 October 2003, http://rds.homeoffice.gov.uk/rds/pdfs2/hosb1203.pdf.

11. Down from 10.2/100,000/year in 1980: James Alan Fox and Marianne W. Zawitz, "Homicide Trends in the United States", *Bureau of Justice Statistics*, 11 July 2007, http://bjs.ojp.usdoj.gov/content/homicide/homtrnd.ctm.

12. Given, *Society and Homicide*, 38, citing David N. Daniels *et al.*, eds., *Violence and the Struggle for Existence* (Boston: Little, Brown, 1970), 249–50.

13. Given, *Society and Homicide*, 38.

14. Halsall, *Violence and Society*; Johannes Fried, ed., *Träger und Instrumentarien des Friedens im hohen und späten Mittelalter* (Sigmaringen: Jan Thorbecke, 1996). Despite their titles, Richard W. Kaeuper, ed., *Violence in Medieval Society* (Woodbridge, Suffolk: Boydell, 2000), concerns mainly late medieval England and Günther Mensching, ed., *Gewalt und ihre Legitimation im Mittelalter* (Würzburg: Königshausen & Neumann, 2003) high and late medieval Germany.

15. Paul R. Hyams, *Rancor and Reconciliation in Medieval England* (Ithaca, NY: Cornell University Press, 2003); Jesse L. Byock, *Feud in the Icelandic Saga* (Berkeley: University of California Press, 1982).

16. Wendy Davies, and Paul Fouracre, eds., *The Settlement of Disputes in Early Medieval Europe* (Cambridge: Cambridge University Press, 1986); Albrecht Classen, ed., *Violence in Medieval Courtly Literature: A Casebook* (New York: Routledge, 2004).

17. Richard W. Kaeuper, *Chivalry and Violence in Medieval Europe* (Oxford: Oxford University Press, 1999); Thomas N. Bisson, *Tormented Voices: Power, Crisis, and Humanity in Rural Catalonia* (Cambridge, MA: Harvard University Press, 1998); Natalie Fryde, and Dirk Reitz, eds., *Bischofsmord im Mittelalter* (Göttingen: Vandenhoeck & Ruprecht, 2003).

18. Dominique Barthélemy, François Bougard, and Régine Le Jan, eds., *La Vengeance, 400–1200* (Rome: École Française de Rome, 2006).

19. Gerd Althoff, "Schranken der Gewalt: Wie gewalttätig war das 'finstere Mittelalter'?" in *Der Krieg im Mittelalter und in der frühen Neuzeit: Gründe, Begründungen, Bilder, Bräuche, Recht*, ed. Horst Brunner (Wiesbaden: Reichert Verlag, 1999), 1–23; Donald J. Kagay and L.J. Andrew Villalon, eds., *The Final Argument: The Imprint of Violence on Society in Medieval and Early Modern Europe* (Woodbridge, Suffolk: The Boydell Press, 1998); Mark D. Meyerson *et al.*, eds., *"A Great Effusion of Blood?" Interpreting Medieval Violence* (Toronto: University of Toronto Press, 2004); William Ian Miller, *Bloodtaking and Peacemaking: Feud, Law, and Society in Saga Iceland* (Chicago and London: University of Chicago Press, 1990); Manuel Braun, and Cornelia Herberichs, eds., *Gewalt im Mittelalter: Realitäten, Imaginationen* (Munich: Fink, 2005); Jutta Eming and Claudia Jarzebowski,

eds., *Blutige Worte: internationales und interdisziplinäres Kolloquium zum Verhältnis von Sprache und Gewalt in Mittelalter und früher Neuzeit* (Göttingen: Vandenhoeck & Ruprecht, 2008).

20. Letaldus of Micy, "Delatio corporis s. Juniani ad synodem Karoffensem", in *Patrologia Latina*, ed. Jacques-Paul Migne, 221 vols. (Paris: Migne, 1844–64), 137: 823–6, as translated in Thomas Head and Richard Landes, eds., *The Peace of God: Social Violence and Religious Response in France around the Year 1000* (Ithaca, NY: Cornell University Press, 1992), 328–9.

21. OED, s.v. "violence", definition 1a.

22. Kelly DeVries, *Medieval Military Technology* (Peterborough, Ontario: Broadview Press, 1992), 32.

23. For a survey and assessment of current debates on this point see George Crowder, review of *Justice, Law, and Violence*, by James B. Brady and Newton Garver, eds., and *Violence, Terrorism, and Justice*, by R.G. Frey and Christoper W. Morris, eds., *The American Political Science Review* 86, no. 4 (1992): 1035–6.

24. OED, s.v. "violence", definition 1: the earliest appearance in English is in 1290.

25. Lewis and Short, s.v. *violentia*.

26. Two exceptions, both from the eleventh century: the Chronicle of Nantes refers to Lambert of Nantes in the 840s dominating lower Anjou *per sua violentia*; the *Miracles* of St. Foy describes people building castles and subjugating people around them *violentia sua*. See Thomas N. Bisson, "The 'Feudal Revolution'", *Past and Present* 142 (1994): 15. The early medieval Law of the Bavarians (*Lex Baiwariorum*) titles an entire section (Title XI) *De Violentia*. The section, however, deals exclusively with forceful violation of protected spaces, namely fields and houses. See Ernst von Schwind, ed. *Leges Baiwariorum*, MGH LL nat. Germ. 5, 2 (Hanover: Hahn, 1926), 396–7.

27. William I. Miller, "Getting a Fix on Violence", in *Humiliation and Other Essays on Honor, Social Discomfort, and Violence* (Ithaca, NY: Cornell University Press, 1993), 53–92 @5.

28. Cf. Andrea Almond, "LA Police Investigate Arrest in Which Suspect Hit with Flashlight after Apparent Surrender", *Associated Press*, 24 June 2004; Mason Stockstill, "Officer May Have Feared Man Beaten During LAPD Arrest Was Armed", *Associated Press*, 26 June 2004; Andrew Glazer, "LAPD Critics Decry May 1 Melee as Latest Example of 'Warrior' Cop", *Associated Press*, 12 May 2007. Cf. the 1969 study cited by Miller, "Getting a Fix on Violence", n. 51, according to which 57% of interviewees believed that police shooting of looters was not an act of violence.

29. Miller, "Getting a Fix on Violence", 57.

30. Ibid., 77.

31. MGH Capit. I, ed. A. Boretius (Hanover: Hahn, 1883), nr. 77, 170–2 @172.

32. OED online, s.v. "norm"; Neil MacCormick, *Institutions of Law: An Essay in Legal Theory* (Oxford: Oxford University Press, 2007), 11, 20.

33. See Elizabeth Colson, *Tradition and Contract: The Problem of Order* (Chicago: Aldine Publishing Company, 1974), 47–9 on a case in which

people might not admit to the norm actually governing a situation. Among the Tonga of central Africa, one supposedly makes gifts of grain out of reciprocity and as insurance against one's own future need; one really does so because one is afraid that if one maintains a grain surplus, a sorceress might strike out of envy.

34. As, for example, when people who prize non-violence are forced for their own survival to be violent; I thank Philip T. Hoffman for pointing this out to me. Nevertheless, their behavior would still reveal a norm, namely that violence for the sake of survival was acceptable.

35. MacCormick, *Institutions*, 23.

36. Cf. Warren C. Brown and Piotr Górecki, "What Conflict Means: The Making of Medieval Conflict Studies in the United States, 1970–2000", in idem, eds., *Conflict in Medieval Europe: Changing Perspectives on Society and Culture* (Aldershot: Ashgate, 2003), 1–35 @7–8.

37. Peter Stein, *Roman Law in European History* (Cambridge: Cambridge University Press, 1999), 4.

38. Warren Brown, "The Use of Norms in Disputes in Early Medieval Bavaria", *Viator* 30 (1999): 15–40.

39. John Hudson, *The Formation of the English Common Law: Law and Society in England from the Norman Conquest to Magna Carta* (London: Longman, 1996), 2–5.

40. Burchard of Worms, "Lex Familae Wormatiensis Ecclesiae", MGH Const. 1, ed. Ludwig Weiland (Hanover: Hahn, 1893), 639–44, @prologue, 640.

41. See Chapter 7.

42. *The Song of Roland*, trans. Dorothy L. Sayers (New York: Penguin Classics, 1957), 62.

43. Ibid., 193–202.

44. As n. 26 above.

45. Michel Foucault, *Madness and Civilization: A History of Insanity in the Age of Reason*, trans. Richard Howard (New York: Pantheon Books, 1965).

46. W.H.C. Frend, *The Early Church* (Minneapolis: Fortress Press, 1982), 58–64.

47. See Miller, "Getting a Fix on Violence", 60–2; Barbara H. Rosenwein, *Emotional Communities in the Early Middle Ages* (Ithaca, NY: Cornell University Press, 2006); idem, ed., *Anger's Past: The Social Uses of an Emotion in the Middle Ages* (Ithaca, NY: Cornell University Press, 1998); Hyams, *Rancor*, 34–67.

48. Cf. Barbara H. Rosenwein, "Controlling Paradigms", in *Anger's Past*, 233–47; idem, *Emotional Communities*, 13–15; Gerd Althoff, "Empörung, Tränen, Zerknirschung: Emotionen in der öffentlichen Kommunikation des Mittelalters", in *Spielregeln in der Politik im Mittelalter* (Darmstadt: Wissenschaftliche Buchgesellschaft, 1997), 258–81; Stuart Airlie, Catherine Cubitt, Mary Garrison, Carolyne Larrington, and Barbara H. Rosenwein, "The History of the Emotions: A Debate", *Early Medieval Europe* 10, no. 2 (2001): 225–6; Guy Halsall, review of Rosenwein, *Anger's Past*, *Early Medieval Europe* 10, no. 2 (2001): 301–3; idem, *Warfare and Society in the Barbarian West* (London: Routledge, 2003), 7.

49. Mancur Olson, "Dictatorship, Democracy, and Development", *The American Political Science Review* 87, no. 3 (1993).

50. Cf. ibid., 568 on Chinese villagers in the 1920s who preferred a stationary bandit to a roving one, even though the former taxed continuously and the latter would have plundered and left. See also a recent application of Olson's model to Vikings: Peter Kurrild-Kiltgaard and Gert Tinggaard Svendsen, "Rational Bandits: Plunder, Public Goods, and the Vikings", *Public Choice* 117 (2003).

51. Gregory of Tours, *Historiarum libri decem*, ed. Rudolf Buchner. 2 vols. (Darmstadt: Wissenschaftliche Buchgesellschaft, 1967–70), v. 2, 388–9; idem, *The History of the Franks*, trans. Lewis Thorpe (New York: Penguin Books, 1974), 586. I have rendered *interficeret* in this passage as "killed" rather than Thorpe's "murdered" for reasons that will become clear in Chapter 2.

52. Thietmar of Merseburg, *Chronicon*, ed. Rudolf Buchner (Darmstadt: Wissenschaftliche Buchgesellschaft, 1957), 232–5; *Ottonian Germany: The Chronicon of Thietmar of Merseburg*, trans. David A. Warner (Manchester: Manchester University Press, 2001), 230–1.

53. The essential though still controversial starting point for the study of medieval "feud" in the Middle Ages is Otto Brunner, *Land and Lordship: Structures of Governance in Medieval Austria*, trans. Howard Kaminsky and James Van Horn Melton (Philadelphia: University of Pennsylvania Press, 1992), translation from the German of *Land und Herrschaft: Grundfragen der territorialen Verfassungsgeschichte Österreichs im Mittelalter*, 4th revised edition (Vienna: R.M. Rohrer, 1959), esp. pp. 14–35 and 90–4. See Kaminsky and Melton, "Translator's Introduction" to *Land and Lordship*, xiii–lxi.

54. Cf. Brunner, *Land and Lordship*, 16–17; Halsall, "Violence and Society", 19–29; Paul Fouracre, "Attitudes Towards Violence in Seventh- and Eighth-Century Francia", ibid., 60–75; Hyams, *Rancor*, 6–10; J.M. Wallace-Hadrill, "The Bloodfeud of the Franks", in *The Long-Haired Kings, and Other Studies in Frankish History* (London: Methuen & Co., 1962), 121–47 @122–3.

55. Max Gluckman, "The Peace in the Feud", *Past and Present* 7 (1955): 1–14 and *Custom and Conflict in Africa* (Oxford: Blackwell, 1959); Jacob Black-Michaud, *Cohesive Force: Feud in the Mediterranean and the Middle East* (London: 1975). Cf. Hyams, *Rancor*, 14–16.

56. See *inter alia* John M. Hill, *The Cultural World in Beowulf* (Toronto: University of Toronto Press, 1995); Miller, *Bloodtaking*; Byock, *Feud in the Icelandic Saga*; Wallace-Hadrill, "Bloodfeud"; Stuart Carroll, "The Peace in the Feud in Sixteenth- and Seventeenth-Century France", *Past and Present* 178 (2003): 74–115.

57. Miller, "Getting a Fix on Violence", 89; Wallace-Hadrill, "Bloodfeud", 126. Cf. Colson, "Tradition and Contract", 37 and *passim*, who similarly argues that to understand order in small-scale, stateless societies one has to take fear into account; people may act like they live in a Rousseauean paradise because they think that the world works in Hobbesian terms.

58. Stephen D. White, "Feuding and Peace-Making in the Touraine around the Year 1000", *Traditio* 42 (1986): 260.

59. MSF, 95–8; English translation: *The Book of Sainte Foy*, trans. Pamela Sheingorn and Robert L.A. Clark (Philadelphia: University of Pennsylvania Press, 1995), 60–3.
60. Brown and Górecki, "What Conflict Means", 6–8; Jean Ensminger, and Jack Knight, "Changing Social Norms: Common Property, Bridewealth, and Clan Exogamy", *Current Anthropology* 38, no. 1 (1997): 1–24; Halsall, *Warfare and Society*, 8–9.
61. Cf. Hyams, *Rancor*, 16–21; Brown and Górecki, "What Conflict Means", 9 n. 17; Ensminger and Knight, "Changing Social Norms", 21.
62. Ensminger and Knight, "Changing Social Norms", Comment VI (Anna Simons), 19 and the critique of this idea proffered by Ensminger and Knight in their "Reply", 21.
63. Fredric L. Cheyette, "Some Reflections on Violence, Reconciliation, and the Feudal Revolution", in Brown and Górecki, *Conflict*, 243–64 @244–59.
64. J. Martindale, ed., "Conventum inter Guillelmum Aquitanorum Comes et Hugonem Chiliarchum", *English Historical Review* 84 (1969): 528–48 @547; "Agreements between Count William of the Aquitanians and Hugh of Lusignan (1028)", in Barbara H. Rosenwein, ed., *Reading the Middle Ages: Sources from Europe, Byzantium, and the Islamic World* (Peterborough, Ontario: Broadview Press, 2006), 213–19 @218.
65. Miller, "Getting a Fix on Violence", 71 and n. 41.
66. Hyams, *Rancor*, 13. Even in this arena, however, national leaders bent on wielding violence will select from friendship/enmity norms or the norms of international law as suits their interests.
67. MacCormick, *Institutions of Law*, 209.
68. Lewis and Short, s.v. *bellum* and *pugna*.
69. Halsall, *Warfare*, 16–17; Janet Nelson, "The Quest for Peace in a Time of War: The Carolingian Brüderkrieg, 840–843", in Fried, ed., *Träger und Instrumentarien des Friedens*, 87–114, @87.
70. Halsall, *Warfare*, 8–9, 14–15.
71. Niermeyer, s.v. *werra* and *bellum*.
72. See Brunner, *Land and Lordship*, 33–5, as well as Chapter 9 below.
73. Here I differ from authors such as Trevor Dean, *Crime in Medieval Europe* (London: Longman, 2001), who use "crime" as a general word for serious wrong.
74. *Chronicles*, 154.

# PART I

# COMPETING ORDERS

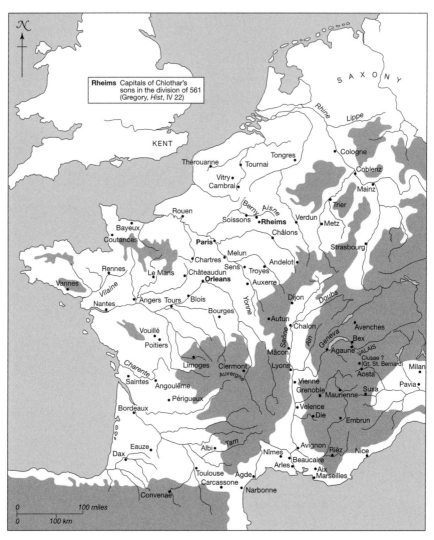

**Map 1**  Gaul in the sixth century (From Alexander C. Murray, ed., *Gregory of Tours: The Merovingians* (Broadview, 2006) p. 271)

## chapter two

# VIOLENCE AMONG THE EARLY FRANKS

Our journey begins in sixth-century Gaul. This was a region in transition. The memory of Roman rule was strong, so strong that the barbarian kings who governed in Gaul still did so at least nominally in the name of the eastern Roman emperor in Constantinople, and life for many of the inhabitants went on just as it had under the last western emperors. Yet from the perspective of the future, the Middle Ages were beginning to stir. In the course of the century, political power in the region would become concentrated in the hands of the Merovingian kings of the Franks. Though they had at their disposal elements of the Roman bureaucracy, military, and tax system, the Merovingians wielded power above all through their own military followings and those of their aristocratic allies. Their success also depended on the support and cooperation of the old Gallo-Roman senatorial aristocracy, which now exercised its influence not through the city senates but through the Catholic-Christian bishoprics. In the course of the century, the Frankish and Gallo-Roman aristocracies would gradually fuse; they would blend Roman with Germanic social, political, and legal traditions into a new social and political order that we can begin to call medieval.[1]

We will look at violence in early Merovingian Gaul from the perspective of four different witnesses. The first is perhaps the most well known from the period: the *Ten Books of Histories* by Gregory, bishop of the city of Tours on the river Loire.[2] The second is a contemporary saint's life: Jonas of Bobbio's *Life of St. Columbanus*.[3] The third, in contrast, is a legal text: the earliest version of the Law of the Salian Franks, the *Pactus Legis Salicae*.[4] The fourth comprises decrees, in the form of capitularies, issued by several of the early Merovingian kings.[5]

## Gregory of Tours

Gregory, who lived from about 539 to 594, belonged to a Gallo-Roman aristocratic family, members of which had long occupied the see of Tours.

He was also a prolific writer; in addition to his *Histories* he wrote books of miracle stories, biographies of holy men and Christian martyrs, and texts on the Psalms and on church liturgy.[6]

Gregory's *Histories* are by far the most extensive and detailed narrative source available for sixth-century Gaul. They are also extremely dangerous. Gregory wrote with purposes and biases that he did not try to hide. He drew on the past to teach political and moral lessons to his present and to the future, to highlight the difference between good and evil as he saw it, to describe his heroes as paragons of virtue and sanctity while casting his antagonists as personifications of evil, and to tell of miracles done by God and by the saints who watched over Gaul. In particular, his story – which extends from Adam and Eve up through his own lifetime – exalts the position and authority of Gregory's own kind, namely the orthodox Catholic bishops and the senatorial aristocracy from which they came. At the same time, it excoriates the enemies of Catholic orthodoxy, particularly the followers of the Arian heresy that was still very much present in his world.

Gregory judged everything and everybody in his story according to these objectives. This makes him devilishly difficult to use as a source for "what happened". Nevertheless, it makes him extremely useful for our purposes. As the *Histories* set out to show what God really wanted and how Gregory and his heroes fitted into God's plan (and how his enemies and anti-heroes did not fit into God's plan) they project a set of norms about violence that Gregory clearly thought were persuasive and ought to dominate people's thinking. Whether or not anybody else accepted them, they are norms that were comprehensible to people in Gregory's world. At the same time, by doing a bit of reading between the lines, we can also pick up from the *Histories* traces of other norms current in Gregory's world, even if they were norms that Gregory did not like.

### Good and Evil

The world as Gregory's *Histories* describe it was definitely violent. Gregory treats us to numerous accounts of hackings, stranglings, stabbings, drownings, live burials, etc., carried out by kings and magnates – and also their wives – but also by bishops and priests, as they competed with each other for power. What is striking, however, is that Gregory himself does not seem to have considered violence to be intrinsically bad or wrong. Instead, it was either good or bad depending on who was wielding it and for what purpose.

Gregory marks bad violence by describing it as random and irrational, and/or driven by boundless rage, greed, lust, or pride. To give one example among many: two evil bishops, Salonius of Embrun and Sagittarius of Gap, upon being raised to the episcopal office let their newfound power go to their heads.[7] "With a sort of insane fury" they disgraced themselves with embezzlement, assaults, homicide, adultery, and many other crimes. For no apparent reason, they assembled a group and attacked a fellow bishop, a saintly man named Victor, as he celebrated his birthday. On getting into a quarrel with members of their own congregations, the pair beat some of them with clubs until, "in their rage", they made blood flow. Gregory admits no rhyme or reason to this violence. These two bishops are simply bad (Gregory also calls them godless, oversexed, luxury-loving gluttons and alcoholics). The random and irrational violence, and the furious rage, are symptoms of their badness.[8]

Bad violence harms good and saintly men, like Bishop Victor. Good violence, however, helps them. Good and bad violence relate to each other in a tit-for-tat fashion; bad violence brings good and legitimate counter-violence. Early on in the *Histories*, for example, Gregory tells how St. Privatus, bishop of Javols, was captured by the barbarian Alemans and beaten because he would not make sacrifices to the Alemans' gods or persuade his townspeople to surrender. The beating was so severe that Privatus died of his injuries. Some time afterwards, the king of the Alemans was himself captured, tortured, and killed. Gregory leaves no doubt about how we are supposed to understand his death: the king had paid "the penalty which he deserved for the sufferings which he had inflicted on God's elect".[9]

Violence can also help God or serve His purposes even when those carrying it out might not have been employing it for the best reasons. The banner example of this principle is provided by the Merovingian king Clovis (r. 481–511). Gregory's Clovis was perfectly willing, even eager, to use violence to help him pursue or maintain power. When he defeated and captured the last military governor in Gaul of Roman descent, Syagrius of Soissons, he had him secretly killed.[10] To eliminate possible threats to his position, Clovis also had other Frankish kings, even his own relatives, killed one by one. In one famous vignette, Clovis bribed the followers of one of his relatives, King Ragnachar, to betray their lord.[11] After capturing Ragnachar, Clovis had him dragged into his presence with his hands bound; he summoned as well Ragnachar's brother Ricchar. Clovis berated Ragnachar for disgracing the Frankish people by allowing himself to be bound and then split his head open with an axe. He then turned to the brother Ricchar, told him that if he had been a good brother he would not have allowed this to happen, and killed him with an axe blow. At this point Ragnachar's bribed followers discovered that they had been paid with counterfeit coins. Clovis responded to their complaints by telling them to be quiet and to be grateful that he had not killed them too. As the story closes, Gregory has Clovis lament how sad it was that he had no relatives to console and help him in times of trouble. Gregory comments, "he said this not because he grieved for their deaths, but because in his cunning way he hoped to find some relative still in the land of the living whom he could kill".

And yet, although he acknowledges Clovis's ruthlessness, Gregory casts Clovis in general in a positive light. Why? First, because Clovis converted himself and the Franks to Catholic orthodoxy. Second, the Frankish king served as God's instrument in spreading orthodoxy in Gaul and combating Gregory's *bête noire*, the Arian heresy. As he narrates Clovis's conversion to Catholicism, Gregory explicitly compares him to the Roman emperor Constantine, who had himself promoted Catholic orthodoxy over Arianism.[12] Gregory moreover has Clovis justify his campaigns of conquest on religious grounds. "I find it hard to see these Arians occupy a part of Gaul," he has the Frankish king remark; "with God's help let us invade them. When we have beaten them, we will take over their territory."[13] Gregory validates everything Clovis had done and would do with the comment, "Day in and day out God submitted the enemies of Clovis to his dominion and increased his power, for he walked before him with an upright heart and did what was pleasing in his sight."[14]

Gregory also has Clovis employ violence to protect the interests of the Gallic bishops and of the Gallic saints. While fighting Syagrius of Soissons and the Visigoths, for example, Clovis's men plundered many churches. From one they stole a marvelous pitcher. The bishop of the church sent messengers to Clovis begging him to have the pitcher returned. Clovis took the messengers with him to Soissons, where the plunder from the recent campaign was being shared out; he promised them that, should the pitcher fall to his share of the loot, he would return it to the bishop. Once he had his men assembled around the large pile of plundered goods, Clovis addressed them and asked for the pitcher over and above his share. Most of the men agreed. However, "a feckless fellow, greedy and prompt to anger", struck the pitcher with his battle-axe and said, "you will have none of this booty except your fair share." Clovis hid his own anger, took the pitcher as his share, and handed it to the bishop's messengers. Some time later, at the end of the year, Clovis mustered his army on a parade ground to inspect its equipment. He found the man who had challenged him over the pitcher; he proceeded to yell at him for the shocking state of his equipment, then grabbed his axe from him and dropped it on the ground. As the man bent over to retrieve the axe, Clovis split his head open with his own axe and shouted, "this is what you did to my pitcher in Soissons." Clovis's army was then dismissed, the men filled with "mighty dread".[15]

## Magnates and their Followings

Gregory tells this story to set Clovis up as a right-thinking supporter of the Catholic bishops and their interests. It is plain, however, that while Clovis returned the pitcher out of respect for a bishop, he killed the man who had challenged him to avenge an insult and deal with a potential threat to his authority. His actions plainly worked; his opponent was dead and his men were filled with a "mighty dread" of his ruthlessness. It is stories like these that allow us to look through the normative framework Gregory is imposing on events and catch a glimpse of the wider world of possible norms governing violence in Gregory's world.

To begin with, this is a world in which the people to whom Gregory pays attention, namely the magnates, used armed followings either to threaten or to wield violence in pursuit of their ends. The Merovingian kings were part and parcel of this world. So were the bishops. To return to the story of the evil bishops Salonius of Embrun and Sagittarius of Gap: after disgracing themselves in assaults, homicides, adultery, embezzlement, etc., they went with what Gregory calls a "company" (*cohors*) to attack Bishop Victor.[16] Gregory of course wants us to see this apparently mindless violence as yet another manifestation of the bishops' evil nature. He nevertheless gives us enough information about the incident to tell that not everyone saw it this way. When word of the assault on Victor reached the Merovingian king of the region, Clovis's great-grandson Guntram, the king ordered an inquiry. A council of bishops found Salonius and Sagittarius guilty of the evil deeds of which they had been accused and removed them from office. The two bishops, however, apparently had their own side to the story, for they promptly appealed their deposition to Pope John III in Rome. After hearing their appeal, the pope ordered King Guntram to reinstate them.

Once the two bishops were back in office, says Gregory, they returned to their bad old ways. He recalls that they once had participated in battle, "armed themselves like laymen and killed many with their own hands". Now, he tells us, is when they got into a violent quarrel with their own parishioners. The people appealed to King Guntram. In response, the king ordered both bishops to be brought to court, but he refused to see them until they had been declared innocent. After Sagittarius ("a fatuous and empty-headed fellow," says Gregory, "much given to garrulous talk") began to spread nasty rumors about the king's mother (the very foolishness of which casts doubt on Gregory's version of events),

Guntram had the pair imprisoned. When one of Guntram's sons fell ill, however, some of the king's associates suggested that perhaps this was God's way of telling him that Salonius and Sagittarius were innocent. Guntram accordingly freed them and ordered them to pray for his sons' health. It seems, then, that the two bishops had allies at court who were able to influence the king on their behalf. These allies must, therefore, have had some understanding, or at least tolerance, for their actions. Nevertheless, the two bishops were unable to escape divine punishment. They fell once more into their evil ways, and, as a result, "the wrath of God descended on their heads".[17]

Gregory wants us to see Salonius and Sagittarius as bad men whose badness was manifested in the irrational violence that got them into trouble. Nevertheless, the story was not so elastic that he could sculpt it at will. The events Gregory describes took place during his own lifetime; he was forced, most likely by common knowledge, to include information that he had to work around. If we strip away his rhetoric of good and evil, we have the following picture: Salonius and Sagittarius were aristocrats who had made their career in the church. They had armed followings and fought in battle like other aristocrats. They felt entitled to prosecute disputes with people both below them and equal to them with violence, and they used their armed followings for this purpose. They were thrown out of church office for doing so. Nevertheless, not everyone around them viewed their actions as entirely reprehensible. They were able to present a plausible defense to the pope that the pope accepted; they had allies at King Guntram's court who apparently tolerated their violence and may well have thought that it was justified.

## Vengeance

In some cases, Gregory tells us why his characters were violent. By far the most common motive is the desire to take vengeance for a perceived injury or insult. Violent vengeance served to save face for the victim and uphold his honor and that of his family. For example, Gregory relates how a saintly bishop named Desideratus had been subjected to the machinations of a man named Syrivald, who had denounced Desideratus to the Merovingian king Theuderich (for what, Gregory does not say). In response, Theuderich had Desideratus deprived of his possessions and tortured. Desideratus' son Syagrius could not forget the wrongs done to his father. After King Theuderich died, Syagrius gathered an armed band (*cum armata manu*), attacked Syrivald's house, and killed him in his bedroom.[18]

There was a counter-norm, however, which Gregory himself seems to have advocated, namely, that while insult or injury might deserve a violent response, the right thing to do was to compensate the victim so that peace might be restored without resort to violence. This ethic of non-violent settlement and compensation plays a central role in one of the most famous stories in Gregory's history, which deals with the conflict among three Franks named Sichar, Austregisel, and Chramnesind.[19] Yet it does not dominate the story. Instead, the norms of non-violent settlement and violent vengeance compete with each other as events unfold, until in the end it is violence that wins out.

The story takes place in and around Gregory's home city of Tours, and Gregory describes himself as a participant in the affair. Sichar son of John was in a village near Tours, enjoying Christmas festivities with a man named Austregisel and some locals. The village priest, who was a friend of Sichar's, sent a servant (*puer*) over to the party to invite some of the men over to his house for a drink. When the servant arrived, one of the men he wanted to invite, who seems to have been a follower of Austregisel, drew his sword and killed him, for no reason that Gregory tells us. Sichar apparently saw this as an insult perpetrated on his friend the priest by Austregisel, because he grabbed his weapons and went to wait for Austregisel at the village church. In response, Austregisel snatched up his own weapons and went after Sichar. A pitched battle ensued. The battle was inconclusive, but Sichar fled to his country estate, leaving behind some of his armed men (*pueri*)[20] who had been wounded, as well as some money and belongings, at his friend the priest's house. Austregisel, however, refused to stop fighting. He launched an attack on the priest's house, killed Sichar's men and took Sichar's gold, silver, and other things.

At this point constituted authority intervened; Sichar and Austregisel were called up before what Gregory calls a citizen's tribunal (*in iudicio civium*) in Tours. Austregisel was judged guilty according to the law (*censura legalis*). Not because his follower had killed the priest's servant, however, or because he had engaged in a fight with Sichar, but because he had killed Sichar's men and taken Sichar's property without a hearing (that is, into whether or not he had a right to it).[21]

A few days after the tribunal had convened, Sichar learned that Austregisel had deposited his property with another family. Sichar apparently felt that this family had wronged him by accepting his property, and that he had the right both to recover his own goods and to exact vengeance. He staged a raid with armed men (*cum armatis viris*) on the family's house in the middle of the night. He killed a man, his brother, and his son while they were sleeping, as well as their servants. He also seized all of their property and animals.

This of course created a new conflict between Sichar and the surviving members of this family, who were represented by a second son of the dead man, Chramnesind. Chramnesind wanted vengeance. It is here that Gregory himself stepped in. Together with a judge (*adiuncto iudice*) he called the parties together and preached to them along the following lines: (1) the wrong done must not spread farther; (2) some sons of the Church have been lost already, we cannot lose any more; (3) peace needs to be kept; (4) whoever has done wrong should pay compensation for it in brotherly love; (5) all should make peace in order to merit heaven, for blessed are the peacemakers; (6) if anyone lacked the money to pay compensation, the Church would pay for it, rather than see the man lose his soul. In short: Gregory casts himself as a peacemaker: he tells us that he appealed to the virtue of Christian peace and offered to back up his appeal with church money.[22]

Chramnesind, however, would have none of it. When he heard a rumor that Sichar had been killed by one of his own slaves (*servus*), he gathered his friends and relations and rushed to Sichar's house. They plundered and burned the house, then they plundered and burned the houses of some of Sichar's neighbors. But the rumor was just a rumor; Sichar was still alive. A judge (*iudex*) then summoned the two parties to the city to plead their cases. Here we learn that according to the law, since Chramnesind had refused to accept compensation and had burned and plundered the houses, he had forfeited his right to be compensated: Gregory tells us explicitly that it was against the letter of the law (*et hoc contra legis actum*), and in an effort to make peace, that a settlement was worked out whereby Sichar was to pay Chramnesind compensation but only half of what he would have paid previously. Gregory himself gave Sichar the money to pay the compensation out of his church's treasury. Both parties then swore an oath that they would make no further trouble.

It looks at first like this settlement ended the dispute. We move on in time, and find that Sichar and Chramnesind became fast friends. They advertised their peace with each other by eating together and even on occasion sleeping in the same bed. But one fateful night, Chramnesind invited Sichar to dinner. Sichar got drunk and began to boast that Chramnesind ought to be grateful to him for having killed his relatives; Chramnesind was now rich because of the compensation he had received. Chramnesind grew sick at heart. He said to himself (according to Gregory) that if he did not avenge his relatives, he would be thought as weak as a woman, "for I will no longer have the right to be called a man".[23] In other words, the norm of violent vengeance for the killing of relatives was so strong that Chramnesind thought he would be sanctioned by his community, not for employing violence, but rather for not employing violence when he was supposed to. So he blew out the candles and hacked Sichar's head in two. He then stripped Sichar's corpse of its clothes and hung it outside on a post in his garden fence. He thus openly declared what he had done and advertised it as a legitimate act.

Chramnesind next went to the Merovingian king in whose kingdom this had all unfolded, Childebert II. He pleaded for his life and told his story point by point, saying that he had killed the man who had in secret killed his own relations and stolen their possessions. Somehow, therefore, Chramnesind had put his own life in danger by killing Sichar. How Gregory does not say. The fact that Chramnesind appealed to the king suggests that the king's authority was now involved, perhaps because Chramnesind had violated a sworn peace settlement. Or perhaps Chramnesind went to the king because the king could protect him from vengeance by Sichar's relatives.

Enter a new party: King Childebert's mother, Queen Brunhild. Brunhild was enraged at Chramnesind, for Sichar had been under her personal protection (*in eius verbo*). Frightened, Chramnesind fled briefly to his relatives, but after a time returned to Childebert's court. Childebert then rendered the following judgment: Chramnesind had to prove that he had killed Sichar in order to vindicate himself (*ut convinceret super se*). This Chramnesind did. Queen Brunhild, however, because Sichar had been under her protection, ordered Chramnesind's property seized and given to one of her retainers. This is important. According to Gregory, the queen did not act because Chramnesind had violated a law that she as queen was responsible for upholding. The matter for her was instead quite personal; he had killed someone under her protection. Nevertheless, her husband the king had sympathy with Chramnesind's position. He was not the only one. The retainer to whom Brunhild had given Chramnesind's property, after some time had passed, quietly returned the property to Chramnesind. Gregory too had some sympathy for Chramnesind. In the middle of telling us how angry Queen Brunhild became with Chramnesind for killing Sichar, Gregory breaks off to give his own opinion of the dead man: he had been a loose-living, drunken, and homicidal[24] person who caused trouble to everyone when he had been drinking. In other words, Gregory thought that Sichar deserved his fate.

### A Violent God

Although he cast himself as a peacemaker, therefore, Gregory did not fundamentally disagree with violent vengeance. Far from it; throughout his *Histories* he tells us that even God and His saints resorted to it. Early on in the work, for example, he describes how two priests rebelled against the saintly bishop Sidonius Apollinaris. But, says Gregory, "God in his clemency did not permit this insult to go long unpunished." One of the priests was found dead in the lavatory; while emptying his bowels he had lost his soul instead. The second priest later fell down dead after his cupbearer learned in a vision that God was going to summon him to judgment for his crimes.[25] God could also exact his revenge through human agents. One Avius committed a series of outrages in the area around Poitiers (including robberies, killings, adultery, and incest). By chance, Avius met a Saxon named Childeric. The pair exchanged insults, and in the fracas that erupted Avius was killed by Childeric's men. Childeric had to pay compensation to Avius's sons. Nevertheless, Gregory was quite pleased by what the Saxon had done. In this way, he says, God in His majesty had avenged the innocent blood that Avius had shed.[26]

Saints too could avenge injuries and affronts with violence. During a campaign by Clovis's son King Theuderich in the Auvergne, the king's troops ran riot in the city of Clermont. Some of them broke into the church of St. Julian, did a great deal of damage, and stole money left there for safekeeping by the poor. Those responsible, says Gregory, were suddenly seized by an unclean spirit and cried out that they were being tortured by St. Julian himself. They then tore themselves to pieces with their own teeth.[27] When a certain Leo alleged that Gregory's own saint, St. Martin of Tours, and his colleague St. Martialis had left nothing of value to the royal treasury, he was "immediately struck deaf and dumb by the miraculous power of the two saints and he died a raging lunatic".[28]

## Saint Columbanus

As the examples discussed throughout the above section illustrate, Gregory's *Histories* do not present violence as fundamentally opposed to Christian culture.[29] On the contrary: violence is a tool that holy people both living and dead, as well as God himself, can use to achieve divine ends. In this regard, the *Histories* resemble the saints' lives written during the Merovingian period. These stories also assume that God works actively in the world, directly as well as through his representatives. They likewise tell of miracles worked by saints or of persecutions and martyrdoms endured by saints. But in contrast to the *Histories*, which like most medieval histories were aimed at revealing God's plan unfolding in the world and teaching virtues and vices by example, hagiography focuses on the saints themselves and seeks to justify their status as Christian heroes and models of sanctity.[30] Saints' lives provide us, therefore, with an opportunity to observe directly how early medieval ideals of holiness and Christian heroism incorporated violence.

The Merovingian period is rich in saints' lives.[31] To try to explore the norms of violence that they express in any comprehensive way would test the limits of a book, much less a chapter. I will, therefore, focus on one example that was written in the generation after Gregory of Tours, about a saint who was Gregory's contemporary: Jonas of Bobbio's *Life of St. Columbanus*. This was one of the most widely copied and most influential of the early western saints' lives, and it was frequently mined for models of sanctity by later hagiographers.[32] As a result, it can provide us with some points of comparison as we repeatedly confront violence and Christian saints throughout our journey.

Columbanus was an Irish monk who left his native country first for Scotland, and then for Gaul, where he arrived around 590.[33] Coming to Burgundy, he founded three monasteries in quick succession. After further extensive travels, Columbanus ended up in northern Italy. There the Lombard king Agilulf gave him a site for a new monastery, at Bobbio, between Milan and Genoa. Columbanus died there in 615.

Shortly after his death, the Irishman's *Life* was written by Jonas, a monk of Bobbio who spent a great deal of time in Francia, including at Columbanus's monastery at Luxeuil. Jonas's text is as much shaped by its author's concerns as are the *Histories* of Gregory of Tours. It reflects in particular the issues important to the second generation of "Columbanian" monks. Chief among these was reconciling the memory of the fierce opposition Columbanus's independent and idiosyncratic brand of monasticism had aroused among the Burgundian bishops and some members of the aristocracy with the *modus vivendi* his successors were reaching with the ecclesiastical and aristocratic establishment of their own day. In Jonas's text, this effort comes at the expense of two people who may well have been Columbanus's patrons, namely Queen Brunhild (whom we met in Gregory's *Histories* trying to punish Chramnesind for killing her follower Sichar) and her grandson King Theuderich. As Gregory tells us, Brunhild, Theuderich, and Brunhild's line fell to the ambitions of King Chlothar II of Neustria (d. 629). Their demise and Chlothar's dominance over Francia allowed Jonas to pin responsibility for all resistance to Columbanus on Brunhild and Theuderich while at the same time making the saint's story (and hence the past of the Columbanian monasteries) fit better with contemporary political realities.[34]

As he described his hero founding monasteries and fighting evil, therefore, Jonas projected his own concerns back on to his subject. Nevertheless, at the heart of his story lies a figure of uncompromising asceticism and independence that must reflect Columbanus himself, as well as his Irish brand of monasticism as his disciples understood it. This figure was not afraid of violence; he both provoked it and used it. The attitudes towards violence displayed by Jonas's Columbanus share a great deal in common with those displayed by Gregory of Tours; used by the right ways by the right people (or divine figures), violence could both protect and promote the interests of the Christian God.

Jonas describes a great deal of violence.[35] Some of it he casts as evil, or as the work of the devil.[36] Much of it, however, he validates because it serves the interests of the saint and ultimately of his employer, God. As in Gregory's *Histories*, these interests included vengeance for injury or insult; Jonas has God and Columbanus working together to avenge themselves violently on those who failed to obey or respect them. Traveling to Brittany after having been forced out of Burgundy, Columbanus and his party took a boat to cross the river Loire. One of the guards in their escort struck a particularly holy man from among the saint's companions. In response, Columbanus threatened the guard with God's vengeance (*divino ultione*). As the guard on his return journey came to the same place to cross the river, he was struck by the hand of God and drowned.[37] God also took aim when necessary at Columbanus's own monks. While isolating himself in a rock hollow near Luxeuil, Columbanus learned by divine revelation that his monks were stricken by disease and that only a few remained well enough to care for the sick. The saint went to the monastery and commanded the sick monks to go to their work threshing the harvest. The obedient ones did as they were told; they were promptly cured of their disease. Those who were disobedient Columbanus chided for their lack of faith and told that they would remain ill for a long time. "Wonderful revenge!" (*mira ultio*) exclaims Jonas; "For the disobedient were so ill for an entire year that they barely escaped death."[38]

Columbanus was even able to browbeat other saints into being violent on his behalf. While traveling, he visited the tomb of St. Martin in Tours. He left his boat with his party's property, including some gold intended for the poor, on the river overnight. The next morning, after having spent the night praying before St. Martin's relics, Columbanus learned that his party's belongings, including the gold, had been stolen from the boat. He promptly went back to the tomb and began to berate Martin; he complained that "he had not watched by the relics of the saint in order that the latter should allow him and his followers to suffer loss". The thief was promptly "tormented and tortured"; he and his associate confessed where they had hidden the gold. The miracle struck such terror into everyone that no one dared further to touch anything belonging to Columbanus.[39]

Much of the violence in the *Life* takes place in the context of the saint's troubled relationship with Queen Brunhild and her grandson King

Theuderich. It is here that we see the same sort of personal and deadly violence used as a tool of power politics that we saw in Gregory of Tours' account of Clovis's career. Here too the way that this kind of violence is evaluated depends entirely on who is doing what to whom and why, and on the values and position of the reporter, in this case Jonas. For Jonas as for Gregory, the most brutal acts of violence among political rivals could, depending on the agent and the circumstances, either reflect the devil's handiwork or be the means by which God's will was fulfilled.

When Columbanus showed up in Burgundy, King Theuderich was quite happy to have such a saintly man in his kingdom. This changed, however, when Columbanus began to reprove him for consorting with concubines rather than taking a wife. Columbanus's criticism also angered Queen Brunhild. The devil, seizing his opportunity, entered into Brunhild; when Columbanus refused to bless Theuderich's illegitimate sons, the queen became enraged. Columbanus promptly left the palace. After he had left, the residents of the palace received a warning of divine anger: a loud cracking noise was heard and the whole house trembled. Undeterred, Brunhild ordered Columbanus's monasteries sealed off from the outside world. In response, Columbanus went to Theuderich, but he refused to enter his palace. Theuderich, seeking to mollify the saint, had food sent out to him. Columbanus not only refused it, he underlined his displeasure with Theuderich by channeling another act of divine violence: the dishes broke, the wine and liquor ran out on the ground, and the food was scattered. Terrified, both Theuderich and Brunhild begged for forgiveness. Columbanus accepted their submission and went home.[40]

Brunhild and Theuderich, however, failed to keep their promises and began to persecute the monasteries once more. Columbanus wrote the king a letter full of reproaches and threatened him with the ultimate spiritual weapon at his disposal: excommunication from the community of the faithful. Brunhild began to marshal supporters. She urged the nobles and others at court to help her incite her grandson against the saint, and she pressed the bishops of his kingdom to attack Columbanus's faith and abolish his monastic rule. The bishops needed no urging. They ordered Columbanus to defend his practice of the faith or leave the kingdom.

King Theuderich then went to Luxeuil and provoked a confrontation: he charged the saint with not allowing lay people to enter into his monastery.[41] Columbanus responded with a sovereign trust in God's willingness to punish an insult: "if you come here to destroy the monasteries of the servant of God and to undermine their discipline and regulations, I tell you that your kingdom will be destroyed together with all your royal family". According to Jonas, Theuderich was determined not to be maneuvered into attacking the saint. He declared, "You want me to honor you with the crown of martyrdom; do not believe that I am foolish enough to commit such a crime." Instead, he said that he would have Columbanus sent back to Ireland. Columbanus responded that he would only leave his monastery if dragged out by force.

As this affair nears its violent end, we get a hint of formal judicial institutions in Jonas's world. Jonas has little respect for them, however, and by no means assigns their judgments any priority over the will of God. King Theuderich had Columbanus forcibly extracted from his monastery and carried off to the town of Besançon. There the saint learned that the local prison was full of condemned men awaiting execution. God helped Columbanus enter the prison without opposition, free the prisoners (who had promised the saint to repent for the wrongs they had done), and protect them from their pursuers.

The action that follows is full of the language of violence and violent vengeance, on both sides. Columbanus, seeing that nobody was watching him, simply left Besançon and returned to his monastery. An infuriated Brunhild and Theuderich ordered a band of soldiers to remove the saint "by violence" (*vim*).[42] The soldiers, however, could not find Columbanus, even though he was sitting in the vestibule of the monastery church, in plain sight, reading a book. Their captain, who alone could see him, called off the search; he recognized that Columbanus was under God's protection. A frustrated Theuderich, "impelled by the madness of his wretched purpose", sent a count and a nobleman to fetch Columbanus. When these could not persuade the saint to come with them, they departed, leaving behind "several men of rough disposition and character". The men begged Columbanus to have pity on them and to think of their peril: "if they did not violently (*violenter*) eject him they would be in danger of death." Columbanus replied that he would not leave unless compelled by violence (*vim*).[43] The panic-stricken men begged for mercy, since they were not obeying their own wishes but rather obeying the commands of the king. Columbanus finally decided to yield so as not to put others in danger. He told his monks that those who wished to share his trials might come with him; the others should stay, "knowing that God would quickly avenge (*ultionem daturum*) their injuries".[44]

And God's vengeance eventually came. Columbanus sent a message to King Theuderich, to the effect that "he and his children will die within three years, and his entire family will be exterminated by the Lord".[45] The way that Jonas describes the end of Theuderich and his family highlights his two-edged message about Merovingian political violence and

God's purposes. Theuderich and his brother Theudebert quarreled over the borders of their kingdoms; each, "priding himself on the strength of his followers", tried to kill the other. Both kings sent to their relative Chlothar (II, King of Neustria) for help. Chlothar, however, was a supporter of Columbanus. When the appeal for aid from Theuderich and Theudebert came in, Chlothar asked Columbanus what he should do. The saint advised him to support neither rival, "for within three years he would receive both kingdoms". Chlothar, "full of faith," sat back to await the outcome. After two defeats in battle, Theudebert was betrayed by his own followers, captured, and sent to Queen Brunhild. Although he was also her grandson, she preferred Theuderich; she shut Theudebert up in a monastery, then after a few days had him killed.[46] But Theuderich was soon struck directly by the hand of God and perished in a fire. Brunhild then crowned his son Sigibert, her great-grandson, as king. Seeing a young and inexperienced king as a ripe target, Chlothar of Neustria gathered an army and invaded. Sigibert was captured, along with his five brothers and Queen Brunhild herself. Chlothar proceeded to have the boys killed one by one. But he reserved special treatment for Brunhild. First he had the old queen placed on a camel and displayed "in mockery" to all her enemies. Then she was tied to the tails of wild horses "and thus perished wretchedly". Columbanus's prophecy was fulfilled.[47]

## The Law of the Salian Franks

Law is not mentioned in the *Life of Columbanus*, though it is implied by the prison from which Columbanus freed the prisoners. Law does, however, appear in Gregory's *Histories*. According to Gregory, the law came into play when people involved in the tit-for-tat of violent vengeance took out others or others' property in the process, or killed the defenseless. The law also appears as a body of norms that claimed to regulate settlements. It did not absolutely determine settlements, but rather served as a point of departure for negotiations.[48]

I would like now to explore the meaning of law in sixth-century Gaul a bit further, through one of the most important legal texts of the period: the law of the Salian Franks, or Salic Law. This title is somewhat misleading, because there really is no such thing as "the Salic Law" in a single and easily identifiable form. Instead, we have a living tradition of texts that refer to themselves as the Salic Law, in over eighty manuscripts and in several versions, that extends from the sixth century into the ninth. These manuscripts also include the texts of decrees, or capitularies (so-called because they are divided up into sections called *capitula*) issued by Frankish kings that were intended to supplement or amend the Salic Law.[49]

For the sake of simplicity, I will focus here on the earliest version of the Salic Law, the so-called *Pactus Legis Salicae*, or "Pact of the Salic Law", that is thought to have been issued sometime between 507 and 511, that is, during the reign of Clovis.[50] This text consists of a Prologue and 65 titles. It shows considerable Roman influence; it was written in Latin, apparently by people trained in Roman legal practice. Yet the legal customs it records look for the most part quite different from Roman law as it appears in the great late antique compilations of the emperors Theodosius II (completed 438) and Justinian (completed 533–4).[51] Most notable is the absence of the distinction between civil and criminal matters present in both Roman law and modern western legal systems.[52] The *Pactus* projects instead a general and undifferentiated sense of wrong; when someone believed that they had been wronged, and the wrong could be proven, the wrong needed to be made right.

It is not immediately obvious what purpose the *Pactus* was intended to serve.[53] To begin with, it offers only a partial picture of what contemporaries understood to be "Salic law". References to the Salic law in other sources often – in fact usually – deal with matters or procedures that are not covered by the written *Pactus* or by any of its later emendations. The *Pactus* therefore records only part of what must have been a much larger world of "law", which contemporaries must have thought of as Salic law even though much of it does not appear in the written text. Moreover, the *Pactus* is not always internally consistent; some clauses are repetitive, others contradict each other. Both of these features make it difficult to imagine how the written text might have been used in a judicial setting.[54]

Patrick Wormald has suggested that the *Pactus* was designed not to serve as a practical judicial resource but rather to make a political statement, that is, to make Clovis look like a ruler in the Roman mold.[55] Late-Roman emperors were by definition lawgivers, and Clovis definitely saw himself as ruling Gaul in their image.[56] From this perspective, issuing the written *Pactus Legis Salicae* would have shown Clovis doing what legitimate Roman rulers did, i.e., issue laws.

Given how hard it is to figure out just what the *Pactus* represents and what aspects of Frankish legal culture it covers, it makes very little sense to assume that when Gregory of Tours referred to the law he meant the written *Pactus*, and to try to figure out what clauses of the *Pactus* applied in a given situation.[57] It makes more sense to treat both Gregory's *Histories* and the *Pactus* as different and independent witnesses to the world that produced them, both of which were shaped by the purposes and worldviews of their creators. The task then becomes to see whether these pale and distorted reflections of early Frankish Gaul share anything in common in their attitudes towards or images of violence.

## Wrong and Compensation

The world with which the *Pactus* presents us is primarily rural and agricultural. Titles II through IX, for example, make this abundantly clear; they deal with the theft of pigs, cattle, sheep, goats, dogs, birds, and bees, as well as with damage to cultivated fields or other enclosures.[58] It is a world with sharp social and political divisions: between free men and women, between freedmen, semi-free persons or *lidi*, and slaves, and between Franks and Romans.[59]

It is also a violent world. The *Pactus* devotes much, in fact most of its attention to acts of violence, carried out against property and animals as well as against persons. Some titles deal with breaking and entering and with the theft of property, with plundering, pillaging, and despoiling property, with arson, with damage to boundary markers, and with violence against slaves (who are treated as property).[60] Others concern harm done to animals, and, interestingly, harm committed via animals; apparently it was not unknown for one Frank to try to hurt his neighbor by turning his animals loose in the neighbor's fields.[61] Still other clauses deal with kidnapping, assault, and rape, with highway robbery, with injury, and with homicide.[62]

The *Pactus* does not stipulate punishment, however, but rather compensation for wrongs, at least as far as free people are concerned. For example, if someone is proven to have robbed a freeman, the text says he is liable to pay 2500 silver pennies (*denarii*) or 62 and one-half gold coins (*solidi*) to his victim; he must also return the objects taken and pay for the time their use had been lost.[63] It is hard to quantify these sums in modern terms. While the ratio between the *denarius* and the *solidus* is consistent throughout the text (at 40 *denarii* to the *solidus*), there is very little evidence either inside or outside the *Pactus* to indicate their purchasing power.[64] The amounts must have been substantial, however, particularly in the case of serious wrongs such as homicide (see below). The *Pactus* assumes that in the last resort, a freeman who could not pay compensation in money stood to lose his property. By implication, then, the highest compensation amounts could ruin a man.[65]

While the *Pactus* allows us only to guess at absolute values, it tells us a great deal about the relative values of wrongs. The amount of compensation stipulated by the *Pactus* varies according to the perceived severity of the wrong and the status of the people involved. To give an example of a status variation: if a Roman were found to have robbed a

Salian Frank he had to pay as stated above. A Frank found to have robbed a Roman, however, had to pay less than half of what a Roman would pay, namely 1200 *denarii*.[66]

Variation according to the degree of wrong is nowhere more clear than in the extensive and often very precise titles that deal with personal injury and homicide.[67] Someone who maims another man's hand or foot, strikes out his eye, or cuts off his ear or nose, for example, is liable for 4000 *denarii*. Cutting off another's hand so that it remains hanging from the body, or piercing another's hand, costs 2500 *denarii*. Cutting off another's thumb or big toe: 2000 *denarii*; cutting the thumb or big toe so that it remains hanging: 1200 *denarii*. Cutting off the second finger of the hand, that is, the finger that a man uses to release arrows from a bow, costs 1400 *denarii*; all of the remaining fingers together are worth 1800 *denarii* (the amounts for these fingers are reduced sequentially for cutting off only two or one, depending on which finger it is). Ears and teeth are worth 600 *denarii*, but cutting out someone's tongue so that he is no longer able to speak costs 4000 *denarii*. One of the most expensive injuries is, perhaps not surprisingly, one affecting the male sexual organ. Castrating a freeman or injuring his penis so that he is incapacitated costs 4000 *denarii*, but cutting the penis away entirely brings a liability of 8000 *denarii*, plus a nine *solidi* payment to the doctor called in to treat the victim.

Losing a penis must have felt like death to a free Frank, because killing a freeman likewise brings a compensation debt of 8000 *denarii*.[68] This compensation for the life of a person is generally called "wergeld", which is a Germanic word meaning "man price" (commonly rendered in modern English as "blood price").[69] Wergeld in the *Pactus* is not a fixed amount, but rather varies depending on a person's rank and status. For example, killing a Roman landholder brings a debt of only 4000 *denarii*.[70]

ʕ Under certain circumstances, a man who killed another could owe more than just his victim's wergeld. The *Pactus* draws a distinction between killing openly, so that the deed was known, and killing secretly or trying to prevent a killing from being discovered. While killing a free Frank normally brings a debt of 8000 *denarii*, throwing him into a well or drowning him costs three times that much: 24,000 *denarii*. Killing someone and then hiding the body with sticks, or bark, or hides – in other words, trying to conceal the fact that one has killed – likewise costs 24,000 *denarii*.[71] The Latin text of the *Pactus* does not reflect this distinction in the quality of the killing with a change in vocabulary; the words used remain, as elsewhere, "homicide" (*homicidium*) or "kill" (*occidere* or *interficere*). However, a set of Germanic glosses added to some of the surviving manuscripts, the so-called "Malberg glosses", does reflect the difference. In most clauses dealing with violent death, the Malberg glosses use the word *leodi*, which is a synonym for wergeld. In clauses dealing with secret killings, however, the gloss uses *matteleodi*, meaning "great man-price", or occasionally *morther*, that is, murder.[72]

Violence towards women comes with its own set of values. The *Pactus* provides a sliding scale of compensation for unwelcome touching, ranging from the hand or finger or arm (600 *denarii*) to the breast (1800 *denarii*). Rape brings a debt of 2500 *denarii*.[73] Women are plainly most important, however, as the bearers of children. Killing a free girl before she can bear children costs the same as killing a free man: 8000 *denarii*. The price for killing a free woman after she has begun bearing children, however, jumps to 24,000 *denarii*. Once she has passed middle age and is no longer able to bear children, her value drops back to 8000 *denarii*.[74]

People in the *Pactus* do not commit wrongs as individuals, but as members of kin groups. Kindreds share in the responsibility for wrongs committed by one of their own, and likewise share in the compensation should a wrong be done to one of their own. If someone kills a man and after having given up all his property still cannot pay all of the compensation due, he must first gather twelve men to swear with him that he has no more property. The debt for the balance then falls to his nearest relatives in sequence: father, mother, brother, his mother's sister and her children, then the next most nearly related from among the paternal and maternal kin.[75] If a father is killed, his children are to receive half of the compensation, while those relatives closest to the dead man's father and mother divide the other half among them.[76] A person can formally remove himself from his kindred. By doing so, however, he loses any share of the money paid to compensate the killing of a relative. If he himself is killed, his compensation no longer goes to his kin, but to the king.[77]

The *Pactus* says little about possible causes or motives for violence (beyond the implied hope of material gain in the case of theft, robbery, or plunder) or about the means by which people carried out violence. Reading it, one finds for the most part only a seemingly endless series of statements like, "whoever . . ." or "if he . . .", then ". . . he shall be liable to pay . . .". Nevertheless, one title does single out the case that a man strikes another's horse "through arrogance or hate".[78] Especially interesting, given what we have seen in Gregory's *Histories*, is the fact that the *Pactus* regards violence at banquets as common or important enough to devote most of a title to it.[79]

The *Pactus* does envision a world in which people sometimes secretly hired others to carry out killings for them (to which the Malberg gloss also applies the word *morther*). The relevant title levies compensation payments on the contractor, the hit man, and on any third party to whom the hit man subcontracts out his work.[80] The *Pactus* also devotes significant attention to violence carried out by armed bands. The text assigns compensation amounts for the case that bands of men attack, break into, and plunder someone's villa (i.e., country home, farm, or estate);[81] it also addresses the case that a band breaks into a freeman's house and kills him,[82] or catches him anywhere outside, in a field, or on a journey and kills him.[83]

## Constituted Authority

The valuation of violent wrong is also influenced by whether or not the Frankish king is involved. The king is able in some cases to increase the level of wrong attached to a violent act by extending his protection over that person or taking him into his following. While killing a free Frank is valued at 8000 *denarii*, for example, killing a sworn follower of the king costs 24,000 *denarii*. Attempting to conceal the killing of a king's follower raises the cost to 72,000 *denarii*.[84] Similarly for Romans: while the death of a normal Roman landowner is compensated with 4000 *denarii*, a Roman who is the king's table companion is compensated at 12,000 *denarii*.[85]

The *Pactus*, as well as some of the capitularies later added to it, occasionally mentions something called the *fredus*, which is generally translated as "peace payment". The *fredus* appears to have been a fine that was levied over and above the compensation due for a wrong committed. An older scholarship regarded the *fredus* as a general fine levied for a breach of the public peace.[86] The evidence does not, however, point unambiguously in this direction. The *fredus* appears in the *Pactus* only eight times; it appears twice more in the capitularies. Two references simply mention it without any statement of who should receive it or why. The first states that if a boy under twelve committed some offense, no *fredus* would be required of him.[87] The second states that if someone kills a particularly valuable slave, such as a household slave, a metalworker, or a specialized farmworker, the *fredus* would be levied along with the compensation due for the injury (*faidus*) and for the time the slave's use was lost.[88] The other six references to the *fredus* come in cases where some sort of constituted authority is involved, such as a count or a judge, or where the king's special protection or rights have been violated. If a creditor is forced to get the help of a count to collect on a promissory note, one third of the collected debt would go to the count as *fredus*; if someone seized a girl who was under the king's protection, a *fredus* of 2500 denarii would be added to the normal compensation due for simply abducting any free girl.[89] The *fredus* thus looks less like a fine for the breach of a general peace and more like a fee that kings could extract when their protection or prerogatives were infringed or they or their officials were involved in settling a conflict.[90]

So far I have focused on acts of violence that the *Pactus* treats as illegitimate, that is, as wrongs that need to be made right by compensation. The *Pactus* also, however, treats some acts of violence as legitimate. The most obvious of these are acts of violent punishment. Here we get an idea of where the society envisioned by the *Pactus* drew a line between "inside" and "outside", that is, between groups to which different rules applied; violent punishments are almost entirely directed towards the slave population. Slaves accused of theft are to be tortured to extract confessions. If the theft is proven, they are, for lesser offenses, to be stretched on a rack and lashed, or, for more serious offenses, castrated. They may, if they are able or their lord is willing to help them, pay to avoid the punishment. In the most serious cases, a slave might be executed.[91]

The world of the *Pactus* does not, however, appear to be one in which such punishments are carried out by the representatives of central authority. Few of the relevant clauses say anything about who is supposed to carry out torture and punishment; they say only that it needs to be done. However, Title XL says that the accuser is responsible for torturing an accused slave. He may do so even if the slave's lord objects, on the condition that he buy the slave. The accuser is also responsible for providing the necessary equipment, that is, a rack and rods.[92]

The *Pactus* does assume that its world had courts to which complaints of wrong could be brought. That the courts were important is indicated by the fact that the very first title of the *Pactus* outlines the procedure for summoning a person before one.[93] A judicial court is called a *mallus*, or occasionally a *mallus publicus*,[94] *mallus* being a word of Germanic origin referring to an assembly held for the purpose of judgment.[95] Sometimes a court is referred to as a *placitum* – in classical Latin literally a forum for determining "that which was agreeable".[96] In most cases, a court is convened by an official called a *thunginus*, or a *centenarius*.[97] Alongside the *thunginus* or *centenarius* act a group of men called the *rachimburgi*; these men appear to be responsible for knowing the law and pronouncing it as it applied to specific cases.[98] Nevertheless, various clauses also refer to cases being taken to counts, or to officials called *sagibarons*, or to the king.[99]

The *Pactus* does not bring these courts into direct connection with acts of violence. Nevertheless, given how the courts appear, it seems that a person in the *Pactus*'s world who felt that he had experienced an illegitimate act of violence would summon his opponent to a *mallus*. If his claim were judged just, a compensation amount would be decreed based on the tables of compensations given by the text. This is, however, as far as the court's involvement goes. Violence is still fundamentally a matter between the accuser and accused, as well as their kindreds. The courts serve as a forum for carrying out a set of procedures and applying a set of rules for determining who owed what to whom and why.

Yet the *Pactus* does occasionally connect violence to what we might call constituted authority, and it indicates that within its sphere that authority should not be ignored or threatened. Should a person have an animal stolen and then find someone else holding an animal that he claims to be the stolen one, he is to have the animal placed in the possession of a third party and let a court decide the right. Should he refuse to do so, and instead seizes the animal by force, he is liable for 1200 *denarii*, for the animal, and for the time the animal's use was lost.[100] This does not necessarily indicate that, in the world of the *Pactus*, resorting to violence rather than to constituted authority (i.e., a court) in general constituted a wrong. The clause simply makes a wrong of choosing violence over a particular kind of legal procedure in a particular kind of case; it appears to be aimed at heading off violent squabbles over the disputed ownership of farm animals. Another clause stipulates that someone who "through arrogance or force takes a bound man away from the count" must pay the amount of his own wergeld.[101] The *Pactus* thus envisions a society in which (1) counts, who *ex officio* acted in the king's name, had a special right to keep bound people, and (2) this right was not always uncontested, that is, that some people occasionally used force to spring captives from a count's custody. Counts themselves, as well as the above-mentioned *sagibarons*, enjoy a higher compensation than normal freemen; killing a count costs 24,000 *denarii* and a *sagibaron* 12,000.[102] The *Pactus* tries to control how people gained these offices. Someone who kills a *sagibaron*, and establishes himself or another as *sagibaron* in his place, is liable for the same compensation as killing a count, i.e., 24,000 *denarii*. Apparently people in the *Pactus*'s world were known to try to gain an office by killing its current occupant.[103] Counts are the ones whom one summons to remove forcibly people who have tried to move to a new village but are not welcomed by the inhabitants.[104] Both counts and local *rachimburgi* also have a special right to seize property owed for debts.[105] A person in such a situation had to be careful, however, for some counts were known to try to profit by taking more than was actually due.[106]

The *Pactus* also connects violence to constituted authority when it comes to outlawry. Outlawry is a modern term that nevertheless captures the outlaw's state: he is placed outside the protection of the law. The terms actually used in the *Pactus* itself vary. A man who digs up and despoils a buried body is literally "made like a wolf" (*wargus*)[107] that is, thrust into the wild, until the kin of the dead man agree that he be permitted once more to come among men and to pay them compensation. Until that time, he may not be given food or shelter, even by his own nearest relatives.[108] A man who refuses a summons to come to a *mallus* or delays in carrying out a judgment by *rachimburgi* is to be summoned before the king. Should he refuse to come, the king is to place him "outside his protection" (*extra sermonem suam*). The guilty man and all his property will belong to the king; he may not be fed or sheltered by anyone until he has made redress for the wrongs with which he was charged.[109] It is some of the capitularies added to the *Pactus* in the reigns of Clovis's sons and grandsons that tell us that outlawry legitimizes violence. A free woman who marries her own slave is to be driven away (*aspellis*). Her relatives may kill her without having to pay compensation; none of her relatives may feed or shelter her.[110] If a person flees into the forest to avoid paying compensation for an evil deed, and no one can compel him to come into the king's presence, he is to be placed outside the king's protection (*nostro sermone*), "so that whoever finds him can kill him in any way without fear".[111]

It is hard to say whether in the ideal (and sometimes internally contra-dictory) world laid out by the *Pactus* and its accompanying capitularies, these outlawry provisions mean that everyone under a king's authority enjoyed a built-in royal protection that a king might revoke. In some of the provisions (despoiling a buried body, or a woman marrying a slave), the law itself places the wrongdoer outside of its protection and legitimates violent vengeance by the affected parties. In the others, however, the king has suffered a direct affront, namely a refusal to obey a summons. Given that other references in the *Pactus* to a king's protection apply to individual people, it seems more plausible that these outlawry clauses pertain to cases in which an affront or wrong has been done specifically to the king. I would suggest, therefore (without claiming to have solved the puzzle for certain), that the law, which includes and embraces but extends beyond the king, legitimizes violence against an outlaw by an injured party. When directly injured, the king may do the same by removing his protection; in such a case, we could think of anyone who might meet and kill the outlaw as the king's agent. But it fits better with the rest of the *Pactus* to suggest that the king's protection is personal, not general. The king might extend his protection, or refuse

to extend it, to specific individuals and in specific cases where his interests are involved.

## What was "Law"?

By far the most important information about how the *Pactus* stands in
relation to the world that produced it, however, comes in a few implicit
but nevertheless telling references to legitimate violence. These references
tell us that there was an entire arena of violence in the Frankish world
that fell outside the *Pactus*'s purview. If a man traveling on a road comes
across a freeman "without hands or feet whom his enemies have left at
a crossroad" and kills him, he is liable for 4000 *denarii*.[112] People in the
world assumed by the *Pactus*, then, were apparently known to seize their
enemies, cut off their hands and feet, and leave them at a crossroad. This
is symbolic violence in the extreme. Such an act declares publicly that
the victim has wronged the perpetrators. To avenge this wrong, the
perpetrators have not killed the victim, but rather rendered him entirely
helpless and left him in a place where people are likely to pass by and
see that their vengeance has been carried out. The *Pactus* treats this as
legitimate and expectable. It gives its attention to, and assigns compensation for, not the mutilation itself but an act carried out by someone
who later comes across the victim. The text does not say whether the
passer-by was supposed to leave the victim alive because it would undermine the effect of the original act of vengeance to put him out of his
misery, because it was unfair to kill a man who could not fight back,
or because interfering with a public display of vengeance might re-open
violent hostilities.[113] But either way, the message is clear: the passer-by
should not interfere.

In one of the variant manuscript traditions of the *Pactus*, two similar
clauses follow immediately upon this one.[114] He who takes a freeman
down from a gibbet without permission is liable for 1800 *denarii*. The
clause says nothing about who might have hanged the freeman and for
what infraction, nor about whose permission was needed to remove him;
however, we do learn that freemen could be hanged and that the authors
of the *Pactus* considered it a wrong for someone to take them down
without permission. More informative is the next clause: he who takes
down the head of a man that his enemies have put on a stick is liable
for 600 *denarii*. Once more we see violent vengeance and symbolic display. An enmity existed which the victim's enemies avenged by killing
the victim. The violence was made as public as possible; its gruesome
results and the identity of the victim were displayed for all to see. The
text regards this violence as legitimate; again, no one should interfere.

In short, there was a world of legitimate violence in the society depicted by the *Pactus* beyond that addressed directly by the *Pactus* itself.[115] In this world, people took violent revenge for perceived wrongs. They made no effort to hide their actions; on the contrary, they advertised them as widely as possible. Far from protesting or condemning this kind of violence, the *Pactus* casts any interference with it as itself a wrong that justified compensation. It does not take much effort to see the link with the story of Sichar and Chramnesind told by Gregory of Tours. After being needled by Sichar for getting rich off the settlement between them, Chramnesind recalled how his family might judge his actions: he had acted like a woman by not taking revenge on the killer of his kin. He promptly killed Sichar and stuck his body outside on a fencepost. King Guntram did not interfere; he asked only for Chramnesind's assurance that he had acted to avenge an insult.

With these observations in mind, I would suggest that the *Pactus* primarily addresses the case that both parties in a dispute agreed, or were forced by community pressure, to a non-violent settlement. The text deals above all with compensation amounts and the procedures by which appropriate compensations were to be determined and paid. It lies near at hand, therefore, to say that this is what "law" was; to resort to the law, for freemen at least, meant to resort to courts, judgment, settlement, and compensation. The law provided a means for settling disputes without violence; the threat of having to pay compensation might well have served to deter some from committing acts of violence. However, the law was not directly opposed to violence. Quite the contrary: beyond the law lay a field of violence that was brutal and deadly but nevertheless legitimate. Opponents who refused to settle their conflict peacefully, and whom their community was unable or declined to sanction, did so violently and personally. Parties to such violence carried it out openly and symbolically; far from hiding the killing of their enemies they advertised it in ways that made it clear what they had done and why. In short, while in some cases community pressure and/or the fear of the consequences of ongoing violence prompted resort to the law, in others violence was left to run its course without interference; the victim got what he deserved.

This picture fits together easily with what we have seen in Gregory's *Histories*. Violent vengeance in Gregory's text is one of several legitimate means magnates and their followings could use to prosecute their disputes with one another. In the Sichar-Austregisel-Chramnesind affair we saw how disputes could move back and forth between violence and the court processes and peaceful settlements that Gregory himself tried to promote. In the end, it ended with Sichar's body on a fencepost, with King Guntram's acceptance (if not that of Queen Brunhild, whose follower had been killed), and even Gregory's grudging approval. The word "law" only appears in connection with the settlement/compensation process. Violent actions that took place outside the law were not *ipso facto* illegitimate. Only when helpless or uninvolved people or property were caught up in violence (Sichar's wounded men killed by Austregisel, Chramnesind's family killed by Sichar, or the houses of Sichar's neighbors plundered and burned by Chramnesind) did the civic authorities step in. And even in its own arena the law was not considered inviolable. The non-violent settlement that at least temporarily halted the enmity between Sichar and Chramnesind contradicted the law; nevertheless, everyone involved agreed to it because they thought it was necessary.

There is no sign in either the *Pactus* or Gregory's *Histories* that the Merovingian kings or their representatives enjoyed any special right to be violent; nor did they have any general right to control or regulate the violence of others. Kings could increase the level of wrong attached to violence in specific cases by extending their protection over a particular person. They could legitimize violence by declaring someone outside their protection, but the law could do this by itself as well. Queens as well as kings could increase the cost of violence with their protection. Certain uses of force belonged to royal representatives and enjoyed some normative safeguards. But in general it seems that in both Gregory and in the *Pactus*, kings and their representatives played within the same system of norms governing violence as did everyone else.

## The Capitularies

In one body of sixth-century texts, however, we find something different, namely in the capitularies issued by Merovingian kings.[116] These capitularies are by definition king-centered documents. So it should come as no surprise that it is here that we find the idea expressed that kings had the right and duty to regulate violence on behalf of the general welfare.

As far as violence is concerned, most of the capitularies associated with the *Pactus Legis Salicae* simply reinforce norms already visible in the original *Pactus*. Unlike the *Pactus*, however, they add an overlay of Christian norms.[117] One example extends the king's protection over fugitives who have sought sanctuary in churches; according to a decree most likely issued jointly by Childebert I (d. 558) and Chlothar I (d. 561), if someone tried to drag a thief or other guilty person from the atrium of a church, he was to be punished according to the canons.[118] This decree does not impose compensation. Instead, it imposes a punishment according to a body of norms lying outside the Frankish legal tradition: the canon law of the Church.[119]

It is from within this overlay of Christian norms that the capitularies cast kings as responsible for upholding peace and order in their kingdoms. The capitulary discussed above calls itself: "The Pact Issued by Kings Childebert and Chlothar for Keeping the Peace." The prologue continues: "Because the madness of many increases and the frightfulness of evil grows, it is necessary [to issue this edict] so that those things that are proper can be reestablished."[120] Therefore, say the king and the greater persons of his palace, proven thieves shall receive the death penalty. The same capitulary decrees that "in order to keep the peace", selected hundredmen be made king's men (that is, be placed "in trust") "so that through their faith and care the above said peace may be observed".[121] In other words, in order to uphold the peace the king might delegate his authority to representatives who would carry out the actual work. The capitulary ends by putting God's imprimatur on the entire enterprise, and by pairing that imprimatur with the royal right to impose violent punishment: "we (i.e., Childebert and Chlothar) have established this pact to keep the peace in the name of God and it is our wish that these prescribed things be observed perpetually; and let it be known that if any judge presumes to violate this decree, he will be subjected to the loss of his life".[122]

A capitulary issued by Chilperic I (d. 584) likewise bills itself as a decree for keeping the peace, and says that it was worked out together with the nobles, king's men, and all the people of Chilperic's kingdom "in the name of God".[123] If we assume that the "peace" which needs to be kept is defined by what follows, it seems to mean something different than a simple absence of violence. As is also implied by the declared intent of the above capitulary to re-establish "those things that are proper", "peace" instead embraces what we might call right order.[124] Keeping the peace means having inheritances follow proper rules,[125] avoiding upsets over minor matters,[126] regulating a lord's responsibility should one of his slaves kill a freeman,[127] providing a procedure for those who must give a pledge that they will go to a court but have nothing with which to give the pledge,[128] forcing lords to submit slaves accused of thefts to an ordeal by lot, dealing with freemen convicted of a wrong who do not have the property to pay compensation,[129] using churches to announce where courts will meet,[130] regulating the process for bringing a case before the courts, handling the cases of people who have fled because they could not pay compensation,[131] and prohibiting theft.[132]

The capitularies also have kings extending the bounds of legitimate violence, though the relevant clauses do not restrict the right to carry out royally-mandated violence to royal officials. A capitulary issued in 595 by Childebert II (d. 596) makes rape, a compensatable wrong in the *Pactus* proper, a capital offense.[133] It empowers a judge to collect what amounts to a posse and kill or outlaw the ravisher. A woman who consented to her own rape, should she seek refuge in a church, was to be sent into exile with her ravisher. If captured, the pair was to be killed and their property given to the relatives or to the king. The same capitulary also generalizes homicide "without cause" into a capital offense.[134] It is hard to say what "without cause" means. Katherine Fischer Drew suggests that it refers to stealth killing of the kind given higher compensation amounts in the *Pactus*. I would suggest, however, that given the evidence we have seen for the legitimacy of killings where the cause was advertised, "without cause" simply means that the grievance behind the killing was not declared. Be that as it may, such a killer is automatically outlawed, and he may be killed without compensation.

Other Merovingian programmatic statements that are transmitted outside of the *Pactus* also project kings as defenders of the Christian faith and of Christian order, and declare kings entitled to use violence in the service of these causes.[135] Already Clovis, in a letter to his bishops, casts himself as the protector of the churches, the religious, and their property; he forbids violence or injury to nuns, widows devoted to the religious life, to clergy, their sons or widows they are supporting, or to church slaves.[136] Childebert I issued an order according to which pagan idols were to be cast down, unfree people who were still carrying out pagan rites were to be lashed, and free people guilty of the same offense were to be punished in another way.[137]

In an edict of 585, King Guntram made the connection between himself, God, and right order explicit.[138] He declared he had been delegated by God to insure justice among the people; as God's agent he was responsible for the stability and salvation of the kingdom. In an echo of the worldview that we saw in Gregory's *Histories* and in the *Life* of St. Columbanus, Guntram notes that the divine being from whom he derived his power had taken violent vengeance for wrongs that his people had committed at the persuasion of the devil; "through diverse worldly tempests" God had caused cattle to be consumed by disease or by the sword. To ward off the divine anger that could fall on him if he failed to do his job, Guntram ordered the bishops to correct the people through their preaching; he forbade any work (except for that necessary to prepare food) or legal activities on Sundays. Judges were to strive to exercise justice, and they and their subordinates were to avoid venality; the transgressions of clerics were not to be ignored. In short: the restoration at the king's command of a right Christian order would prevent divine violence and bring about the desired peace and concord.

The Merovingian capitularies from the sixth century in general reflect the same world that produced our other sources. Because they are direct acts of lawgiving by Catholic Christian kings, however, they directly address the relationship between the king, God, right order, and violence. The king had the duty as God's representative on earth to uphold Christian peace, which meant not the absence of violence but rather proper Christian order.[139] He himself was able to use violence to carry out this duty. He could in particular extend or retract the bounds of legitimate violence. Nevertheless, the early Merovingians were far from enjoying, or even claiming, a monopoly on the legitimate use of violence. This latter point is especially important, because in the next chapter we will see a Frankish ruler, in very different circumstances, building on what we have seen here to make a very different claim.

## Notes

1. See Paul Fouracre, ed., NCMH I; Ian Wood, *The Merovingian Kingdoms 450–751* (London and New York: Longman, 1994); Patrick J. Geary, *Before France and Germany: The Creation and Transformation of the Merovingian World* (New York and Oxford: Oxford University Press, 1988); Wallace-Hadrill, *The Long-Haired Kings*.
2. Gregory of Tours, *Historiarum libri decem*/Thorpe, ed., *History of the Franks*. All quotations below will be drawn from Thorpe unless otherwise noted.
3. Bruno Krusch, ed., *Vita Columbani abbatis discipulorumque eius libri duo auctore Iona*. MGH SSRM 4 (Hanover: Hahn, 1902), 64–108. English translation of Book I: Jonas, "Life of St. Columbanus", in *Monks, Bishops and Pagans: Christian Culture in Gaul and Italy, 500–700*, ed. Edward Peters, trans. William C. McDermott (Philadelphia: University of Pennsylvania Press, 1975), 75–113. All quotations will be drawn from McDermott unless otherwise noted.
4. Karl August Eckhart, ed., *Pactus Legis Salicae*, MGH LL Nat. Germ. 4, 1 (Hanover: Hahn, 1962). English translation: *The Laws of the Salian Franks*. trans. Katherine Fischer Drew (Philadelphia: University of Pennsylvania Press, 1991 – henceforward Drew). All quotations below will be drawn from Drew unless otherwise noted.
5. Alfred Boretius, ed., MGH Capit. I (Hanover: Hahn, 1883), 1–23; *Pactus Legis Salicae* editions as n. 4 above.
6. See *inter alia*: Martin Heinzelmann, *Gregor Von Tours (538–594): "Zehn Bücher Geschichte": Historiographie und Gesellschaftskonzept im 6. Jahrhundert* (Darmstadt: Wissenschaftliche Buchgesellschaft, 1994), translated into English by Christopher Carroll as *Gregory of Tours: History and Society in the Sixth Century* (Cambridge: Cambridge University Press, 2001); Kathleen Mitchell and Ian Wood, eds., *The World of Gregory of Tours* (Leiden: Brill, 2002); Walter A. Goffart, *The Narrators of Barbarian*

*History (A.D. 550–800): Jordanes, Gregory of Tours, Bede, and Paul the Deacon*
(Princeton: Princeton University Press, 1988).

7. Gregory V/20, v. 1, 324–9/Thorpe, 285–7.
8. Cf. also, for example, Gregory IV/16, v. 1, 214–17/Thorpe, 211; IV/36, v. 1, 246–7/Thorpe, 231; VI/36, v. 2, 62–7/Thorpe, 366–70.
9. Gregory I/32, v. 1, 36–9/Thorpe, 88–9; I/34, v. 1, 38–9/Thorpe, 89–90.
10. Gregory II/27, v. 1, 110–11/Thorpe, 139. On Syagrius of Soissons see Wood, *Merovingian Kingdoms*, 39–41.
11. Gregory II/42, v. 1, 138–41/Thorpe, 156–8.
12. Gregory II/31, v. 1, 116–19/Thorpe, 143–4. On Constantine see Richard Gerberding, "The Later Roman Empire", in NCMH I, 13–34, @21–3.
13. Gregory II/37, v. 1, 128–31/Thorpe, 151.
14. Gregory II/40, v. 1, 136–7/Thorpe, 156.
15. Gregory II/27, v. 1, 110–13/Thorpe, 139–40. Cf. Clovis protecting the interests of St. Martin: Gregory II/37, v. 1, 128–31/Thorpe, 151–2.
16. Gregory V/20, v. 1, 324–9 @324–5/Thorpe, 285–7 @285. I have chosen to translate *cohors* as "company" rather than Thorpe's "mob"; see Lewis and Short and Niermeyer, s.v. *cohors*.
17. Gregory V/20, v. 1, 328–9/Thorpe, 287.
18. Gregory III/35, v. 1, 188–9/Thorpe, 191; Cf. Gregory VI/36, v. 2, 62–7/Thorpe, 366–70.
19. Gregory VII/47, v. 2, 152–7/Thorpe, 428–30 and IX/19, v. 2, 256–9/Thorpe, 501–2. See Patrick J. Geary, "Gabriel Monod, Fustel de Coulanges et les «Aventures de Sichaire». La naissance de l'histoire scientifique au xixᵉ siècle", in Bougard, *La Vengeance*; Guy Halsall, "Violence and Society", 1–2; Wallace-Hadrill, "Bloodfeud", 39–41.
20. Thorpe translates *puer* throughout this story as "servant". However, *puer*, literally "boy", can in this period mean anything from a slave to a royal agent; it was frequently used to describe armed followers. Sichar's wounded men were plainly his "boys", i.e., members of his armed retinue. See Niermeyer, s.v. *puer*, def. 3.
21. Gregory VII/47, v. 2, 154–5/Thorpe, 428.
22. Cf. Edward James, "*Beati Pacifici*: Bishops and the Law in Sixth-Century Gaul", in *Disputes and Settlements: Law and Human Relations in the West*, ed. J. Bossy (Cambridge: Cambridge University Press, 1983), 25–46.
23. Gregory IX/19, 256–7/Thorpe, 501.
24. Thorpe, 502 translates *homicida* here as murderous; for reasons that will become clear below I prefer to render it as homicidal.
25. Gregory II/23, v. 1, 104–9/Thorpe, 135–7.
26. Gregory VII/3, v. 2, 96–7/Thorpe, 390.
27. Gregory III/12, v. 1, 158–9/Thorpe, 171–2. Cf. also Gregory III/16, v. 1, 170–1/Thorpe, 179.
28. Gregory IV/16, v. 1, 214–17/Thorpe, 211. Cf. also, for example, Gregory III/16, v. 1, 170–1/Thorpe, 179 (St. Julian again); IV/18, v. 1, 218–21/Thorpe, 214 (God and St. Martin); IV/36, v. 1, 244–9/

Thorpe, 230–2 (God and St. Nicetius); IV/39, v. 1, 248–51/Thorpe, 233–4 (God); IV/48, v. 1, 266–7/Thorpe, 244–5 or VI/10, v. 2, 24–5/ Thorpe, 340–1 (St. Martin again); etc.

29. On this point I disagree with Fouracre, "Attitudes Towards Violence", 62.

30. Cf. the comprehensive introduction to medieval hagiography offered by Thomas Head at ORB: **http://www.the-orb.net/encyclop/religion/ hagiography/hagindex.html**.

31. See *inter alia*, František Graus, *Volk, Herrscher und Heiliger im Reich der Merowinger: Studien zur Hagiographie der Merowingerzeit* (Prague: Nakladatelství Československé akademie věd, 1965); J.M. Wallace-Hadrill, *The Frankish Church* (Oxford: Oxford University Press 1983); Raymond Van Dam, *Saints and their Miracles in Late Antique Gaul* (Princeton: Princeton University Press, 1993); Paul Fouracre and Richard Gerberding, eds., *Late Merovingian France: History and Hagiography, 640–720* (Manchester: Manchester University Press, 1996).

32. Fouracre and Gerberding, *Late Merovingian France*, 43.

33. See *inter alia*: Wood, *Merovingian Kingdoms*, 184–9; Geary, *Before France and Germany*, 169–71; Heinz Löwe, ed., *Die Iren und Europa im früheren Mittelalter* (Stuttgart: Klett-Cotta, 1982); Friedrich Prinz, *Frühes Mönchtum im Frankenreich: Kultur und Gesellschaft in Gallien, den Rheinlanden und Bayern am Beispiel der monastischen Entwicklung (4. bis 8. Jahrhundert)* (Vienna: Oldenbourg, 1965).

34. See Clare Stancliffe, "Jonas's *Life of Columbanus and His Disciples*", in *Studies in Irish Hagiography: Saints and Scholars*, eds. John Carey, *et al.* (Dublin: Four Courts Press, 2001), 189–220; Barbara H. Rosenwein, *Negotiating Space: Power, Restraint, and Privileges of Immunity in Early Medieval Europe* (Ithaca, NY: Cornell University Press, 1999), 59–73; Ian Wood, "The *Vita Columbani* and Merovingian Hagiography", *Peritia* 1 (1982): 63–80.

35. The following examples are all drawn from Book I of the *Vita Columbani*.

36. See *Vita Columbani* C. 20, 92/McDermott C. 38, 99–100; C. 25, 99/McDermott C. 49, 106; C. 27, 103/McDermott C. 54, 108–9. See also temptation cast as diabolical violence in C. 3, 68/McDermott C. 7, 77 and C. 7, 73/McDermott C. 14, 82.

37. *Vita Columbani* C. 21, 93/McDermott C. 40, 100.

38. *Vita Columbani* C. 12, 78; McDermott C. 20, 87.

39. *Vita Columbani* C. 22, 96/McDermott C. 44, 103.

40. *Vita Columbani* C. 19, 87–8; McDermott C. 32, 94–5.

41. *Vita Columbani* C. 19, 88/McDermott C. 33, 95–6; Rosenwein, *Negotiating Space*, 70–1.

42. *Vita Columbani* C. 20, 90/McDermott C. 35, 98.

43. *Vita Columbani* C. 20, 91/McDermott C. 36, 99.

44. *Vita Columbani* C. 20, 92/McDermott C. 37, 99.

45. *Vita Columbani* C. 22, 95–6/McDermott C. 43, 102–3.

46. *Vita Columbani* C. 28, 105/McDermott C. 57, 111.

47. *Vita Columbani* C. 29, 106/McDermott C. 58, 111.

48. Cf. also Gregory VI/31, v. 2, 54–5/Thorpe, 360.

49. Drew, introduction to *Laws of the Salian Franks*, 52; Rosamond McKitterick, *The Carolingians and the Written Word* (Cambridge: Cambridge University Press, 1989), 40–60.
50. Drew, introduction, 28.
51. Stein, *Roman Law*, 28–9, 34–5.
52. Jill Harries, "Violence, Victims, and the Legal Tradition in Late Antiquity", in *Violence in Late Antiquity: Perceptions and Practices*, ed. H.A. Drake (Aldershot: Ashgate, 2006), 85–102.
53. Drew, introduction, 28–31; Wood, *Merovingian Kingdoms*, 108–13 and "Disputes in Late Fifth- and Sixth-Century Gaul: Some Problems", in Davies and Fouracre, eds., *Settlement of Disputes in Early Medieval Europe*, 7–22 @10–22; Geary, *Before France and Germany*, 90–1; LDM, s.v. "Lex Salica".
54. Though see the argument made from the manuscripts by McKitterick, *Written Word*, 40–60.
55. Patrick Wormald, "Lex Scripta and Verbum Regis: Legislation and Germanic Kingship, from Euric to Cnut", in *Early Medieval Kingship*, ed. P.H. Sawyer and Ian N. Wood (Leeds: University of Leeds, 1977).
56. Cf. Steven Fanning, "Clovis Augustus and Merovingian Imitatio Imperii", in Mitchell and Wood, *World of Gregory of Tours*, 321–35; Michael McCormick, *Eternal Victory: Triumphal Rulership in Late Antiquity, Byzantium, and the Early Medieval West* (Cambridge: Cambridge University Press, 1986), 335–8.
57. Cf. Patrick J. Geary, "Gabriel Monod", 87–99.
58. *Pactus* II–IX, 20–51/Drew, 65–74; Drew, 49.
59. Drew, introduction, 47–9.
60. See *Pactus* X, 51–5/Drew, 74–6; XI, 55–7/Drew, 76–7; XVI, 71–5/Drew, 81–2; XXI, 85–6/Drew, 84–5; XXVII, 98–109/Drew, 88–91; XXXIV, 126–8/Drew, 96–7; LXVc, 235/Drew, 126.
61. See *Pactus* II/5, 22/Drew, 66; VI/3–4, 38/Drew, 71; XXXVIII/13, 141/Drew, 101. Damage via animals: IX/9, 50–1/Drew, 74.
62. See *Pactus* XIII–XV, 59–71/Drew, 77–80; XVII, 75–80/Drew, 82–3; XIX–XX, 81–4/Drew, 83–4; XXIV–XXV, 89–96/Drew, 86–7; XXVIII–XXIX, 110–17/Drew, 92–4; XXXI–XXXII, 120–3/Drew, 94–5; XXXV, 128–32/Drew, 97–8; XLI–XLIII, 154–67/Drew, 104–8; LIV, 203–4/Drew, 117–18; LVIII, 218–21/Drew, 121–2; LXI–LXIII, 226–30/Drew, 123–25; LXVb–e, 234–5/Drew, 126–7.
63. *Pactus* XIV/1, 64/Drew, 79.
64. See Philip Grierson, and Mark Blackburn, *Medieval European Coinage* (Cambridge: Cambridge University Press, 1986), 81–111 and esp. 102–6.
65. Drew, introduction, 50.
66. *Pactus* XIV/2–3, 64–5/Drew, 79.
67. *Pactus* XXIX, 112–17/Drew, 92–4; cf. also XVII, 75–80/Drew, 82–3.
68. *Pactus* XV/1, 70/Drew, 80; XLI/1, 154/Drew, 104.
69. The word "wergeld" is almost never used in the *Pactus* itself. Only a variant text of LI/3, 197/Drew, 115, given by the MGH edition as H 10, says that a count who collects more than a just debt shall pay with his life

or redeem himself with his wergeld (*uuereguldum suum*). For uses of the term in the capitularies attached to the *Pactus* see Capitulary VI, II/3, 268/Drew, 158 and Capitulary VI, III/3, 268/Drew, 158.

70. *Pactus* XLI/9, 157/Drew, 105.

71. *Pactus* XLI/1-4, 154-5/Drew, 104.

72. See XXVIII/1-3, 110-11/Drew, 92; XLI/2, 4, 155/Drew, 104. In LXIII/2, 230/Drew, 125 the word *mother* [sic] is also used for the case of a king's man (antrustion) killed while serving in the army. On the Malburg glosses see Drew, introduction, 52-3; Heinrich Brunner, *Deutsche Rechtsgeschichte*, 2nd edn (Munich: Duncker & Humblot, 1906-1928), v. 1, 432-3.

73. *Pactus* XX, 83-4/Drew, 84.

74. See also *Pactus* XXIV, 89-92/Drew, 86 and XLI/15-17 and 19, 160-1/Drew, 105-6.

75. *Pactus* LVIII, 218-21/Drew, 121-2.

76. *Pactus* LXII, 227-8/Drew, 124.

77. *Pactus* LX, 225/Drew, 123.

78. *Pactus* XXXVIII/13, 141/Drew, 101.

79. *Pactus* XLIII/1-2, 165-6/Drew, 107.

80. *Pactus* XXVIII, 110-11/Drew, 92.

81. *Pactus* XIV/6-8, 66-7/Drew, 79-80.

82. *Pactus* XLII, 162-5/Drew, 106-7.

83. *Pactus* XLIII/3, 166-7/Drew, 107-8.

84. *Pactus* XLI/5-7, 156/Drew, 104.

85. *Pactus* XLI/8, 157/Drew, 105.

86. See Brunner, *Deutsche Rechtsgeschichte*, v. 1, 230-1, 333-4.

87. *Pactus* XXIV/7, 92/Drew, 86.

88. *Pactus*, XXXV/9, 132/Drew, 98.

89. *Pactus*, XIII/6, 60/Drew, 78; L/3, 192-5/Drew, 114-15. See also LIII/2, 4, 6, 8, 201-3/Drew, 116-17; Capitulary II, LXXXVIII, 252/Drew, 140; LXLII, 252/Drew, 141-2. Pactus, LXVg/1-11, 236/Drew, 127-8 may represent a list of *fredus* amounts; see Drew, 127 n. 68.

90. Cf. Wallace-Hadrill, *The Long-Haired Kings*, 148-248 @188; Dilcher, "Friede Durch Recht", in Fried, *Träger und Instrumentarien des Friedens*, 203-7 @208.

91. *Pactus* XII, 58/Drew, 77; XXV/5-7, 94-6/Drew, 87; XL, 145-54/Drew, 102-4.

92. *Pactus* XL/4 and 6, 146-9/Drew, 102-3.

93. *Pactus* I, 18-20/Drew, 65; Drew, introduction, 32-9.

94. *Pactus* XLVI/6, 181/Drew, 111.

95. DRW, s.v. *mallus*.

96. Lewis and Short, s.v. *placeo*.

97. *Pactus* XLIV/1, 168-9/Drew, 108; XLVI/1, 176-7/Drew, 110; L/2, 190-2/Drew, 114.

98. *Pactus* LVII, 215-17/Drew, 120-1.

99. Counts: *Pactus* L/3-4, 192-5/Drew, 114-15. *Sagibarons*: LIV/4, 204/Drew, 117-18. King: XVIII, 80/Drew, 83; XLVI/6, 181/Drew, 111.

100. *Pactus* XXXVII/3, 135/Drew, 99; cf. also LXI/3, 155/Drew, 124.
101. *Pactus* XXXII/5, 123/Drew, 95.
102. *Pactus* LIV/1–2, 203–4/Drew, 117.
103. *Pactus* LIV/3, 204/Drew, 117.
104. *Pactus* XLV/2, 173–5/Drew, 109–10.
105. *Pactus* L/3, 192–5/Drew, 114–15; LVI/6a, 214/Drew, 120.
106. *Pactus* LI/3, 197/Drew, 115.
107. WGS, s.v. *varga*.
108. *Pactus* LV/4, 206–7/Drew, 118.
109. *Pactus* LVI/1–6, 210–13/Drew, 119.
110. *Pactus* Capitulary III, LXLVIII, 255/Drew, 144.
111. *Pactus* Capitulary IV, CXV, 263/Drew, 152.
112. *Pactus* XLI/11, 158/Drew, 105.
113. For this latter suggestion I thank Jason Glenn.
114. *Pactus* XLI/11a and 11b, 158/Drew, 105.
115. I disagree, therefore, with Drew's comment @235 n. 41.
116. On the Merovingian capitularies see Drew, introduction, 52; Ingrid Woll, *Untersuchungen zu Überlieferung und Eigenart der merowingischen Kapitularien* (Frankfurt: P. Lang, 1995).
117. Only three clauses in the *Pactus* proper hint at Christian influence, by setting compensations for plundering or burning a basilica, including one that covers a dead body, that contains relics, or that has been blessed: LV/6–7, 209/Drew, 118–19 and LXVb, 234/Drew, 126. LV/6–7 do not appear in the earliest redaction of the *Pactus*; LXVb is restricted to one manuscript tradition. See Drew, introduction, 119 n. 56 and 126 n. 63; cf. Wood, *Merovingian Kingdoms*, 112.
118. "Pactus pro tenore pacis domnorum Childeberti et Chlotarii regum", *Pactus* Capitulary II, 250–4/Drew, 137–43 @LXL, 252/Drew, 141; Woll, *Untersuchungen*, 13–17, 50–73, 143–6.
119. On the development of canon law in this period: James A. Brundage, *Medieval Canon Law* (London: Longman, 1995), 18–26.
120. *Pactus* Capitulary II, prologue, 250/Drew, 137. I have translated *digna* as "those things that are proper" instead of Drew's "good order".
121. *Pactus* Capitulary II, LXLI, 252/Drew, 141.
122. *Pactus* Capitulary II, LXLIII, 252/Drew, 142.
123. "Edictus domni Chilperici regis pro tenore pacis": *Pactus* Capitulary IV, CVI, 261/Drew, 148; Woll, *Untersuchungen*, 29–33, 50–73, 142–3.
124. Cf. Thomas Renna, "The Idea of Peace in the West, 500–1150", *Journal of Medieval History* 6 (1980): 145–8; Brunner, *Land and Lordship*, 18–19.
125. *Pactus* Capitulary IV, CVI, CVIII, CIX, CX, 216–62/Drew, 148–9.
126. *Pactus* Capitulary IV, CVII, 262/Drew, 149. Drew translates *scandalum* as "breach of the peace"; in my opinion this is too specific.
127. *Pactus* Capitulary IV, CXI, 262/Drew, 149–50.
128. *Pactus* Capitulary IV, CXII, 262/Drew, 150.
129. *Pactus* Capitulary IV, CXIII, 262–3/Drew, 150–1.
130. *Pactus* Capitulary IV, CXIV, 263/Drew, 152.

131. *Pactus* Capitulary IV, CXV, 263/Drew, 152.

132. *Pactus* Capitulary IV, CXVI, 263/Drew, 152.

133. "Decretus Childeberto rege": *Pactus* Capitulary VI, 267–9/Drew, 156–9, esp. II, Maestricht/Treiectum 595, 268/Drew, 157–8; Woll, *Untersuchungen*, 36–40, 50–73, 137–42.

134. *Pactus* Capitulary VI, II/3, 268/Drew, 158.

135. Wood, *Merovingian Kingdoms*, 104–8.

136. "Chlodowici regis ad episcopos epistola, 507–511", MGH Capit. 1, 1–2; Woll, *Untersuchungen*, 168–75.

137. "Childeberti I. regis praeceptum, 511–558", MGH Capit. 1, 2–3; Woll, *Untersuchungen*, 6–13, 47–8, 135.

138. "Guntchramni regis edictum, 585. Nov. 10", MGH Capit. 1, 10–12; Woll, *Untersuchungen*, 33–6, 49–50, 136–7.

139. Cf. Philippe Buc, *The Dangers of Ritual: Between Early Medieval Texts and Social Scientific Theory* (Princeton: Princeton University Press, 2001), 107–11.

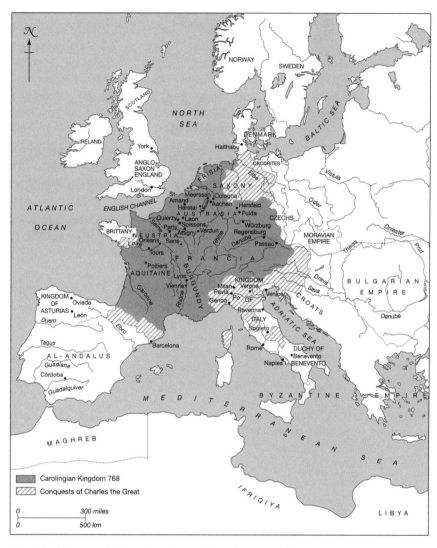

**Map 2** Europe during the reign of Charlemagne (From B.H. Rosenwein, *A Short History of the Middle Ages* (Broadview, 2004) p. 109)

## Chapter three

# CHARLEMAGNE, GOD, AND THE LICENSE TO KILL

The kindred that would replace the Merovingians as kings of the Franks emerged at the end of the seventh century and the beginning of the eighth.[1] In contrast to the family of Clovis, which came from what would become Neustria, this family was propertied to the east, in Austrasia. The names that defined its leading members were originally Arnulf and Pippin. It was with Charles, nicknamed the "Hammer" or in Old French Martel (c. 688–741, sole mayor of the Frankish palace from c. 720), that a new leading name entered the family tradition and gave the family its final label: the Carolingians.

The Carolingian ascendancy came to a climax in 751, when Charles Martel's son Pippin III deposed the last figurehead Merovingian and took the title king of the Franks.[2] Despite the realities of his power, Pippin was not of Merovingian royal blood. He had, therefore, in order to secure his position vis à vis the rest of the Frankish magnates, to put his kingship on a different basis. He looked for this basis to Christianity; he had himself anointed king on the model of the great kings of the Old Testament,[3] possibly with the approval of the bishop of Rome, Pope Zacharias.[4] In 753, Pope Stephen II travelled to Francia and anointed Pippin again, together with all of his immediate family. In other words, Pippin legitimated his family's claim to royalty according to a different political ideology from that of his predecessors. Although he and his Carolingian successors continued to rule in tandem with the great Frankish magnates much as the Merovingians had, their position in the relationship was based, not on being born kings, but rather on an image of sacred Christian kingship overtly derived from biblical precedent.

This shift in the ideological basis of Frankish rulership had been a long time building. As we have seen, the Merovingian kings of the sixth century had proclaimed in their capitularies that they were acting on God's behalf; they thus cast both their restrictions of violence and the violence they legitimated in a Christian hue. From the middle of the seventh century, this hue becomes more pronounced in a wide variety of sources, at least in part because of a change in the nature of Frankish political conflict.[5] A series of child kings led factions of Frankish aristocrats to compete directly with each other for control of the royal courts and of the young kings. Prominent among these aristocrats, by virtue of their wealth and power, were the Frankish bishops. As the competition for control particularly of the office of mayor of the palace intensified, so too do reports of political violence in both history and hagiography. Much of this violence involved powerful bishops both on the giving and on the receiving ends. With kings no longer directly legitimating political violence by leading it, the use of sanctity as a propaganda tool became increasingly important. Accordingly, the later seventh century saw a burst of new hagiography, in particular lives of bishops who were martyred in the course of political conflict. These late Merovingian martyr stories put violence and its legitimacy at center stage. They cast violence as something morally and religiously significant, that is, as a form of action that was imbued with religious significance and had to be understood according to religious norms. Violence was evil when it struck a saintly bishop, yet it provided a vehicle for the bishop's martyrdom and sainthood. Victory in factional conflict, including victory achieved by violence, was a sign of divine favor. Successful violence was, therefore, itself a justification for political power.

The early Carolingians took full advantage of this normative framework, especially after they achieved the kingship and were in a position to influence more widely how history was written.[6] The victories of the mayors Pippin II and his son Charles Martel against their Austrasian and Neustrian rivals are presented by Carolingian texts as signs of divine favor and of their right to rule. Once they reach the reign of Pippin III as king, these texts downplay factional conflict within the Frankish aristocracy. Instead, they highlight the kings and a united aristocracy fighting foreign enemies. Nevertheless, religious norms remain essential to the ideology of Carolingian power. Victory in battle was a sign of God's favor. Once victory had been achieved, and the Carolingians' right to rule had been demonstrated, the Carolingian kings served as God's agents, in the mold whose contours were originally shaped by the Merovingians whom they had replaced.

This chapter will focus not on Pippin III, but rather on his son Charles, who became a king of the Franks on Pippin's death in 768 and sole king after his brother Carloman died in 771. The reign of Charles – better known as "Charles the Great" or in Old French Charlemagne – was a watershed in medieval history. It is the period in which Charlemagne finished the task started by his grandfather Charles Martel and his father Pippin and firmly united all of what had been the Merovingian realm under the rule of the Carolingian house. More than this, in an unprecedented burst of military expansion he pushed the boundaries of the Frankish realm into regions where the Franks had never securely ruled, or had not ruled at all: Saxony, Bavaria and its eastern March, Lombardy, and northern Spain. The lands and treasure that flowed into Charlemagne's hands from his conquests enabled him to attract the loyalty of much of the European aristocracy; his armies coerced the co-operation of the rest. As a result, he was able to erect a political structure in Europe whose extent went unmatched until the European Union of the twentieth century. The magnitude of Charlemagne's achievement was symbolically expressed on Christmas Day of the year 800, when he was crowned emperor in Rome by Pope Leo III.

Charlemagne's reign is important for our purposes because in the process of building and maintaining his empire, Charlemagne and his court circle made new claims about the power of central authority to regulate the use of violence. To be specific, Charlemagne took the idea that a Christian king was responsible for promoting and maintaining God's peace to justify an effort to limit sharply the use of violence by anyone but himself or his agents. The norms governing violence that came out of this effort had an impact on how some Franks, or at least some Franks who left traces in the sources, thought about violence. They had, however, to compete with far older norms that were still well entrenched among the Franks, namely the norms surrounding the personal right to violence and violent vengeance. It seems in fact that they had only a limited impact at the time that they were made. Nevertheless, the framework of norms regulating violence that Charlemagne tried to set up survived his death in 814, as part of a powerful ideology and image of Christian kingship that he left for the European rulers of later periods to inherit.

### Charlemagne's Capitularies

It is in Charlemagne's capitularies that we find the king's sense of his own rights and responsibilities most strongly expressed. Charlemagne relied on the capitulary like no other Frankish king before him as a tool for recording his decisions and decrees and transmitting them to his agents in the localities.[7] Some of his capitularies are extensive, formal documents; others are quite simple, offering only lists of decrees or sometimes only lists of subjects. Some capitularies were produced in the context of great assemblies or ecclesiastical synods. In these Charlemagne appears at the center of a great collaborative government, surrounded by his partners the counts and other secular magnates, and by the archbishops, bishops, and abbots who were their ecclesiastical counterparts. Others were simply issued. The capitularies' content is eclectic. While we can see them as legislative texts (and we know that some contemporaries understood some of them that way), they do not represent statute law in the modern sense. Instead, they generally record specific legal decisions made in specific times and places. Few if any of the capitularies deal solely with one issue or program. Most move back and forth among various issues or problems that were at hand at the time they were issued. They deal, often in the same text, with everything from specific judicial or administrative matters to general judicial or administrative organization, military affairs, Church government and morality, the economy, the protection or extension of royal rights, etc. The capitularies were transmitted to the localities in several stages. Copies were written out by scribes attached to the court. These copies could be complete, or simple aids to memory consisting of lists of subjects. They were then given to people returning home from assemblies, or to royal agents sent out (*missi*) on royal business or to oversee royal interests, to be recopied for local distribution and use.

When one looks at Charlemagne's capitularies, one sees right away that the great Carolingian had picked up the ideological and normative threads left to him by his Merovingian predecessors.[8] In his General Admonition of 789, for example, which was aimed at the reform of the Frankish Church, Charlemagne presented himself as the source of God's right order in the world. He ordered that there be "peace and concord and unanimity with all Christian people, among bishops, abbots, counts, judges, and all people everywhere whether greater or lesser".[9] In a capitulary of 802 (called by its editor the "General Capitulary for the *Missi*"), Charlemagne appears as the wellspring of right and justice. He directed his *missi* to go out and correct whatever injustices they found so that all men "might live a good and just life in accordance with God's commands".[10] Counts and *centenarii* were to strive to see that justice was done, so that evil "might be removed from among our Christian people".[11] Everyone, lay and ecclesiastical, powerful and less powerful, should obey the emperor's decrees "in order that everything should be good and well-ordered for the praise of almighty God . . . to the eternal reward both of ourselves and of all our faithful people".[12]

Like his Merovingian predecessors, Charlemagne assumed that he had the right to both extend and retract the bounds of legitimate violence. He extended them by mandating violent punishments for certain wrongs. At Herstal in 779, for example, he precisely regulated the maiming of robbers. For the first offense robbers were to lose an eye, for the second their nose, and for the third they were to die.[13] In a capitulary of 803, Charlemagne addressed the case that someone accused of being unfree (*servus*) might kill one of his relatives to prevent him from testifying to his status. Should this occur, the killer was to die and all of his blood relations were to be placed in servitude.[14] In 805 the emperor mandated that the authors of any sworn conspiracies that succeeded in doing any evil were to die; those that helped them were to be flogged and have their noses cut off.[15]

The most spectacular examples come in a capitulary issued in Paderborn and traditionally dated to 785 that was directed at the Saxons.[16] Charlemagne had been trying to conquer the pagan Saxons since 772. Faced with their stubborn resistance to Frankish rule and to the forced Christianization that went along with it, Charles reacted with ferocity. Anyone in Saxony breaking into, stealing from, or setting fire to a church was to die. Anyone eating meat during Lent, unless they were forced to do so by necessity, was to die. Killing a priest, carrying out pagan rituals, or remaining unbaptized brought death, as did conspiring against the king, killing one's lord or lady, or raping the daughter of one's lord. Only by turning to the church and the priesthood for sanctuary and forgiveness could someone guilty of one of these offenses save his life.

Also like the Merovingians before him, Charlemagne retracted the bounds of legitimate violence by extending his special protection around specific people. Those violating that protection were to pay with their lives.[17] What is new, however, is the degree to which Charlemagne extended his personal protection beyond specific individuals to encompass entire classes of people. Starting from the premise that the king, as God's representative, was the protector of the church, widows, orphans, pilgrims, the poor, women, and other defenseless people, he declared violence towards members of these groups to be an offense against the king himself.

The Merovingians had been perfectly familiar with the concept of injuring the king by harming a member of a protected group of people. But the primary group the Merovingians protected in this fashion was not at all poor and defenseless; it consisted of the king's sworn following, the so-called *antrustiones*. The status of the men sworn into the king's trust raised the amount of their blood price. Compensation for their death was payable not to the king but rather to their kin.[18] In addition, Clovis had cast himself in a letter to his bishops as the protector of churches, clerics, their sons and/or their widows, of nuns, religious widows, and church slaves.[19] Building on this precedent, Charlemagne extended his protection beyond churchmen to encompass pilgrims, widows, orphans, the poor, etc. as classes of people. This protection stemmed from his duties as a Christian ruler. Harming such people was an offense against God; by extension, therefore, it was an offense against the king personally as

God's representative. As the general capitulary of 802 put it, ". . . no one should presume to commit fraud or theft or any other criminal act against God's holy churches or against widows or orphans or pilgrims; for the lord emperor himself, after God and his saints, has been appointed their protector and defender".[20]

The consequence for violating the king's special protection for these groups was compensation paid not to those affected, but rather to the king. Charlemagne's capitularies describe this compensation in terms of what they call the king's "ban" (*bannus*). The word *bannus* has traditionally been understood to refer to the royal power to command and to levy a fine for failure to obey. It is hard to tell, however, despite the term's obvious Germanic origin, to what degree the *bannus* as a fine preceded Charlemagne. The *Pactus Legis Salicae*, as well as some of the Merovingian capitularies added to it, do occasionally reflect a sense of a general peace whose violation brought a fine when they mention the *fredus* or "peace payment" that was levied over and above (or deducted from) the compensation due for the wrong committed. As discussed in the previous chapter, this fine appears mostly in cases where some sort of constituted authority is involved, such as a count or a judge, or where the king's special protection has been violated.[21] The term *bannus*, however, does not appear in the *Pactus*, nor in any of the Merovingian capitularies. Trace references in other sources suggest that the word was used under the Merovingians, but in its more general sense of command.[22] It is only under Charlemagne that *bannus* starts to refer unequivocally to a royal fine.[23]

The *bannus* first appears in Charlemagne's capitularies in the capitulary of Herstal from 779.[24] From then on it is hard to avoid. In most cases, it refers to a money fine of 60 *solidi*[25] payable for a violation of the king's special protection, a violation of a royal command, or an injury to royal interests.[26] When it appears, Charlemagne is presented as if he himself were the wronged victim deserving of compensation, no matter who had actually gotten hurt. This makes sense when the *bannus* is mandated for harming royal justices; these were, after all, his officials.[27] But Charlemagne also claimed the ban as punishment for harming the church, widows, orphans, the helpless, etc.[28] This starts to look like a claim to a quasi-public responsibility for protecting large swaths of the Frankish population. An injury to a member of one of these protected groups was an injury to the king/emperor not because he was a member of the victim's kin, or the victim's lord, or because he had extended his royal protection to that person individually. It was an injury to the king/emperor because the king/emperor had been charged by God with protecting all people like the victim.

At the same time as Charlemagne was delegitimizing violence to God's followers and particular favorites, he was also trying to delegitimize other kinds of violence. Some of his efforts were limited in scope. For example, at a synod held in Frankfurt in 794, Charlemagne ordered all people to be peaceable towards one another during mass.[29] He also forbade abbots of monasteries to blind or mutilate their monks no matter what sin they had committed.[30] Other attempts were broader. As early as 779, Charlemagne went after the main weapon of the Frankish magnate: the armed following. The relevant clause of this capitulary, which was issued at Herstal, is short and to the point: "concerning the raising of an armed following (*de truste faciendo*): let no one do it".[31] Charlemagne also tried to get the clergy to stop being violent. In 802 he forbade clergy to carry on armed fights or get involved in any quarrel with their neighbor.[32] At around the same time he ordered priests, deacons, and all other clergy to refrain from carrying arms, and instead to place their trust in the protection of God.[33] In 811, the emperor declared that those who had renounced the world, i.e., religious, were not to bear arms, nor were they to have armed followings.[34]

Charlemagne went so far as to cast certain categories of violence as injuries to the king, by making them subject to the *bannus* alongside injuries to his protected classes of people. The kinds of violence so cast included rape, arson, and violent entry into or destruction of dwellings.[35] Most significantly, he sought to regulate violence aimed at avenging wrong. In the Herstal capitulary of 779 he decreed that those people who were unwilling to accept compensation for an injury instead of engaging in violent conflict (*pro faida*) were to be sent to him and he would place them where they could not hurt anybody.[36] He thus claimed to be able to restrict violent vengeance and to require that parties in conflict pay and accept compensation. Charlemagne returned to the subject ten years later. In his General Admonition of 789, the king forbade homicide for the sake of revenge or out of avarice and thievery. When a homicide did take place, no private party was to respond. The case was to be judged by royal judges according to law, and no man was to be killed unless the law demanded it.[37]

Later on in the same text, Charlemagne put his attempt to control violent vengeance on a moral footing; he branded (among other things) enmities, contentions, animosities, anger, brawls, dissension, and homicides all as works of the devil.[38] In 802, the emperor explicitly connected his duty to regulate homicide and violent vengeance with his mission to uphold God's order. In his general capitulary of that year, he declared that homicide was to be shunned on Christian grounds. Particularly reprehensible was the slaying of sons or brothers. As God's representative, the king was responsible for punishing homicide as severely as possible. However, to avoid an increase in crime and enmity among Christians when the devil did make them kill someone, the guilty should make amends and pay compensation as quickly as possible to the relatives of the dead. He expressly forbade the victim's kin to choose hostility over making peace; they were to accept the payment offered them, as long as the guilty man was not too slow in paying it. Anyone who scorned to pay compensation should be deprived of his inheritance pending the emperor's judgment. In addition, anyone who killed a relative was to go immediately to his bishop to receive the appropriate penance.[39]

Three years later came a set of really radical claims. In a capitulary of 805, Charlemagne forbade all carrying of weapons within the fatherland.[40] Then he raised the issue of what the text calls *faida*. *Faida* as it appears here and elsewhere in the capitularies refers to a disagreement between two parties that is being prosecuted with violence.[41] Charlemagne set himself against it. If someone was involved in a *faida*, the capitulary says, it should be determined which of the parties was in the wrong (how is not stated). Then they should be forced to make peace, even if they did not want to. If they refused, they were to be brought to the king, who would enforce a peace. And if after this one of the parties should go ahead and kill the other anyway, he was not only to pay compensation to the victim's kin; he was to lose the hand with which he had sworn peace and pay a royal ban.[42] In short: Charlemagne was mandating the settlement of violent disputes in such a way that not only required a non-violent settlement and the payment of compensation, but also turned a homicide following a settlement into an injury to the king. Had Gregory of Tours' Chramnesind lived under these rules rather than those of the sixth century, after killing Sichar he would have had his hand cut off and been forced to pay both compensation to Sichar's kin and 60 *solidi* to the king.

By trying to shut down some of the central features of Frankish violence, namely the right to raise armed followings and the right to use violence to avenge a perceived injury, and by trying to enforce the norms and mechanisms of non-violent settlement, Charlemagne effectively delegitimized all violence save that which he had authorized. This seems to at least suggest, if not get close to, a claim to a royal monopoly on legitimate violence.

### Ideal and Reality in the Capitularies

The capitularies offer a good deal of evidence, however, that Charlemagne was pushing his norms of violence out into a world in which many people thought about violence quite differently. There was plenty of violence going on; its reality is implicit in what Charlemagne tried to forbid. There were violent robbers; people broke into, plundered, and destroyed dwellings and barns.[43] Some people fought with each other during masses; some abbots blinded or mutilated their monks as punishment for their sins. People prosecuted disagreements violently; in some cases they killed other people, including near relatives. Some people were willing to kill their own relatives to avoid falling into servitude. Churchmen and monks bore arms, sometimes maintained armed followings, and on occasion prosecuted their disputes violently.

In the Herstal capitulary of 779 Charlemagne forbade counts and/or bishops acting as judges from maiming men through hatred or ill-intent, on penalty of losing their office and being subject to the penalty they had sought to inflict. This sounds very much as if some counts or bishops heading courts were using their positions to pursue their own grievances against their enemies, and doing it violently under the cover of judicial authority.[44] The general capitulary of 802 refers to imperial judicial officials being killed; perhaps some locals thought that by violently silencing the king's judge they could handle a dispute in a way more to their liking.[45] Other capitularies similarly indicate that the emperor's judicial officials sometimes ran into armed resistance. In one, Charlemagne forbade anyone to come to a *mallus* or *placitum* armed with a shield and a lance (which also suggests that armed groups at courts might attack each other).[46] In another, he forbade anyone to use an armed gang to block the *missi* in their work, on pain of death.[47]

On occasion Charlemagne himself appears to acknowledge the personal right to violence and even to work within its terms. In a capitulary issued from his residence in Aachen, he addressed his own sworn followers, as well as people holding imperial property as benefices, and essentially ordered them to render each other armed support at need. Should someone bound to the emperor by oath and/or by property be asked to help a peer (*aliquem de conparis suis*) fight an enemy and refuse, he declared, that person was to lose his benefice.[48] Towards the very end of his reign, Charlemagne addressed himself to violent quarrels among men (*faidosis hominibus*) that spilled over into Sundays, other holy days, and the Easter season. This he prohibited, "lest they presume to do it".[49] Implicit in this declaration is the understanding that people would violently quarrel on other days.

This latter prohibition is interesting for another reason. It says people should not be violent on Christian holy days. This puts violence in a new light. Up to this point, violence itself has appeared in our sources as morally neutral; it was the use to which violence was put and the motives for its use that determined whether a given source cast it as good or bad. Here, however, Charlemagne presents violent quarrels, regardless of their rhyme or reason, as offenses against the holy and therefore to be avoided on Christianity's holy days. This makes violence itself out to be a symptom of unavoidable but nevertheless sinful human behavior. Violence on days important to God was an offense against God. It was the duty of the Christian emperor, therefore, to prohibit it.

## Violence Outside the Capitularies

The next logical step is to look at evidence about violence from outside the capitularies. At this point, however, I have to acknowledge a remarkable silence in the sources. There is very little direct evidence outside of the capitularies for the forty-six-year reign of Charlemagne that reveals people being violent.[50] Charlemagne's judicial diplomas, that is, documents in which he intervened directly in the settlement of a dispute, all appear to reflect non-violent settlements. So too the surviving judicial documents, or *placita*, issued by his *missi*.[51] An argument from silence is always dangerous; it may well be that the evidence we seek has been lost to the vagaries of time. Nevertheless, the silence might provoke one to wonder whether Charlemagne's vast prestige and authority did in fact cause many of his empire's inhabitants to back away from their long-established attitudes towards violence, and to turn towards processing their disputes through courts and judicial officials.

There are, however, a few sources that we can bring to bear. The evidence that these sources offer is equivocal. It suggests that Charlemagne's norms of violence did affect how some people thought about violence, but that their ultimate impact was limited. Some of this evidence matches what the capitularies prescribe, without telling us whether or not it was produced in response to the capitularies. This is the case with several formula collections from the period of Charlemagne's reign or shortly afterwards. The formula collections, mostly but not entirely compiled and kept by churches and monasteries, comprise copies of various types of documents that have had all specific details, such as names, dates, places, etc., removed. They most likely served as templates or as sources of language for students learning to write documents and for scribes drafting real documents. We cannot always say for certain that the formulas were actually used as the basis for other documents. The most we can say is that the collections covered a spectrum of documents that their compilers thought might be useful in some fashion at some point.[52] A few of these formulas deal with violence; they do so in a way that is entirely consonant with the capitularies. We have, for example, formulas representing written securities for wergeld payment; the kinsman or lord of someone who had been killed gives the killer a receipt for the compensation payment and indemnifies him against future claims.[53] One of these takes place in the context of a count's court.[54] We also have a letter from bishops designed to be carried by the recipient. Addressed to the world at large, it says that the bearer had killed a close relative and had come to the bishop to receive a penance. The bishop had assigned him to wander on pilgrimage and therefore asked all whom he might meet to give him support and shelter on his journey.[55] It seems, therefore, that the compilers of these collections thought it was at least within the realm of possibility that people would kill others, including close relatives. And they have the killers doing just what the capitularies said they should do: paying compensation and seeking out their bishop for penance. It is just hard to say whether these formulas reflect a response to the capitularies or rather their drafters' belief that the only homicide cases that could possibly generate documents were those that ended in a wergeld payment and/or a penitential pilgrimage.

Some saints' lives from the period tell us that Charlemagne affected how at least some hagiographers thought about violence. As we saw in the previous chapter, writers in the sixth and early seventh centuries such as Gregory of Tours and Jonas of Bobbio present an image of Christianity that is perfectly comfortable with violence as long as it is used by the right people for the right ends. Not only do human actors use violence to achieve their ends and take vengeance for injuries and affronts, so too do God and his saints. In contrast, two examples of Carolingian hagiography delegitimize violent vengeance and highlight law and judicial process.

The first example is the life of an Anglo-Saxon saint named Willibrord who carried out a mission to the Frisians in the decades on either side of 700.[56] A century later, Willibrord's *Life* was written by a fellow Anglo-Saxon who spent his career very close to Charlemagne: Alcuin.[57] Alcuin was originally from Northumbria. An extremely well educated man, he came to Charlemagne's attention during a chance encounter in Italy in 781 and was asked by the king to take charge of education at his court. In 796, Alcuin was rewarded for his service with the post of abbot of the monastery of St. Martin in Tours.[58]

In his *Life* of Willibrord, Alcuin describes the efforts by the saint and his companions to plant Christianity on patently hostile territory. The story is pervaded by the ethic of violent vengeance. The Frisians take vengeance on the missionaries for insulting and hurting their deities.[59] Willibrord's companions want to take vengeance on the Frisians for insulting, threatening, and hurting them.[60] Everyone seems to think that violent vengeance is justified, except, however, for St. Willibrord himself. In one miracle story, the saint comes to a village where he finds an ancient pagan idol. Moved by zeal, he smashed it to pieces before the eyes of its custodian. The pagan custodian naturally became angry, and moved to strike Willibrord with a sword "as if to avenge the insult paid to his god". Seeing this, Willibrord's companions rushed forward to kill the man, but Willibrord himself rescued the pagan and let him go free. Alcuin then gives us a lecture about the virtue of refusing to avenge wrongs.[61]

Alcuin was about as high up at Charlemagne's court as one could get. It is not terribly surprising, therefore, that he would reflect a court ethic that sought to make violent vengeance illegitimate. But it is not just in Alcuin's hagiography that we see signs of a shift in attitudes towards violence and royal power. To illustrate this, we need to move back to a Merovingian life, the *Life* of St. Balthild from the late seventh century.[62] Balthild is a typical figure in hagiography from a century that saw the Frankish kingdoms riven by the factional conflict that set the stage for the Carolingians' climb to power. Balthild was a queen. She was married to King Clovis II of Neustria, and after the death of her husband in 657 she had served as regent for their young son Clovis III. She earned her title of saint by patronizing monasteries; she seems to have used her connections to the holy as a tool in political competition in the same fashion as most of her contemporaries.

What is important for us here is the story of Balthild's exile from the Neustrian court, which took place around 664 or 665. In the oldest version of her life, which was written shortly after her death in 680, the story goes as follows: the queen had long expressed the desire to retire to a particular monastery she had founded, but the Neustrian aristocrats would not let her because they loved her. Then a rebellion erupted, in which a leading role was played by Bishop Sigobrand of Paris. After the rebellion had been put down, a dispute arose at court because the Neustrians had killed Bishop Sigobrand against Queen Balthild's will. Fearing that the queen would hold the killing against them and wish to avenge (*vindicare*) Sigobrand, the Neustrians at court "immediately permitted her to go into the monastery".[63] It does not take much imagination to see what must have happened underneath the pious spin that Balthild's hagiographer put on events. The rebellion against the faction in power at the Neustrian court was instigated by Bishop Sigobrand with Queen Balthild's support. The victors were afraid that Balthild would find a way to take vengeance for the bishop's death, so they packed her off to her monastery to remove her from the political scene.[64]

About a century later, sometime during or shortly after Charlemagne's reign, a new version of Balthild's life was written by an unknown author.[65] This version tells the above story in a different way. We start as before: Balthild wanted to retire to her monastery. However, the Franks did not want to let her because the palace was governed by her wisdom and she was loved by all for her holy conversation. The Franks would not have let her go but for the rebellion launched by the miserable Bishop Sigobrand. The rebellion was put down as before, but a dispute arose because the Franks had killed the bishop against Balthild's wishes without discussing the matter and "against the law" (*contra legem*). They were afraid that the saintly queen would hold this gravely against them and would wish to punish such an evil deed. Beaten down "by the fear of judicial law" (*timore legis iuditialis*), they permitted the queen at last to do what she had always wanted to do, namely retire to her monastery. In other words, fear of vengeance in the late seventh century is replaced around the turn of the ninth by fear of the law and of judicial process as a possible and threatening consequence of violent action. Plainly the second hagiographer had run the story through Carolingian filters.

According to the evidence discussed so far, some people, or at least some members of the Carolingian court and some hagiographers, picked up on and responded to Charlemagne's attitudes towards violence. Others, however, did not. A fragment of an imperial judgment, that has been dated to sometime during Charlemagne's reign, has the king dealing with a particularly heinous use of violence and thus gives us an idea of what "particularly heinous" meant. It concerns a man who had seized an unfree person (*servus*) and forced him to kill his lords.[66] The lords were children; one was nine years old and the other eleven. Once the *servus* had carried out the killings, the man who had given him the order threw him into a pit, where he died. Somehow the man was caught and brought before Charlemagne. The king ordered that he pay a triple wergeld for the younger boy and a double wergeld for the older. In addition, he was to pay a triple wergeld for the *servus* and on top of everything the royal ban. The report itself drips with disapproval. In particular, it uses the highly unusual word "murdered" (*mordritum*) to describe the death of the *servus*, instead of the more usual "killed". This, and the triple wergeld for the *servus*, very likely reflect the fact that the killer tried to hide the killing by throwing the *servus* into a pit.[67] The man who ordered the killing also violated the most basic ties of loyalty when he ordered a *servus* to kill his own lords and then betrayed the *servus*. We do not learn anything about norms of legitimate violence from this case, but we see clearly here what norms have been violated.

Different is a dispute case described by a charter from one of the out-lying regions of the Empire that Charlemagne himself had conquered: Bavaria. This charter stems from the cathedral church at Freising. It describes a dispute settlement that took place in 808, that is, some twenty years after the Carolingian conquest of the duchy.[68] It describes a dis-pute between the bishop of Freising, named Atto, and a local landowner named Kyppo. Originally the two men had agreed to some sort of prop-erty exchange; the details are not specified. Then, for some reason that is also not given, Kyppo backed out of the exchange. As a result, a quar-rel erupted between the two men. We are not told what course that the quarrel took, only what the terms were of the agreement that settled it. Kyppo gave a piece of property to Atto's church. For his part, Atto agreed to undo the original exchange. He then gave Kyppo "one horse and a woolen garment and another of linen for the buildings which had been destroyed in that dispute". It seems highly unlikely that Atto would have compensated Kyppo for destroyed buildings unless the buildings were Kyppo's and Atto was somehow responsible for their destruction. And this from a bishop whom we know from other sources was firmly pro-Carolingian and who had actively helped smooth the way into Bavaria of Charlemagne's judicial officials.[69] This fact notwithstanding, Atto was apparently perfectly willing to use violence (or, more likely, have his men use violence) to prosecute a grievance with a local landowner. It is hard to say more without more information, but the story suggests that Atto took violent action against Kyppo's buildings as part of the dance of pressure and negotiation that led ultimately to the settlement.[70]

A dispute described in a set of letters shows us Charlemagne's author-ity clashing with local interests whose defenders, including ordinary towns-people, played according to the norms of honor and vengeance. At the same time, it reveals that the emperor was perfectly willing to accept violence carried out or threatened by armed followings as long as it was in his own interests to do so. Caught in the middle of the dispute was our acquaintance Alcuin. In 802, Alcuin had been abbot of the monastery of St. Martin in Tours for six years. In that year he became entangled with a person with whom he had a troubled relationship, namely Theodulf, the bishop of Orléans.[71] The affair also got him crossways with his former employer, namely Charlemagne. The letters written and received by Alcuin in the course of the dispute, including one he sent to two of his former students who were at court and a second he wrote to Charlemagne himself, lay out the story for us.[72] A prisoner, convicted of some unspecified crime, escaped from Bishop Theodulf's custody and ended up in Tours, where he sought sanctuary in the church of St. Martin. There the convict confessed his sins and begged to be allowed to see the emperor. Alcuin and his monks nevertheless handed him over to some men sent by Theodulf to retrieve him. At this point interesting things started to happen. Theodulf's men, who must have been unarmed, heard a rumor that an ambush had been laid for them on their return journey; apparently the convict had some allies. So they abandoned their captive and left. Shortly afterwards another and larger group of men, whom Alcuin expressly says "belonged" to Theodulf, showed up "in a hostile manner"; this suggests, as Alcuin actually confirms later, that they were armed. This band, accompanied by the archbishop of Tours, broke into the church, seized the prisoner, and, according to Alcuin, broke past the altar rails, thus insulting Saint Martin himself. The outraged monks of St. Martin's counterattacked and drove the attackers away from the altar.[73]

In the meantime, word had spread throughout the city about what was happening. Responding to rumors that "enemies had come from Orléans to profane the sanctuary of St. Martin" and that these enemies were going take by force a man who had sought sanctuary there, crowds of people came to defend their saint. In the uproar, the monks of Tours managed to rescue the bishop's men and then drove everyone out of the church. When Charlemagne heard what had happened, he was angry. He made it clear that he wanted the prisoner returned to Bishop Theodulf. He also sent an envoy to inquire into the matter.

I will not go into details about how Alcuin in his letters tried to defend the sanctuary rights of his church and his monks' desire to protect the honor of their saint to his former employer, who thought (says Alcuin) that a man already convicted of a crime had no right to seek sanctuary and appeal to his august person. I am more interested in what the story tells us about violence. To begin with, we learn that Bishop Theodulf of Orléans had an armed following. He was willing to use this following to march on Tours and seize an escaped man from somebody else's church, in somebody else's diocese. Equally interesting is the fact that, according to Alcuin, Charlemagne sanctioned Theodulf's use of his armed men to carry out what was in essence a judicial mission. This suggests that the emperor was perfectly prepared to tolerate the maintenance and use of a personal armed following as long as it was used in his interests by someone loyal to him. Theodulf was very much Charlemagne's man. A refugee from Visigothic Spain, Theodulf owed his job to the emperor, who had installed him as bishop of Orléans into a city and an area where he had no connections or support network of his own.[74] In essence, Theodulf and his men were Charlemagne's, which made their use of violence legitimate.

Theodulf also had a personal interest in the matter, though that interest is not given explicit expression in Alcuin's letter: his honor and authority had been challenged when the convict fled. They had been challenged again by the threat of an ambush to rescue the convict, and yet again when the monks and townspeople of Tours had fought his men. Theodulf plainly had affronts to avenge. For their part, the monks and townspeople of Tours were also avenging injured rights and honor. The monks of Tours drove Theodulf's men away from St. Martin's altar to defend the rights and dignity of their church and saint. So too the townspeople of Tours; according to Alcuin it was the disrespect to St. Martin, the outrage to his sanctuary, and the violation of the church's sanctuary rights that led them to attack Theodulf's men. Alcuin himself was caught in the middle. He wanted to defend his monks and their saint, as well as the rights of his church, but at the same time he had to justify himself to his emperor.[75]

## The Reign of Louis the Pious

According to the evidence discussed so far, some people in late eighth- and early ninth-century Europe did pay attention and respond to Charlemagne's norms of violence. Others, however, continued to act according to the older norms associated with the personal right to violence. On occasion, the king himself acknowledged these norms; he was even willing to work with them if doing so would help him achieve his own ends.

If it is hard to say exactly how much of an impact Charlemagne's norms of violence had during his reign, it becomes easier when we move to that of his son Louis the Pious. Louis was Charlemagne's sole surviving legitimate son and therefore inherited the Carolingian empire undivided when his father died in 814.[76] He ruled the empire successfully for almost two decades, until the 830s, when rebellions by his sons began to shake the structure that his father had built. While he remained unchallenged, Louis continued to pursue many of his father's aims. In particular, he made essentially the same claims to regulate violence as Charlemagne had. Nevertheless, the culture of personal and violent vengeance remained alive and well during his reign; the evidence suggests that, Louis's pronouncements notwithstanding, it may in fact have dominated the behavior of the powerful.

Louis issued capitularies at a steady clip. His capitularies continued to project the emperor as responsible for upholding God's peace and order and continued to condemn violence.[77] They also dealt with specific acts of violence in a way that both shows Louis continuing his father's policies and reveals more about the kinds of violence going on that could provoke an imperial response. Homicide, rape, arson, plundering, amputation of limbs, theft, robberies, and invasion of others' property were defined as serious matters (*maiores causas*) that needed to be handled by a count's *mallus*.[78] Homicide carried out by necessity was to be compensated with the appropriate wergeld; anyone who refused to pay or accept compensation was to be brought to the emperor, who would send him into exile until he agreed to do what was right.[79] Homicide carried out for no reason, or for a frivolous one, was likewise to be compensated with wergeld, but the perpetrator was also to be sent into exile, even though he had paid.[80] Wergeld could be paid with anything except hawks and swords, because people sometimes lied about how much these were worth.[81] The imperial palace at Aachen was not to serve as a haven for people who had committed crimes including theft and homicide. Moreover, anyone who witnessed an altercation at the palace and did not intervene to stop it would have to join the participants in paying compensation.[82] Nor were people attached to imperial estates to think that they could carry out killings or other injustices with impunity; the emperor ordered his agents to make them pay just like everyone else.[83] Armed gangs and followings were apparently still seen as a problem. In 829 Louis forbade the formation of such gangs (*collectae*) "for the purpose of carrying out evil". If they were formed, and were led by someone who bore an official title (such as provost, advocate, or *centenarius*), that person was to be brought before the emperor.[84] If unfree (*servi*) formed a band and carried out any violence (*vim*), such as homicide or arson, their lords were to pay the imperial ban.[85] The defenseless also drew their share of attention. Louis dealt on two separate occasions with the rape of women who were betrothed to others, and once with the rape of widows (whether willing or unwilling).[86] Imperial *missi* were to take care that their negligence did not lead to poor people being tortured unnecessarily.[87] Only once did Louis appear to validate the personal resort to violence. This instance concerned an accusation of unfreedom. If a man thought another man was not free, and in an effort to expose him struck him, it was the victim who had to defend himself; he had to verify his free status by gathering oath-helpers and swearing an oath.[88]

If there was a change in attitudes towards violence at the Carolingian court, it was that Louis was even more focused on how violence affected the Church than his father had been. As his nickname suggests, Louis took his role as guardian of the Frankish Church very seriously. His decrees about violence correspondingly reflect a greater concern for churches, their clergy, and religious people as possible victims of violence rather than as potential perpetrators. In addition, Louis supported his decrees much more often than had his father with references to canon law. In a capitulary issued in 818 or 819, Louis mandated death for anyone who committed homicide in a church. He also set up a procedure for the case that a violent quarrel starting outside a church was brought into a church. If one party to such a struggle killed the other inside the church and claimed he had acted in self-defense, he had to provide either direct witnesses or oath-helpers prepared to support his claim. Even if he was successful, he had to pay compensation to the violated church as well as the royal ban, and do penance according to canon law. The person he had killed, however, was to remain uncompensated.[89] In the same capitulary, the emperor dealt with people striking clergymen with clubs, and he forbade the killing of people doing public penance, on pain of paying a triple ban on top of the victim's wergeld.[90] Another capitulary from the same period contains a vehement prohibition against raping nuns, supported by a decretal of Pope Gelasius I.[91] In a fragmentary capitulary from the following decade, the first title simply states: "concerning priests bound and whipped by laymen".[92] Only once did Louis treat clergy as potential perpetrators. In the same capitulary in which he forbade the rape of nuns, Louis quoted a decree of the Council of Chalcedon, to the effect that if a member of the clergy raped a girl, they were to lose their grade, while laymen were to be anathematized.[93]

When one looks beyond Louis's capitularies, however, the culture of violent vengeance dominates the scene. Some notable evidence for this comes from the writings of another person who was closely connected to the Carolingian court: Einhard. Einhard was a student in his early twenties at the monastery of Fulda when the abbot recommended him to Charlemagne as a scholar. Einhard arrived at Charlemagne's court about a decade after Alcuin; the two men were there together for about four years before Alcuin left for Tours. After Charlemagne died, Einhard apparently remained connected with Louis's court for about a decade. In the 820s he started what turned out to be a long process of retiring from court life and supporting himself from the rich estates and offices with which Louis had rewarded him.[94]

As a wealthy man with high connections, Einhard was a natural intercessor and patron for people who needed help. One such person, named Gundhart, approached Einhard by letter sometime between 822 and 840, prompting Einhard to write a letter on Gundhart's behalf to the abbot of his old monastery at Fulda, Hrabanus Maurus.[95] Gundhart was Hrabanus's man, and as such was obligated to join any military contingent that Hrabanus mustered from the resources of his monastery to join the imperial army. One such muster was about to be conducted, but Gundhart begged Einhard to intercede on his behalf with Hrabanus so that he would not have to go. Gundhart needed to stay home, says Einhard, because he had been threatened with violence (*faidosus sit*) by enemies who would also be on the expedition. These enemies had threatened his life; they included the count who was supposed to lead his contingent and who was, Gundhart said, his bitterest foe. Gundhart therefore wanted Hrabanus to allow him to stay home; he would pay the fine due for missing an imperial muster himself and not trouble Hrabanus about it. Einhard asked Hrabanus for his help in this matter, saying that he would not have bothered him had he not learned for certain that Gundhart was in fact in grave danger.

So during Louis's reign, Frankish magnates, including counts, were prosecuting their enmities with violence. This is in and of itself nothing terribly surprising; Louis's capitularies imply as much. What is important about this letter of Einhard's is that it makes no apologies for the culture of violent vengeance. Gundhart was involved in an ongoing hostile relationship with a group of people headed by the count; the members of this group were advertising openly that they would kill Gundhart given the chance. Einhard himself fully acknowledged the existence of the vengeance ethic and was prepared to work within its terms. He did not tell Gundhart to levy a complaint against his enemies to the emperor, nor did he offer to do so himself. Instead, he recognized that Gundhart's life really was in danger, and that the best way to help him was to get Hrabanus Maurus to let him skip the muster (which, by the way, also tacitly reveals that Einhard expected Hrabanus likewise to acknowledge the norms of vengeance and act accordingly).

It was not just magnates who killed in the course of disputes; so did people farther down the social scale. Faced with such a case, Einhard helped to arrange a settlement. Sometime between 828 and 840, an unfree man (*servus*) belonging to an unnamed archbishop came to Einhard's church at Seligenstadt.[96] The man begged Einhard to gain him forgiveness for an evil deed (*scelus*) that he had committed; he had gotten into a quarrel with a companion and had killed him. His master the archbishop was therefore entitled to take his life. In response, Einhard wrote a letter to the archbishop (which is our source for this story). He asked the archbishop that since the *servus* had taken refuge in the church of Saints Marcellinus and Peter (the patrons of Einhard's church at Seligenstadt), his life should be spared out of reverence for the saints. Einhard urged the archbishop instead that the *servus* be allowed, after he had been whipped, to pay compensation for his companion's death.

Einhard also gives voice to the culture of violent vengeance in another kind of text: his account of the translation of the relics of Saints

Marcellinus and Peter from Rome to his homeland in 827 and the miracles that went along with it.[97] This is a fascinating work, because it shows Einhard stretching all of his considerable literary and theological skill to cast what amounted to patent relic theft as a pious act. Be that as it may, in one vignette Einhard uses a case of violence and enmity to give one of his saints a chance to perform a miracle. After their long journey from Rome, some of the relics of St. Marcellinus had ended up at the imperial residence in Aachen.[98] After considerable effort, Einhard gained custody of them. He then set out for his church in Seligenstadt so that the relics could rejoin the rest of the saint. About two miles down the road from the palace, at a bridge across a stream, the party stopped to allow people who had followed them a chance to pray before the relics before returning home. Among the people who approached the relics were two men. The first led his companion by the hand to the relics and then said, "You killed my father and for that reason we have been enemies. But now, for the love of God and this saint, I want to end our enmity[99] and to make and enter into an agreement with you that henceforth we shall maintain a lasting friendship between us. Let this saint be a witness to the reconciliation we have promised each other and let him punish the first person tempted to destroy this peace."

Einhard clearly wanted to present this incident as an example of Marcellinus's marvelous powers and as validation for his efforts to reclaim the relics from Aachen. The saint, by performing a wondrous deed, displayed his consent to and approval of what was transpiring. The miracle consisted of bringing formerly warring people to peace and ending an ongoing enmity. Whether or not this incident actually occurred, Einhard plainly wanted his readers to believe that it occurred. He therefore assumed that his audience would see it as plausible. The story itself assumes a culture of enmity and violent vengeance; it takes it as given that one man could kill another's father and that such an act would create a lasting enmity between the killer and the victim's son. Had the saint not happened by and intervened, presumably the enmity would have persisted and possibly spawned more violence, including from the relatives whom the dead man's son must have had his eye on when he asked the saint to punish anyone tempted to violate the peace.

### Violence and the Carolingian God

The idea that violence was a legitimate response to wrong was in fact woven into the fabric of Carolingian society, or at least of that part of Carolingian society that left written evidence of its habits of thought.

It manifests itself in the persistent assumption that God took violent vengeance for wrong. This assumption is visible whether we look at the reign of Charlemagne or of Louis the Pious, and whether we look at capitularies or at hagiography.[100] For example, in the vignette discussed above from Alcuin's *Life* of St. Willibrord, the pagan whom Willibrord saved from the attempted vengeance of his own men, and then freed, was immediately afterwards seized and possessed by the devil. Three days later he died in misery. After relating the man's fate, Alcuin quotes Romans 12:19: "Vengeance is mine, I will repay, says the Lord."

This assumption is also easy to find in the works of Einhard. In Book IV of his report of the translation of Saints Marcellinus and Peter, for example, Einhard tells the story of a nun who suffered from paralysis.[101] The miserable woman had a vision; a figure in the form of one of her neighbors told her to go to the town of Maastricht, where the relics of Marcellinus and Peter had arrived. The nun was reluctant to trust the vision and did not go. A second time the vision came, and a second time the nun failed to follow the figure's instructions. The vision came once more; this time the figure was so angry at the nun's disobedience that it struck her with a rod.

A more extensive example comes from the same text and concerns one of Einhard's most interesting characters: Wiggo the demon.[102] Wiggo is a fascinating personality. Einhard tells us that he was very well spoken and well educated, and moreover that he had had his words and thoughts written down in a book. Einhard came into possession of this book and tells a story from it in which Wiggo describes how he took possession of a sixteen-year-old girl. The girl's desperate parents, in order to drive the demon out of their daughter, brought her to the monastery at Lorsch. There the priest of the monastery church started to perform the rite of exorcism. In the middle of the rite the priest paused to ask Wiggo how and when he had entered into the girl. The demon answered, not in the girl's native language of German, but in flawless Latin. He identified himself as one of Satan's assistants and disciples; he then bragged about the destruction, disease, plague, and pestilence he and eleven of his companions had wreaked upon the kingdom of the Franks. The priest asked why such power had been given him. Wiggo replied with a long diatribe which must reflect Einhard's own view of the state of his society and which boils down to this: the Franks were sinful and corrupt and had been ignoring the commands of God. Because of their disobedience, Wiggo and his companions were ordered to do what they had done, so that the Franks "might pay the penalty for their lack of faith". Among the misdeeds that Wiggo had been sent to punish were homicide and rape.

## Conclusions

The men who surrounded Charlemagne, as well as the emperor himself, believed that violent vengeance for wrong was fundamentally legitimate, and that God himself avenged wrongs to himself, his followers, or his interests on a regular basis. But what they had done was to mold the ideology of Christian kingship to assert that, among men, only the king or emperor, in his capacity as God's representative, had the right to take such vengeance. In other words, Charlemagne and his advisors took a pre-existing image of Christian kingship and expanded its implications beyond all precedent, in order to provide a normative basis for royal claims to power. This fits with Charlemagne's general *modus operandi*, that is, with the ways that he took pre-existing tools, such as the capitularies, reshaped them, and used them in innovative ways to do unprecedented things. He couched novelty and innovation in the clothing of the traditional.

It was Charlemagne's enormous military expansion, and the economic and political resources that came with it – as well as the prestige that he earned and the fear that he inspired – that made it possible for him to intervene in the political and social behavior of his subjects over a wide area. For some he provided opportunities and rewards; for others he posed a grave threat. To rule and govern as well as reign, to control local, regional, and imperial aristocracies as well as work in tandem with them, Charlemagne had to try to reshape the traditional relationship between king and aristocracy in his own interests. As part of this effort, he sought to absorb and control habits of violence, and to insert himself into them. He delegitimized violent vengeance and sought to reinforce the ethic of compensation. In his legislation, he made himself and his officials the focus of judicial authority. Most important, he cast violent injuries to certain broad classes of people, and certain serious acts of violence, as injuries to God and therefore injuries to him, for which he was entitled to compensation or to which he could respond with violent vengeance of his own on God's behalf. In the process, he came very close to articulating, without doing so explicitly, both a claim to a royal monopoly on the legitimate use of violent force and a right to use that monopoly on behalf of what we might call a "public".

Charlemagne's claims to regulate violence had an impact on the sources, as well as on the reality behind them. Nevertheless, they do not constitute that reality; the world into which Charlemagne pushed his claims was much messier than the capitularies make it appear. His norms had to compete with very old assumptions about the personal right to use violence that were very much alive and well. Moreover, Charlemagne himself seems to have been perfectly prepared to work with the old norms when it was in his interests to do so.

Whatever the impact of Charlemagne's norms during his lifetime, that impact was ultimately limited and transitory; it had already begun to fade after his death. It would fade further over the next couple of centuries, in some places to the point of invisibility. Yet the attitudes towards violence and royal power that Charlemagne had projected never disappeared completely, and they would be revived when circumstances made it in the interests of the powerful to do so.

## Notes

1. Paul Fouracre, *The Age of Charles Martel* (London: Longman, 2000), "Francia in the Seventh Century", in NCMH I, 371–96; Fouracre and Gerberding, *Late Merovingian France,* 1–58; Geary, *Before France and Germany,* 151–231.

2. See *inter alia* Rosamond McKitterick, ed., NCMH II; idem, *Charlemagne: The Formation of a European Identity* (Cambridge: Cambridge University Press, 2008) and *The Frankish Kingdoms under the Carolingians, 751–987* (London: Longman, 1983); Pierre Riché, *Les Carolingiens: une famille qui fit l'Europe* (Paris: Hachette Littératures, 1983), translated into English by Michael Idomir Allen as *The Carolingians: A Family Who Forged Europe* (Philadelphia: University of Pennsylvania Press, 1993).

3. e.g., 1 Samuel 9.16-10.1 (Saul) and 16.1-13 (David); 2 Samuel 19.10 (Absalom); 1 Kings 1.39, 45 (Solomon); 2 Kings 9.4, 6 and 11.12 (Jehu).

4. Cf. Rosamond McKitterick, *History and Memory in the Carolingian World* (Cambridge: Cambridge University Press, 2004), 133–55.

5. See Fouracre, "Attitudes Towards Violence", 60–75; Fouracre, "Conflict, Power and Legitimation in Francia in the Late Seventh and Eighth Centuries", in *Building Legitimacy: Political Discourses and Forms of Legitimacy in Medieval Societies,* ed. Isabel Alfonso, Hugh Kennedy, and Julio Escalona (Leiden: Brill, 2004), 3–26.

6. McKitterick, *History and Memory.*

7. For the Carolingian capitulary the essential starting points are: F.L. Ganshof, *Was waren die Kapitularien?* (Weimar: H. Böhlaus Nachfolger, 1961) and "Charlemagne et l'usage de l'écrit en matiére administrative", *Le Moyen Age* 57 (1951): 1–25, English translation as "The use of the written word in Charlemagne's administration", in idem., *The Carolingians and the Frankish Monarchy,* trans. Janet Sondheimer (London: Longman, 1971), 125–42. See also Janet L. Nelson, "Kingship and Government", in NCMH II, 383–430 @409–11; McKitterick, *Written Word,* 25–37. On the capitulary manuscripts and their transmission: Hubert Mordek, *Bibliotheca capitularium regum Francorum manuscripta: Überlieferung und Traditionszusammenhang der fränkischen Herrschererlasse* (Munich: MGH, 1995).

8. Cf. Thomas M. Buck, *Admonitio und Praedicatio: Zur religiös-pastoralen Dimension von Kapitularien und kapitulariennahen Texten (507–814)* (Frankfurt: Peter Lang, 1997).

9. *Admonitio Generalis,* MGH Capit. I, 52–62 @c. 62, 58.

10. *Capitulare missorum generale* a. 802, MGH Capit. I, 91–9 @c. 1, 92; English translation in Patrick J. Geary, ed., *Readings in Medieval History,* 3rd edn (Peterborough, Ontario: Broadview Press, 2003), 315–19 @315. I thank Jennifer R. Davis for the point about the title.

11. Ibid. c. 25, 96/Geary, *Readings,* 316.

12. Ibid. c. 40, 98/Geary, *Readings,* 319.

13. *Capitulare Haristallense,* MGH Capit. I, 46–51 @c. 23, 51; English translation in Geary, *Readings,* 297–9 @299.

14. *Capitulare legibus additum* a. 803, MGH Capit. I, 111–14, @c. 5, 113.

15. *Capitulare missorum in Theodonis villa datum secundum, generale* a. 805, MGH Capit. I, 122–6 @c. 10, 124; English translation in Rosenwein, *Reading,* 182–5 @184.

16. *Capitulatio de partibus Saxoniae* a. 775–790, MGH Capit. I, 68–70 @c. 2–14, 68–69; English translation in Geary, *Readings,* 299–302 @299–300. Ganshof, *Kapitularien,* 164, dates this capitulary to 785, Mordek, *Biblioteca capitularia,* 1083, to 782.

17. Cf. *Capitulare missorum generale* a. 802, c. 30, 96–7/Geary, *Readings,* 317. Cf. the *Capitularia missorum specialia* a. 802, MGH Capit. I, 99–102, specifically the *Capitulare missorum Parisiacum et Rotomagense* @c. 15, 101, English translation in Geary, *Readings,* 319–20 @320; *Capitulare missorum item speciale* a. 802?, MGH Capit. I, 102–4 @ c. 54, 104.

18. *Pactus* XLI/5, 156/Drew, 104; XLI/8, 157/Drew, 105. See also *Pactus,* Capitulary I, LXX/2 and LXXI/2, 241/Drew, 131; Capitulary III, LXLIV, 254/Drew 143 and CIV/7, 260/Drew, 148.

19. Chapter 2 above @n. 136. Cf. the "Chlotharii II Edictum" (614), MGH Capit. I, 20–3, @c. 14, 22 and c. 18, 23; "Chlotharii II Praeceptio" (584–628), MGH Capit. I, 18–19, @c. 7–8, 19.

20. *Capitulare missorum generale* a. 802, c. 5, 93/Geary, *Readings,* 316. See also *Capitulare Baiwaricum,* a. 810?, MGH Capit. I, 158–59, @c. 3, 158.

21. See Chapter 2 above @nn. 86–90.

22. According to the MGH Capit. index, the word *bannus* first appears in the Herestal capitulary of 779. The verb *bannire* shows up in the formula Marculf I/40 (late seventh century), in which a count is to summon (*bannire*) his pagenses in response to a royal command: "Marculfi Formulae", in *Formulae Merowingici et Karolini aevi,* ed. Karl Zeumer, MGH LL 5 (Hanover: Hahn, 1886), 32–112 @68, English translation in "The Formulary of Marculf", in *The Formularies of Angers and Marculf: Two Merovingian Legal Handbooks,* trans. Alice Rio (Liverpool: Liverpool University Press, 2008), 103–244 @176. The adjective *bannitus* appears in Lex Ribuaria, 68.1 and 69.3; it refers to someone having been commanded into the king's service or the army: *Lex Ribuaria,* ed. Franz Beyerle and Rudolf Buchner, MGH LL nat. Germ. 3, 2 (Hanover: Hahn, 1954),

119, 121, English translation in *Laws of the Salian and Ripuarian Franks*, trans. Theodore John Rivers (New York: AMS Press, 1986), 201, 203. The Lex Rib. most likely originated in the early seventh century, but its surviving manuscripts are all Carolingian. Lex Rib. 68.1 mandates a fine of 60 *solidi* for failure to obey a command to the king's service or army; the coincidence of the amount with the *bannus* of the capitularies raises the possibility that it too is Carolingian.

23. The term *fredus* continues to be used in the Carolingian period: François Louis Ganshof, *Frankish Institutions under Charlemagne*, trans. Bryce and Mary Lyon (Providence: Brown University Press, 1968), 41–2.

24. *Capitulare Haristallense*, c. 9, 48/Geary, *Readings*, 297.

25. The Carolingian *solidus* was valued at 12 *denarii*: Grierson and Blackburn, *Medieval European Coinage*, 102–6.

26. e.g. *Capitulare Haristallense*, c. 9, 48/Geary, Readings, 297; *Capitulare Saxonicum*, a. 797, MGH Capit. I, 71–2 @c. 1–2, 71, English translation in Geary, *Readings*, 302–3 @302; *Capitula cum primis constituta*, a. 808, MGH Capit. I, 139–40 @c. 5–6, 140; *Capitulare missorum Aquisgranense alterum*, a. 809, MGH Capit. I, 151–2 @c. 7, 152.

27. *Capitulare missorum generale* a. 802, c. 31, 97/Geary, *Readings*, 317.

28. *Capitulare Saxonicum*, a. 797, c. 1, 71/Geary, *Readings*, 302; *Capitularia missorum specialia*, a. 802, c. 18, 101/Geary, *Readings*, 320; *Capitula a misso cognita facta*, a. 803–13, MGH Capit. I, 146 @c. 1, 146; *Capitula ad legem Baiwariorum addita*, a. 801–13, MGH Capit. I, 157–8 @c. 1, 157; *Capitula singillatim tradita Karolo magno adscripta*, MGH Capit. I, 213–15 @nr. 104, c. 6, 214; *Summula de bannis*, MGH Capit. I, 224.

29. *Synodus Fraconofurtensis*, a. 794, MGH Capit. I, 73–8 @c. 50, 78, English translation in Geary, *Readings*, 303–8 @307.

30. *Synodus Fraconofurtensis*, c. 18, 76/Geary, *Readings*, 305–6.

31. *Capitulare Haristallense*, c. 14, 50/Geary, *Readings*, 298; cf. *Brevarium missorum aquitanicum*, a. 789, MGH Capit. I, 65–6 @c. 15, 66: *De truste non faciendo*.

32. *Capitula a sacerdotibus proposita*, a. 802, MGH Capit. I, 105–7 @c. 18, 107; cf. *Capitulare missorum generale* a. 802, c. 22, 95–6 (not translated in Geary, *Readings*) re canons.

33. *Capitulare missorum item speciale*, a. 802?, c. 37, 103.

34. *Capitula de causis cum episcopis et abbatibus tractandis*, a. 811, MGH Capit. I, 162–4 @c. 4 and 8, 163.

35. *Capitulare Saxonicum*, a. 797, c. 1–2, 71/Geary, *Readings*, 302; *Capitularia missorum specialia*, a. 802, c. 18, 101/Geary, *Readings*, 320; *Summula de bannis, Capitula ad legem Baiwariorum addita*, a. 801–13, c. 2, 157–8.

36. *Capitulare Haristallense*, c. 22, 51/Geary, *Readings*, 298.

37. *Admonitio Generalis*, c. 67, 59; terms repeated in *Capitulare missorum item speciale* (802?), c. 42, 104.

38. *Admonitio Generalis*, c. 82, 61; English translation in Rosenwein, *Reading*, 182. Cf. also *Capitulare missorum item speciale* (802?), c. 31, 103.

39. *Capitulare missorum generale*, a. 802, c. 32, 97 and 37, 98/Geary, *Readings*, 317–18. Cf. also *Capitulare Baiwaricum*, a. 810?, c. 5, 159; *Capitula Karoli magni*, a. 803–13, MGH Capit. I, 143 @c. 3, 143, which puts an extra penalty on killing a close relative.

40. *Capitulare missorum in Theodonis villa datum secundum, generale*, a. 805, c. 5, 123/Rosenwein, *Reading*, 183.

41. Niermeyer, s.v. *faida*.

42. *Capitulare missorum in Theodonis villa datum secundum, generale*, a. 805, c. 5, 123/Rosenwein, *Reading*, 183.

43. *Capitula Karoli apud Ansegisum servata*, a. 810 or 811?, MGH Capit. I, 159–60 @c. 2, 160.

44. *Capitulare Haristallense*, c. 11, 49/Geary, *Readings*, 298.

45. *Capitulare missorum generale*, a. 802, c. 31, 97/Geary, *Readings*, 317; cf. *Capitulare missorum item speciale*, a. 802?, c. 55, 104.

46. *Capitula a misso cognita facta*, a. 803–13, c. 1, 146.

47. *Capitula Karoli apud Ansegisum servata*, 810 or 811?, c. 1, 160.

48. *Capitulare Aquisgranenses*, a. 801–13, MGH Capit. I, 170–2 @c. 20, 172.

49. *Capitula origins incertae*, a. 813 vel post, MGH Capit. I, 175 @c. 2, 175.

50. I thank Jennifer R. Davis for this observation.

51. Rudolf Hübner, *Gerichtsurkunden der Fränkischen Zeit* (Aalen: Scientia Verlag, 1971, reprint of the original edition, Weimar, 1891–3).

52. Zeumer, *Formulae*; Warren C. Brown, "Die karolingischen Formelsammlungen – warum existieren sie?", in Peter Erhardt, Karl Heidecker, and Bernhard Zeller, eds., *Die Privaturkunden der Karolingerzeit* (Dietikon-Zurich: Urs Graf Verlag, 2009), 95–101.

53. "Formulae Turonenses vulgo Sirmondicae dictae", in *Formulae*, 128–65 @nr. 38, 156.

54. "Formulae Salicae Lindenbrogianae", in *Formulae*, 265–84 @nr. 19, 280–1. On the dating of the Lindenbrog and Tours collections and their manuscripts see Alice Rio, *Legal Practice and the Written Word in the Early Middle Ages: Frankish Formulae, c. 500–1000* (Cambridge: Cambridge University Press, 2009), 101–10, 112–17; Bernhard Bischoff, *Salzburger Formelbücher und Briefe aus Tassilonischer und Karolingischer Zeit* (Munich: Verlag der Bayerischen Akademie der Wissenschaften, 1973), 11–12.

55. "Formulae Salicae Lindenbrogianae", nr. 20, 281.

56. Ian Wood, "Christianisation and the Dissemination of Christian Teaching", in NCMH I, 710–34 @717–18.

57. *Vita Willibrordi, archiepiscopi Traiectensis auctore Alcuino*, ed. Wilhelm Levison, MGH SSRM 7 (Hanover: Hahn, 1920), 81–141; English translation: Alcuin, "The Life of Saint Willibrord", in Thomas F. X. Noble and Thomas Head, eds., *Soldiers of Christ: Saints and Saint's Lives from Late Antiquity and the Early Middle Ages* (University Park: Penn State Press, 1995), 189–211. All quotations are taken from Life of Willibrord unless otherwise noted.

58. Noble and Head, *Soldiers of Christ*, 189–90.

59. *Vita Willibrordi*, c. 11, 125–6/Life of Willibrord, c. 11, 199–200.

60. *Vita Willibrordi*, c. 14–15, 127–9/Life of Willibrord, c. 14–15, 201–2.
61. *Vita Willibrordi*, c. 14, 127–8/Life of Willibrord, c. 14, 201–2.
62. *Vita Sanctae Balthildis*, ed. B. Krusch, MGH SSRM 2 (Hanover: Hahn, 1888), 475–508; English translation: "The Life of Lady Balthild, Queen of the Franks", in Fouracre and Gerberding, *Late Merovingian France*, 97–132. All quotations are taken from Life of Balthild unless otherwise noted.
63. *Vita Balthildis*, c. 10, 495–96/Life of Balthild, c. 10, 126–7.
64. Cf. Fouracre and Gerberding, Commentary to Life of Balthild, 112–13.
65. This is the B version of the *Vita Balthildis* given by Krusch in his edition in a parallel column next to the oldest, or A version; see Fouracre and Gerberding, Commentary to Life of Balthild, 115–16.
66. *Iudicatum regium*, MGH Capit. I, 257.
67. This suggestion was made to me by Jennifer R. Davis.
68. Theodor Bitterauf, *Die Traditionen des Hochstifts Freising* (Aalen: Scientia Verlag, 1967, reprint of the original edition, Munich, 1905), vol. 1, nr. 275, 242.
69. Warren C. Brown, *Unjust Seizure: Conflict, Interest and Authority in an Early Medieval Society* (Ithaca, NY: Cornell University Press, 2001), 73–101.
70. Ibid., 135–8.
71. L. Wallach, *Alcuin and Charlemagne: Studies in Carolingian History and Literature* (Ithaca, NY: Cornell University Press, 1959), 97–140.
72. E. Dümmler, ed., "Alcuini sive Albini epistolae", MGH Epist. 4 (Berlin: Weidmann, 1895), nrs. 245–9, 393–404; English translations of 245 and 249 in Paul Edward Dutton, ed., *Carolingian Civilization: A Reader* (Peterborough, Ontario: Broadview Press, 1993), 116–19.
73. In letter 249, Alcuin downplays the role of the monks in resisting the incursion into the church, a role that he had highlighted in letter 245.
74. LDM, s.v. "Theodulf, Bf. Von Orléans".
75. A letter from Alcuin, possibly to his close friend Archbishop Arn of Salzburg, suggests that the affair may have ended with Alcuin sending the refugee into a safe Bavarian exile: see letter 248.
76. McKitterick, *Frankish Kingdoms*, 106–39; Riché, *Carolingians*, 145–59; Peter Godman and Roger Collins, eds., *Charlemagne's Heir: New Perspectives on the Reign of Louis the Pious (814–840)* (Oxford: Clarendon Press, 1990).
77. *Ordinatio imperii*, a. 817, MGH Capit. I, 270–3; *Prooemium generale ad capitularia* (818–19), MGH Capit. I, 273–5; *Admonitio ad omnes regni ordines*, 823–5, MGH Capit. I, 303–7, esp. c. 2, 8, 303–4.
78. *Constitutio de Hispanis in Francorum regnum profugis prima* (815), MGH Capit. I, 261–3 @c. 2, 261.
79. *Capitula legibus addenda* (818–19), MGH Capit. I, 280–5 @c. 13, 284. Cf. also *Capitula missorum 819*, MGH Capit. I, 288–91 @c. 12, 290.
80. *Capitula legibus addenda* (818–19), c. 7, 282.
81. Ibid., c. 8, 282.
82. *Capitulare de disciplina palatii Aquisgranenses*, c. 820?, MGH Capit. I, 297–8, @c. 3–4, 298.

83. *Capitulare Missorum Wormatiense* (829), MGH Capit. II, ed. A. Boretius and V. Krause (Hanover: Hahn, 1890), 14–17 @c. 9, 16.
84. *Capitulare Missorum Wormatiense* (829), c. 10, 16.
85. *Capitula missorum* (821), MGH Capit. I, 300–1 @c. 1, 300.
86. *Capitula legibus addenda* (818–19), c. 9, 282; *Capitula incerta* (814–40), MGH Capit. I, 315 @c. 1, 315; *Capitula legibus addenda* (818–19), c. 3, 281.
87. *Capitulare Missorum Wormatiense* (829), c. 14, 16–17.
88. *Capitula incerta* (814–40), c. 2, 315.
89. *Capitula legibus addenda* (818–19), c. 1, 281.
90. Ibid., c. 2, 281 and c. 5, 282.
91. *Capitulare ecclesiasticum* (818–19), MGH Capit. I, 275–80 @c. 25, 279.
92. *Capitula incerta* (829?), MGH Capit. II, 11 @c. 1, 11.
93. *Capitulare ecclesiasticum* (818–19), c. 23, 278.
94. Paul Edward Dutton, ed., *Charlemagne's Courtier: The Complete Einhard* (Peterborough, Ontario: Broadview, 1998), esp. xi–li.
95. K. Hampe, ed., "Einharti epistolae", MGH Epist. 5 (Berlin: Weidmann, 1899), 105–45 @nr. 42, 131; English translation: "The Collected Letters", in Dutton, *Charlemagne's Courtier*, 131–65 @nr. 17, 137–8.
96. Einharti epistolae, nr. 49, 134/Collected Letters, nr. 25, 140–1. Cf also Einharti epistolae, nr. 48, 133–4/Collected Letters, nr. 18, 138.
97. *Translatio et miracula SS. Marcellini et Petri auctore Einhardo*, ed. G. Waitz, MGH SS 15, 1 (Hanover: Hahn, 1887), 238–64; English translation: "The Translation and Miracles of the Blessed Martyrs, Marcellinus and Peter", in Dutton, *Charlemagne's Courtier*, 69–130.
98. *Translatio*, Book II, c. 8, 247; Translation, 89–90.
99. Dutton translates *deposita simultate* as to "end [our] feud". Cf. Lewis and Short, s.v. *simultas/tatis*.
100. Capitulary of Charlemagne: *Capitulare missorum generale* a. 802, c. 32, 97/Geary, *Readings*, X; of Louis the Pious: *Hludowici et Hlotharii epistola generalis* a. 828, MGH Capit. II, 3–6, version B.
101. *Translatio*, Book IV, c. 14, 261–2/Translation, 126.
102. *Translatio*, Book III, c. 14, 253–4/Translation, 104.

# PART II

# LOCAL AND ROYAL POWER
# IN THE ELEVENTH CENTURY

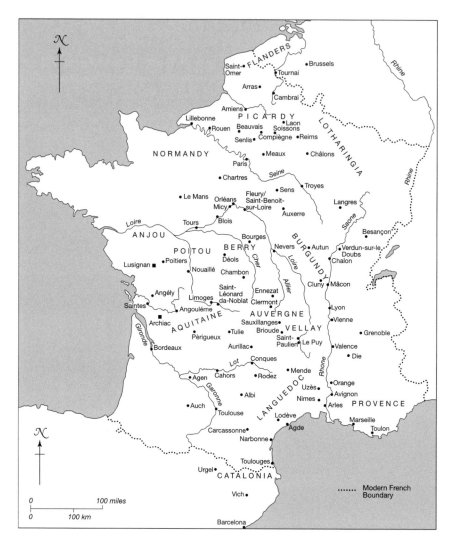

**Map 3**  France c. 1000 (From Thomas Head and Richard Landes, eds., *The Peace of God: Social Violence and Religious Response in France around the Year 1000* (Ithaca, NY: Cornell University Press, 1992) p. 5)

*chapter four*

# VIOLENCE, THE ARISTOCRACY, AND THE CHURCH AT THE TURN OF THE FIRST MILLENNIUM

We now move forward in time, to the decades around the turn of the first millennium. We will begin with the regions west of the river Rhine, that is, in the part of Europe that was on its way to becoming France. A great deal has happened here since Charlemagne ruled.[1] To begin with, the political edifice that he erected has disappeared. In its place, after over a century and a half of civil war, violent political competition, and Viking incursions, is a kingdom of the western Franks. This kingdom is led not by Carolingians, but by descendants of the Roberting counts of Paris, who in 987, in the person of Hugh "Capet", took the west Frankish throne from the last Carolingian contender and inaugurated the line of the Capetian Kings of France.

The political landscape of this west Frankish kingdom is fragmented. Robertings and Carolingians alike had been forced to bid for support from other western magnates with the tools they had available. These tools comprised not only whatever military prestige the leaders of each house could gain by fighting Vikings or each other, but also rights, privileges, and an ever shrinking pool of royal lands. By the time Hugh Capet took the throne, he had the advantage of royal anointment, as well as a strong base of inherited lands in the area around Paris. But he faced a kingdom that was largely controlled by magnates on whose good will he depended and who, save for anointment, thought themselves every bit his equal. The great magnates were in just as precarious a position, however, for their power similarly depended on attracting or coercing the support of those beneath them.

At the same time, west Francia boasts two rather remarkable novelties: the knight and the castle. The earliest castles were generally wooden towers placed on natural or artificial hills and surrounded by stockades. From the late tenth century onwards they appear in the sources as bases for small troops of heavily armed and armored mounted warriors.[2] Such mounted warriors were in themselves nothing new.[3] But what is new is their deployment in castles to fight small brush wars (*werrae* or *guerrae*) with each other. These early knights quickly developed a bad reputation, particularly in ecclesiastical circles. Contemporary texts written above all by clerics and monks from the central and southern parts of the kingdom complain in bitter and outraged terms about depredations and killings carried out by castle-based lords and their mounted followers against ecclesiastical property and persons.

How can we explain the appearance of the knight and his castle and the concomitant rise in complaints about knightly violence?[4] One powerful hypothesis argues that they reflect a new relationship between violence and political power.[5] According to this argument, while the power of the Frankish aristocracy had always rested on its ability to wield violence, this power had been contained or co-opted by the Carolingian kings. As the range of royal authority in the west Frankish kingdom contracted in the course of the tenth century, however, magnates farther and farther down the social and political scale found themselves increasingly free to use their power as they wished without having to be accountable to kings. As a result, the political order created by the Carolingians broke down. Regional lords and their followers simply pursued their local interests, which mainly concerned the control of land, men, and income, by force. To this end, they planted armed and mounted followers in castles, supported by fiefs of income and/or land, to dominate and exploit local populations and to ward off attacks by any nearby competitors. In some parts of central and southern France, distance from cities or difficult geography made it especially hard for anybody to assert political control over a wide area. Here the political infighting became so local and so fierce that commanders of castle garrisons, called castellans, themselves took to playing the lordship game and imposed their power on the peasants around them with few, if any, limits.

This kind of lordship was based not on any ideology or set of political traditions, but rather on naked violence loosed from the chains of royal restraint (though sometimes its purveyors claimed to be exercising delegated royal powers that had been enforced by the royal ban – hence the term "banal lordship" that is sometimes applied to it). It divided the world into two kinds of people: those who could wield violence and those who could not, perpetrators and victims. The victims of this violence comprised above all the peasants who worked the land and who fed everyone else. But they also included the churches and monasteries, which possessed vast resources in land and manpower that could be seized or plundered to support the power and military activities of the lords and their followers. Direct symptoms of the new violent lordship, there-fore, were not only the chorus of complaints about knights in clerical and monastic texts, but also the so-called Peace of God councils that are attested from the last decades of the tenth century. These ecclesiastical councils brought together not only clergymen and monks but also laypeople of both high and low status. They represented an effort in the most violence-riven areas to counter lordly power with spiritual weapons, that is, oaths sworn on the relics of the saints to uphold God's peace, and the threat of excommunication.

This narrative is often called the "feudal transformation" or "feudal mutation" because its advocates see it eventually producing that flexible combination of homage, fiefs, and military service that came to character-ize much of medieval society and that later ages would call feudalism.[6] Some have gone so far as to call it the "feudal revolution" because they see it taking place very rapidly, within only a few decades on either side of the year 1000. The narrative is powerful because it makes a great deal of sense and brings much of the evidence together in a logical and internally consistent way. It has not gone without challenge, however. Its critics point out that the actual exercise of power in the early Capetian realm, though it took place on a more local scale, worked in essentially the same way as it had under the Carolingians. Violence had always been one tool used by Frankish magnates to exert local power, and Carolingian control of that violence was never as effective as Charlemagne's cap-itularies would make it seem. Courts similar to those visible under the Carolingians continue to appear in tenth- and eleventh-century west Francia, and they brought about settlements in ways comparable to their ninth-century predecessors. What disappeared in early Capetian France was the language of royal restraint; as the millennium approached this language was replaced in sources increasingly disconnected from kings by language more accurately reflecting what had been going on all along. Moreover, close study of accusations written by monks about rapacious and violent laymen sometimes reveals them to be tactical rhetoric; when such accusations are peeled away from an account of a given dispute, it can emerge that the dispute may not have involved what we would call violence and that even if it did, the monks' lay opponents may have understood their actions as something other than evil provoked by the devil.[7]

Viewed from our particular perspective, the feudal mutation narrative depends on a set of basic assumptions about violence. To begin with, it assumes that violence itself can work as a tool of power outside of any framework of legitimation; the ability to wield violence alone ("I do this because I want to and because I can") is itself the basis for the new lordships. Second, it assumes that violence is a negative and disruptive force that needs to be restrained. Lordly violence had been kept in check by royal authority but was being restrained no longer. Therefore, the restoration of order, or the creation of a new order, depended either on restoring old mechanisms of restraint or erecting new ones. Third, the narrative assumes that violence was wielded, and used as a tool of power, by one group within early Capetian society: those with the swords, the horses, and the castles. The members of this group acted entirely out of self-interest, using violence opportunistically in the pursuit of wealth and power. Those at the high end of the socio-political ladder used it to compete with each other and to exploit the resources of those below them. At the low end, mounted thugs only barely removed from the peasantry oppressed their neighbors to avoid falling into the ranks of the oppressed themselves.

In this chapter, we will test these assumptions about violence in early Capetian west Francia against an array of sources of different kinds. These sources mostly stem from or deal with the south-central regions of the west Frankish kingdom, that is, Poitou, Anjou, the Touraine, La Marche, Angoulême, and Aquitaine. These are among the regions where the evidence about violence is most thick on the ground, and they are the homeland of the Peace councils. Some of our texts, however, come from Burgundy, from the Capetian homelands near Paris, and from Flanders.

These sources leave no doubt that we are in a profoundly different world from that of Charlemagne. The regionalism of political identity is readily apparent; "France", that is, the Capetian domains around Paris, is a land distinct from other areas of the west Frankish realm such as Aquitaine and Burgundy, or Poitou and the Touraine. The world of our sources is populated by the lords of castles with their troops of horsemen, as well as by bishops, by abbots and monks, and by peasants. The old Latin word for soldier, *miles*, has become a term peculiar to mounted warriors, leaving footsoldiers to be called *pedites*; the old Carolingian benefice has begun to mutate into the fief (*fevum*). Kings, while not invisible, are scarce. Figures bearing what we might call "official" titles, that is, titles that under Charlemagne had signaled authority delegated from the king, are also rarer. When they do show up, they are likely to be dukes, counts, or viscounts. Much more often, however, lay wielders of power are simply called "lords". Judicial institutions are not completely absent; we still see gatherings for the purpose of settling disputes that resemble, and are even described as, *placita*. However, what judicial records say about disputes has changed. They tell us that people competed with each other not only for property, but overtly and explicitly for rights to collect or levy streams of income from properties and people, from tolls, mills, or courts. These income sources had lost the official or royal labels that had previously defined and legitimated them. They were now legitimated simply by having previously existed, and are therefore called "customs" (*consuetudines*). Many disputes hinged on questions of whether such customs were old and customary exactions and therefore good, or whether they were new impositions and therefore bad.

There is no question that the knights were violent; violence is what they did for a living and what they lived to do. They seized property to supply themselves and their men; they burned down buildings and cut down crops to hurt their opponents economically; they hurt and killed not only each other but also clerics, monks, and peasants. Nevertheless, the purveyors of violence did not work in a normative vacuum. They were heirs to long traditions of violence and of norms governing violence, traditions that offered options and that could be played off against each other. Nor were they all knights. Looking at how a variety of people in this period worked with the norms available to them, therefore, may help us to understand better why the sources say to us the things that they do about violence and political order.

### Hugh of Lusignan

Our first source captures lay magnate violence from the perspective of a lay magnate, namely Hugh IV, lord of Lusignan in the Poitou. The text records the settlement of a series of disputes between Hugh and his lord, William V, count of the Poitevins and Aquitanians (r. 990–1029).[8] Although the earliest manuscript of the text most likely stems from the middle of the eleventh century, the events it describes took place some-time between 1022 and 1028.[9] The settlement regulated the rights and responsibilities of Hugh and William with respect to each other, and gave Hugh control of a castle and the land and rights that went with it. It is prefaced with an extensive narrative from Hugh's perspective that was apparently dictated if not written by Hugh himself.[10] Like those opening many an earlier dispute record, this narrative tells the history of the conflict that the agreement was supposed to settle. It is, however, unusually long, and it is unique in the view it gives of an early eleventh-century power struggle between a man and his lord.

The events Hugh describes all took place within an area of less than one hundred kilometers diameter in eastern Poitou. His tale is all about control of castles and of the lands and income that pertained to them, a military and economic unit that the text often refers to as an honor.[11]

The characters are lords and vassals and their armed and mounted followers. The vassals, such as Hugh, needed castles and/or land and income to maintain or increase their power. The lords controlled the castles, lands, and incomes and gave them out as fiefs, either directly, or by allowing their vassals to marry women who had inherited rights to them. Lords and vassals were bound together by oaths of fealty as well as by fiefs. While it was castles that Hugh was after, therefore, it is the rights, obligations, and expectations created by promises and oaths between lords and vassals that form the normative framework for Hugh's story. This story is sometimes outrageously slanted in Hugh's favor. Hugh presents himself as the injured and aggrieved party who struggled to behave well even when it was not to his advantage. Count William, in contrast, consistently failed to behave towards Hugh as a lord should. He broke promises to Hugh, he did things that directly harmed Hugh's interests, and he claimed arbitrary authority over Hugh. Precisely because it is so biased, however, it gives us a very good idea of the norms of proper behavior in Hugh's world that Hugh could invoke in order to blacken William and support his case.

As he starts his narrative, Hugh presents us with a tangled and confusing web of relationships and obligations, of alliances and betrayals. He says that he held land from Count William and had been promised another honor.[12] But Viscount Savary of Thouars seized some of Hugh's land. William promised not to make any agreement with Savary's brother Ralph until the land was returned. The count nevertheless proceeded to give the seized land to Ralph. Hugh tried to get the land back by marrying Ralph's daughter, but was persuaded "out of love and fidelity for the count", and by a promise from William to give him whatever he wanted, to back out of the marriage. William started to keep his promise by arranging for his neighbor, Count Fulk Nerra of Anjou, to give Hugh another honor and the widow of the man who had held it. Ralph of Thouars, however, persuaded William not to follow through on the deal. He then approached Hugh again to offer his daughter and the land his brother Savary had seized if only Hugh would help him against William. Hugh, "out of his love for Count William", refused. When Ralph went ahead and launched a dispute (*litigatio*) against the count, Hugh displayed his loyalty to his lord by launching one against Ralph. By his own testimony, he suffered heavy loss.

As the end of this story indicates, a *litigatio* involved violence. When violence broke out, the outcome was most often burned castles and captured horsemen – though men could be mutilated or killed. Not all violence was licit, however. We know this not because Hugh explicitly says so, but because he admits that while he was fighting Ralph on Count

William's behalf, he committed an unspecified wrong (*malefactum*).[13] Hugh's misdeed prompted Ralph's nephew Geoffrey to take vengeance, by attacking one of Hugh's castles and burning it, then capturing Hugh's horsemen and cutting off their hands. Hugh wanted to negotiate a settlement, but William (ever the neglectful lord) failed to help him in any way.

Hugh resorted to violence on his own behalf in an effort to gain some bargaining power vis à vis the Thouars kindred; he attacked Ralph's family castle at Thouars itself and captured forty-three horsemen. Hugh claims that he should then have been able to reclaim his seized lands and settle his dispute with Ralph's nephew Geoffrey, and in addition score a nice ransom for the horsemen.[14] But Count William intervened; he asked Hugh to give him the captured horsemen, promising in exchange either to arrange a settlement with Geoffrey and finally get Hugh's land delivered to him or return the horsemen to Hugh. Putting his "trust in God and in the count", Hugh complied. But he was betrayed once more; he received neither the land nor the settlement nor the horsemen.[15]

The story continues in more or less the same vein. Hugh claimed castles because he believed William had promised them to him or because members of his family had once held them.[16] He commended himself to other lords at William's request (or at William's order; Hugh charges at one point that William told him, "you owe so much to me that if I should tell you to make a peasant into a lord you should do it").[17] He fought for castles to which he thought he was entitled; in the process he suffered great losses "in men and many other things".[18] He joined with William in attacking castles to avenge wrongs that others had done to William.[19] William made promises to Hugh and broke them. These promises included one to hold a judicial hearing (*placitum*) at which he would try to get Hugh's property claims settled or, if he could not, give him a castle he had built.[20] Evidently, Hugh did not see such hearings as fora for adjudication but rather for negotiation.

Hugh makes no distinction whatever between the behavior of lay magnates and that of clerics. He describes bishops acting in exactly the same way as everybody else. At one point he says that he agreed to commend himself to Bishop Isembert of Poitiers for a share of a castle that his uncle had held from the bishop's predecessor.[21] Later on, he sought advice from Bishop Gerald of Limoges. Together he and the bishop built a castle against Hugh's opponent of the moment. Count William, however, seized the new castle and burned it.[22]

While Hugh focuses on the actions of lords and their followers, he does reveal that others were affected by what they did. Non-combatants were swept up in the violence, to their cost. An opponent burned the settlement around one of Hugh's castles, after plundering it and taking prisoners and doing "plenty of other evil deeds".[23] Some time afterwards, Hugh himself burned a castle, captured both men and women, and carried off plunder.[24]

After more negotiating and fighting, and an abortive appeal before the count's court, Hugh finally broke off his fidelity to William, "except what he owed for the city [of Poitiers] and his own person" – evidently a memory of the public authority once inherent in the office of count of Poitou.[25] Only after still more fighting, however, was Hugh able to reach the agreement with William that ends the text. After forcing William to renounce trickery by invoking God and the Holy Cross, Hugh renewed his sworn fidelity to William and his son and renounced his claims to all that he had claimed from William in the past. In exchange, William agreed to give Hugh the honor that had belonged to his uncle.[26]

### Monasteries

Hugh's narrative gives us an idea of the claims and grievances with which lords both great and petty justified their use of violence as they pursued the castles, lands, and incomes on which their positions and power depended. It is, of course, an idea shaped by Hugh's own position and perspective. We can get some other perspectives on magnate violence by looking at monastic charters.

A rewarding cache of charters comes from the Poitevin monastery of Saint-Maixent.[27] Saint-Maixent lies in the same region covered by Hugh of Lusignan's text; indeed, some of Hugh's descendants show up in the monastery's charters. Monastic charters are by nature principally concerned with a monastery's property rights. When the Saint-Maixent charters report violence, therefore, it is violence that affected the monastery's property and dependants.

An example from the year 1041 tells us that a nobleman named Walter had engaged in conflict with his enemies.[28] "Seizing the opportunity", Walter plundered (*predavit*) the lands of Saint-Maixent, laid waste (*vastavit*) to villas and drove out their inhabitants just as he pleased. In other words, a *guerra* was under way, and in the course of hostilities Walter plundered property belonging to Saint-Maixent. He did not, however, do so with impunity. Like Hugh of Lusignan, he was embedded in a network of relationships; members of this network put pressure on him to make amends. "With the counsel of his friends", Walter publicly acknowledged that he had done something wrong (*reatum*); he agreed to compensate the monastery for the evil deeds (*pro malefactis*) he had committed. In penitent humility, therefore, before a gathering of witnesses that included Count William (VII of Aquitaine and Poitou, William V's grandson) and Countess Agnes (the count's grandmother),[29] he gave a church along with a complex of properties to Saint-Maixent for the redemption of his soul and those of his parents. Explicitly consenting to the settlement were one Maingot of Metulus and his sons. Maingot was Walter's lord; the charter says that he had given Walter the church that Walter gave to Saint-Maixent. It appears, then, that Walter's lord did what Hugh of Lusignan had accused Count William V of not doing, namely help him to make good a wrong. The monks of Saint-Maixent did their part as well; they lessened Walter's humiliation with a counter-gift, namely 40 *solidi* in cash and a horse valued at 200 *solidi*.[30]

This case is clear-cut: magnate violence harmed monastery property and dependants. The monks of Saint-Maixent could not rely on consti-tuted authority for protection or recompense; instead they depended on a conviction among Walter's friends that he had committed a wrong and on the willingness of Walter's lord to give him the means to make amends. The wrong appears to have consisted of harming a party not involved in the original *guerra*; it is also possible that Walter's friends and lord were unwilling to risk angering the monastery's patron saint. Even so, the monks still had to pay to ease Walter's shame. Count William added his prestige to the proceedings, but as far as the charter was concerned, he did little else.

Other examples, however, show just how hard it can be to grasp what was going on when monks accused someone of plunder. In 1079, the monks of Saint-Maixent charged Hugh VI of Lusignan (grandson of Hugh IV) with plundering (*predam fecit*) one of their properties.[31] The monastery's provost challenged Hugh to a judicial duel over the matter. The charter says that Hugh, terrified by his sin, refused to accept the duel. Instead, he relinquished "that bad custom" (*malam consuetudinem*) in perpetuity. The change in terminology – from plunder to custom – suggests that what was at issue here was a dispute over rights to impose an exaction. It is possible that Hugh VI had tried to impose a new exaction on property and people that were not his. It is also possible, however, that he had asserted what he believed to be his right. How much violence was actually involved we cannot say. But regardless of whether Hugh had acted with actual coercive force, the monks plainly thought that illicitly extracting income from their property constituted plunder.

The monks of Saint-Maixent were willing to aim such language not only at lay magnates but also at other monks. In a case from the very end of the eleventh century, they charged another monk named Mascelinus, prior of the monastery of Saint Gildasius at the castle of Talniacus, with having "unjustly invaded" (*injuste invaserat*) a church and the property attached to it, and possessing it with "tyrannical power" (*virtute tirannica*).[32] An appeal to the bishop of Saintes led to a hearing, at which a monk of Saint-Maixent took an oath vindicating his monastery's claim. Mascelinus returned the church, in exchange for 110 *solidi* as compensation for building works that he had carried out there. This last step probably represented a counter-gift to ease Mascelinus's dishonor. It also raises questions, however, about Saint-Maixent's rhetoric. Since Mascelinus had invested resources to improve the church and/or its property, he may well have taken possession thinking that he had legitimate rights to it.

In the above two cases, Saint-Maixent won clear-cut victories. One final example, however, records a compromise that left the monks of Saint-Maixent in an ongoing and amicable relationship with their opponent. Here the rhetoric of violence is absent. A charter written between 1040 and 1044 states that a knight named Albuin had built a mill and bakery on a villa belonging to the monastery without permission.[33] This was not an altruistic effort on Albuin's part to provide a service. Lords built mills and bakeries so that they could force the people who lived near them to grind their grain and bake their bread there, for a fee of course; mills and bakeries were a source of income.[34] Abbot Archimbald of Saint-Maixent responded by arranging a settlement (*placitum vel convenientiam*). The settlement did not remove the burden of the mill and bakery from the villa's inhabitants, however. Instead, the parties agreed that Albuin could continue to hold the mill and bakery for his lifetime. After his death, half of the mill and bakery (i.e., of their revenues) were to go to the monastery (where the other half was to go is not specified). Albuin sealed the deal with an annual gift to the monastery of a jug of wine. In this case, then, the monks appear perfectly willing to have a layman extort revenue from their dependants as long as they got a cut of the proceeds. No one involved seemed to object to the fact that the villa's residents now had to pay to use Albuin's mill and bakery; Abbot Archimbald was apparently happy to see a new source of revenue constructed. He just wanted to make sure that his monastery got its rightful share. Given the previous examples, one can imagine that had the monks not been willing to accept the mill and bakery, Albuin would have been surrounded by charges of plunder and unjust seizure.

The Saint-Maixent charters discussed above deal with claims of violent seizure of monastic property or violence done to monastic property rights or people. In contrast, a set of charters from the abbey of St. Mary of Noyers in the Touraine, studied in a seminal article by Stephen D.

White, were written because violent disputes among magnates ended in settlements that involved the abbey.[35] These highlight violence as a tool of vengeance. An example from c. 1088 reports that a man named Boso de Chillo was killed.[36] Boso's sons held one Aimericus of Saint-Savigny responsible. They therefore began a dispute with Aimericus's sons and killed one of them. Boso's sons later repented of their action, why we are not told, and repeatedly tried to reach a settlement with the slain man's brother, Aimericus II. Eventually a settlement was reached that triggered the production of this charter: Boso's sons gave property to the abbey at Noyers to support a monk who would pray for the soul of the slain man. As in the first Saint-Maixent example, this settlement was apparently brought about with the help of – or as the result of pressure from – Boso's lord, one Aimericus of Faye-la-Vineuse; the witness list is dominated by Aimericus of Faye-la-Vineuse and men in his following.[37]

The impulse to violent vengeance could be triggered by humiliation. Bartholomaeus, lord of L'Isle-Bouchard, together with his friends attacked a castle held by Count Fulk Rechin of Anjou.[38] The party burned the castle and captured the garrison. Among those captured was one Guarnerius Maingodus. Bartholomaeus ordered a man named Paganus to fold Guarnerius up in a small coffer. Guarnerius was outraged by this treatment. After his release (says the charter) he felt such loathing for Paganus that he swore an oath to kill him. The terrified Paganus activated his network of relationships; he tried to arrange a settlement with Guarnerius through friends and acquaintances, but did not succeed. Finally Paganus's father asked Abbot Stephen of Noyers to intervene. Abbot Stephen went to Guarnerius and preached to him about giving up anger. Then he took Guarnerius to see Archbishop Radulf of Tours, who preached to him some more. Finally overcome, Guarnerius agreed to make peace with Paganus if Paganus and his family would give some property to the abbey at Noyers, for the sake of acquiring his love and to help him overcome the sin he had committed by swearing an oath to kill Paganus. Paganus, his father, and his brothers agreed.

As the above examples indicate, the magnates around Noyers were very ready to fight each other to avenge subjectively perceived wrongs. Nevertheless, they had a sense of at least one line that could not be crossed. It was not licit to take out the helpless and uninvolved, at least if the helpless and uninvolved were aristocratic women and children. Sometime around 1074, one Acharias was entangled in a violent conflict with three other lords.[39] He was losing badly, having already lost his own castle and lands. One night, Acharias rode out with his men on a plundering raid. The band found a group of men gathered at the house of a peasant and attacked. The people of the house fled to a cave below the house. So Acharias and his men burned the house down on top of the refugees, killing them all. Unfortunately for Acharias, among the dead were women and children, including some members of a local aristocratic kindred: the sister of Walter of Les Puys and her sons, and the mother of Bernard, brother of Hubert of Les Puys.

That same night, Acharias was captured by his own nephew. He turned for help to the monks of Noyers. Realizing his sin (according to the charter), he asked for the monks to pray for him and offered in exchange to release some of the monastery's fishermen he had been holding (for what reason the text does not say). When the monks arranged for his release, he asked them to help him make peace with the kin of the men he had killed. The monks brought the victims' kin to their church and reconciled them with Acharias. In exchange, Acharias asked for two hundred masses to be said for the slain. He also released to the monks half of a river landing-place that he had previously claimed from them, so that he might be freed of the sin of homicide through St. Mary's intercession. Among the witnesses to the settlement were Walter and Bernard of Les Puys.

Two different normative frameworks are visible in this story. The charter itself, which was written to record the property and liturgical arrangements that underlay the settlement, puts things in a monastic framework. It says that the wrong Acharias had committed consisted of killing the refugees in general and especially the women and children; he needed Mary's intercession, to be won through the prayers of the monks, to be freed from his sin. But, as White has noted in his discussion of this case, the speed with which Acharias sought a settlement, and the detailed list of the Le Puy family members affected, indicates that Acharias himself had other concerns. On the losing side of a *guerra*, the last thing he needed was to open up a second conflict with the Les Puys; he was not in a position to deal with their vengeance. He already had a strained relationship with the monks (since he was holding their fishermen and disputing rights to their landing-place); he had further strained his relationship with God by burning innocent women and children to death. He had been humiliated, betrayed by his own nephew, captured, and imprisoned. It is likely that not only his own fortunes but also the loyalty of his following depended on making a quick and decisive settlement. Acharias was not concerned about the peasants; he had launched his attack on their house as soon as he saw them gathered there. But he had crossed a line by killing aristocratic women and children who had sought refuge. He had to act quickly and decisively to repair the damage and avoid a new conflict that he could not handle.

## The Miracles of Saint Foy

In the sources we have looked at so far, magnates resorted to violence because they believed that they had grievances: claims to property and/or income that were not honored, injuries to themselves, their interests, their followers, or their families that needed to be made good, insults that needed to be avenged. They fought on their own behalf, and on behalf of their lords, allies, or followers. Their violence was not without limits, however. Lords and their knights in this region had a sense of legitimate and illegitimate violence, of lines between the acceptable and the unacceptable. Moreover, each of them was embedded in a set of vertical and horizontal relationships that connected friends and relations, lords and followers, monks, clerics, and saints. When their acts of violence threatened the interests of members of their larger community, pressure surrounded them like a cocoon and forced them to settle with their opponents. The settlements balanced face with rights and material claims, and included the prayers of monks and the favor of saints in the balance. None of the above, however, appears so far to have encompassed those below the ranks of the lords, knights, monks, or clerics – that is, the peasants. Implicit or explicit in all of the stories told so far are burned villages, wasted fields, and peasants injured or killed, or forced to deal with exactions imposed by both secular and ecclesiastical lords.

Members of the ecclesiastical establishment participated in this culture of violence in a variety of ways. According to Hugh IV of Lusignan, some bishops played the game for castles and lands alongside their lay counterparts. In contrast, our monastic charters show that abbots and monks resisted the violent encroachment of lay lords on their monastery's properties, or at least tried to make sure they got a fair share of the revenues. They also served as peacemakers, applying spiritual pressure and the power of prayers purchased by gifts of land to help end violent conflicts among the people who lived around them.

At least some monks in the region, however, thought about violence in the same way as did the knights and their lords. Evidence for this comes from a collection of miracle stories, the *Book of the Miracles of Saint Foy*.[40] St. Foy of Conques (in English, St. Faith) was according to legend a young girl who in the early fourth century was martyred by the Roman authorities.[41] In the ninth century, her relics were acquired (or, more properly, stolen) from their original home by monks from the monastery of Conques in the Rouergue.[42] St. Foy displayed her pleasure with her new home by performing miracles, with the result that by the turn of the eleventh century Conques had become a premier pilgrimage site.

Shortly after the turn of the first millennium, a man named Bernard, head of the cathedral school at Angers, decided to go south to Conques to investigate and record Foy's miracles for himself. The result was two books of miracle stories written between 1013 and 1020. Spurred on by Bernard's work (and possibly by some of his notes), the monks of Conques produced two more books between 1020 and 1050.[43]

St. Foy's miracles occurred in a world dominated by warrior lords with their armed followings who lived in the castles scattered throughout the area around the monastery. These lords and/or their knights[44] fought with each other and they attacked monks. Their enmities and their acts of violence were recorded in the collection because they frequently prompted St. Foy's miraculous intervention. In a good example, a high-ranking abbot named Peter set out to visit Conques, but was ambushed by one of his enemies with a party of armed men.[45] However, divine intervention prevented the attackers from seeing their prey, and Peter made it safely to Conques. On Peter's return journey, the same enemy again sought to attack him. St. Foy's intercession produced a second group of armed men, who were likewise Peter's enemies but also enemies of the first group. The first and second groups of Peter's enemies were soon embroiled with each other, and Peter escaped in the confusion.

The *Miracles* do not, however, simply pit rapacious and violent lay lords and knights against peace-loving monks. Far from it; members of the clergy also violently persecuted St. Foy and her followers. A pious man aroused the hatred and jealousy of a priest, because the priest thought the man had made advances to his mistress.[46] Despite the man's pleas of innocence, the priest had his men hold him down while he himself ripped his victim's eyes out. St. Foy restored the man's sight. A knight left his castle to journey to St. Foy's church. He was captured by an evil priest and held in chains. He was only released when St. Foy struck the priest from head to foot with sores running with a "discharge so foul that his whole household found it intolerable".[47]

The ranks of St. Foy's followers included at least one monk who made violence his business. A monk and prior of Conques named Gimon kept weapons and armor above the foot of his bed and a fully equipped warhorse in the stable, which he used to take "vengeance against evil-doers".[48] When "wicked men invaded the monastery with hostile intent" Gimon would ride at the head of his armored ranks, giving courage to the fearful to face victory or martyrdom. When it happened that he found himself so outnumbered that his own people melted away, he would plead his case to St. Foy, alternating prayers with threats to flog the saint's reliquary and even throw it into a river or well unless she took action immediately. According to Bernard of Angers, God seems to have accepted this as simply Gimon's way of doing things, because in every other respect the monk was morally excellent. It was not normally considered proper for a monk to go on armed expeditions, but Bernard declares: "if only lazy monks would put aside their cowardly sloth and act as bravely to the advantage of their monasteries!"

Perhaps the most violent character in the entire collection is St. Foy herself. The saint responded violently in particular to those who injured her followers or threatened her property. A knight living in the castle of Conques stole everything he could from the monastery's property, mutilated the men who worked the monastery's land, and harassed the monks themselves with insults.[49] The senior monks prayed for St. Foy's assistance, unfurled "the banner of the Lord's victory" in the public square, and placed alongside it a cross, reliquary boxes, and St. Foy's image. The knight and his children were promptly stricken with disease and the tower of Conques castle fell down. St. Foy did not even spare her fellow women. A noble woman who obsessively coveted a field of St. Foy's that adjoined her own continually abused the men who worked it and eventually succeeded in driving them away.[50] As she set a plowman of her own to work the field, "her whole body shriveled instantly and she croaked and hissed horribly" as she died.

St. Foy also avenged affront or insult with violence. The lord of a famous castle seized a farm that the monks of Conques believed belonged to them. In response, the monks processed to the farm carrying St. Foy's reliquary. One of the lord's knights, sitting at a banquet surrounded by armed followers and servants, declared that those who served the saint "were a pile of shit" and that he would trample the saint's reliquary underfoot. A windstorm sent from heaven caused the roof of the knight's house to collapse; the falling debris killed him, his wife, and five of his servants, but no one else.[51] A cleric spread "some silly foolishness" about St. Foy's reliquary and dissuaded people from making offerings to it.[52] That night, the saint appeared to the cleric in a dream and beat him with a rod for the insult; he died the next day.

Most significantly, St. Foy was just as capable as any knight of violently seizing property that she wanted, even if it did not belong to her. The monks of Conques decided that the high altar of the saint's church needed a new frontal.[53] To make it, they needed gold. As Bernard of Angers puts it, "this is the reason that few people are left in this whole region who have a precious ring or brooch or armbands or hairpins, or anything of this kind, because Sainte Foy, either with a simple entreaty or with bold threats, wrested away these same things for the work of the frontal". One woman from the area, knowing that the saint was requisitioning gold, decided to hide a gold ring. St. Foy promptly visited the woman with a painful fever for several nights in succession until she gave up and handed the ring over. Another ring had been promised to the monastery by a married woman. When the woman died, her husband and his second wife decided to keep the ring. St. Foy proceeded to torture the second wife with severe pain until she admitted her fault, at which point the pain disappeared.[54]

The monks of Conques thoroughly approved of their patroness's violence. Count Raymond II of Rouergue had made a gift of property and treasure to Conques. After the count's death, the gift was contested by the wife of a man named Bernard the Hairy.[55] The woman claimed that Count Raymond had stolen the property from her first husband. When a meeting at Conques failed to settle the dispute, the monks and their opponents gathered for a second hearing at the site of the disputed property itself, over which Bernard the Hairy himself presided. Bernard, despite his marriage to the plaintiff, ruled in favor of the monks. His wife's party was reduced to raving like madmen. The ruling only set the stage for negotiations, however, at the end of which Bernard's wife agreed to drop her charge in exchange for money. This compromise was promptly challenged by a noble and powerful but belligerent and bombastic young man. The challenger leapt into the midst of the assembly, urged his party to stand up for their rights (all the while rolling his eyes, gnashing his teeth, and flailing his fists), and called for a judicial combat. "For I shall win the day," he declared, "and then afterwards neither Sainte Foy nor those utterly corrupt servants of hers will dare to demand again the right and ownership of our fief". As tensions rose and mass violence threatened to erupt, the monks fled. The raving young man set out with fifty of his knights to attack the monks on their road home. St. Foy then stepped in. With a flash of light and a horrifying rumble, the young man was struck dead by an arrow of heaven to the brain and burnt to charcoal. The monks were delighted; they rejoiced that they had recovered their property and been "avenged on their worst enemy".

The *Miracles* tell us quite a bit about violence in the world around Conques. Members of lay families fought with each other over claims to property.[56] They fought over women.[57] They also, of course, fought for the sake of vengeance, and feared the threat of it. A bold knight from the Auvergne was stricken with a malady, in the course of which part of his intestines erupted into his scrotum.[58] Eventually he could no longer ride a horse, and so was turned from a knight into a footsoldier (*de milite pedes factus*). He prayed to St. Foy, who told him to look up a local blacksmith and have the blacksmith put the affected part of his body on his anvil and strike it as hard as he could with his hammer. When the suffering man went to the blacksmith and told him what he had to do, the blacksmith was horrified. Not only would the man die, the blacksmith protested, but the man's kin would come after him to exact vengeance (they went through with the process anyway, and the sufferer was miraculously cured).

St. Foy accepted violent vengeance when the grievances behind it were legitimate (which is not surprising, since she took such vengeance herself). She only intervened when people seeking vengeance attacked people who were not involved in their grievances, or when they hit the wrong target. For example, a young man named Stephen set out to attack a castle that he hated because his father had been killed there.[59] On his way, he seized a young man who had nothing to do with his father's death in order to extort from him a particularly attractive piece of land. St. Foy freed the captive.

It was in fact dangerous *not* to be violent in this world; a knight who wanted to protect his wealth and status needed everyone around him to know that he was willing and able to defend his interests. A brave knight from the Auvergne became ill and lost all his hair.[60] With his hair went his self-confidence, and the knight abandoned all martial activities. The lords living near his lands promptly began seizing his fiefs from every side, acting with impunity and without opposition. A vision prompted him to go to Conques, where he was cured by the power of St. Foy's intercession.

As they pursued their grievances with each other, the knights around the monastery at Conques did a great deal of damage to the local peasantry, which naturally drew St. Foy's attention. The saint intervened to protect or avenge both peasants who were her own,[61] and some who were not. An example of the latter connects plundering to what the knights involved apparently thought of as seizing the supplies that they needed to fight. Bernard the Hairy laid siege to a castle.[62] His men, in order to supply themselves, tried to plunder the area around the castle, but the people of the area had collected their belongings and taken refuge in a church. One of Bernard's horsemen, "driven by necessity", broke into the church and violently took a bundle of straw from a peasant. St. Foy froze the man's horse in place. The horseman returned what he had stolen and confessed his guilt before the crowd. The peasant, however, realized that St. Foy had intervened. For love of her he gave the straw back to the horseman. After hearing this story, three other horsemen sought to plunder the same peasants. They took bread and wine, and declared their intent to return and take the peasants' plow horses and bedding as well. The peasants appealed to St. Foy, who arranged to have the leader of the marauders killed in battle.

Peasants were not always defenseless victims, however; they too could fight. A lord held a castle that lay next to a village belonging to St. Foy.[63] In a "fit of anger" he attacked the monk who oversaw the village and tried to kill him. But the peasants of the village fought back, so that the lord and his men were driven off. To "avenge the indignities that had been inflicted on him", the lord next tried to ambush his enemy at night with five accomplices. But divine intervention confused him as he stood in the doorway of his enemy's house. A young man in the house awakened, grabbed a sword, and drove the invaders away. The lord's accomplices later found their master stricken helpless with his mouth wrenched back towards one ear.

Nor were peasants always innocent. A monk built a small church in honor of St. Foy, which became a customary place for peasants to pray on their way to clear the nearby forest. One peasant, however, teased his colleagues for what he called their credulity, saying "I think you would be as likely to get salvation from a doghouse!"[64] He promptly fell prostrate on the ground, his knees pulled up to his chin, and rolled around witless in the sand. Only the fervent prayers of the other peasants convinced St. Foy to have mercy on him and restore him to health.

### The Peace of God

It is against the backdrop of texts like the ones examined above that we have to understand the gatherings collectively known as the Peace of God councils.[65] It is not easy to grasp these councils. They are depicted in different ways by different kinds of sources that represent different perspectives and purposes. Nevertheless, after looking at some examples, and some references to them in other sources, we will be able to draw some general conclusions about them.

On June 1, 989, Gunbaldus, archbishop of Bordeaux, convened a council of his fellow bishops of Aquitaine at the monastery at Charroux. Charroux lay in what would become Hugh IV of Lusignan's haunts between Angoulême, Poitou, and La Marche; it is less than fifty kilometers southeast of Lusignan itself. According to the surviving record of this council,[66] the bishops, as well as clerics, monks, and laypeople of both sexes, had gathered to eradicate the offences (*noxia*) that had by pernicious habit been sprouting up in their districts because of the long delay in calling a council, and to replace them with more rightful activity (*utilia*).[67] The bishops issued the following decrees: (1) if anyone attacked the holy church or took anything from it by force, and compensation was not provided, he was to be anathema; (2) if anyone took as booty sheep, oxen, asses, cows, female goats, male goats, or pigs from peasants or from other poor people, he was to be anathema, unless it were the fault of the victim or unless the perpetrator failed to make reparations; (3) if anyone robbed, seized, or struck a priest, or a deacon, or any person from the clergy who was not bearing arms (that is, a shield, a sword, a breastplate, or a helmet) but was rather simply going about his business or remaining at home, and if after examination by his own bishop the perpetrator were found guilty of a crime, then he was to be judged guilty of sacrilege. Furthermore, if the perpetrator did not come forward to make satisfaction, then he was to be excluded from God's holy church.

This brief text targets violence towards churches, as well as the uncompensated seizure of church property. It also attacks the uncompensated seizure of animals from peasants and poor people, whether or not they were connected to the church. But this concern with violence is not absolute. The phrase "unless it is due to the fault of the victim" in the second clause indicates that when a peasant or pauper had done something for which reparations were due, someone else was entitled to seize his property. The same clause also allows someone to seize the listed animals from peasants or the poor as long as he paid for them. Particularly interesting is the third clause forbidding assaults on unarmed clergy. It leaves unsanctioned an entire world of potential violence against clergy bearing shields, swords, breastplates, and helmets who were not going about their business or remaining at home. By implication, such clergy would be doing what we have in fact seen them do in other sources: fighting. In other words, the council assumed the existence of clergymen who were wealthy enough to own such weapons and who used them – and it regarded violence against them as legitimate.

Sometime between 1000 and 1014, another council was held at Poitiers. The acts of this council differ from those of Charroux in some important ways.[68] To begin with, the moving force behind the council at Poitiers was not the clergy but rather a lay lord: our acquaintance William V, here called Duke of Poitiers. William summoned a gathering of five bishops and twelve abbots for the purpose of restoring peace. Before the assembly William himself along with other princes swore to restore peace and justice, provided hostages to guarantee their oath, and accepted the threat of excommunication for violations. In contrast to Charroux, however, these council acts cast peace and justice in terms of secular judicial authority. Whenever someone claimed that his possessions had been usurped during the five years preceding the council, or at any time afterwards, the parties involved were to stand trial in the presence of the prince of that region or of a judge of that county. Should one party refuse to do so, the prince or the judge was to compel his attendance or risk losing the hostages he had given the council. Should the prince or judge be unable to compel his attendance, the princes and bishops who had called the council were to gather and together "destroy and trouble" the recalcitrant one until he agreed to do proper justice.

This decree presents Duke William in a very Carolingian light. Like Charlemagne before him, William had convened a church council. He used the acts of that council to proclaim his own judicial authority and that of his representatives. What is different is the enforcement mechanism. It was not William himself but the lords who had convened the council, both secular and ecclesiastical, who claimed the right and the duty to wield violence if necessary to uphold the duke's judicial authority. They were bound by oath, by their hostages, and by the threat of excommunication, to support the judicial system with armed force.

The acts from Poitiers go on to invoke the decrees of the council of Charroux. But then they continue in a direction that has nothing to do with violence. Bishops were not to demand gifts for penance or confirmation, or for any gift of the Holy Spirit; such gifts could be accepted only if they were freely given. Priests or deacons who had women in their houses, that is, who kept them with the intent to fornicate, were to lose their clerical orders. These two decrees are aimed at separating the clergy from the temptations of the world, temptations in which many of them were apparently indulging. They also, however, again make the man who had summoned the council, Duke William, look Carolingian. Like Charlemagne, William had convened a church council that concerned itself with the internal well being of the church.

The impulse to hold peace councils did not remain in the south. In 1023, Bishop Warin of Beauvais, which lies c. 75 kilometers northwest of Paris, proposed a peace oath to the Capetian king Robert the Pious.[69] Bishop Warin's lengthy text consists of a detailed list of promises not to commit certain actions. It is interesting both for what it aims to prohibit and for what it does not. The oath is broadly concerned with protecting church property from seizure and unarmed clergy from assault. It also seeks to protect merchants, pilgrims, women, and members of the lower orders of society from attack, from the arbitrary or uncompensated seizure of their property, and from being caught in the middle of fighting amongst their betters. It makes a particular point of protecting mules and horses from seizure during planting and harvest season, i.e., from the first of March to the end of October.

However, the oath leaves alone two kinds of violent activity. First, it permits violence by knights and their followers against their enemies, and it protects access to the supplies needed to carry out this violence as long as the supplies were paid for, belonged to the person seizing them, or were somehow necessary for military purposes. For example, houses were not to be destroyed unless there were an enemy horseman inside and unless the house were joined to a castle. One could not destroy a mill, or seize the grain in it, unless one were on a cavalcade (*cavallicata* – i.e., a mounted military expedition),[70] with the royal army, or the mill was on one's own land. When building or besieging a castle, when in the host of kings or bishops, or when on cavalcade, one could not break into the protected areas of churches unless the churches refused to sell one what one "needed to live". The oath assumes that those participating in such violence would include at least some members of the clergy; only clergy not carrying at least a spear and a shield were to be protected from attack.

Second, the oath protects violence carried out for the purpose of enforcing justice and punishing wrongs. One could invade a church to catch someone who had committed homicide or someone who had broken this peace oath (or to catch a stray horse). One could seize someone's horse if its rider was in the process of committing a crime or the horse was taken as compensation for an uncompensated wrong – though one had to give fifteen days warning first. One could attack merchants or pilgrims and take their possessions if they were committing misdeeds. The kind of judicial activity assumed by this oath is quite different from that projected by the decrees of the council of Poitiers. If that council sought to reinforce constituted judicial authority, this oath assumes that a broad range of people had the right to punish crimes and avenge wrongs. Particularly empowered to do so were the very people whose behavior the oath aimed to regulate.

Bishop Warin's oath also introduces a couple of interesting novelties. First, it forbids parties to the oath from attacking unarmed horsemen or taking their possessions during the period from the beginning of Lent to Easter. This provision suggests that a certain kind of violence was not proper for Christians to carry out during this most solemn and penitential part of the Christian year; it thus echoes the hint of this attitude that we saw in a capitulary of Charlemagne.[71] It also implies, however, that it would have been legitimate for someone to attack armed horsemen (i.e., for the likely parties to the oath, their peers) during this period, and that violence against unarmed horsemen was legitimate for all the rest of the year. Second, at the very end the oath text voids all of its provisions for the case that the king himself was leading a *werra* [sic].[72] A royal war legitimated everything.

The penitential attitude towards violence suggested by Bishop Warin's oath was pushed further a few years later. In 1027, a council was held far to the south in a meadow at Toulouges, in the county of Roussilon.[73]

No one in the county, or in the diocese of Elne, was to attack any enemy from the ninth hour on Saturday to the first hour on Monday, "so that everyone would render the honor owed to the Lord's day". In other words, all violence against one's enemies, no matter what its reason, was categorically prohibited on the Sabbath; violence *per se* was something that good Christians were to avoid to render proper honor to the Lord. As at the council of Poitiers, these provisions form part of a larger set of reforms. The assembled at Toulouges "established this pact or truce (*pactum sive treugam*) because the divine law and almost all of the Christian way of life had been reduced to naught . . . and because iniquity was rife and love was becoming cold". The council therefore forbade incestuous marriages (up to the sixth degree of kinship). It also prohibited anyone from associating with people who had been excommunicated, and told the clergy exactly how to properly separate the excommunicate from Christian society. In short, while violence draws much of the council's attention, that concern is once again embedded in a broader concern for the proper order and functioning of Christian society.

This concern is quite visible in the work of a monk of Angoulême, Ademar of Chabannes. Sometime between 1025 and 1033, Ademar wrote a chronicle that refers to two peace councils.[74] The chronicle's horizon mainly covers the central and southern regions of the west Frankish kingdom. Its actors are generally magnates, both lay and ecclesiastical, at the level of duke and bishop and below; Ademar himself was related to some of them. Ademar's chronicle is by no means a piece of unbiased reporting. His story is shaped by his desire to have the patron of the monastery where he was educated, St. Martial of Limoges, recognized as one of Christ's apostles, and by Ademar's profound antipathy towards secular canons, who he thought posed a threat to Benedictine monasticism.[75]

As he sought to achieve his polemic ends, Ademar described a world that looks very much like that of Hugh IV of Lusignan and the *Miracles* of St. Foy: it is full of magnates fighting over castles and land and violently pursuing enmities, settlements, alliances, etc. These magnates included bishops and abbots as well as laymen. Ademar had nothing against any of this violence *per se*. Like most other people in his society, he judged violence according to his sense of the motives of the people (or divine figures) who wielded it.[76]

It is against this backdrop that Ademar describes a council held at Limoges in 994.[77] The council was provoked by an outbreak of disease. A pestilence burned throughout the region of the Limousin; an invisible fire was devouring the bodies of men and women. In response, the abbot of St. Martial, Gosfrid, and the bishop of Limoges, Alduin, held a council together with Duke William V of Aquitaine and proclaimed a three-day fast. All the bishops of Aquitaine attended, as did the bodies of numerous saints, including Ademar's "patron of Gaul" St. Martial. As a result of the council, great joy filled everyone present, and the sickness ceased. A pact of peace and justice was then concluded by the duke and his lords.

Ademar does not, unfortunately, go into specifics. One can only presume that this pact consisted of some sort of oath buttressed by the threat of excommunication, as at other councils. Whatever it encompassed, Ademar does not present the pact as a particular response to unrest or lay violence against the Church. The council was convened to ward off, by an act of penance, the divine wrath implicit in a terrifying pestilence. The pact of peace and justice was a response to God's mercy and the power of his saints in ending the sickness.

The second council described by Ademar was held at the abbey of Charroux in 1027 or 1028.[78] Ademar likewise puts this effort to uphold peace in the context of a larger effort to reform Christian society.[79] The assembly of bishops, abbots, and the princes of Aquitaine was summoned, he says, by Duke William in order to exterminate the heresy being spread among the people by the Manicheans. William commanded the lords of Aquitaine to protect the peace and venerate the Church. If in Limoges it was an act of penance and thanksgiving for the lifting of divine anger, here it is part of an effort to combat heresy.[80]

Ademar does note on several occasions that peasants and the poor suffered from the violence wielded by their betters. Like the *Miracles* of St. Foy, however, he also tells us that peasants could fight. Moreover, they sometimes did so not to defend themselves against rapacious lords but to help their own lords. He tells us that Gaubert, lord of the castle of Malemort, was captured by Eble, viscount of Comborn. But Gaubert had God's support. As a consequence, "one fine morning" the peasants of Gaubert's domain launched an attack on the castle in which their lord was being held. They took the castle, freed their lord, and burned the castle to the ground.[81]

Ademar gives no sign that he thought constituted authority enjoyed any special right to be violent or to regulate the violence of others. His attitude towards kings in particular is ambivalent. He reveals some veneration for the memory of Charlemagne, but has nothing but scorn for the Capetians, whom he regarded as pitifully ineffective.[82] He treats William V of Aquitaine, however, as nothing short of a hero. And his hero image fits entirely within the old Carolingian tradition. William was glorious and powerful, yet friendly; he gave wise counsel, was generous, and a defender of the poor. He was a father to monks, a builder of sanctuaries, a friend of churches and of the Holy Roman Church as an institution. Wherever he went, he held courts. He gave off the impression of being a king rather than a duke. Indeed, William was treated as an equal by the king of the Franks, and he wielded uncontested power in Aquitaine, crushing any lord who dared rebel against him.[83]

That Carolingian norms of rulership were still in circulation in the west is also attested by another narrative source, this one from Flanders. Titled the *Deeds of the Bishops of Cambrai*, it explicitly connects what it thinks the peace councils were trying to do with what it thinks kings ought to have done.[84] But it does so because the man responsible for it did not like the councils. Commissioned by Bishop Gerard I of Cambrai (r. 1012–51) and written by an anonymous author between 1024 and 1025, the *Deeds* represent an entirely different perspective from the sources we have looked at so far. The diocese of Cambrai lay on the border between the west Frankish kingdom and the east Frankish Empire. The *Deeds* therefore reflect Bishop Gerard's efforts to document not only his actions as bishop of a diocese that perforce looked westwards, but also his loyalty to the emperors in the East, to whom he owed his job and who were, as we will see in the next chapter, rulers of much greater political consequence than the Capetian kings.[85]

In Chapter 27 of Book III, the author sets the stage for the councils by declaring that the foundation of the realm was tottering because of the incompetence of the king and the sins of men; the laws, ancient customs, and all kinds of justice were being confounded and profaned. Bishop Berold of Soissons and Bishop Warin of Beauvais tried to save "much of the public interest" (*multum rei publicae*) by following the precedent of the bishops of Burgundy. These latter, though "surely devoid of all authority", had tried to constrain all men by an oath to become the servants of peace and justice. Bishops Berold and Warin tried to persuade Bishop Gerard to join in their effort. But Gerard indignantly refused to follow this "pernicious and impossible" counsel. The very idea was inappropriate, because the bishops were claiming "for themselves what was royal right". They were thus confounding the condition of the holy Church, which ought to be administered by two persons: the priestly and the royal. The job of the latter was to fight for the health of the fatherland, that of the former to pray.[86] It was the king's job to put down sedition with strength, rein in fighting, and to spread the commerce of peace. The bishops' proposed decree was dangerous, because all had to swear to it or face anathema; everyone would therefore be caught up in a common sin. In response, the other bishops charged Gerard with not being a friend of peace. They added pressure in the form of an appeal from the abbots of Saint-Vaast and Saint-Bertin, until Gerard finally agreed to participate.

This passage offers us a very Carolingian vision of royal power; it is the king's duty and right to wield violence against violence in support of order. Gerard's argument does not at all match the reality of early Capetian life projected by our other sources. However, it would have appealed very much to the German emperors, who were continuing to project a vigorously Carolingian image of their office and rights.[87]

Several chapters later, our anonymous author returns to the subject of the peace councils.[88] He tells us first that the German Emperor Conrad II summoned the bishops of diverse regions to a synod. There Bishop Gerard, with moderation and wisdom and in accordance with the custom of the ancient fathers, helped the other bishops resolve a question about the celebration of fasts falling on the same day. Then we learn that the bishops of France had also promulgated a decree for their subjects. One of the bishops claimed to have received a letter from heaven demanding that peace on earth be renewed. He told this to his fellow bishops and gave the following directives to the people: (1) no one should bear arms or attack for plunder, (2) a victim of bloodshed who wanted to take vengeance should be compelled to forgive the attackers, (3) all were to fast on bread and water every Friday and abstain from meat and fat on the Sabbath, and be content with this fast for the satisfaction of all sins. All were to confirm with an oath that they would observe these decrees, on pain of excommunication. Bishop Gerard was alarmed "by this novelty". He prepared a sermon in response, showing that the human race had been divided from the beginning into prayers, farmers, and fighters and that each of these should foster the others with his right and left hands. We are then treated to the entire text of Gerard's sermon, which describes at length his image of the three orders of society and once again assigns the job of upholding peace to the fighters.[89]

Moderation, wisdom, and ancient custom rest with Bishop Gerard, who acts for the common good at the command of his emperor. Dangerous novelty and a potential breakdown in the proper divisions of society follow the bishops of Francia, who, armed with the dubious letter from heaven, dared to trespass on the preserve of secular authority. Once again, we have a good, Carolingian-style image of proper order. Through his critique, however, our author gives us his perception of what the western bishops were doing. He understood them to be concerned with controlling violence; he also recognized that this concern was part and parcel of a broader concern for Christian religious behavior.

It is hard to say to what degree the decrees of the peace councils actually affected anyone's behavior. Nevertheless, the councils were noticed. Journeys to the councils taken by the saints (in the form of their relics) provided monastic writers with welcome opportunities to advertise their miracles.[90] And in at least one case, the norms about the proper order of Christian society that the councils broadcast were picked up and re-broadcast because they were useful in a dispute. A charter from Saint-Maixent, written in the year 1032, begins by telling us that the holy Church was in danger of foundering; innumerable diabolically inspired crimes were destroying holy religion.[91] In response, church councils were convened in every city. These councils, attended by an innumerable multitude of people both noble and powerless, were supposed to treat matters concerning the Catholic faith and God's holy Church, so that God could affirm "a faith improved in all things". The charter then notes that a particular council was convened at Poitiers, by Duke William V's son William VI (the "Fat", r. 1030–8). The council decreed that if any man dishonestly or violently took possession of the property of the holy Church, or unjustly seized it, they should restore it so that the Church might hold the lands of the monasteries whole and free.

The charter thus starts by describing an effort by both secular and ecclesiastical authority to reform religion and the Church through a series of councils and in particular to protect monastic property from unjust seizure. This effort provided the monks of Saint-Maixent with a useful normative framework for their particular problem. While all this was going on, the monks sued William VI, saying that judges and provosts were exercising "unjust justice through falsehood and cupidity" on the monastery's lands and condemning poor people. After summoning elderly witnesses to tell him what the customs of the area had been in earlier times, William accepted the monks' position.

It is only when the customs are specified that we learn what this process was all about. On a set of specified lands, for cases of seizure, theft, and homicide, the secular judge or *vicarius* was to receive one half of the judicial revenues, the monks of Saint-Maixent the other. Within the lands of Saint-Maixent the monks were to do justice, outside the monastery's lands the *vicarius*. If a claim were brought outside of the monastery's lands against a person belonging to Saint-Maixent, no judge was to exercise justice unless a monk were present, and the monks were to have the revenue. Furthermore, no secular official was to send a judicial summons to anyone on the lands concerned.

In other words, the monks were upset about secular judicial officials unjustly exercising their office on monastery lands and collecting judicial revenues from the monastery's people. In the monks' mind, this constituted the dishonest and violent seizure of monastic property. "The proper practice of holy religion" in this case meant having judicial revenues go where they were supposed to, and dividing them properly in the serious cases where secular and monastic authority overlapped.

## *Conclusions*

The peace councils reflect the imperatives of bishops and abbots, clerics and monks who thought that Christian society needed to be reformed to avoid God's wrath. The crowds that gathered around or alongside them highlight the similar fear of the people in the countryside that God was punishing them for their sins. The portents that both high born and low, educated and uneducated experienced gave them plenty of evidence that God's anger was real and dangerous.

Among the moral failures that the councils targeted was what the people behind them considered to be the illicit and dangerous use of violence. Violence was a real and serious problem for many in early Capetian France. Some magnates took control of church and monastic property, and tried by force to impose customs or exactions where they could. As they fought each other, some magnates seized food and supplies for themselves and their followers, chased each other into sacred spaces, ransacked and violated church and monastic buildings, and plundered peasant holdings and villages. In response, the councils tried to use the tools of the communal oath and the threat of excommunication against particular kinds of violence, that is, to defend the sanctuary rights of churches, to protect church property from uncompensated seizure, to protect the property of the peasantry from unjustified and uncompensated seizure, and to prevent violent conflict from harming innocent bystanders. Outside of these limits, however, the councils not only tolerated but even validated a great deal of violence.[92]

Other sources we have examined in this chapter make it clear why this was so. The resort to violence was not exclusive to members of any one social or political group in the early Capetian West. There was little difference in the ways that most clergy and most lay magnates thought about violence; both clerics and laymen shared common attitudes towards it. And these attitudes are familiar. The use of violence was good or bad depending on who was using it for what. Lay magnates of course wielded violence quite frequently to build their followings and to protect or extend their power over others, as they had done for centuries. Their use of violence was also driven by a very subjective sense of right and wrong; they and their followers used violence to protect or assert their (subjectively perceived) rights and honor and to avenge (again subjectively perceived) injury and insult. They were also aware, or were forced by their communities to be aware, of boundaries that separated the legitimate from the illegitimate use of violence – at least within their own class. The same holds true for churchmen and monks. Many bishops and priests, and clerics and monks, used violence in much the same way as lay magnates, with the same weapons and for similar reasons. Even those who did not, such as the good Christian monks of Conques (leaving aside the warrior monk Gerard), celebrated acts of violence when that violence helped them to achieve their goals or defend their interests. Their attitudes towards violence mirrored a supernatural world in which God and his saints too were violent, and in the same way and for the same reasons as their earthly followers.[93] As usual, with peasants it is a different story. Lords and their followers were perfectly willing to hurt peasants, whether their own or somebody else's; some monks were not unduly disturbed by a custom newly imposed on their people by a lay neighbor if they could profit from it. When peasants insulted a saint, they paid. Peasants, however, were not always passive victims. They could and did wield violence on their own behalf, both in their own defense and on behalf of a lord whom they valued.

These attitudes towards violence were by this point already ancient. What had changed was the political environment. In the decentralized political world particularly of central and southern France, most lords (not to mention the Capetian kings) were unable to exercise the control, or attract the self-interested cooperation, necessary to make those capable of wielding violence, or the writers of most of our sources, invest in Carolingian-style norms of order. As a consequence, it was not Charlemagne's norms of violence but rather those associated with the personal right to violence that were dominant and thus are most prominent in the sources. In other words, the political transformation visible in the early Capetian sources did not replace public order with violent disorder. Instead, it provoked a large-scale shift in the normative order governing west Frankish society. One idea of order was placed in the shadows by another that had always been there, but now, because it better matched the realities of power and thus better served the interests of more people, had become dominant.

These observations also have implications for the speed with which the transformation of western political society took place. The attitudes towards violence that predominated in the eleventh century are the same that predominated in the sixth. They are also visible on the margins at the height of the Carolingian period, but already under Louis the Pious they are no longer marginal. It makes sense to assume, then, that the norms associated with the personal right to violence not only persisted but gradually gained strength as royal authority in the West waned throughout the late ninth and the tenth centuries, until they, like the associated norms of personal fidelity, became the dominant way of understanding power and order in a world that had by the turn of the first millennium changed profoundly.

However, the norms of violence associated with Carolingian-style kingship did not disappear entirely. Some people clearly did think that the new conditions of the late tenth and eleventh centuries represented disorder. If we give priority to their voices, and look at early Capetian society exclusively from their perspective, then we will see conditions as they did. The people who believed that disorder had replaced order were those who were invested in Carolingian-style norms of royal order. The bishops and abbots who promoted the peace councils, as well as the ordinary people who flocked to them, felt that the kings were no longer protecting the churches and the powerless, as Charlemagne had done. Bishop Gerard of Cambrai likewise preserved a belief in public order, but – with an eye cocked towards the emperor in the East – he thought that it was the peace councils themselves that represented disorder.

Also remembering Carolingian norms was Duke William V of Aquitaine. William appears in the acts of the council held at Poitiers very much like a Carolingian king, summoning a council that tried to restore the proper order of Christian society. Highlighting his efforts to appear king-like, William's "peace" prioritized the workings of secular justice in addition to the welfare of the weak and the well being of the Church. It was plainly to his advantage to take advantage of the peace movement to project himself as a Carolingian-style ruler acting on God's behalf.[94] Even if in practice he had (as had Charlemagne before him) to play off strong-willed followers against each other, and even if his courts (like those of Charlemagne before him) more often served as fora for negotiating settlements, he stood to gain a significant ideological boost for his claims to power.

The efforts of the reformers behind the peace councils to regulate violence and restore the moral health of Christian society resemble those of Charlemagne two centuries before. The reformers were simply working through the mechanisms of councils that they summoned themselves, rather than through the initiatives and decrees of the king. While their general aims are similar to those visible in Charlemagne's capitularies, however, the particulars are different. The profusion in the central and southern parts of the west Frankish kingdom of lords, knights, and castles, and the fierce competition for property and power that resulted, made the uncompensated seizure of property, and violence against the weak and uninvolved, figure more strongly among other more general concerns, such as clerical chastity, simony, and the proper regulation of fast days, than they had before.

The early eleventh century did see a new norm of violence emerge, or better re-emerge. In some peace council acts and narrative sources we see recorded attempts to enforce, by oath and excommunication, an abstinence from violence of any kind, by anyone for any reason, on certain holy days or in certain holy times.[95] We saw a flicker of this attitude appear in a capitulary of Charlemagne, but in this time and place it stands out more strongly.[96] This Truce of God ethic reflects an attitude towards violence that saw it not as a morally neutral tool but rather as intrinsically undesirable. Like sex, which clerics and monks had been trying to limit on holy days for centuries, violence could not be avoided; it was part of the sinful human condition.[97] Nevertheless, and again like sex, good Christians could be brought to abstain from it occasionally out of respect for the holy.

## Notes

1. On the post-Carolingian West: Timothy Reuter, ed., NCMH III, esp. pts. I and II; Jean Dunbabin, *France in the Making, 843–1180*, 2nd edn (Oxford: Oxford University Press, 2000).
2. Robert Fossier, "Rural Economy and Country Life", in NCMH III, 27–63 @47–9; Dunbabin, *France in the Making*, 40–3.
3. Cf. Janet L. Nelson, "Ninth-Century Knighthood: The Evidence of Nithard", in *Studies in Medieval, History: Presented to R. Allen Brown*, ed. C. Harper-Bill, C. Holdsworth, and J.L. Nelson (Woodbridge, Suffolk: Boydell and Brewer, 1989), 235–66.
4. For an excellent survey of this discussion, with bibliographic references, see Dunbabin, *France in the Making*, Introduction to the 2nd edition, xiii–xxvi @xiv–xxv.
5. Bisson, "Feudal Revolution", and *The Crisis of the Twelfth Century: Power, Lordship, and the Origins of European Government* (Princeton: Princeton University Press, 2008), 22–83; Jean-Pierre Poly and Eric Bournazel, *La mutation féodale: Xe–XIIe siècle*. 3rd edn (Paris: Nouvelle Clio, 2004), first edition (1980) translated into English by Caroline Higgitt as *The Feudal Transformation, 900–1200* (New York: Holmes and Meyer, 1991).
6. See fundamentally F.L. Ganshof, *Qu'est-ce que la féodalité?* (Brussels: Office de Publicité, 1947), translated into English by Philip Grierson as *Feudalism*, 3rd edn (Toronto: University of Toronto Press, 1996); Susan Reynolds, *Fiefs and Vassals: The Medieval Evidence Reinterpreted* (Oxford and New York: Oxford University Press, 1994). See also the Internet Medieval Sourcebook: **http://www.fordham.edu/halsall/sbook1i.html#Feudalism**.
7. Dominique Barthélemy and Stephen D. White, "Debate: The 'Feudal Revolution': Comment 1, Comment 2", *Past and Present* 152 (1996): 196–223; Timothy Reuter, Chris Wickham, and Thomas N. Bisson, "Debate: The Feudal Revolution: Comment 3, Comment 4, Reply", *Past and Present* 155 (1997): 177–225; Stephen D. White, "From Peace to Power: The Study of Disputes in Medieval France", in *Medieval Transformations: Texts, Power, and Gifts in Context*, ed. Esther Cohen and Mayke B. de Jong (Leiden: Brill, 2001), 203–18; Dominique Barthélemy, *La mutation de l'an mil, a-t-elle*

*eu lieu?: servage et chevalerie dans la France des Xe et XIe siècles* (Paris: Fayard, 1997), expanded and translated into English as *The Serf, the Knight, and the Historian*, trans. Graham Robert Edwards (Ithaca, NY: Cornell University Press, 2009).

8. Martindale, "*Conventum inter Guillelmum Aquitanorum comitem et Hugonem Chiliarchum*" (henceforward *Conventum*), 528–48. English translation: "Agreements between Count William of the Aquitanians and Hugh of Lusignan (1028)", in Rosenwein, *Reading*, 213–19. All quotations below are from Agreements unless otherwise noted. Cf. Martindale, "Dispute, Settlement, and Orality in the *Conventum inter Guillelmum Aquitanorum Comitem et Hugonem Chiliarchum*: A Postscript to the Edition of 1969" and "Peace and War in Early Eleventh-Century Aquitaine", in *Status, Authority and Regional Power: Aquitaine and France, 9th to 12th Centuries* (Aldershot: Ashgate, 1997), 1–36 and 147–76; Stephen D. White, "Politics of Fidelity: Hugh of Lusignan and William of Aquitaine", in *Georges Duby: L'écriture de l'histoire*, ed. Claudie Duhamel-Amado and Guy Lobrichon (Brussels: De Boeck, 1996), 223–30.
9. Martindale, "Notes and Documents" in *Conventum*, 528–41 @530.
10. Martindale, "Dispute, Settlement, and Orality", 10 and n. 28.
11. Niermeyer, s.v. *honor*, esp. definition 14.
12. *Conventum*, 541–2/Agreements, 214, cols. 1 and 2.
13. *Conventum*, 543/Agreements, 215, col. 1.
14. *Conventum*, 543/Agreements, 215, col. 1.
15. *Conventum*, 543/Agreements, 215, col. 2.
16. Civray castle: *Conventum*, 543/Agreements, 215, col. 2. See also Hugh's claim to Chizé castle: *Conventum*, 547/Agreement, 218, col. 1.
17. *Conventum*, 544/Agreement, 215, col. 2.
18. *Conventum*, 544/Agreement, 216, col. 1.
19. *Conventum*, 544/Agreement, 216, col. 1.
20. *Conventum*, 544/Agreement, 216, col. 1.
21. *Conventum*, 543/Agreement, 215, col. 2.
22. *Conventum*, 545/Agreement, 216, col. 2.
23. *Conventum*, 545/Agreement, 216, col. 2.
24. *Conventum*, 546/Agreement, 217, col. 1.
25. *Conventum*, 547/Agreement, 218, col. 1.
26. *Conventum*, 548/Agreement, 218, col. 2; 219, cols. 1 and 2.
27. SM. English translations are by the author.
28. SM 95, 115–18.
29. Dunbabin, *France in the Making*, 384.
30. For similar examples cf. SM 117 (1060–61), 147–8 and SM 124 (1069), 156.
31. SM 144, 174.
32. SM 188, 219–20.
33. SM 105, 130–1.
34. Steven A. Epstein, *An Economic and Social History of Later Medieval Europe* (Cambridge: Cambridge University Press, 2009), 200.
35. White, "Feuding and Peacemaking".

36. Ibid., Case 2, 221–5.
37. Ibid., 222, 224–5.
38. Ibid., Case 7, 241–6.
39. Ibid., Case 1, 214–21.
40. MSF. All quotations are from Sheingorn, *The Book of Sainte Foy*, unless otherwise noted.
41. Sheingorn, introduction to *The Book of Sainte Foy*, 1–31, @8–10.
42. Patrick J. Geary, *Furta Sacra: Theft of Relics in the Central Middle Ages*, 2nd edn (Princeton: Princeton University Press, 1990), 58–60.
43. Sheingorn, 24–5.
44. Sheingorn translates the Latin *miles* in this context as "warrior" in order to avoid the anachronistic chivalric associations of the English word "knight". Since the text is clear that *miles* means mounted warrior as opposed to footsoldier (*pedes*), I have decided to translate it as "knight", with the explicit understanding that any overtones of chivalry in the later medieval sense are indeed anachronistic.
45. MSF 2.9, 171–4/Sheingorn, 132–5.
46. MSF 1.1, 78–86/Sheingorn, 43–51.
47. MSF 3.24, 214–15/Sheingorn, 175. Cf. also MSF 2.5 and 2.6, 162–8/ Sheingorn 124–9.
48. MSF 1.26, 128–31/Sheingorn, 93–7.
49. MSF 3.17, 205–7/Sheingorn, 166–7. Cf. also MSF 1.5, 94–5/Sheingorn, 58–60.
50. MSF 3.16, 205/Sheingorn, 165–6.
51. MSF 1.11, 106–8/Sheingorn, 70–3.
52. MSF 1.13, 112–14/Sheingorn, 77–9. See also MSF 1.1, 78–86/Sheingorn, 43–51; MSF 1.6, 95–8/Sheingorn, 60–3; MSF 1.8, 103/Sheingorn, 68; MSF 3.20, 209–11/Sheingorn, 169–71.
53. MSF 1.17–22, 117–23/Sheingorn, 82–8.
54. Cf. MSF 1.16, 116–17/Sheingorn, 81–2.
55. MSF 1.12, 108–12/Sheingorn, 73–7.
56. See MSF 3.5, 188–90/Sheingorn, 149–51; MSF 3.15, 203–5/Sheingorn, 164–5; MSF 4.8, 233–8/Sheingorn, 191–6.
57. MSF 3.18, 207–8/Sheingorn, 167–8.
58. MSF 4.28, 263–6, given in Sheingorn as 4.23, 215–18. Cf. also MSF 4.3, 225–7/Sheingorn, 183–5.
59. MSF 3.15, 203–5/Sheingorn, 164–5. See also MSF 1.30, 134–6/Sheingorn, 99–101.
60. MSF 3.7, 191–3/Sheingorn, 152–4.
61. See MSF 3.13, 201–2/Sheingorn, 161–2.
62. MSF 3.21, 211–12/Sheingorn, 171–3.
63. MSF 3.10, 197–8/Sheingorn, 158–9.
64. MSF 4.23, 258–9; given in Sheingorn as 4.21, 212–13.
65. Foundationally: Hartmut Hoffman, *Gottesfriede und Treuga Dei* (Stuttgart: Hiersemann, 1964) and Georges Duby, "Les laics et la paix de Dieu", in *I laici nella "societas christiani" dei secoli XI e XII* (Milan: Vita e pensiero, 1968), translated into English as "Laity and the Peace of God", in *The*

*Chivalrous Society*, trans. Cynthia Postan (Berkeley: University of California Press, 1977), 123–33. More recently: Thomas Head and Richard Landes, eds., *The Peace of God: Social Violence and Religious Response in France around the Year 1000* (Ithaca, NY: Cornell University Press, 1992); Dominique Barthélemy, *L'an mil et la paix de Dieu: la France chrétienne et féodale, 980–1060* (Paris, Fayard, 1999); Thomas Head, "The Development of the Peace of God in Aquitaine", *Speculum* 74/3 (1999): 656–86.

66. Mansi vol. 19, 89–90; English translation in Head and Landes, eds., *Peace of God*, 327–8. All quotations for this and the following peace texts will be taken from Head and Landes unless otherwise noted.

67. *Noxia* and *utilia* may carry specifically juridical overtones and be translated as criminal and lawful activity respectively, as the Head and Landes translation has done. Cf. Lewis and Short, s.v. *noxius* and *utilis*.

68. Mansi vol. 19, 265–8; English translation in Head and Landes, eds., *Peace of God*, 330–1.

69. Christian Pfister, *Etudes sur le règne de Robert le Pieux (996–1031)* (Paris: F. Vieweg, 1885), LX–LXI; English translation in Head and Landes, eds., *Peace of God*, 332–4.

70. Niermeyer, s.v. *caballicata* [sic].

71. Chapter III, @n. 49.

72. . . . *nisi de werra regis*; Pfister, *Etudes*, LXI.

73. Mansi, vol. 19, 483–4; English translation in Head and Landes, eds., *Peace of God*, 334–5.

74. Ademar of Chabannes, *Ademari historiarum libri III*, ed. D.G. Waitz, MGH SS IV (Hanover: Hahn, 1841), 106–48; French translation starting with C. XVI of Book III (where Ademar's original material sets in) in *L'an mille: Oeuvres de Liutprand, Raoul Glaber, Adémar de Chabannes, Adalberon, Helgaud*, ed. and trans. Edmond Pognon (Paris: Gallimard, 1947), 145–209.

75. Richard Landes, "Between Aristocracy and Heresy: Popular Participation in the Limousin Peace of God (994–1032)", in Head and Landes, eds., *Peace of God*, 184–219 @184, 213; idem, *Relics, Apocalypse, and the Deceits of History: Ademar of Chabannes (989–1034)* (Cambridge, MA: Harvard University Press, 1995).

76. See, for example, Ademar 3.25, 3.28, 3.29, 3.31, 3.34, 3.42, 3.43, 3.50, 3.60, 3.67, 126–32, 135, 138–9, 144, 147/Pognon, 165–76, 183–4, 190, 200–1, 207–8.

77. Ademar 3.35, 132/Pognon, 176–7.

78. Ademar 3.69, 148/Pognon, 208–9.

79. Ademar does report one direct ecclesiastical response to lay violence. In 3.35, 132/Pognon, 177, after describing the council of Limoges, he notes, with evident disapproval, that Bishop Alduin suspended divine services in the churches and monasteries as a response to lay brigandage. But he depicts Alduin's actions as his own response to his own situation; he does not present them as part of the pact of peace and justice reached at the council of Limoges.

80. A similar view of the peace councils is visible in the *Five Books of Histories* by the Burgundian monk Rodulf Glaber. Glaber presents the councils as a

response to the divine wrath manifested in a great famine. He notes that they sought to protect the laity as well as clergy from violence, but also to promote proper religious behavior, in an effort to ward off God's anger in the future. Glaber has an idea of a public weal promoted by good rulers (for example Henry II of Germany), and he writes with evident disapproval about a great deal of magnate violence in France. Like Ademar, however, he writes with approval about violence carried out by lay magnates as well as by God and the saints when that violence served God's purposes as he understood them. See *Rodulfi Glabri Historiarum libri quinque* = *The five books of the histories*, edited and translated by John France (Oxford: Clarendon Press, 1989). On the peace councils: 4.5.10–17, 187–99. On the public weal: 1.5.23, 39–41 and 4. Preface, 171–3. On violence as a force for good or instrument of God's will: 1.4.12, 25–7; 3.7.24, 133–7; 3.9.39, 163–5; 5.1.8, 225–9; 5.2.19, 243–5.

81. Ademar 3.48, 137/Pognon, 187–8.
82. Charlemagne: Ademar 3.31, 129–31/Pognon, 170–4. Capetians: 3.34 and 51, 131–2, 139/Pognon, 175–6, 190–1.
83. Ademar 3.41, 134–5/Pognon, 181–3.
84. *Gesta episcoporum Camaracensium*, ed. L.C. Bethmann, MGH SS 7 (Hanover: Hahn, 1846), 402–89; English translation of some of the relevant passages in Head and Landes, *Peace of God*, Appendix A, 335–7.
85. LDM s.v. "Gerhard I, Bischof von Cambrai" and "*Gesta episcoporum Cameracensium*".
86. Cf. Charlemagne's similar declaration to Pope Leo III: Alcuin, *Epistolae*, nr. 93, 136–8.
87. See Chapter 5.
88. *Gesta* 3.51–2, 485–6.
89. See Georges Duby, *Les trois ordres: ou, l'imaginaire du féodalisme* (Paris: Gallimard, 1978), translated into English by Arthur Goldhammer as *The Three Orders: Feudal Society Imagined* (Chicago: University of Chicago Press, 1980).
90. See, for example, Letaldus of Micy, *Delatio corporis s. Juniani*, 823–36; English translation in Head and Landes, eds., *Peace of God*, 328–9.
91. SM 91, 109–11; note that the citation to this text in Head and Landes, eds., *Peace of God*, 337 is incorrect.
92. Halsall, "Violence and Society", 32.
93. White, "Feuding and Peacemaking", 201–2.
94. Cf. Geoffrey Koziol, *Begging Pardon and Favor: Ritual and Political Order in Early Medieval France* (Ithaca, NY: Cornell University Press, 1992), 109, 135–6.
95. See also Glaber, *Histories*, 5.1.15–16, 237–9.
96. *Capitula origins incertae*, a. 813 vel post, MGH Capit. I, 175, c. 2.
97. Vern L. Bullough and James A. Brundage, eds., *Handbook of Medieval Sexuality* (New York: Garland, 2000), 107.

**Map 4**  Germany in the late tenth century (From D. Matthew, *Atlas of Medieval Europe* (Facts on File, 1992))

*chapter five*

# VIOLENCE AND RITUAL

One thread running through our story so far has been violence that sent messages. We have seen single acts of violence carried out in such a way as to declare that vengeance had been taken for a grievance. We have also seen parties to disputes violently advertise their willingness and ability to use force as they maneuver along the path to a settlement. These observations point towards the world of ritual. The term "ritual", as the modern scholarship uses it, denotes above all the visible performance of actions or gestures that communicate symbolic meaning. It can encompass single acts that carry specific meanings as well as sequences of such acts that communicate more complex messages. Violent rituals can thus comprise individual acts of violence designed to send specific messages (I have killed this man to avenge a grievance) or several violent acts that fit together with other symbolic actions like words in a sentence (I have thrown the staff that represents my allegiance to you on the ground, assaulted and captured your castle, and cut off the right hands of its garrison to show that, while I expect to reach a settlement with you, you cannot simply dictate its terms to me).

Medieval society was pervaded by ritual.[1] Admittedly, medieval texts do not as a rule employ the term "ritual". Instead, as Philippe Buc has noted, they reveal symbolic behavior by employing descriptive words or phrases such as "properly" (*rite*), "according to custom" (*secundem morem*), "solemnly", "honorably", or "humbly" (*solemniter, honorifice, humiliter*). As a noun they might use "ceremonies" (*caerimonialia*), especially in a religious context.[2] Nevertheless, sources from across medieval Europe in both time and space describe political actors doing things that we can comfortably call rituals. Magnates gave or withheld the kiss of peace to signal the quality of their relationship to one another. A supplicant needing a favor from his lord prostrated himself at the lord's feet to declare his dependence on the lord's generosity, thus allowing the lord to appear greathearted by fulfilling his request.[3] Those arranging processions or banquets set participants' places in line or at table very carefully to display hierarchies of prestige or power – or to inflict a calculated insult.

Such rituals were, according to the texts that describe them, carried out publicly. They therefore tended to commit those participating in them to behave as expected or risk community sanction (a supplicant prostrating himself in front of an audience before a lord, for example, made it hard for the lord to refuse his request). Such was ritual's power to compel that the precise contours of a publicly staged event were often negotiated in advance, so that everyone involved knew and agreed to what they were going to do in public.[4]

It lies near at hand to wonder, therefore, whether political rituals and the norms that they expressed could by themselves have formed a basis for order in times and places where central authority could not impose its own norms.[5] The argument that they could and did has been made particularly strongly in Germany. Germany, seen from the perspective of the modern, centralized nation-state, has had a long history of fragmentation. German historians have therefore spent a great deal of time studying those periods in the more distant past when Germany "succeeded", that is, when most or all of the German-speaking lands seem to have been bound strongly together. One such period stretches roughly from the second half of the tenth century to the middle of the eleventh. At this point, the East Frankish/German kingship, held by the Ottonian and Salian dynasties in succession, was much more effective than its Capetian neighbor to the west; it is a time ripe with the promise of a powerful and united German kingdom.[6] Part of the explanation for this lies in geography and economics. Germany, with its open frontier against pagan or quasi-pagan Slavic peoples to the east and its control of the Alpine passes, had plenty of room for the large-scale offensive warfare and concomitant seizure of land and plunder that tended to keep the interests of aristocrats focused on the kings and on the great dukes, from whose ranks the kings came. The Ottonians in particular also benefited from the discovery of rich silver mines in the Harz Mountains of their native Saxony. Part of the explanation must also, however, lie in the accidents of biology and personality. The later tenth and early eleventh centuries saw a succession of capable German kings who could not only fight and win, as did Otto I when he inflicted a catastrophic defeat on Hungarian invaders near Augsburg in 955, but who also often benefited from the good luck that their contemporaries saw as evidence of divine favor.

German and Austrian historians of the later nineteenth and early twentieth centuries, viewing the medieval past through the lens of the bureaucratic monarchies of their own time, tried to understand this apparently strong German kingdom by looking for its legal, administrative, and judicial institutions. A new generation of historians, in contrast, has argued that such institutions did not yet dominate political life.[7] Political order in Ottonian and Salian Germany, they contend, was based primarily on personal relationships of lordship and vassalage, patronage and clientage, and sworn friendship among members of the ruling class like those we have observed at a local and regional level in early Capetian France. Because the German kings remained important sources of reward and prestige, however, these relationships bound magnates together over a much wider area and culminated in the kings themselves. Their dynamics were regulated by unwritten but commonly understood norms that were expressed through rituals. The kings, while perhaps the most powerful players in the game of politics in their kingdom, did not dominate it. They followed the unwritten rules, or ignored them at their peril.[8]

One such ritual has garnered particular attention because it appears to have regulated violent conflict among those magnates who were powerful enough to threaten political order. Gerd Althoff has called it, because of the act that forms its centerpiece, the *deditio* or surrender ritual.[9] In an idealized form, it runs roughly as follows: a magnate declares a grievance against the king. He then rebels and holes up with his followers in a castle (perhaps after plundering some of the king's lands first). The king publicly displays the appropriate angry emotions and then lays siege to the castle (perhaps after plundering the rebel's lands first). After a bit, mediators with connections to both sides help work out a deal whereby the rebel and his garrison surrender unconditionally in exchange for their lives. The castle itself might be destroyed; it might also, however, be only damaged in a token fashion. Then the rebel prostrates himself before the angry king to demonstrate his surrender (*deditio*); in the case of a collective rebel like a town, the leading citizens come before the king barefoot with nooses around their necks. The rebel is condemned and thrown in prison; all of his offices and properties are taken away. But after a short while, someone intervenes with the king on the rebel's behalf and appeals to his duty as Christ's vicar to be merciful. The king releases the captive, who shortly afterwards reappears in possession of his former lands and honors.

This sequence of actions allowed the king to display publicly that he was strong and firm, and that he had the right to punish rebels unconditionally, but that he was also merciful. The rebel was humiliated, but in exchange for the loss of face came out of the affair without substantial damage. Magnates could thus express grievances in a way that did not fundamentally threaten the stability of the realm. The violence involved was demonstrative but caused no lasting harm (at least to those who mattered). This is precisely the kind of behavior that is predicted by the "peace in the feud" model discussed in Chapter 1. The ritual even fits the model's assumption of a small-scale, relatively egalitarian society, because it demarcated the political elite. Only the highest of the high – that is, the king and those likely to come into conflict with the king – enjoyed the privilege of taking part in it.

The idea that political ritual of this kind could serve as a framework for political order has some problems. To begin with, the very study of ritual in the past carries with it a built-in danger. By identifying patterns of public behavior, describing them in a generalized form, and giving the resulting generalization a name, the historian risks imposing a modern analytical construct on living, thinking, and feeling people. These people may have felt that they could react to or manipulate their society's symbolic language in a variety of ways for a variety of purposes, rather than plugging themselves into a script that dictated their actions. The analytical construct is useful, but only if it is treated as a starting point for questions and analysis, not as a real artifact of the past.

Second, rituals do not always lead to predictable outcomes. Ritual can in fact be dangerous; that is, it can be hijacked and turned to ends different from those that its instigators might have intended.[10] A king or great magnate approaches a city expecting to participate in the ritual of the *adventus*, or ceremonial arrival, by which a community expresses its acknowledgment of his authority.[11] The citizens, however, refuse to carry out their part of the ritual, the *occursus*, in which they meet their ruler at some point outside the city walls. The outraged ruler therefore attacks the city and slaughters its inhabitants. According to the Ottonian chronicler Bishop Liutprand of Cremona, just this happened in the late ninth century to the Carolingian emperor Arnulf when he tried to enter the Italian town of Bergamo.[12] In the *Miracles* of St. Foy, Bernard of Angers similarly describes St. Foy torturing a girl who failed to react properly to her *adventus*, that is, the monks of Conques in procession with her reliquary.[13]

Third, rituals can only promote order and consensus if everyone understands their meaning in the same way. This was not always the case. We are faced with written descriptions of medieval rituals. These descriptions were composed by authors who were, as we have seen, often highly partisan and who wrote history for their own purposes, whether moral or polemical. Their accounts may or may not bear any relationship to what other observers thought had happened, or in fact to what actually took place, if anything. They may well have been written stage-plays designed to cast the world and its players in the author's own image.

In other words, a description of a ritual in a given source describes a normative framework that its author wants to validate rather than one that everyone tacitly agrees organizes society. Even when several authors reported the same rituals, they often struggled mightily to control how those rituals were understood, for example by claiming that those who had staged them were acting deceitfully or hypocritically. The arbiter of interpretation and motive was, of course, the author himself.[14]

The very fact that authors from the period so often reported rituals and tried to control how their readers understood them, however, indicates that rituals good and bad, consensus expressing or dangerous, were a central feature of their society. In order for an author to persuade, what he depicted had to be something that could plausibly have happened.[15] Just as disputants in any given time and place had competing normative frameworks available to them, then, so too there were competing rituals, or competing efforts to control the outcome of rituals, or competing efforts to control the meaning of rituals. This left plenty of room for both spontaneous and predictable behavior, for surprises as well as for rituals that reflected the outcome of behind-the-scenes negotiations, and for authors to describe rituals that may not have taken place or that might not have meant the same thing to everyone who participated in or witnessed them.

In this chapter, we will look at violence and ritual in tenth- and eleventh-century Germany. I have chosen this time and place not because ritual was unique to Germany – it was not – but because much of the modern historiographical debate on ritual and political order in medieval Europe centers on Germany in this period. We will look for violence that formed part of ritual patterns of behavior, but we will also look for violence that did not. We will examine the ways that the norms expressed by the former interacted with those expressed by the latter, and try to decide under what circumstances which set of norms took precedence. Our stories will turn above all around the Ottonian kings and emperors. These rulers moved around on a much wider stage than did their western counterparts. As a consequence, the historians of their reigns tell stories whose horizons are often equally broad. Therefore, although we will still focus as much as possible on violence carried out at the local level and that involved individuals or small groups, we will repeatedly brush up against violent conflict at the level of kings, dukes, and archbishops, carried out on a scale that based on numbers alone we might want to call warfare. Yet the sources talk about violence on this scale in essentially the same terms as they do smaller-scale violence. It too, then, can illuminate how power was exercised and violence was performed in the Ottonian world.[16]

## *Thietmar of Merseburg*

We will enter into this world through one of the great sources from the period: the *Chronicon* by Thietmar, bishop of the Saxon diocese of Merseburg.[17] Thietmar belonged to a family that held the office of Count of Walbeck, as well as that of Margrave of the Saxon northern march. He therefore knew the great personalities involved in German politics during the reigns of Otto III and Henry II, and he was related by blood or by marriage to many of them. His *Chronicon*, which he began writing in 1012, offers in eight books essentially a "lives and times" of the Ottonian rulers. It begins with the reign of Henry I (Book I), and then continues with the reigns of Ottos I, II, and III (Books II, III, and IV). The final four books are devoted to the reign of Henry II up to 1018. For the earlier sections of his work, Thietmar relied on a variety of earlier sources, such as Widukind of Corvey's *Deeds of the Saxons* and the Annals of Quedlinburg. As his history drew closer to his own lifetime, he was increasingly able to draw on the memories of relatives and acquaintances. By the time he reached Book VIII, Thietmar was writing more or less contemporaneously with events.[18]

It is not hard to see where Thietmar's interests lay. He was above all a champion of his diocese of Merseburg, which had been established by Otto I in 968 as a suffragan diocese of the new archbishopric of Magdeburg. Merseburg was a diocese whose interests needed defending. In 981 it was suppressed by Otto II and its property redistributed among neighboring dioceses and landholders, in order to end quarrels among those whose territorial interests had been affected by the creation of the archdiocese of Magdeburg. Merseburg was re-established by Henry II in 1004, but its bishops remained embroiled in struggles to regain what they thought should be theirs.

Thietmar also charts the course of his own immediate family members through the seas of Ottonian high politics. The course has its high and low points, and Thietmar's assessment of his own kin is not always positive. But he does keep reminding us, by directing his spotlight on them, of the central role played (from his perspective) of his kin in the affairs of the realm.

The political culture that Thietmar describes was pervaded by public, symbolic communication. It was also marked by a great deal of violence. Violence and symbolic communication came together quite often. Nevertheless, Thietmar's stories tell us that the norms that captured and limited violence within rituals had to compete with, or at least to operate alongside, other persistent and familiar norms of violence. People in Thietmar's world resorted to very real and dangerous violence to assert or protect their rights as they understood them, to defend their honor, and to take vengeance for wrongs they felt had been committed against them.

## The Ottonians

Thietmar generally casts the Ottonians, and especially Henry II, in a positive light. He of course owed his position and the very existence of his diocese to Henry, whom he knew personally and who spent a great deal of time at the royal palace in Merseburg. However, Thietmar was not afraid to criticize the kings, especially when something they did, or had done, affected his interests or those of his fellow bishops. Indeed, Thietmar's primary message in the *Chronicon* is essentially the same as Gregory of Tours' over four centuries previously: good kings always had to support their bishops.[19] Also like Gregory, Thietmar moved in the circles of power. He and his fellow churchmen appear therefore as political as well as religious figures, as powerful men who fought as well as prayed.

Nevertheless, Thietmar does say some things about violence that are similar to what the peace councils on the other side of the Rhine were saying at about the same time. After telling how King Henry I had suppressed human sacrifice among the Northmen, for example, he declares the only sacrifice acceptable to God to be that which refrains from spilling human blood. For indeed the Lord declared, he says, "you should not kill the innocent and pious."[20] His account of Otto II's reign begins with a laudatory poem that presents peace as a sign of the love of Christ. The violence of the "vengeful sword" which brought sadness to Otto's later years (and which particularly affected Merseburg, says Thietmar) was the tool of the devil and penance for the sin of rejecting the truth.[21] He gives a hint of the Truce of God ethic when he notes sadly that a man in his own diocese had killed his own brother during Lent.[22]

When Thietmar makes broad ideological statements about kingship, he does so in good Carolingian style. His poem praising Otto I at the beginning of Book II draws a direct link between Otto and Charlemagne; not since the death of Charles had the world had such a great patron. Otto too had erected new bishoprics, had subdued the Lombards, and was made emperor by Rome herself. He was a friend of peace and he suppressed violence.[23] Similarly, Henry II brought peace and justice back to the land, drove out highborn robbers, and controlled them with harsh law.[24] Very occasionally, Thietmar evokes an idea of a public political order. It was all the princes of the realm (*rei publicae principes*), for example, who in 936 had elected Otto I king.[25] In 1017,

Henry II settled several disputes at a great assembly at Allstedt, which Thietmar calls a *publicus principum conventus*.[26]

As his image of weak kingship Thietmar uses the West Frankish kings; the consequence of their weakness is disorder. West Francia was a land of darkness and sin. It was ruled by robbers and persecutors of justice because the kings and great men had little power. It was rife with illicit marriages and other "unspeakable deceptions", and no one paid any attention to the bishops' excommunications.[27] The king of Burgundy, Rudolf (III, r. 993–1032), did not keep his promises and danced to the tune set by his magnates. As a result, bishops were forced to serve local magnates as if the magnates were kings, and the "madness of wicked men [continued] without restraint".[28] In short: good kings promoted peace and justice and suppressed violence with law. They also listened to and protected their bishops. Bad kings ignored bishops and failed to protect them. They let the balance of power tilt too far in the direction of the magnates, with immorality and rampant violence as the result.

When moral failure combined with diabolical influence, however, even the eastern kings could be wrongfully violent. The consequences could last for generations. One Maundy Thursday (the Thursday before Easter), says Thietmar, Henry I became very drunk. Although the church prohibited sexual relations on this day, Henry, driven on by the devil, forced his strongly protesting wife Queen Mathilda to consent to sex. The queen became pregnant. The devil promptly appeared to an elderly woman and claimed ownership of the newly conceived son. The woman warned the queen; she told her to always have bishops and priests with her and to wash the devil's influence from the boy with the waters of baptism. When the child was born, the frustrated devil came to the woman again, declaring that although he had been blocked, his companion Discord would stay with the boy and his offspring. The boy became Duke Henry I of Bavaria; his son followed him and was nicknamed Henry "the Quarrelsome". During their lifetimes "disruption was frequent and tranquility uncertain". The devil's curse was put to rest only with the accession of the third in their line as King Henry II.[29]

## Violence and Ritual

Such stories do not mean, however, that Thietmar saw all violence as diabolical. Far from it; he validates a great deal of violence. The role that kings and other praiseworthy magnates played in this perfectly legitimate (from Thietmar's perspective) violence indicates that for all of the Carolingian-like ideological statements he makes, both Thietmar and his kings understood violence differently.

Much of the violence in Thietmar's chronicle hinges on castles and land. Some of it involved members of Thietmar's own family. Writing of events that took place in February of 1017, for example, Thietmar notes that his own first cousin Berthold bribed the guard at the castle Monreburg and forced his way inside along with his followers. He was met by a vassal of Count Wichmann named Balderich, who along with his companions offered stout resistance. Nevertheless, Berthold killed Balderich and took the castle.[30]

Thietmar also assumes without question that his fellow clergymen were violent. He tells us that Bishop Michael of Regensburg (941–72) was honored as "a brave warrior (*miles bonus*) by all the clergy and the best of pastors by the people" for killing a Hungarian warrior in single combat.[31] A young count, after having been trained in earthly and divine law by his uncle the archbishop of Trier, was sent to Brun, archbishop of Cologne and brother of Otto I, to be trained in military matters (*res militares*).[32] In short, there was no division whatsoever between lay and ecclesiastical behavior in Thietmar's mind. Counts and bishops all came from the same families and participated in the same political and military activities.

Many of the violent conflicts that Thietmar describes follow the contours of Althoff's *deditio*. When they do, they involve the highest of the high, that is, at least a member of the royal family if not the king himself. A good (and romantic) example again involved a member of Thietmar's own family.[33] A marriage had been arranged between Thietmar's first cousin Werner, son of Margrave Liuthar III of the Saxon northern march, and Liudgard, daughter of Ekkehard, Margrave of Meissen.[34] Ekkehard, however, tried to back out of what had been a sworn agreement. Thietmar confesses that he did not understand why, though he suggests that perhaps the overt favor of Otto III prompted Ekkehard to seek a more prominent match for his daughter. The rejected groom Werner decided to take matters into his own hands. While Ekkehard was with Otto III in Italy, Werner and his cousins, Thietmar's brothers Henry and Frederick, gathered a group of "excellent warriors". They headed for the fortress at Quedlinburg, where the girl Liudgard was being educated under the care of Mathilda, abbess of Quedlinburg, aunt of Otto III, and regent for the emperor in his absence. Driven by "love of the girl and fear of public dishonor", Werner and his companions scaled the walls of the fortress. They seized the girl by force, despite her resistance and complaints, and rode off with her to the family castle at Walbeck.

On hearing of the abduction, Abbess Mathilda "was greatly disturbed". She tearfully complained to all the leading men, asking and demanding that they arm themselves and quickly pursue the lawbreakers; "having captured or killed them", they were to return the girl to her. A pursuit was duly launched. But the pursuers soon learned that their quarry had reached Walbeck in safety. Moreover, Werner and his companions had declared that they would defend themselves there or die trying. So the pursuers turned back. Werner's father Liuthar then went to Walbeck to find out what the girl's wishes actually were. He was persuaded (says Thietmar) that Liudgard wished to remain with Werner after all. When Abbess Mathilda heard this, she consulted with her leading men. They told her that it would be best if an assembly were held in Magdeburg, to which the betrothed and his bride-to-be should come. All of Werner's helpers should come as well and admit themselves guilty or be forced into exile. The assembly was duly held. Werner and his accomplices appeared barefoot before a large crowd of people. Werner returned Liudgard to Mathilda and offered compensation. At the urging of the assembled princes, he and his companions were then forgiven. Mathilde took Liudgard under her wing again "to strengthen her in the fear of God".

To boil this story down to its essentials: first there was a grievance. Werner was dishonored by Ekkehard of Meissen's attempt to renege on his promise to give him his daughter.[35] Werner responded with violence; he forcibly abducted Liudgard. Then came emotional displays on both sides: Abbess Mathilda displayed sorrow and anger, and asked her men to recover the girl and capture or kill her abductors. Werner declared his intent to fight to the death for his rights. Then came mediation and negotiation. Werner's father Liuthar told Mathilda that Liudgard wanted to stay with Werner. Mathilda's counselors advised a settlement. The settlement was carried out publicly and symbolically: Werner and his companions appeared in a posture of penitence and humiliation and returned what before they had been willing to fight for. The princes inter-vened publicly on their behalf, providing Mathilda with the opportunity to forgive the penitents without loss of face.

We could interpret this sequence of events as a spontaneously negoti-ated settlement of an awkward situation. Everybody concerned recog-nized the power of the youthful male ego and hormones, as well as the fact that the girl's father Ekkehard had violated his oath. They therefore worked out a way to settle the matter so that no one got hurt. It also fits the evidence, however, to assume that the young Werner knew in advance what would happen. He must have known that he and his companions could not possibly have withstood the armed might at Mathilda's disposal. But he had a legitimate grievance. He may have triggered the conflict knowing full well that it would conclude as it did. In the end, he did not suffer any permanent damage. Moreover, he avenged the insult that Ekkehard had inflicted on him with a bold act of violence that declared his willingness to fight for his rights and his bride. The ceremony that settled the dispute was worked out behind the scenes. It balanced Werner's self-abnegation with the princes' intervention and Mathilda's act of mercy. If we assume that Werner indeed felt he could predict the course of events, then this does qualify as a ritual, that is, as a series of publicly staged, symbolic actions that led to an expected outcome.

It is important to note Thietmar's own role in this story. Werner was Thietmar's own first cousin. In addition, Thietmar became very good friends with the girl Liudgard, who after Ekkehard's death did marry Werner.[36] It is not surprising, therefore, that Thietmar casts these events as what Philippe Buc calls a "good ritual", that is, as a series of symbolic steps that restored equilibrium and consensus.[37]

The sense that Thietmar is describing here a ritual pattern understood by his society at large is reinforced by the number of times that stories following similar patterns recur in his narrative.[38] An extended example has drawn attention in the scholarship as a classic case.[39] Another of Thietmar's cousins, Margrave Henry of Schweinfurt (a son of Thietmar's aunt Eila of Walbeck),[40] was hurt and dishonored by Henry II's refusal to grant him the Duchy of Bavaria, as he had sworn to do if the margrave supported his claim to the throne. The angry margrave distanced himself from the king and then, in the spring of 1003, joined Duke Boleslav Chrobry of Poland in open revolt. Thietmar himself was torn by his cousin's actions. He admitted that it was wrong of Henry II to violate a sworn promise, but the margrave's obedience to the king as God's representative should have trumped his own personal grievance.[41] As the dispute escalated, both sides plundered and devastated lands of their opponents and their allies. Castles were captured, but not all of them were destroyed; on at least two occasions, after men loyal to the margrave had surrendered castles to the king in exchange for their lives, the castles were only partially damaged. One of these was Margrave Henry's own castle at Schweinfurt. When the bishop of Würzburg and the abbot of Fulda arrived at the castle with orders to burn it, Margrave Henry's mother (and Thietmar's aunt) Eila retreated to the castle church and declared that she would die in the flames rather than submit to the castle's destruction. Faced with an impasse, the archbishop and the abbot decided to pull down only the walls and outbuildings of the castle. They then promised Eila that they would have the damage repaired whenever the king's favor permitted it.[42]

Finally, in early 1004, "trusted mediators" came to King Henry to ask for forgiveness on the margrave's behalf. At the urging of two close counselors, the king agreed to forgive the margrave on the condition that he be able to keep him in custody for as long as he wished. Thereupon Margrave Henry came before the king, shedding tears and clothed as a penitent; he confessed his guilt and surrendered himself. The king ordered him imprisoned in a castle and guarded night and day. Shortly afterwards, however, while in Prague, the king heard a mass sung by Bishop Gottschalk of Freising. The bishop preached that Christians needed to be mindful of God's mercy and to be merciful themselves. He then, directly and publicly, asked the king to forgive Margrave Henry. Moved by the appeal, the king agreed. So once more: injury and insult provoke violent rebellion. Both sides make plain their willingness to fight; lands are plundered and castles are burned, but some of the margrave's castles, including the one most important to him, are left in repairable condition. Mediators negotiate a settlement that is then acted out in a public ceremony. The margrave acknowledges the king's power by his penitent garb, by his overt display of sorrow and guilt, and by his surrender to imprisonment. In the end, however, the bishop of Freising appeals to the king's duty as God's representative to be merciful, giving Henry the opportunity to let mercy prevail over justice and readmit the margrave to his favor.

However, not all conflicts among the highest nobility in the Ottonian realm were handled this way. According to Thietmar, kings could act punitively, though at times they faced condemnation from their magnates if they did so. During the reign of Otto II, one Waldo accused Count Gero of Alsleben of some unspecified wrong.[43] Gero was captured and held in custody by Thietmar's father and uncle (Count Siegfried of Walbeck and Margrave Liuther III). Then the leading men of the realm gathered at Magdeburg; Gero and his accuser Waldo fought a judicial duel. Gero wounded Waldo seriously, but Waldo managed to knock Gero down with a strong enough blow that Gero conceded defeat. Waldo then put down his weapons and fell down dead. Otto II nevertheless ordered Gero beheaded because he had lost the duel. Thietmar notes that many were displeased by Otto's verdict; the emperor was rebuked for "allowing such a great man to be condemned on such a petty charge". Thietmar himself implicitly criticized Otto's action by casting Gero as blessed. He reports that Abbot Liudolf of Corvey saw Count Gero's head floating above his altar, and that the count's body was found uncorrupted three years after his burial.[44]

A king could unilaterally punish a great magnate without apparent opposition, however, when his opponent had already gone through a ritual settlement and then violated its terms. After the death of Otto III, Duke Hermann II of Swabia put himself forward for the kingship and at first enjoyed considerable backing. The support of most of the

German magnates eventually shifted to Henry II; nevertheless, Duke Hermann continued to fight.[45] When it finally became clear that he would not win, Hermann asked through intercessors for Henry's forgiveness. Henry received Hermann, who appeared humbly and made amends for the damage he had caused, and gave him his grace. While celebrating Christmas of 1002 in Frankfurt the king again received Duke Hermann, publicly reconciled himself to him, and treated him with overt esteem (another contemporary chronicler, Bishop Adalbold of Utrecht, adds the detail that Hermann appeared barefoot, with intercessors, and formally asked for the king's favor on bended knee).[46] Afterwards, however, Hermann, in company with Duke Dietrich of Upper Lotharingia, tried in some unspecified way to undermine the king while Henry was trying "benevolently to give the law to all, whatever their need". In response, Henry ordered that one of Hermann's castles be torn down and never rebuilt.

If Thietmar's stories accurately reflect the practices of his society, the ritualized settlements that he describes comprised chains of symbolic actions, put together in a variety of ways depending on particular circumstances, that allowed aggrieved parties to air their grievances without serious consequences, at least for the principals involved (not, of course, for those living on the lands that were plundered and devastated). The acts of violence that preceded the settlements signaled that the parties involved were ready and willing to assert and protect their rights and honor, or avenge injuries. The carefully timed intercessions, the ceremonial surrender, the appeals to Christian mercy, etc. captured this violence and steered conflicts towards peaceful settlements. The magnates expected the steps of this dance to be followed, at least the first time around.

### Violent Vengeance

Is this then "peace in the feud"? Not quite. Making these settlements work was the threat of violent vengeance. But ritual settlements could not always capture and control that threat; sometimes vengeance won out. During the reign of Otto III, in 994, Thietmar's cousin Margrave Henry of Schweinfurt (the son of Thietmar's aunt Eila) suffered unspecified injuries at the hands of "an accomplished but overly proud knight (*miles*)" of the bishop of Würzburg named Eberger. In response, Margrave Henry seized Eberger and blinded him. Messengers from Eberger's lord the bishop protested to Otto III, who sent Margrave Henry into exile. A short time later, however, he restored Henry to favor and reconciled him to the bishop by paying an appropriate indemnity. The bishop acknowledged the peace by inviting Henry and his uncle Leopold, margrave of Austria, to attend his celebration of the mass of St. Kilian (July 8, 994). So far, the familiar pattern is intact. That evening, however, while Margrave Leopold was indulging in war games with his knights, he was shot with an arrow by a friend of the blinded Eberger. The Austrian margrave died two days later. Plainly Eberger's friend did not feel himself in any way bound by the bishop's settlement with Henry; he still had to avenge Eberger's injury (though why he shot Henry's uncle instead of Henry himself is never explained).

Thietmar not only openly acknowledges vengeance; quite often he validates it. In his account of Henry II's ascent to the throne in 1002, he describes the fate of Margrave Ekkehard I of Meissen, who along with Duke Hermann of Swabia had contested Henry's claim.[47] Thietmar admits that Ekkehard had opponents as well as supporters, and that Ekkehard's arrogant behavior towards the sisters of the dead Otto III had only inflamed the hostility.[48] Yet Thietmar expresses outrage and bafflement as he tells of an ambush launched on the sleeping Ekkehard and his followers at Pöhlde.[49] He tells how Ekkehard, "a man praiseworthy in both domestic and military matters", fought for his life and how two of his faithful knights were killed. Ekkehard himself finally fell to a javelin thrust. His attackers swarmed over him, cutting off his head and then plundering his corpse. Thietmar calls this a "savage crime" and labels "cowards" the followers of Ekkehard who had stood nearby but had "neither helped their besieged lord nor attempted to avenge his death". Not only did Thietmar think that vengeance was warranted in this case; as he sought to explain the attack he could only do so in terms of vengeance. Some said (he reports) that the future Henry II had been flogged by Otto III at Ekkehard's urging and that Henry nursed the grievance, leading his followers to attack Ekkehard. Others (including Thietmar himself) thought that the attack was carried out to avenge Ekkehard's treatment of the sisters of the dead emperor.

Thietmar's attitude towards violent vengeance changes depending on his perspective. Sometimes, vengeance is bad. In 1013, followers (*satellites* or later *milites*) of Margrave Gero of the Saxon eastern march attacked the men of Bishop Arnulf of Halberstadt because the bishop had allegedly insulted their lord by correcting one of his priests.[50] Thietmar charges them with displaying an arrogance that "the faithful Christian should be astounded at". In 1016, four brothers, Aelli, Burchard, Dietrich, and Poppo, gathered a warband and attacked a good knight (*miles*) named Bern who had often treated them with contempt. Though Bern was accompanied by more than one hundred armed men, his attackers managed to kill him. Thietmar places the killing in a litany of evils which he says God imposed on Christians in that year to punish them for their sins.[51]

Sometimes, however, vengeance is good because its result is good. When Gottfried, Duke of Lower Lotharingia, attacked the "much hated" Count Lambert of Löwen and his companions and killed Lambert himself, Thietmar found the battle regrettable but praised the killing itself. Lambert, he says, was the "worst of men. Indeed, he had strangled many people in churches, with bell ropes. No one can count the number of men he had disinherited or killed. Nor did he ever do penance for his shameful deeds."[52]

Thietmar sometimes found himself caught between conflicting loyalties that compelled him to validate an act of violence from one perspective, but to admit that from another perspective it was wrong. In 1009 Count Dedi accused Thietmar's cousin Margrave Werner (the boy who had abducted his future bride in the story above, now entered into his inheritance as margrave of the Saxon northern march) of unspecified misdeeds before the king. As a result, Werner was in danger of losing both the king's favor and the benefices he held from him.[53] Werner fell ill, forcing a delay in the proceedings. Count Dedi's accusations reminded him, however, that Dedi had helped to pillage and burn a castle that had belonged to his father.[54] After recovering from his illness, Werner gathered twenty armed men and, together with Thietmar's brother Frederick, attacked Dedi as he was issuing with some of his men from one of his own castles. Dedi's allies fled and Dedi himself was killed along with one of his retainers. Thietmar reports all of this in terms favorable to his cousin. He says that the insults from Dedi (whom he makes clear he does not like)[55] had "roused the spirit of the excellent young man's heart". However, Werner had been wrong to attack Dedi; after the incident Werner "justly lost that which he had previously come close to losing unjustly through Dedi's slander", namely his march and his royal benefices, which were taken from him by King Henry.

Thietmar's comments about the motivations of parties in conflict are based on assumptions that allow us to get a good view of the economy of honor and shame at work in his world. Perhaps the best example covers several chapters of Books VII and VIII. It describes the death in 1016 of Wichmann III, count in Westfalia and in the Düffelgau, at the instigation of Balderich, count in the Drenthegau.[56] Thietmar tells us directly where his loyalties lie. Wichmann "was a man very valuable for our homeland", while Balderich was "a second Herod". The two men had been involved in a long conflict. In the back and forth fighting, Balderich had often been defeated. As a consequence, the other leading men of the realm "treated him with great disdain". This was humiliation crying out for vengeance. Wichmann sought to end the conflict with a peaceful settlement. He invited Balderich to his house and tried to placate him with hospitality and gifts. Balderich apparently accepted these "new bonds of affection", and invited Wichmann to his house in return.

But the devil had other plans. "The ancient serpent" hissed to Balderich through his wife that he should try to capture by cunning the man whom he had not been able to master by force. Accordingly, when Wichmann arrived at Balderich's house he was treated well but slipped a poisoned drink. Wichmann became quite ill and the following day was forced to set out for home. Balderich and his wife sent him off with signs of affection and abundant gifts, says Thietmar, but by a ruse they held back Wichmann's knights. Unobserved, a servant slipped forward and killed Wichmann. Balderich, says Thietmar, "made no effort to avenge the deed". Instead, he revealed his guilt by fleeing. The rumor of the killing spread. Finally it reached the ears of Thietmar's maternal cousin, Bishop Dietrich of Münster, who was bound to Wichmann in friendship.[57] Bishop Dietrich gathered his neighbors and relatives to take vengeance. With a strong force he besieged Balderich in the castle of Uflach, and devastated and burned the lands round about. Shortly afterwards another cousin of Thietmar's, Duke Bernhard II of Saxony,[58] arrived to take over the siege as ward for Count Wichmann's young son.

The ending of this affair tells us a great deal about Thietmar and especially about his frustration when a clash of norms did not go his way. News of the siege reached the emperor Henry II, who hurried to the scene. Balderich was allowed to leave, but the castle was destroyed. To Thietmar's outrage, however, Balderich's wife was also allowed to depart with all of her belongings:

> May all the afflictions that Job called down upon himself, also strike this woman who so clearly deserves them. May she endure so much suffering in this life that she may at least hope for forgiveness in the future. Whoever aided her in this matter should turn to God, fervently confess his sin, and make worthy restitution. Indeed, through the hissing of this poisonous adder, the church lost a great defender.[59]

Pages of Thietmar's chronicle go by with no more mention of the incident. Then we hear that two years later, King Henry discovered that Balderich had never made amends for killing Wichmann, and that he was still in a state of rebellion with his companions.[60] More silence follows. Then, near the very end of the chronicle, comes a bitter comment from Thietmar: "Balderich was reconciled, and the divine promise was forgotten."[61] What "the divine promise" (*promissio divina*) means here is not clear. But apparently Thietmar did not think that the king should have made peace with Balderich. He wanted vengeance or satisfaction. However, his desires (and those of anyone who agreed with him) were overridden by the interests of the king and the magnates allied with him. As at the trial of Ganelon in the *Song of Roland* Charlemagne's magnates had urged him to make peace with Ganelon and his kin, so too here Henry II's magnates (one suspects among them the archbishop of Cologne) had urged a reconciliation with Count Balderich – and with success.[62]

## Ritual and Power

From Thietmar's accounts it appears that the path a conflict took was determined by the constellation of power among the people involved. People far below their betters in power never got the chance to take part in a ritual surrender. In a vignette derived from Widukind of Corvey's *Deeds of the Saxons*, Thietmar describes the culmination of a rebellion against Otto I.[63] Thietmar either misunderstood or deliberately reshaped what he read in Widukind, for his version of the story is different from Widukind's in several ways. Nevertheless, it apparently reflects Thietmar's sense of what the great Otto had been capable of. The rebellion centered, he says, around Thankmar (or Tammo), Otto's son.[64] Thietmar has Otto besieging Thankmar in a castle, and finally driving his exhausted rival into the castle church. There one of Otto's men, Maginzo, pierced Thankmar in the back with a lance which he pushed from outside through a window. Thankmar died. Instead of rewarding Maginzo for helping to end the rebellion, Otto had him punished "with a cruel death".[65] Later in his chronicle, Thietmar tells how Margrave Ekkehard of Meissen had a knight blinded.[66] Henry II himself, as part of what Thietmar calls an effort to root out "the authors of all iniquity" in Saxony, had one of his own retainers hanged; shortly afterwards he did the same to a pair of Slavic magnates along with their followers.[67]

Magnates could also act with impunity when their opponents were unable to rally support from their community. In one example, Thietmar himself was unable to force someone to settle because his fellow bishops would not support him. Some people subject to Margrave Ekkehard I of Meissen committed a theft in the village of Görschen.[68] Görschen apparently belonged to the bishop of Merseburg, because Thietmar says that "our people" captured, accused, and hanged the thieves. Thietmar's people were unaware, however, that they should have notified the thieves' lord Margrave Ekkehard. Ekkehard was accordingly enraged; he ordered his knights to arm themselves and exact revenge. Ekkehard's men promptly surrounded Görschen and carried off all the men of the village with their belongings; they only released them after the payment of a heavy fine. When Thietmar learned of this "outrage", as he calls it, and was told that no one was going to force Ekkehard to pay compensation, he could only sputter. "The secular power should not rage in this fashion," he complains; the case should have been settled by the judgment of the bishops according to the authority of the canons. "The stubborn audacity of wicked men" would not have been reinforced in this way "if the will of my episcopal colleagues was unified".

The most extreme cases of power imbalance came, of course, when God and his saints got involved in human affairs. God and his saints did not engage in ritual settlements, nor does Thietmar think that they should have. When their followers and favorites were harmed, deadly vengeance followed. While the emperor Otto III was in Rome, for example, knights of Duke Hermann II of Swabia forcibly seized a meadow belonging to the monks of St. Paul Outside the Walls.[69] They refused to give up the meadow, despite the monks' humble entreaties. Thereupon dark clouds appeared and lightning flashed, "thereby revealing the anger of the Lord". Terrible thunder followed, killing four of the best of Hermann's knights and prompting the rest to flee. Thietmar's comment: "This proved that, even in this world, the paupers of Christ should not be held in contempt. Merciful God is their protector. He rewards those who honor them and render assistance in time of need, and punishes their persecutors, either here, which is lighter, or for eternity, which is worse."

Thietmar's saints were likewise violently dangerous when insulted. The martyrs Crispin and Crispinian, for example, killed a young monk who had treated their relics carelessly.[70] In one case, however, these particular saints were violent for reasons that Thietmar did not understand. Crispin and Crispinian were the patrons of the bishopric of Osnabrück. After the death of Bishop Dodo of Osnabrück, the martyrs visited the chamberlain of Archbishop Giselher of Magdeburg, Gunther, in a vision.[71] They asked Gunther if he would like to receive their bishopric. When Gunther answered, "If God wills it and it is pleasing to you", they pierced him with two spears. When Gunther awoke, he could not get up from bed without help. The emperor heard of Gunther's illness and promptly gave him the bishopric. Gunther eventually took up his office, and lived for "four years more, in great pain". Thietmar was baffled; he could only assume that the martyrs had a grievance of some sort. "I do not know," he says, "if something in him was displeasing to God or his holy martyrs. I both saw and heard from others that he was a just and God-fearing man, mild and chaste." Later signs proved that he was indeed valued by God, who "does not punish the same mistake twice".

Thietmar's God was happy to achieve his aims through human violence. In the summer of 1017, Duke Gottfried (II, of Lower Lotharingia) and Count Gerhard (of Alsace) met together with their supporters to settle a long-standing dispute between them by a judicial duel.[72] Something happened, however, that turned the meeting into a pitched battle. Count Gerhard's followers fled, and no less than three hundred of them were killed. Among the dead was a cleric named Walter Pulverel. Thietmar cannot say enough bad about Pulverel, who was so called "because he was accustomed to reduce his opponents to dust". Clothed as a cleric, he was really a bandit. He only considered a day well spent when his spear was covered with human blood and he could see a church burning. God's mercy prevented him from surviving this encounter and "ensured that his customary outrages would not continue".

Two lovely little stories have God taking his vengeance through animals. Very early in his chronicle, Thietmar describes a strange incident that took place at the palace of King Henry I.[73] In the sight of everybody present, a dog wandered in. Spying a certain man sitting among the assembled, the dog moved forward and quickly bit off the man's right hand. The dog then exited with his tail wagging, "as if having done something very good". The astonished bystanders asked the wounded man what he had done to deserve the attack. The man answered that what had just happened constituted divine retribution. He explained that he had found the master of that particular dog asleep, and, "like a miserable wretch", had killed him. The dog had attacked him repeatedly, but he had managed to escape. "Now," he went on, "after hoping that all was forgotten, but still guilty, I have met him again. Now, I know that no criminal can hide from judgment without penalty, whether in this world or the next." In a second example, a knight (*miles*) who had seized property of the monastery of St. Clement refused to offer satisfaction.[74] He was then attacked in his room by "an indescribable number of mice". At first, the knight tried to fight off the mice with his fist, and then with his sword, but to no avail. Finally, in desperation, he had himself enclosed in a chest that was then hung from the ceiling by a rope. After the mice had finally disappeared, the chest was opened to free the knight. But it was found that still other mice had managed to enter the chest and had gnawed the knight to death. Thietmar: "the vengeful anger of God alone had consumed him as payment for his crime".[75]

Although God himself never participated in ritual settlements, he did sometimes intervene to make sure that all of the steps of such a settlement were carried out. The factor determining whether He did so was of course Thietmar's own sense of right and wrong. The brother and successor of Margrave Ekkehard I of Meissen, Gunzelin, was engaged in a violent conflict with his nephews, Hermann and Ekkehard II, over Ekkehard's inheritance.[76] Thietmar comments that the conflict was carried out "in a manner unusual for our region", possibly referring to the bitter destructiveness with which each side went at the assets of the other. After failing to capture one of Hermann's castles, Gunzelin turned to one that was less well defended and burned it to the ground. In return, Hermann and Ekkehard attacked a castle that Gunzelin particularly valued and in which Gunzelin had stored his treasure. They captured the castle, divided the treasure between them, and destroyed the castle by fire. When the emperor Henry II heard about the fighting, he rushed to Merseburg and took statements from each party. He then assigned all the blame to Gunzelin. Thietmar supports Henry's judgment with a litany of Gunzelin's misdeeds (including accusations that he had sold the dependants of other people to the Jews, had engaged in unrestrained banditry, and had flirted with treason). He then has Henry ask his leading men for their opinion. The leading men showed some sympathy for Gunzelin and advised the king to go through the familiar steps:

> "We recognize that this man's behavior towards you is not inexcusable. It is our opinion that he should submit himself unconditionally to your mercy. You, however, following the admonitions of our most merciful God, should provide an example to all who might wish to turn to you, namely by displaying that mercy of which you possess an abundant supply and by rejecting the model of behavior that he himself has followed."[77]

Henry accordingly received Gunzelin's submission and placed him in the custody of Bishop Arnulf of Halberstadt. He also took care to protect Gunzelin's home base of Meissen against further attack. That, however, is as far as Henry went. If he had followed the pattern as we have seen it in other examples, he should eventually have had Gunzelin released and restored to his office. Instead, on the advice of his counselors, he gave the march of Meissen to Gunzelin's nephew Hermann. Thietmar apparently did not like this result, for somewhat later he has God step in.[78] God himself released Gunzelin from his long captivity; he "caused the chains to fall effortlessly from Gunzelin's feet, without falling apart".

## Conclusions

Thietmar has left us a text that is the product of his own biases and purposes. It is a polemic supporting the rights and interests of his diocese of Merseburg. It is a history charting the political fortunes of his family. And it is a warning to secular powers, especially to the king, of their duty to uphold and protect the rights and interests of the bishops, especially the Saxon bishops. In short, it is a text that was not a passive report of events, but rather one that was intended to impact the very political world that it describes.

We can safely assume that Thietmar's stories, and the normative frameworks in which he packaged them, were at least plausible to his contemporaries, even if some of those contemporaries might not have agreed with how he cast them. Thietmar refers explicitly or implicitly to normative frameworks that either did govern people's behavior in his world, or that he thought should have governed people's behavior, and that therefore were viable elements of his world's mental and normative landscape. At the same time, his stories were, to some degree at least, limited by the living memories of those in a position to read or hear the text; he was not entirely free, especially in his later books, to construct his stories at will. We can, therefore, reconstruct normative frameworks that competed with Thietmar's preferred ones by looking closely at what he says happened. This task is made much easier by the fact that Thietmar did not always try to hide motivations of which he did not approve. In several cases, Thietmar freely admits why his characters behaved as they did, even when he did not agree with their motives. On occasion, Thietmar admits that he did not understand why someone was (or some saints were) violent. Yet he always tries to come up with an explanation. His attempts to do so reveal still more about his sense of both the possible and the dominant norms that governed his contemporaries' behavior.

Thietmar gives us plenty of evidence for ritualized violence. Quite a number of violent conflicts in his chronicle end up following the contours of what Althoff has called the *deditio*, that is, a staged, public, and symbolic surrender followed by a merciful forgiveness. The pattern appears in Thietmar's text often enough, and is regular enough, to qualify as ritual. The sense of the ritual in these affairs is reinforced by Thietmar's accounts of behind the scenes negotiation and advance planning, and especially by his accounts of magnate criticism when kings chose not to act as they thought he should. The violence that formed part of the ritual, such as seizing a girl and barricading oneself in a castle, or damaging a castle in a significant but repairable fashion, communicated symbolically one's readiness to use violence to assert or defend one's rights and honor. It reminded one's opponents of the latent threat of real, dangerous violence that made settlement preferable.

This blending of violence with ritual and symbolic communication reflects a culture of disputing visible in sources from both east and west of the Rhine throughout the period covered by our story so far. We have already seen hints of it in Gregory of Tours' *Histories*, in a dispute record from Carolingian Bavaria, and in the *Agreements* of Hugh IV of Lusignon.[79] Philippe Buc has pointed out that rituals of humiliation and pardon, mediated in advance, were as common in early Merovingian Gaul as they were in Ottonian Germany.[80] Geoffrey Koziol and Stephen White have noted similar rituals of surrender in a variety of early Capetian texts.[81] In Germany, the pattern appears both before and after Thietmar. It can be seen, for example, in the earlier *Deeds of the Saxons* by Widukind of Corvey and in the later *Deeds of the Emperor Conrad II* by Wipo of Burgundy.[82]

But to say that the threat of violence was always processed through such rituals is incomplete and does not do justice to the evidence. Thietmar does not show us "peace in the feud". Violence in his chronicle is not always symbolic, nor does it always lead to a settlement (nor does it in other sources, as we have seen).[83] Thietmar reports a great deal of very real and often deadly violence. He tells us about people being killed and castles being destroyed. This violence was driven by the desire to take revenge for a subjectively perceived injury or insult and by the belief that doing so was legitimate. Thietmar himself participated fully in this normative culture; he validates and even valorizes violent vengeance when he agrees with its motives and targets. He cheers when vengeance is taken on someone whom he thought deserved it, and is critical when he thinks it should have been taken and was not.[84] God and His saints, of course, also took violent vengeance for wrongs, and Thietmar regarded this as a normal and necessary element of his world's order.

The choice of which path to take, that is, whether to try to end a dispute by violent fiat or to participate in a ritualized settlement process, depended on the concrete circumstances surrounding a particular dispute. Playing a large and perhaps even determinative role were the relative power relationships among the parties involved. When one side was significantly more powerful than the other, there was a greater likelihood that the more powerful side would choose simply to end a dispute in its favor by force. In such a situation there was little that the weaker party could do, unless powerful friends chose to get involved, or unless vengeance took priority over self-preservation (as was likely the case with the man who killed Margrave Leopold of Austria to avenge his friend's blinding. One wishes one knew – or perhaps not – what happened to him. Unless he had powerful friends, however, it was not likely to have been pleasant).

Differences in relative power were pronounced when a conflict pitted a great magnate against a knight, or a magnate against a non-aristocrat, or God against anyone. When a duke came into conflict with another duke, however, or with a king, there was a much greater chance that an effort by one side to push through its view of its rights or grievances by force would seriously endanger the political order (not to mention the countryside and its inhabitants). It tells us a great deal about the relative power of the kings and the great magnates in the Ottonian kingdom that the kings were clearly not in the position, as Charlemagne had been, to deal with conflict in a preemptory fashion.[85] Despite their prestige and the range of their power, the Ottonians could not act like Charlemagne; they could not try to impose their will unilaterally on their magnates. They were anointed rulers, and they enjoyed the prestige of the kingship, but in all other respects they were first among other, more or less equal magnates.

Thietmar does give voice to the old Carolingian idea that the king, as God's representative, was the source of right order and was responsible for upholding peace. He was perfectly capable of thinking in terms of a public order that a king was supposed to uphold and that violence disturbed. Yet he only projects this idea when he is making broad, ideological statements. In his descriptions of events, the image disappears in favor of a world in which the use of violence by members of the aristocracy, to defend and/or assert their rights and honor, was considered legitimate. Even kings could and did revenge themselves for insult or injury, although according to the ideology of their office they were not supposed to.[86] The kings do appear bathed in a Christian light. It is not, however, the light of a king who as God's representative took vengeance on God's behalf. It is instead that of a king beholden to his duty as a sacred ruler to be merciful; this was the point of appeal that allowed him in dangerous situations to let mercy prevail over justice.

### Coda: The Law of the Episcopal Community at Worms

Thietmar hardly mentions people below the level of the aristocracy. When he does, it is either to caricature or castigate them. It is a loose-tongued peasant (*rustici unius incontinens lingua*) who tells the forces of Henry II where those of Margrave Henry of Schweinfurt are camped; it is a presumptuous serf (*servili presumptione*) who kills Count Wichmann at the instigation of Count Balderich.[87] For the most part, however, the common people remain faceless and voiceless. We learn nothing about how they were affected by the violence of their betters, or were violent themselves. We can only assume that they suffered under the plundering, burning, and laying waste that were a regular feature of aristocratic conflict.

A different kind of text, in contrast, and one that was written only a few years after Thietmar's death, offers us a rare flash of insight. Titled the Law of the Episcopal *Familia* at Worms, it was written sometime between 1023 and 1025 by the bishop of Worms, Burchard. This is a legal text, one of the first, in fact, to surface on the continent after the Carolingian period. It represents Bishop Burchard's effort to set limits on the behavior of members of his *familia*, that is, his episcopal community. This community included the clergy who served under him, the servants of his household, his knights and officials, the townspeople of Worms, and all of the tenants and serfs on his manors.[88] A number of the problems that Burchard felt compelled to address involved violence. What he says about them looks generally familiar. He specifies wergeld amounts for particular classes of people within the *familia*, and regulates how people were to swear oaths in cases of violent conflict ( *faida*).[89] The bishops of Worms seem to have taken over the old Carolingian *bannum*; Burchard levies his ban, in the amount of 60 *solidi*, for the violent deaths of members of his *familia*, for each piece of a girl's clothing that a rapist had gone through to reach his goal, for striking someone to the ground within the city, or for readying a sword, bow, or lance for the purpose of killing someone.[90]

The real prize, however, is chapter 30. Here Burchard lets loose with a diatribe against the "killings (*homicidia*) which arise daily in the *familia* of St. Peter as though among wild beasts".[91] These killings took place, says Burchard, often for no reason, or because one person was insanely raging against another, or on account of drunkenness or pride. As a consequence, 35 guiltless servants (*servi*) of his church had been killed by other servants (*servi*) of his church. But the killers are more glorified and exalted, he laments, than given up to repentance.

To deal with this violence, Burchard, having taken counsel with his sworn followers, issued the following orders. If any member of his *familia* should kill another member of the *familia* without cause – cause being defined as self-defense, resistance to a brigand, or defense of one's goods and family – he was to lose his skin and hair and be branded on either side of his jaw. Moreover he was to pay the dead man's wergeld and make peace with his victim's kin in the accustomed way. The kinsmen of the victim would be constrained to accept the settlement. If the victim's kin nevertheless wanted to take vengeance on the killer's kin, even if the killer's kin were able to clear themselves of complicity, they too would lose their hair and skin and be branded on the jaw. If the killer fled and could not be caught, his property would be seized and his kin would be protected from retaliation. If the killer wished to stay and defend his innocence, he could fight a duel with a kinsman of the deceased. If none of the victim's kin wished to fight him, then he could clear himself by undergoing the ordeal of boiling water in the presence of the bishop. If he passed the ordeal, he would still have to pay the victim's wergeld, but he would have peace from the victim's kin.

The chapter goes on in more or less the same vein. It deals with the possibility that the victim's kin would try to circumvent the bishop's law by persuading members of an outside *familia* to intervene. It also deals with killings carried out by people not belonging to the bishop's *familia* but who nevertheless were working the bishop's land. These latter, if they could not be punished with the loss of hair and skin and branding, were explicitly left open to reprisals from members of the Worms *familia* and/or by the bishop's advocates. Killers who served in the bishop's own court were to be judged by the bishop himself and his sworn followers (*fideles*).

When discussing people below the level of the aristocracy, I have for the most part used the term "peasant", for these are the people – the farmers and agricultural workers, or people living in country villages – who would have been most affected by aristocratic violence. There were certainly some peasants among Bishop Burchard's *familia*. But there were also household servants, townspeople, clerics, knights, and episcopal officials. Nevertheless, Burchard focuses on *servi*, that is, on people who were in some way unfree. It was *servi* killing *servi* that had drawn his ire. And through Burchard's outraged condemnation we can see some familiar norms at work. There was apparently little difference in the way that Burchard's *servi* and Thietmar's magnates thought about violence. *Servi* too, at least in Worms, thought about violence, honor, and vengeance in the same way as their betters. They killed because they were drunk, and they killed because they were angry. They killed because their pride had been injured. When they successfully killed, at least in a cause that their community supported, they were celebrated. When their kin were killed, they sought vengeance, either against the killer himself or his kin. Peaceful settlement was something apparently that the bishop had to try to impose. Members of his *familia* sometimes resisted his efforts, to the point of reaching outside the *familia* for allies who would carry out vengeance. If the killer were not a member of the *familia*, however, and could not be punished, the bishop got out of the way and let vengeance take its course.

### Notes

1. Althoff, *Spielregeln*, 1–17, esp. 11.
2. Buc, *Dangers of Ritual*, 6–7.
3. Koziol, *Begging Pardon and Favor*.
4. Gerd Althoff, *Die Macht der Rituale: Symbolik und Herrschaft im Mittelalter* (Darmstadt: Primus Verlag, 2003) and *Spielregeln*, esp. "Das Privileg der *deditio*", 99–125 @101.
5. Cf. Koziol, *Begging Pardon and Favor*, esp. 289–324, and "The Dangers of Polemic: Is Ritual Still an Interesting Topic of Historical Study?", *Early Medieval Europe* 11 no. 4 (2002): 367–88; Buc, *Dangers*, esp. 1–12, and

"The Monster and the Critics: A Ritual Reply", *Early Medieval Europe* 15 no. 4 (2007): 441–52.

6. Timothy Reuter, *Germany in the Early Middle Ages, c. 800–1056* (London: Longman, 1991).

7. Althoff, *Spielregeln*, 1–17.

8. Foundationally: Karl J. Leyser, *Rule and Conflict in an Early Medieval Society: Ottonian Saxony* (London: Edward Arnold, 1979). More recently: Althoff as n. 4 above, as well as (*inter alia*) *Verwandte, Freunde und Getreue: Zum politischen Stellenwert der Gruppenbindungen im frühen Mittelalter* (Darmstadt: Wissenschaftliche Buchgesellschaft, 1990), translated into English by Christopher Carroll as *Family, Friends and Followers: Political and Social Bonds in Medieval Europe* (Cambridge: Cambridge University Press, 2004), *Die Ottonen: Königsherrschaft ohne Staat* (Stuttgart: Kohlhammer, 2000); Gerd Althoff and Hagen Keller, *Heinrich I. und Otto der Große: Neubeginn und karolingisches Erbe*, 2nd edn (Göttingen: Muster-Schmidt, 1994); Timothy Reuter, "Unruhestiftung, Fehde, Rebellion, Widerstand", in *Die Salier und Das Reich*, ed. Stefan Weinfurter (Sigmaringen: J. Thorbecke, 1991), 297–325 @299–300.

9. Althoff, "Privileg der *deditio*"; Reuter, "Unruhestiftung", 320–1.

10. Buc, *Dangers*, 8–9.

11. McCormick, *Eternal Victory*.

12. Buc, *Dangers*, 41–2.

13. MSF 1.15, 115–16/Sheingorn, 80–1; Buc, *Dangers*, 42.

14. Buc, *Dangers*, 9–10, 79 and "Monsters", 448; Hanna Vollrath, "Konfliktwahrnehmung and Konfliktdarstellung in erzählenden Quellen des 11. Jahrhunderts", in Weinfurter, ed., *Die Salier*, 279–96.

15. Cf. Buc, *Dangers*, 76: "The ambient political culture's assumptions and commonplaces concerning what could and should happen can be recovered from ninth-century sources."

16. Cf. Reuter, "Unruhestiftung", 302.

17. Thietmar of Merseburg, *Chronicon*, ed. Rudolf Buchner (Darmstadt: Wissenschaftliche Buchgesellschaft, 1957); English translation: David A. Warner, trans., *Ottonian Germany: The Chronicon of Thietmar of Merseburg* (Manchester: Manchester University Press, 2001). All quotations will be taken from the Warner translation unless otherwise noted.

18. Warner, "Introduction: Thietmar, bishop and chronicler", in *Ottonian Germany*, 1–64.

19. Reuter, "Unruhestiftung", 308.

20. *Chronicon* I/17, 22–3/Warner, 80.

21. *Chronicon* III/Prologue, 84–5/Warner, 126.

22. *Chronicon* VIII/7, 448–9/Warner, 366.

23. *Chronicon* II/Prologue, 32–3/Warner, 89.

24. *Chronicon* V/Prologue, 192–3/Warner, 205.

25. *Chronicon* II/1, 34–5/Warner, 89. See also II/20, 54–5/Warner, 106–7; IV/52, 168–9/Warner, 188–9; V/4, 198–9/Warner, 208; VIII/34, 476–7/Warner, 385. Cf. Reuter, "Unruhestiftung", 306–7.

26. *Chronicon* VII/50, 408–9/Warner, 343; Reuter, "Unruhestiftung", 306–7 and n. 54.

27. *Chronicon* IV/14, 130–1/Warner, 160–1.
28. *Chronicon* VII/30, 385/Warner, 328.
29. *Chronicon* I/24, 26–9/Warner, 85. On the Bavarian Henries and Thietmar's depiction of them see Warner, "Introduction", 32–3.
30. *Chronicon* VII/53, 412–15/Warner, 346; Warner, Genealogy 1 (Walbeck and Querfurt), xiii.
31. *Chronicon* II/27, 64–5/Warner, 112.
32. *Chronicon* IV/31, 148–9/Warner, 174–5.
33. *Chronicon* IV/39–42, 154–9/Warner, 179–81.
34. Warner, Genealogy 1, xiii.
35. So was Werner's father Liuthar, to whom Ekkehard had made the promise, but Thietmar does not mention his reaction.
36. Warner, "Introduction", 48–51.
37. Buc, *Dangers*, 16–50.
38. In addition to the examples discussed below see *Chronicon* II/5, 38–9/Warner, 93–4; II/6–8, 40–3/Warner, 95–7; VI/35, 280–3/Warner, 261–2.
39. *Chronicon* V/14, 206–9/Warner, 214; V/32–8, 226–35/Warner, 226–31; VI/2, 244–5/Warner, 237–8; VI/13, 256–9/Warner, 236–7; VI/16, 260–1/Warner, 248–9. Cf. Gerd Althoff, "Königsherrschaft und Konfliktbewältigung im 10. und 11. Jahrhundert", in *Spielregeln*, 21–56 @24–31; Reuter, "Unruhestiftung", 320 and n. 136.
40. Note Warner's error 214 n. 42 in calling her a daughter of Liuthar III; she was his sister: Genealogy 1 and 2, xiii–xiv.
41. *Chronicon* V/32, 226–9/Warner, 226–7.
42. *Chronicon* V/38, 232–5/Warner, 230–1. See also V/35, 230–1/Warner, 228–9.
43. *Chronicon* III/9, 94–5/Warner, 133–4.
44. *Chronicon* III/10, 94–7/Warner, 134–5.
45. Warner, "Introduction", 24; *Chronicon* IV/54, 170–1/Warner, 190; V/3, 196–7/Warner, 207–8; V/11–13, 204–7/Warner, 213–14; V/20, 214–15/Warner, 219.
46. *Chronicon* V/27, 222–3/Warner, 223–4; see also Warner, 223 n. 73.
47. Warner, "Introduction", 24.
48. *Chronicon* V/4, 196–9/Warner, 208.
49. *Chronicon* V/6, 198–201/Warner, 209–10.
50. *Chronicon* VI/96–8, 344–7/Warner, 301–2.
51. *Chronicon* VII/44, 400–3/Warner, 338. Cf. Reuter, "Unruhestiftung", 306 and n. 51. See also VI/52/Warner, 273–4.
52. *Chronicon* VII/46, 402–5/Warner, 339–40.
53. *Chronicon* VI/48, 296–7/Warner, 270–1.
54. *Chronicon* VI/49, 296–9/Warner, 271–2.
55. See *Chronicon* VI/50, 298–9/Warner, 272.
56. *Chronicon* VII/47–9/Warner, 340–2.
57. Warner, Genealogy 3, xv.
58. Ibid.
59. *Chronicon* VII/49, 406–9/Warner, 342.

60. *Chronicon* VIII/7, 446–9/Warner, 366.
61. *Chronicon* VIII/18, 460–1/Warner, 374.
62. Reuter, "Unruhestiftung", 297–8 and n. 2.
63. *Chronicon* II/2, 34–7/Warner, 90–1.
64. He was actually Otto's half-brother: Warner, 91 n. 10.
65. Widukind reports that Maginzo died in battle sometime later: Widukind, as n. 81 below, II/17, 102–5.
66. *Chronicon* IV/67, 182–3/Warner, 198.
67. *Chronicon* VI/28, 272–3/Warner, 256.
68. *Chronicon* IV/73, 188–91/Warner, 202.
69. *Chronicon* IV/59, 174–7/Warner, 193.
70. *Chronicon* IV/70, 184–7/Warner, 200.
71. *Chronicon* IV/69, 184–5/Warner, 199.
72. *Chronicon* VII/62, 422–5/Warner, 351–2.
73. *Chronicon* I/27, 30–1/Warner, 87.
74. *Chronicon* VI/82, 330–1/Warner, 292.
75. See also *Chronicon* II/7, 40–3/Warner, 96–7; V/12, 206–7/Warner, 213–14; VI/9, 252–3/Warner, 243–4.
76. *Chronicon* VI/53–4, 300–3/Warner, 274–5 and n. 109.
77. Warner, 275.
78. *Chronicon* VII/66, 426–9/Warner, 354.
79. See Chapter 2 @n. 23; Chapter 3 @n. 70; Chapter 4 @nn. 13–26. See also Brown, *Unjust Seizure*, 124–39.
80. Buc, *Dangers*, 103–5.
81. Koziol, *Begging Pardon and Favor*, esp. 185–7; White, "Feuding and Peacemaking", 256–7.
82. Widukind of Corvey, *Rerum gestarum Saxonicarum libri tres = Die Sachsengeschichte des Widukind von Korvei*, in *Quellen zur Geschichte der sächsischen Kaiserzeit. Widukinds Sachsengeschichte, Adalberts Fortsetzung der Chronik Reginos, Liudprands Werke*, ed. A. Bauer and R. Rau (Darmstadt: Wissenschaftliche Buchgesellschaft, 1971), 1–183: see II/6–7, 92–5; II/13, 100–1; 19, 106–7; 25, 110–11; 27, 112–13; 28, 112–15. Wipo of Burgundy, "The Deeds of Conrad II", in *Imperial Lives and Letters of the Eleventh Century*, ed. Robert L. Benson, trans. Theodore E. Mommsen and Karl F. Morrison (New York: Columbia University Press, 2000 – reprint with new bibliographical essay of the 1962 original), 52–100: see XIII, 77–8; XVI, 79; XXI, 82–3. Cf. Althoff, "Privileg der *deditio*"; Buc, *Dangers*, 31.
83. See also Buc, *Dangers*, 19–20.
84. Reuter, "Unruhestiftung", 299, 304–6.
85. Cf. Althoff, "Privileg der *deditio*", 113–14.
86. Note Wipo, III, 67–8, on Conrad becoming another kind of man when he became king, namely one who renounced revenge for injuries. Cf. Reuter, "Unruhestiftung", 303–4, 306–7, 312 and Koziol, *Begging Pardon and Favor*, 233.
87. *Chronicon*, V/34, 228–31/Warner, 228; VII/47, 404–5/Warner, 340.
88. Burchard of Worms, *Lex familae Wormatiensis ecclesiae*, ed. L. Weiland, MGH Const. 1 (Hanover: Hahn, 1893), 639–44. English translation by

S. Lane, at the Internet Medieval Sourcebook, **http://www.fordham.edu/ halsall/source/lexworms.html**. See Benjamin Arnold, *Power and Property in Medieval Germany: Economic and Social Change c. 900–1300* (Oxford: Oxford University Press, 2004), 33–4; Peter Landau, "The Development of Law", in NCMH IV/1, ed. Luscombe and Riley-Smith, 113–47 @115.

89. *Lex familae Wormatiensis ecclesiae*, c. 9, 641; c. 18, 642.
90. Ibid., c. 20, 642; c. 23, 642–3; c. 27–8, 643.
91. Ibid., c. 30, 643–4. I have chosen not to follow Lane, who translates *homicidia* here as "murders".

# PART III

# TWELFTH-CENTURY TRANSFORMATIONS

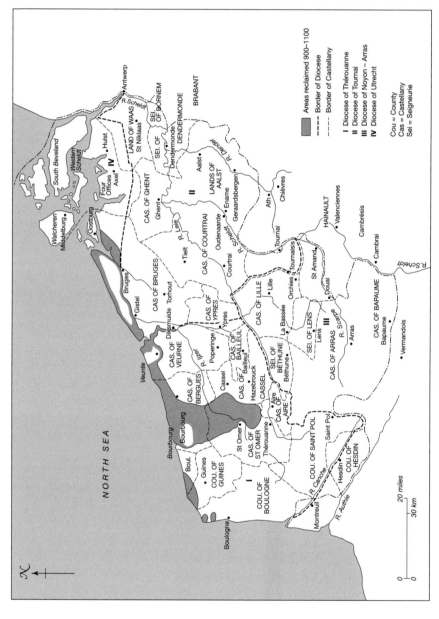

**Map 5**  Flanders c. 1100 (From F.L. Gansof, *La Flandre Sous les Premiers Comtes* (*La Renaissance du Livre*, 1943))

## chapter six

# VIOLENCE, THE PRINCES, AND THE TOWNS

We move again in time and place, to the first half of the twelfth century and to the county of Flanders, which at this point covered what are today the western regions of Belgium and parts of northern France. In this period, Flanders was undergoing economic and social changes that would soon transform all of Europe. These changes affected how people in Flanders deployed the norms of violence available to them. They also introduced new players on the political field with their own set of interests and imperatives, whose use of violence brought new norms of violence in their wake.

In the centuries prior to the year 1000, the economy of Europe north of the Alps was fundamentally rural and agricultural.[1] This is not to say that there was no commerce or manufacture. Quite the contrary; recent scholarship has made it clear that trade networks connecting western and central Europe with the civilizations of the Mediterranean persisted after the western Roman Empire dissolved.[2] Nevertheless, the fundamental economic basis for political power remained land, that is, the ability to exploit the produce of the land and the income of the people who worked the land. Towns, mostly survivors of Roman *civitates*, were kept alive by local commerce but above all by the Christian bishops and their administrations. Smaller settlements surrounded monasteries or castles and helped to satisfy their economic needs.

The seeds of change lay in a warming climate that had already begun to affect Europe before 800. While the extent and duration of this warming trend are still hotly debated, it is clear that average temperatures in Europe did go up to a significant degree.[3] Climate change made it worthwhile to clear more land; more land meant more food to feed a growing population that could clear more land, etc. More land also meant more wealth for landlords.

By the year 1000, economic growth was also being encouraged by relative stability. Attacks by Vikings and others had largely ceased. The

Northmen had either returned to Scandinavia to find their place in the developing Christian kingdoms of Denmark and Norway, or had settled down to become a permanent part of the political landscape, as did large numbers of Danes in England and as did the *Nordmanni* or Normans around the mouth of the Seine river in France. Stability helped trade; traders dealing in the products of (still rare but less rare than before) agricultural surpluses, or in products made by the growing number of people in the towns who were supported by those surpluses, took to the roads and rivers in greater numbers. Towns and cities increased both in size and in number as demand for labor grew and new markets sprang up. Lords were for the most part happy to promote these developments, by protecting and granting rights to merchants and townspeople, for they stood to profit from the tolls and taxes that they could levy from increasing economic activity.[4]

In some areas of western Europe, some lords were able to take advantage of their particular economic circumstances to erect larger-scale principalities that took on some permanence. The dukes of Normandy, for example, had by the eleventh century assembled a territorial power base secure enough that Duke William "the Conqueror" could in 1066 invade England and make himself king of the English without having the duchy of Normandy disappear. Economic trends also helped the Capetian kings of France. As we saw previously, in the early eleventh century the Capetians hardly attracted any notice in the south of what was formally their kingdom. In their own domains between Paris and Orléans, however, they enjoyed the advantages of rich agricultural lands and the excellent communications and transportation for trade provided by the Seine. Successive Capetians carefully managed their estates with a growing army of estate administrators, or *prévots*, and aggressively pressed their claims to lands and incomes from secular and ecclesiastical lords alike. Growing ever richer as a consequence, the Capetians were already by the end of the eleventh century showing signs of the resurgence that would lead ultimately to rule over France in fact as well as name.[5]

Flanders provides a particularly precocious and prominent example of this phenomenon.[6] The region had been known since Roman times for its woolen cloth, which was made from wool taken from sheep pastured on coastal dunes. In the tenth and eleventh centuries, Flemish manufacturers and merchants concentrated on making and exporting fine woolen fabrics. By 1100, Flanders' export textile industry was trading cloth throughout the known world; it was at the start of a trajectory that would see towns such as Arras, Bruges, Ghent, Lille, and Ypres develop from towns into cities that were magnets for rural labor. At the same time, Flanders became a vast market for wool, food, and other goods from

England, northern France, the Low Countries, and Germany needed to feed its looms and supply its growing population. By 1200, it had become the most densely urbanized area of Europe. An important symptom of the Flemish towns' growth: they developed enough of a sense of their corporate interests, and were wealthy enough to afford, to build city walls. St. Omer was the first to do so, around 1000. Others followed suit in the course of the eleventh century; Bruges put up its first walls around 1100.

The counts of Flanders benefited tremendously from Flanders' economic transformation. They enjoyed what had been royal rights in the region; most important from an economic perspective were the rights to collect tolls on trade and to mint coins. As flooded land in the west of the county was reclaimed, they asserted regalian rights and took it for themselves. By the tenth century they were already being recognized as being more than counts; they were effectively as rich and powerful as dukes or margraves and sources occasionally label them as such. By the turn of the first millennium, their reach had extended far enough that it confronted the territorial ambitions to the south and west of the dukes of Normandy and the Capetian kings, and to the east of the Ottonian and later Salian emperors. Count Arnulf II (r. 965–88), for example, had to struggle with Otto II to assert his claims to lands east of the river Scheldt, and Thietmar of Merseburg describes conflict between Henry II and Count Baldwin IV (r. 988–1037).[7]

To increase their own income, the counts fostered commerce by establishing fairs, where merchants and manufacturers could meet to exchange wares. By the second quarter of the twelfth century there were fairs at Ypres, Lille, and Tourhout. The counts also developed what was by the standards of the time a sophisticated administration to handle their growing tax and toll revenues. The provost of St. Donatian's church in Bruges became in 1089 the count's chancellor; as chancellor he administered the count's income, aided by a bureaucracy of clerics whose duties were primarily administrative and financial rather than ecclesiastical. The chancellor was matched by a chamberlain who had physical control of the treasury and of all disbursements from it.

The counts also exploited the idea of peace councils in an attempt to extend their authority over everyone in Flanders. In 1024, Count Baldwin IV pressured Bishop Gerard of Cambrai into declaring the Peace of God at Douai. In 1030, after a rebellion by his son, Baldwin together with the bishop of Tournai successfully extracted a peace oath from all Flemish knights. In 1042–3 a peace was jointly proclaimed by Baldwin V and the bishop of Thérouanne.[8] Count Robert I "the Frisian", who had seized power in 1071 by usurping the place of his young nephew, deliberately cast himself as a protector of the public peace; he forbade anyone to build castles without his authorization and claimed to be the protector of roads, merchants, widows, orphans, and travelers. In 1092 he swore to uphold a Truce of God. Robert II (r. 1093–111) repeated his father's decree about fortifications and issued a Peace of God in his own name. He also sought support from the Flemish towns by proclaiming a peace for markets and punishing violators severely.[9]

There was a limit, however, to what the counts could do to impose their idea of order. Flemings cherished their personal right to violence.[10] When Robert the Frisian ordered a record made of all homicides committed in the area around Bruges, for example, it led to an assassination plot.[11] The counts could freely execute low-status malefactors, but when it came to the powerful, or even knights, they often had to finesse compromises.[12]

By the time our particular story starts, the structure of power in Flanders was multilayered and interlocking. The traditional landed, military aristocracy, that is, the great peers of Flanders such as the eastern lords of Dendermonde or Aalst, and lesser lords with or without offices, drew income from their lands and/or from judicial or toll rights in their territories. These lords in turn had their followers, that is, their knights, and their castles. Below the aristocracy perhaps in social standing but rapidly catching up to them in actual wealth and power were the mercantile and artisan aristocracies in the walled towns, whose citizens were increasingly organized, trained, and armed for defense. The two groups were often connected; castellans exercised power on behalf of the counts from old castles that overlooked or were built into the fabric of towns; magnates held offices such as chancellor or chamberlain with oversight over comital incomes from towns; members of aristocratic families held high church offices in towns (such as the bishops of Thérouanne or Cambrai, or the abbots of St. Peter's in Ghent), or served as canons in urban churches (such as the chapter of St. Donatian's in Bruges). Straddling all were the counts, who had their fingers as much as possible in all of the pies. Below everyone were the peasants who worked the land growing grain or tending sheep, and the urban laborers who moved goods or worked the looms.

Each of these interest groups had their own attitudes towards legitimate violence. Sometimes these attitudes overlapped; sometimes they did not. In moments of crisis, they could clash, making it easier for us to see them. Just such a crisis came in March of the year 1127. Count Charles of Flanders, nicknamed "the Good", was killed by members of one of the leading aristocratic clans in Flanders, the Erembalds. The assassination touched off a civil war in Flanders that lasted until the summer of 1128. We know about this affair in great detail because of an account written by a notary in the comital administration in Bruges, a cleric named Galbert.[13] Galbert's text captures a moment of upheaval and social change, in which different norms of violence collided, in which people had to choose between norms, and in which some newly powerful groups, who were not among the traditional holders of power, were able to wield violence in support of their own claims and ambitions.[14]

## The Murder of Charles the Good

In 1119, Charles had succeeded the childless Baldwin VII as Count of Flanders.[15] Charles had a good, though not outstanding, blood claim to the county. He was the son of Robert the Frisian's daughter Adela, who had been married to King Cnut of Denmark; he and Baldwin VII were thus cousins. He had been raised at the Flemish court since childhood, and Baldwin had designated him his successor on his deathbed. Charles immediately faced opposition. Baldwin VII's mother Clementia launched a revolt in favor of William of Ypres, an illegitimate but nevertheless direct male line descendant of Robert the Frisian. She had the support of many of the magnates of southern Flanders, as well as (in secret) that of the Capetian King Louis VI of France. Charles quickly crushed the revolt, but he evidently felt insecure, because he moved to assert his control over the Flemish aristocracy.

His efforts to do so (the details of which we will look at below) brought him into conflict with one of the most powerful aristocratic kindreds in Flanders, the Erembalds, so named after the first prominent member of their line. The Erembalds controlled the offices of castellan of Bruges and, more important, of chancellor of Flanders, in the person of Bertulf, provost of St. Donatian's church. According to the extant sources, as tensions grew between the count and the Erembalds, Charles learned that the Erembalds had once been serfs belonging to the counts. The count promptly declared his intent to restore the Erembalds to their proper status. When he intervened in a violent dispute between the Erembalds and their bitter enemy Thancmar of Straten, and supported the latter, the Erembalds decided that he was about to move against them directly. So in a preemptive strike, on March 2, 1127, members of the clan killed the count as he knelt in prayer at St. Donatian's church.

The Erembalds, led by the provost Bertulf, apparently believed that the other leading magnates of Flanders (many of whom had their own difficulties with Count Charles) would support them. But to their surprise, most of the Flemish barons refused to back them up, turning instead to deriving whatever they could for their own advantage out of the situation. The Erembalds soon found themselves besieged in Bruges castle. At this point King Louis VI of France intervened. He saw in the murder and resulting power vacuum a chance not only to assert his own formal overlordship over Flanders (or at least over that major part of it that did not fall under the lordship of the German emperor), but also to help arrange for a new count who would best help him in his ongoing competition for power with the dukes of Normandy and kings of England. He placed the weight of his prestige, his money, and his knights behind William Clito, or William of Normandy. William had no blood claim to Flanders. However, he had the advantage (from Louis's point of view) of being the nephew of King Henry I of England but Henry's enemy and competitor for the duchy of Normandy. With the agreement of the Flemish barons, William Clito was elected to replace Charles. The besieged Erembalds were soon defeated, captured, and executed. William Clito, however, provoked a rebellion by (allegedly) breaking some agreements he had made with the Flemish towns. A protracted civil war followed and other claimants to the countship entered the fray. In the summer of 1128, William Clito was killed in battle. His main competitor, Thierry of Alsace, who like Charles was also a cousin of Baldwin VII, became count of Flanders.

Our principle source for these events, Galbert of Bruges, was a cleric, but he seems to have worked mostly as a bureaucrat in the county's fiscal administration. It is clear that he was in Bruges while all this was happening and that he was collecting information, taking notes, and writing as events unfolded. It is equally clear, however, particularly since the work in 2001 of Jeff Rider, that his account of Charles's assassination and its aftermath is far from a neutral piece of reporting.[16] Galbert idolized Count Charles. Accordingly, after Charles's death he set out to write a Passion of his hero. But then, as the civil war turned an apparently finished story into an unfinished one, Galbert extended and reworked his text to produce a narrative showing how God was at work in Flanders, defeating the devil, taking vengeance on the guilty, rewarding the virtuous, visiting the sins of past generations on their descendants, and finally restoring a just order to a battered county.

### The Good Count

It is in the Prologue and the first few chapters of Galbert's text that we get the clearest picture of Count Charles as Galbert's ideal, and of the norms of violence that Galbert associated with this ideal. Charles, ordained count by God, was defender of the fatherland and protector of the Church, the poor, and the defenseless. He strengthened the peace and reaffirmed the laws of the realm, restoring order (*pacis statu* – literally the "condition of peace") little by little in all parts of Flanders so that by the fourth year of his reign "everything was happy and joyful in the security of peace and justice".[17] Charles paid especial attention to the Flemish towns, decreeing that throughout Flanders all who attended markets or lived in towns should live together peaceably without arms, otherwise they would be punished "by the very arms they bore". People henceforward, says Galbert, attacked their enemies not with weapons but rather in courts, with the strength and eloquence of their rhetoric and oratory.[18] Galbert thus casts Count Charles in what with the benefit of historical hindsight looks like the image of his great Carolingian name-sake. He is ruler of Flanders *dei gratia*; he protects the Church and the helpless; he upholds peace and order and strengthens the law. Reflecting his own context, Galbert adds an extra element to this image by high-lighting in particular Charles's care for the towns.

Galbert does note an unintended consequence of Charles's attention to law and courts. There were many unlettered people (*illiterati*: not necessarily illiterate in the modern sense; the word can also mean unedu-cated) whom nature had endowed with such gifts "of eloquence and rational methods of inference and argument" that those who actually had rhetorical training could not resist or refute them. These natural talents used their skills to bring actions in court against the innocent, that is, "the faithful and the lambs of God, who were less wary". It appears from this charge that some people may have taken advantage of the newly important comital courts to pursue grievances against their enemies. Whatever the case, God did not long endure it. He took vengeance, says Galbert, by inflicting famine and afterwards death on the entire realm.[19]

For his part, Count Charles upheld the laws not only of men but also of God. His piety expressed itself in his personal morality and in regu-lar prayer and almsgiving; "in his merits he excelled the leaders and many philosophers of the Christian faith".[20] He reacted accordingly to the above-mentioned famine. He distributed alms and bread in the towns, and intervened directly to make sure that crops were grown that could feed the poor quickly and that merchants did not try to profit from the scarcity. He moreover fed paupers from his own table and even provided some of them with clothes.[21]

There is one significant difference between Galbert's image of Count Charles and the neo-Carolingian image of rulership we have been track-ing for the last few chapters, however. Charles was a knight and gloried in the fact. As soon as the young Charles had gained the honors of knight-hood, Galbert tells us, he fought with distinction against his enemies and gained a fine reputation and glory for his name among the rulers of the earth.[22] After he became count, when he had no enemies around his land, he "undertook chivalric exploits for the honor of his land and the training of his knights" in Normandy or France and even beyond, and "there with two hundred knights on horseback he engaged in tourneys, in this way enhancing his own fame and the power and glory of his county". In this one arena, Charles ignored the Church, which did not like tournaments.[23] Galbert excuses his hero with the comment that "whatever sin [Charles] committed by this worldliness he redeemed with God many times by almsgiving".[24] This characteristic of Galbert's Charles reflects the gradual process by which the practitioners of mounted warfare, ranging from princes to magnates to the lowest *milites*, were drawing together into a common military aristocracy separated from everyone else by the practice of their profession. "Knight" was becoming a badge of honor for counts and kings as well as their armed followers, and displays of skill at violence, or prowess, while essential to the ruler's image throughout the periods we have looked at so far, were taking on a more individual and characteristically knightly cast. Charlemagne had conquered lands and people; Count Charles of Flanders and his knights won tournaments.[25] In this regard, Galbert's image of his ruler-hero echoes the Charlemagne of the *Song of Roland* as well as the Charlemagne of the ninth-century capitularies.[26]

## The Evil Magnates

Galbert's good count, then, enforced peace and order in his county and protected the Church, the townspeople, and the powerless, while gaining honor and glory by fighting enemies or displaying prowess. Galbert's corresponding image of evil comes, of course, in the form of Charles's eventual killers, the Erembalds. Galbert says some rather nasty things about the clan, headed by the provost and chancellor Bertulf, the castellan of Bruges Didier Hackett, and Bertulf's nephews, chief among them the knight Borsiard.[27] The Erembalds' position was built on everything that Charles was not: treachery, deceit, contempt for the Church, the inversion of proper status, and the illegitimate use of violence. To begin with, according to Galbert, they were serfs. Erembald, father of the provost Bertulf, was an armed serf in the following of the then castellan of Bruges. An ambitious man, Erembald began an affair with his lord's wife. One night, while everyone was on a boat, the castellan got up to urinate over the side and Erembald pitched him overboard. He then married the wife and used her money to buy the position of castellan for himself.[28] Galbert tells us that Erembald and his descendants proceeded to do everything possible to make sure that their origins were forgotten as they climbed the ladder of power. One tactic they chose was to marry young

Erembalds to the daughters or sons of free knights who wanted to hitch their wagon to the family's rising star. This tactic worked until a knight who had married an Erembald girl challenged another knight to a judicial duel in Count Charles's presence. The second knight refused, saying that since his challenger had been married to a servile woman for more than a year, he too was a serf; free knights did not fight judicial duels with serfs. Through this exchange, Count Charles learned that the Erembalds were unfree, setting in motion the train of events that led to his murder.[29]

The Erembalds also looked for ways to display their power through violence. Galbert describes how the provost Bertulf (who he says was proud and arrogant, and accuses of having freely sold positions in the chapter of St. Donatian's church to whoever would pay) sought to advance the careers of his nephews. After the nephews were "finally girded with the sword of knighthood", Bertulf, "trying to make their reputation known everywhere", armed them for "strife and discord; and he found enemies for them to fight in order to make it known to everyone that he and his nephews were so powerful and strong that no one in the realm could resist them or prevail against them".[30] This is the mirror image of Galbert's image of Count Charles. Charles had fought with his knights to defeat his enemies, and he had participated in tournaments to increase his fame and glory and that of Flanders, as well as to train himself and his knights. The Erembalds too sought out violence in order to increase their reputations and thus their power. But according to Galbert they did so by fomenting discord and by actively trying to find enemies to fight. Because the Erembalds were bad, their actions were bad; illegitimate violence served to increase the power of an evil family.

The Erembalds and Count Charles first clashed directly in a way that is very revealing, both about the norms of violence that Galbert wants to project and about the competing norms under which the Erembalds appear to have been operating. While Count Charles was out of the country, a conflict broke out between the provost Bertulf's nephews and their bitter enemy, Thancmar of Straten. Bertulf used his influence and money to call all of the knights he could to aid his nephews. The assembled Erembald force then attacked Thancmar in his fortified house; the besiegers broke through the gates of the outer wall and cut down Thancmar's orchards and hedges. The perfidious Bertulf, says Galbert, while pretending he knew nothing about the affair, illicitly took tools from his church and sent them to be used in the attack, thus adding desecration of church property to his crime of violence and deceit. Once the besiegers had done all the damage they wanted (without, apparently, being able to get at Thancmar), they returned to Bruges, whereupon Bertulf threw them all a party in the cloister of his church.[31]

While all this had been going on, however, some of the Erembalds' knights and squires had plundered the nearby peasants, taking their flocks and cattle and seizing the peasants' belongings for their own use. An outraged Galbert declares that "none of the counts from the beginning of the realm had allowed such pillaging to go on in the realm, because great slaughter and conflict come to pass in this way".[32]

Count Charles found out about the affair on his return to Flanders, says Galbert, not from either of the disputing parties but from the peasants. A delegation of about 200 peasants found him in the town of Ypres. They knelt, begged him for his "customary paternal help", and asked for him to have their goods returned. In response, Charles took counsel with his advisors, who urged him to punish the Erembalds by burning down the house of the knight Borsiard, Bertulf's nephew, "for as long as it stood, so long would Borsiard indulge in fighting and pillaging and even killing, and would continue to lay waste the region". Count Charles promptly went to Borsiard's house and "destroyed the place to its foundations".[33]

The anxious Erembalds then sent mediators to the count who begged him to receive the provost and his nephews back into his friendship. The count replied that he would be perfectly happy to act with justice and mercy if they would give up their fighting and pillaging; he would also build a new house for Borsiard, as long as it was far away from Thancmar's. Otherwise, Borsiard "would do nothing but fight and quarrel with his enemies and the people with pillage and slaughter".[34] Galbert portrays the mediators as not very serious about their business. He says, rather implausibly, that they failed to pursue reconciliation and instead did their best to drink as much of the count's wine as possible. Charles of course, ever the gracious host, supplied them with as much as they wanted until they went home.[35]

I have gone into this affair in depth because it shows two sets of norms clashing, one which Galbert projects through the actions of his hero Charles and the other implicit in the behavior of the Erembalds. To start with the former: according to Galbert, the attack on Thancmar's house by the Erembalds was bad. But the real wrong came when the Erembald knights and squires started plundering the peasantry. Galbert immediately casts this as a violation of the count's authority. Then we get the peasants appealing for help to the father of the fatherland. The count, in good neo-Carolingian style, follows his duty to protect the weak and acts as a supreme judicial authority; he seeks advice from his counselors and decides on a punishment. The punishment is violent: Charles destroys Borsiard's house. In the negotiations that follow, Charles makes it clear that his goal is to stop Borsiard's violence. In short: violence among the magnates, especially when it harms the peasantry, is illegitimate. The count is responsible for the well being of all the people of Flanders, including the peasants. He may, therefore, and in fact should use violence to punish wrongful violence and keep it from continuing.

When we tune out Galbert's efforts to control how we understand this affair, however, and simply look at what happened, another set of norms emerges. The Erembalds had some sort of grievance with Thancmar. They dealt with it by gathering their armed followers and friends and attacking his house. They did not destroy the house, however; they simply damaged it and plundered the grounds, and then went home to drink and feast. This is an entirely typical *guerra* involving magnates and their followers. If the affair had taken place a century earlier, we might have expected it to follow the ritual surrender pattern we saw in Thietmar of Merseburg's *Chronicon*. Galbert in fact has the Erembalds going through the opening steps of the dance. The Erembalds were dealing with their equivalent of a king, namely the count of Flanders; they were powerful enough to expect him to take their positions seriously or risk serious unrest. By harming people under his protection, they injured and offended him. The count responded by burning down the house of an important member of the clan. The Erembalds then approached the count through mediators and offered to make satisfaction. They apparently expected that after some display of self-abnegation and surrender Charles would indeed, as Galbert says, "receive them mercifully back into his friendship".[36]

In other words, when we look at this affair against the backdrop of everything we have learned so far about magnate violence, it appears that the Erembalds thought they had the right to employ violence to prosecute their grievances with other magnates, and that they did so according to a common and well-established pattern. They also assumed that Count Charles would play according to the same rules, that is, that when he intervened he would act not as what we might call a "public" authority, but rather within the network of magnate alliances and enmities. Galbert says straight out that when Charles stepped in, the Erembalds reacted as if he had taken sides in their dispute with Thancmar: "the count had clearly lent aid and comfort to their enemies".[37] They assumed that if they acknowledged Charles's rights and authority publicly, the matter would end with everyone satisfied: Charles would have his authority acknowledged and then would receive the Erembalds back into his friendship – but the Erembalds would still have humiliated Thancmar.

According to Galbert, Charles did offer to build Borsiard a new house, but he insisted that the Erembalds stop prosecuting their disputes with violence. He thus posed a threat to the Erembalds and their ambitions as potentially mortal as his threat to reclaim them as his serfs. He had shamed them, and he had made it impossible for them to recoup their lost reputation or to continue to extend their power in Flanders through further acts of violence. The count justified his stance on the claims that he had the duty to protect the peasantry throughout Flanders and that he had the right to use force to do so.

## The Assassination and its Aftermath

From this point on, the battle lines were drawn in a struggle for power and survival between Count Charles and the Erembalds. This was in Galbert's mind a black and white struggle between good and evil. Count Charles was doing the work of God, that is, maintaining peace with a firm hand, preserving the proper order of the world by keeping everyone to their divinely ordained status, and protecting and honoring the Church.[38] The devil was working through the Erembalds to achieve the opposite: illegitimate violence, disorder and inversion of status, and the violation of the church.[39] Galbert describes in detail secret meetings in which the Erembalds and their supporters plotted the death of Count Charles. Even here, however, he acknowledges the normative framework within which they were operating; he says that their excuse for the assassination was Charles's destruction of Borsiard's house.[40] In other words: vengeance for wrong.

On the morning of March 2, 1127, Borsiard, together with his knights and serfs, killed Charles in the gallery of St. Donatian's church, as he was kneeling in prayer and distributing coins to the poor.[41] Galbert, his language vibrant with outrage, describes the chaos that followed the killing, as Borsiard and the other Erembald nephews fanned out through the streets of Bruges and hunted down everyone they thought had supported Charles and harmed them. He accentuates the Erembalds' evil by surrounding them with pejorative emotional language. He repeatedly casts them, for example, as taken beyond the bounds of reason by anger. Borsiard and his cousin Isaac, who was Count Charles's chamberlain, appeared "maddened with rage" as they pursued the knight Walter of Loker into the choir of the church; their swords drawn and bloodstained, "they were indeed furious and ferocious in countenance, tall and savage in stature, inspiring terror in everyone who saw them".[42]

Along the way, Galbert makes small judgments about good and bad violence that give us more information about the palette of norms with which he was working. Bad violence was not only illegitimate by virtue of who wielded it against whom and why; it was carried out in a way that humiliated or dishonored its victim. The killing of Themard, castellan of Bourbourg, is paradigmatic. Immediately after killing Count Charles, Borsiard and his men attacked the castellan, who had gone up into the gallery of the church with the count. First "wounding him mortally", they then "dragged him ignobly by his feet . . . to the doors of the church and dismembered him outside with their swords".[43] Two of Themard's sons, named Walter and Gilbert, heard of the count's death and immediately tried to flee. They were, says Galbert, paragons of knighthood, "brothers in blood, peers in knighthood, handsome in appearance, worthy to be loved by all who knew them".[44] A "wicked knight" named Eric, a member of the Erembald conspiracy, pulled one of the fleeing brothers off his horse and with his companions killed him on the spot. Galbert repeatedly associates this kind of brutal, dishonorable violence with status. For example, the second of the Bourbourg brothers was caught at the entrance to his lodgings. His pursuers pierced him through with their swords. It was not a knight but rather a citizen, one Lambert Benkin, who "cut him down as if he were a piece of wood".[45] After finally capturing Walter of Loker, Borsiard wanted to kill him immediately, but was persuaded by clerics of St. Donatian's to wait at least until the captive knight could be taken out of the church. So Borsiard and his men led Walter, begging for mercy, to the court of the castle and "threw him to their serfs to be killed. How quickly the serfs put him to death, beating him down with swords and sticks, clubs and stones".[46]

With the restraint of Count Charles's authority gone, the Erembalds set about taking vengeance on old enemies. The deaths of Walter of Loker and the castellan of Bourbourg were part and parcel of this effort; both had been members of Count Charles's inner circle and were opposed to the Erembalds' ambitions.[47] The Erembalds also, as soon as they were able, attacked Thancmar of Straten again. Thancmar and his men, however, had already learned that their comital protector was dead, and they had prudently fled their strongholds and farms. Undeterred, the Erembalds proceeded (as Galbert presents things) to demonstrate their evil natures some more. They overran Thancmar's castle and farm, seized all of his arms and equipment, and plundered the flocks and clothes of the manor's peasants. Others of their party set out deliberately (and, charges Galbert, with malice aforethought) to attack members of one of Count Charles's protected groups; they caught merchants on their way to the fair at Ypres and plundered their goods.[48] Somewhat later, the Erembalds managed to catch Thancmar and his men, but "after suffering a most humiliating defeat, they returned to the castle [at Bruges] in fear and shame".[49]

As always, however, the value of violence is relative. Galbert fundamentally accepts violent vengeance as legitimate. In a lengthy excursus foreshadowing the course of his story, he looks forward to the vengeance that will fall on the killers of "the most pious count".[50] The first blow is struck by a knight named Gervaise of Praat and his following, who undertook "vengeance more forcefully and quickly than was thought possible at that time". Gervaise displays rage, but his rage is righteous; "gathering his wrath, with the whole strength of his following, he vented his rage against those criminals, who had slain the best of all princes, pious and just in the service of God".[51] As a first step, Gervaise and his men on March 7 besieged an Erembald stronghold named Raverschoot. They could not breach the defenses, so they did exactly as the Erembalds had done to Thancmar's property; they plundered the neighborhood, taking sheep from the flocks of the castle and of others nearby. The very fact of the attack, however, so terrified the garrison of Raverschoot that it surrendered to Gervaise in exchange for life and limb. After plundering and burning the castle, Gervaise and his men moved on Bruges. His arrival on March 9 forced the Erembalds in the town to take refuge in Bruges castle and prepare themselves for a siege.[52]

Dishonor too, is relative. Violence carried out in such a way as to dishonor was a sign of evil when carried out by evil men (and especially by lower-status people against those of higher status), but it was perfectly appropriate when carried out by the champions of good. In this arena, Galbert proves to have been quite sensitive to the symbolic use of violence. He highlights in particular symbolic violence as a way to make brutal and public statements about people and about vengeance, in a way that evokes the heads on fenceposts and bodies at crossroads of Gregory of Tours and the Salic Law. As Gervaise of Praat and his men forced the Erembald party into Bruges castle, a knight named George, "the most powerful knight among the traitors" and one of the men who had actually taken part in the killing of Count Charles, was intercepted. He was caught by the knight Didier, who was an Erembald but who had not taken part in his relatives' conspiracy. Didier knocked George from his horse and cut off both of his hands. The mutilated George fled, but was denounced to one of Gervaise's knights. This knight ordered one of his men to kill George. The "fierce young swordsman" did not do George the honor of killing him directly, however. Instead, he knocked him down with his sword, dragged him by the feet to a sewer, and dumped him in to drown.[53] Later on during the siege, an Erembald knight trying to escape fell while trying to slip over the castle walls and was killed. His body was seized, tied to the tail of a horse, dragged through the streets of Bruges, and finally thrown in a sewer and decapitated.[54]

## *Knights*

It is tempting to see in Galbert's micro-judgments about individual acts of violence hints of an ethic of violence that he associated with knights.[55] Virtually all of the people Galbert judges favorably in this part of his story are knights, while those he judges unfavorably are either bad knights or no knights at all. His good knights fought fairly and honorably, except when their opponents had disgraced their rank through treachery. His bad knights fought brutally and unfairly, and had their lower-status or unfree accomplices kill good men disgracefully. That Galbert's judgments break down in this way, however, may simply reflect where his attention is focused at this stage in his narrative; later on he speaks approvingly of violence carried out by members of other social groups. In general, when Galbert talks about knights *per se* he focuses not on the ethics of their fighting but on their manner of fighting and whether or not they were good at it. His knights fought in a way that distinguished them from everyone else, namely on horseback. Even in situations where mounted combat was of little value, they still found a way to do so. On two occasions, Galbert describes sieges of towns, Ypres and Oostkamp respectively, in which knights from both sides engaged in encounters that he calls *tornationes* – which is the same word he uses for tournaments.[56] In other words, even in sieges the knights fought each other as their training and station demanded, on horseback, with lance, sword, and shield. In the Oostkamp case, Galbert explicitly connects this fighting style with knighthood: "how many deeds of knighthood, how many encounters (*tornationes*) knights in both armies engaged in!"

For Galbert, to be good at knighthood did not mean to constrain violence within a set of ethics but rather to be good at the kind of violence that knights practiced, that is, to display prowess.[57] The prime example is William Clito, the first successor to Charles the Good as count of Flanders. Although Galbert casts William in a positive light when he comes on the scene, his characterization of Flanders' new count grows ever more negative as William progressively alienates town after town.[58] Nevertheless, when Galbert reports William's death in July of 1128 during an assault on the castle of Aalst, he notes that men on both sides of the conflict "started up" to mourn "the fall of such a great and famous knight".[59] Somewhat later he says that nothing remained to William "of all he possessed in life except fame, for he was called good in knighthood".[60]

When the chips were down even knights on the side of the good and the righteous fought dirty. A knight named Guy of Steenvorde, whom Galbert openly criticizes but nevertheless calls "a famous and strong knight", had been one of Count Charles's chief counselors but had joined the Erembald conspiracy because he had married a niece of the provost Bertulf. Another knight named Herman the Iron challenged Guy to a judicial duel "because he had vilely betrayed his lord". The combat started with both men on horseback. Guy was able to knock Herman off his horse and keep him "down with his lance just as he liked whenever Herman tried to get up". But Herman managed to disembowel Guy's horse with his sword, forcing his opponent to join him on foot. The pair then went at each other with swords and shields for a while, until, exhausted, they both threw away their weapons and resorted to wrestling. Herman ended up on the ground, with Guy on top of him smashing his face repeatedly with his iron gauntlets. Galbert continues:

> But Herman, prostrate, little by little regained his strength from the cool-ness of the earth . . . and by cleverly lying quiet made Guy believe he was certain of victory. Meanwhile, gently moving his hand down to the lower edge of the cuirass where Guy was not protected, Herman seized him by the testicles, and summoning all his strength for the brief space of one moment he hurled Guy from him; by this tearing motion all the lower parts of the body were broken so that Guy, now prostrate, gave up, crying out that he was conquered and dying.[61]

Guy was promptly taken away and hanged.

### The Townspeople

Principal players in the siege of the Erembalds in Bruges castle were the citizens of Bruges. The Brugers in 1127 were armed to the teeth. They first started threatening to use their weapons as magnates from outside the town began to react to Charles's murder. The first of these was Gervaise of Praat, who had to reach an agreement with the leading citizens of the town before they would let him and his following into Bruges.[62] A few days later the great peers and barons of Flanders showed up. They too had to swear an oath that they would respect the town's area and property as inviolate before they were permitted to enter.[63]

It was not just against magnates that the Brugers asserted themselves; they were also prepared to defend their interests by force against people from other towns.[64] Immediately after the death of Count Charles, the Erembalds asked the abbot of St. Peter's monastery in Ghent, which was a principal burial place for the counts of Flanders, to come and take Charles's body.[65] The Brugers, however, would have none of this. Many of them already regarded Charles as a holy martyr whose bodily pres-ence and intercession would protect the city and its church from God's anger at his murder. The following day, when the abbot of St. Peter's appeared and the provost and his men began to prepare the body for transport, the clergy of the church resisted. A group of the citizens gathered, and finally the bells of St. Donatian's were rung.[66] Soon "all the citizens of the place . . . came running with arms . . . and with drawn swords surrounded the bier of the count, ready to resist if anyone should try to take it away" (it is at this point that Galbert reveals his own belief in the count's saintly status, by telling of a crippled man lying under the bier who was suddenly cured).

On March 14 and 15, armed citizens of Ghent arrived at Bruges to take part in the siege of Bruges castle.[67] According to Galbert, their castellan had ordered them to "assemble their communal forces and come, armed and girded for fighting, to make an attack on their own on the castle, by themselves, inasmuch as they were men with a name for conflict and battle who knew how to demolish defenses in sieges". Galbert betrays here his perspective as a Bruger; he tells us that the Ghenters, accompanied by a band of "plunderers, murderers, thieves, and anyone ready to take advantage of the evils of war", were there only to collect the money they thought they could gain if the besieged surrendered to them. The citizens of Bruges, however, met the Ghenters at the gates of the town prepared to fight. They only allowed them inside after they promised to share as equal partners in the rights and duties of the siege and to respect the Brugers' property.

On the 19th, after Bruges castle had fallen and the besiegers were trying to penetrate St. Donatian's church itself, the Ghenters made one final attempt to get hold of Count Charles's body.[68] They were met by irate Brugers, and an armed conflict broke out (with the gleeful Erembalds attacking both sides). The fight was only stopped when "the more sensible men among the victors" urged postponing a decision over the body's fate until a legitimate count of Flanders could decide.

The citizens' collective military power earned them a pivotal place at the bargaining table when it came to electing a new count. King Louis VI and the barons of the siege had elected William Clito, but they had to get the Flemish towns to agree to their choice. As the price for their consent, the Brugers extorted what Galbert calls "a little charter of agreement", which granted them among other things freedom from tolls or rent to the count and his successors. William Clito also agreed, as an additional incentive, to let the citizens correct their own laws from day to day and to change them as circumstance demanded.[69] Similar charters were granted to the other towns of Flanders; some, for example that for Aardenburg, limited the count's right to summon military levies from the towns without their consent.[70]

The connection between the towns' ability to use violence in defense of their own rights and interests and their ability to extort concessions from the traditional holders of power is made wonderfully clear in Galbert's description of William Clito's ceremonial entry, or *adventus*, into the town of St. Omer. Galbert has the townspeople of St. Omer and the count acting out the connection through a charming but at the same time menacing ritual. His story highlights ritual's effectiveness as a way to act out negotiations and to communicate messages. On Sunday, April 17, 1127, the new count and his men rode towards St. Omer. They were met by boys from the town armed with bows and arrows. The boys advanced towards the count as if they were going to resist his entry; their bows were drawn, their arrows were at the ready. Seeing them, the count sent a messenger to ask what they wanted. The boys replied that they wanted a kind of "fief" that they had obtained from his predecessors, namely, the right to wander the woods freely on feast days and in the summertime, to catch birds, shoot arrows at squirrels and foxes, and engage in other kinds of play. The boys claimed to have done all this freely in the past, and now asked the count to confirm their liberties.

This is all very charming, save for one thing: the adult male citizens of the town were drawn up behind the boys and were likewise armed. William Clito, however, knew what he was about. Himself still young, he granted the boys' request and then playfully seized their banner. The boys began to sing his praises and dance around him. When the townspeople saw that William had been formally accepted by the boys, they came out as well, and the town clergy began the ceremonies of the *adventus*.[71] This symbolic dance allowed the adult holders of power to clarify their relationship to each other. Without having to overtly threaten William, the citizens of St. Omer signaled their ability and readiness to use violence to protect their liberties, and William signaled his acceptance of their terms without having to go through the potential humiliation of doing so before the adults.

The point that towns could force the aristocracy and their rulers to recognize their claims by threatening violence is important because it reflects a normative shift brought about by a change in the landscape of power in Flanders. The claims asserted and rights gained by the towns of Flanders in 1127 were unprecedented, for all of Galbert's efforts to have the citizens claim them as customary and ancient.[72] However, the towns of Flanders had by 1127 reached a position of considerable economic and therefore military power. After Charles's murder, the traditional holders of power were broken into factions and had to compete for the towns' support. As a consequence, the towns were able to step forward, make new claims to influence and independence, and have those claims accepted. They thus tacitly expressed, and gained recognition for, their belief that towns as collectives could use armed force to assert and protect their own honor, rights, and interests.

The threat of violence from the towns was real, as William Clito soon learned to his cost. At the beginning of August, 1127, he had his knights chase a runaway serf into the market at Lille. Outraged at the violation of the peace of their market, the citizens of Lille "rushed to arms and chased the count and his men outside the town". William only got control of the situation by laying siege to Lille and forcing the citizens to pay him 400 marks of silver.[73] The next month, William got in trouble with the citizens of Bruges, when he broke his promise to waive tolls in exchange for their support.[74] The following February the citizens of St. Omer rebelled against the castellan William had put in charge there, because he was allegedly taking their property.[75] A week later a similar conflict broke out in Ghent.[76] William soon had a full-blown rebellion on his hands, led not only by the citizens, but also by some opportunistic magnates.[77]

## The Personal Right to Violence

As is probably already clear, and as becomes more clear throughout Galbert's description of the civil war, the Flemish townspeople were using violence to defend their economic interests, that is, the security of persons and property, and the freedoms, necessary for commerce and money-making. Many townspeople, however, displayed at least sympathy for the norm that the Erembalds had followed, namely that violence was a legitimate way to respond to a grievance of any kind. For all of his efforts to portray the Erembalds as iniquitous serfs and tools of the devil, Galbert does not hide the fact that many Brugers quite admired and loved them.[78] He notes that some people voluntarily joined the Erembalds once they were shut up inside Bruges castle, though they had not been involved in the murder.[79] Many Brugers thought that the provost and his kin had been religious men and good lords, who had been friendly and had treated everyone in Bruges and in Flanders honorably.[80] When the siege was over, some citizens shed tears of pity when they saw their lords held captive.[81]

The best evidence that the Erembalds' point of view was widely shared, however, appears in the very strange way that blame for Count Charles's murder gradually shifts from the Erembalds to their enemies Thancmar of Straten and his nephews. The story emerges as Bruges castle falls, the Erembalds are driven back into St. Donatian's church, and Thancmar and his nephews take possession of the provost Bertulf's former house.

The citizens were so outraged by the Stratens' presumption that they began to look "for an opportunity for fighting and killing them".[82] It turns out that the citizens held Thancmar's nephews responsible for Count Charles's death. The argument runs like this: Thancmar and his nephews had by their "deceit, discord, and influence" prejudiced Count Charles against their lords the provost and his brothers and nephews.[83] They had done so by provoking Borsiard and the other Erembald nephews into attacking them, thus drawing Count Charles to crack down on the Erembalds. This had prompted the Erembalds to kill Count Charles. *Ergo*, Charles's murder was the Stratens' fault; the Erembalds had acted throughout in an understandable way.[84] Galbert himself seems finally to have agreed. When one of Thancmar's nephews, Walter, was captured by the knight Gervaise (who had become castellan of Bruges), Galbert remarks, in the first person plural: "finally, after so many evils, so much looting and burning of houses, and so many murders which had been inflicted on us, we had captured that Walter who was the source and beginning of all the misfortunes of our land, by whose cunning Count Charles had been betrayed; not that he himself had betrayed him but he had forced his enemies, Borsiard and his men, to the act of betrayal". Galbert adds that the townspeople would have hanged Walter immediately or "destroyed him by some new and unheard of kind of death" had their new count, Thierry of Alsace, not stopped them.[85]

In short, the Erembalds were justified in attacking the Stratens because the Stratens had provoked them; personal violence to pursue a grievance was legitimate. The Erembalds had then been forced to kill Count Charles because the conflict with the Stratens had prompted Charles to threaten their position. Killing to protect one's honor, status, and power, therefore, was at least understandable. Or the citizens had accepted the Erembalds' line that they had killed Count Charles to avenge the injury of having Borsiard's house burned down. In any case, the only way to explain the story of the Stratens' responsibility is to conclude that the Erembalds had acted throughout according to widely understood and shared norms about the legitimate use of violence.

Galbert projects these norms onto the person who is really the main protagonist in his story: God. Galbert's God uses violence to pursue enmities, to protect his interests and his followers, and to avenge injuries just like any Flemish aristocrat. As we saw at the beginning, for example, while order and justice reigned under Count Charles's firm but benevolent rule, some people were misusing their skill at eloquence and argument in the courts "against the faithful and the lambs of God, who were less wary"; in response, God inflicted a terrible famine on Flanders.[86] After Charles's murder, those who took up arms against the Erembalds served as instruments of God's vengeance. To return to the knight Gervaise: "On March 7, Monday, God unsheathed the swords of divine punishment against the enemies of His Church, and He moved the heart of a certain knight Gervaise to undertake vengeance . . ."[87] As Gervaise fought in the siege, God himself fought beside him.[88] God also tracked down and killed people involved in Charles's murder who had managed to evade the consequences. For example, one of the peers of Flanders, Walter of Vladslo, had been an accessory to the murder and had helped some of the besieged to escape, but he had switched sides at the right moment and had thus avoided punishment. But no one gets away from God: "by the severe and horrible judgment of God" Walter was hurled from his horse, was shattered, and died.[89]

In a rather impressive burst of normative gymnastics, Galbert in fact explains the entire course of events in 1127–8 in terms of God violently settling scores. The original Erembald had murdered his lord by throwing him off a boat; God punished his descendants by having them thrown off a tower in Bruges after their capture. Count Charles's grandfather Robert the Frisian had become count by betraying and having his men kill the legitimate heir to the county; therefore Count Charles, for all his goodness and piety, had to die by God's hand and Flanders had to be devastated. The Erembalds were thus the tools "through whom the dispensation of God was accomplished, the treachery fulfilled, the fatherland desolated, pillage unleashed, the hand of each armed against all".[90] The citizens of Bruges had provoked God to wrath because they had abandoned William Clito and accepted Thierry of Alsace; although William Clito deserved to die because he had broken his faith with the towns, he had been set over them as count by God and therefore God took revenge on those who had betrayed him.[91]

### Conclusions

Galbert's story is not about norms of violence *per se*, of course. It is instead about power. Count Charles needed to assert himself in what was an insecure and contested position. To justify his efforts to do so, he reached for Carolingian-style norms of rulership. He apparently broadcast them loudly enough that Galbert picked them up and rebroadcast them as part of his image of the ideal count. As we have seen, the norms and ideals of rulership that Charlemagne had projected remained available in European political culture. We saw them appear sporadically in texts from early Capetian France; Thietmar of Merseburg advanced them in his idealized portraits of the Ottonians; Charles the Good's own predecessors in Flanders as far back as the tenth century had advanced them when it was to their advantage.[92] As Geoffrey Koziol has noted, the first thing that successful princes in the eleventh century did was to try to act like Carolingian kings.[93] In his particular context, Charles the Good invoked this image of rulership as a way to strengthen his position vis à vis his competitors. The long tradition of strong counts in Flanders, the wealth of the county, and the concomitant sophistication of the comital administration made it possible for him to do so with some chance of success (whether it was a smart thing to do remains open to question; it got him killed). In short, the norms of rulership handed down from Charlemagne provided a normative resource to which Charles the Good could resort when his context made it possible and it was in his interests to do so.

The norms of violence that Count Charles projected (or that Galbert projected on behalf of Count Charles) asserted, like those of Charlemagne, that the ruler had the right to deploy violence to protect the weak and the Church, and to shut down the use of violence by others in his realm. Once more, we see something approximating a claim to a monopoly on the legitimate use of violent force. The claim was helped along by the now well-established tradition of the sworn peace. This tradition was well on its way to becoming the ruler's peace, a peace that the ruler could extend to specific interest groups within society, such as merchants.

The Erembalds had no interest in buying into Count Charles's view of rulership. They were ambitious and had much to lose. They had exploited their military and administrative offices within Flanders to rise from unfreedom and obscurity to a wealthy, powerful, and prestigious position. They were not disliked for this; as we have seen, Galbert tells us that many people loved and respected them. But they viewed power politics through an entirely different normative lens: men were entitled to use violence, on their own authority, to avenge a perceived injury or insult and to increase their reputations and attract followings. When they were confronted by Charles over their fighting with Thancmar of Straten, Galbert has them trying to deal with the threat in a way consonant with this attitude. But when Charles insisted on imposing his terms on a settlement, the Erembalds were faced with a stark choice; either accept Charles's view of his powers and his rights, and the diminution of their powers and freedoms that would have come with it, or fight. They chose to fight.

But the changing context in Flanders was not just affecting the count and the magnates. The Flemish towns as collectives were also growing in wealth and power. As communities they had subjectively perceived rights and interests to assert and defend. They believed that they had the right to threaten or use violence to do so. What was new was not this norm *per se*, but the idea that towns as armed collectives could act this way, and the fact that their rights and interests concerned self-government and the stability, order, and freedoms necessary for commerce and money-making. The towns wanted maximum freedom to pursue their economic and political interests, and minimal interference from such things as tolls and taxes, or claims on their military power by the counts. When Flanders exploded in 1127 as a result of the clash between Count Charles and the Erembalds, the towns seized the chance to assert themselves, and to have their claims and interests – and the claims to use violence that went with them – recognized by the traditional holders of power.

In this case, then, we are not seeing the appearance of new norms *ex nihilo*, but rather the evolution of older norms into something new in response to a changing social and political landscape. So too with the norms asserted by Count Charles; they derived from a by then ancient view of the ruler *dei gratia* who was entitled to use violence, on God's behalf, against the misdeeds of God's subjects and in the interests of God's favorites, the Church and the powerless.[94] In this particular context these neo-Carolingian norms of rulership had evolved to include the protection of the towns as well the displays of violence demanded by the ruler's knighthood.

All three of the normative frameworks visible in this text derived from the same basic principle, namely that individuals or groups were entitled, and sometimes even required, to use violence to assert or protect their rights as they understood them and to avenge injury or insult. Throughout our journey so far we have seen magnates and their followings act according to these imperatives. God and his saints did so as well, and it is from this understanding of the divine that Charlemagne had derived his view of his duties and powers; he was God's representative and was responsible for acting on God's behalf to uphold God's interests and view of right order. The Flemish towns in the crisis of 1127–8 asserted their rights to wield violence as collectives to assert and defend their own interests and honor. In Galbert's Flanders, therefore, what we see are three branches from the same normative tree crossing as different groups within Flemish society reworked and reshaped the same basic principle to fit their own needs and interests in response to changing circumstances and new opportunities.

### Notes

1. Adriaan Verhulst, "Economic Organisation", in NCMH II, 481–509; Fossier, "Rural Economy and Country Life".

2. Michael McCormick, *Origins of the European Economy: Communications and Commerce A.D. 300–900* (Cambridge: Cambridge University Press, 2001).

3. See *inter alia* E. Jansen *et al.*, "Paleoclimate", in S. Solomon *et al.*, eds., *Climate Change 2007: The Physical Science Basis. Contribution of Working Group I to the Fourth Assessment Report of the Intergovernmental Panel on Climate Change* (Cambridge: Cambridge University Press, 2007), esp. 468–9, online at **http://www.ipcc.ch/pdf/assessment-report/ar4/wg1/ ar4-wg1-chapter6.pdf**.

4. Peter Johanek, "Merchants, Markets, and Towns", in NCMH III, 64–94; Epstein, *An Economic and Social History*, esp. 10–128.

5. Dunbabin, *France in the Making*, 133–222.

6. David Nicholas, *Medieval Flanders* (London: Longman, 1992), 14–61.

7. *Chronicon*, VI/29, 272–5/Warner, 256–7.

8. Nicholas, *Medieval Flanders*, 49.

9. Ibid., 60–1; Geoffrey Koziol, "Monks, Feuds, and the Making of Peace in Eleventh-Century Flanders", in Head and Landes, eds., *Peace of God*, 239–58.

10. Bisson, *Crisis*, 151–4.

11. Ibid., 151; Nicholas, *Medieval Flanders*, 59.

12. Nicholas, *Medieval Flanders*, 60.

13. Jeff Rider, ed., *Galbertus notarius Brugensis de multro, traditione, et occisione gloriosi Karoli comitis Flandriarum* (Turnhout: Brepols, 1994). English translation: Galbert of Bruges, *The Murder of Charles the Good*, trans. James Bruce Ross (Toronto: University of Toronto Press, 1982). All quotations will be taken from *Murder* unless otherwise noted.

14. For analyses of the crisis of 1127–8 from different perspectives and including other sources see Bisson, *Crisis*, 259–69; Hanna Vollrath, "Probleme um die Landfrieden: Fragen an Geschichte und Rechtsgeschichte", in *Landfrieden: Anspruch und Wirklichkeit*, ed. Arno Buschmann and Elmar Wadle (Paderborn: Ferdinand Schöningh, 2002), 11–29 @21–8.

15. Nicholas, *Medieval Flanders*, 62–70.

16. Jeff Rider, *God's Scribe: The Historiographical Art of Galbert of Bruges* (Washington, DC: The Catholic University of America Press, 2001).

17. *De multro*, c. 1, 5/*Murder*, c. 1, 83.

18. *De multro*, c. 1, 7/*Murder*, c. 1, 83–4.

19. *De multro*, c. 1 and 2, 7/*Murder*, c. 1 and 2, 84; *Murder*, 85 n. 3.

20. *De multro*, c. 6, 15/*Murder*, c. 6, 94.

21. *De multro*, c. 3, 9–11/*Murder*, c. 3, 87–9.

22. *De multro*, c. 1, 5/*Murder*, c. 1, 82.

23. Maurice Keen, *Chivalry* (New Haven: Yale University Press, 1984), 94–7.

24. *De multro*, c. 4, 13/*Murder*, c. 4, 92.

25. Jean Flori, "Knightly Society", in NCMH IV/1, 148–84; Matthew Strickland, *War and Chivalry: The Conduct and Perception of War in England and Normandy, 1066–1217* (Cambridge: Cambridge University Press, 1996), 142–53.

26. This point was suggested to me by John Hudson.

27. *Murder*, 316–17.

28. *De multro*, c. 71, 125–6/*Murder*, c. 71, 238–9.

29. *De multro*, c. 7, 17–19/*Murder*, c. 7, 96–100. On the Erembalds' status see also R.C. Van Caenegem, "Galbert of Bruges on Serfdom, Prosecution of

Crime, and Constitutionalism (1127–28)", in Bernard S. Bachrach and David Nicholas, eds., *Law, Custom, and the Social Fabric in Medieval Europe* (Kalamazoo: Medieval Institute Publications, 1990), 89–112 @93–100.

30. *De multro*, c. 13/33–5/*Murder*, c. 13, 114–16.
31. *De multro*, c. 9, 21–3/*Murder*, c. 9, 102–4.
32. *De multro*, c. 9, 23/*Murder*, c. 9, 104.
33. *De multro*, c. 10, 23–5; *Murder*, c. 10, 105–6.
34. *numquam nisi lites, seditions in hostes et in cives cum rapina et cede ageret*: *De multro*, c. 10, 25. Ross, *Murder*, c. 10, 107 translates this passage to read that Borsiard "would never do anything but fight and feud with his enemies, and pillage and slaughter the people", which in my opinion slightly changes the meaning.
35. *De multro*, c. 10, 25/*Murder*, c. 10, 106–7.
36. *De multro*, c. 10, 25/*Murder*, c. 10, 106.
37. Ibid.
38. *De multro*, c. 7, 17/*Murder* c. 7, 96–7; *De multro*, c. 37, 86/*Murder*, c. 37, 167.
39. *De multro*, Prol., 5; *Murder*, Introduction, 81; *De multro*, c. 6, 17; *Murder*, c. 6, 95.
40. *De multro*, c. 11, 25–9 and c. 10, 25/*Murder*, c. 11, 108–11 and c. 10, 106.
41. *De multro*, c. 12, 29–31/*Murder*, c. 12, 111–12 and *De multro*, c. 15, 35–7/*Murder*, c. 15, 118–19.
42. *De multro*, c. 17, 43/*Murder* c. 17, 126. See also *De multro*, c. 12, 29/*Murder*, c. 12, 112 and *De multro* c. 41, 91/*Murder* c. 41, 176.
43. *De multro*, c. 16, 37/*Murder*, c. 16, 120.
44. *De multro*, c. 16, 39/*Murder*, c. 16, 121–2.
45. *De multro*, c. 16, 39/*Murder*, c. 16, 122.
46. *De multro*, c. 17, 43/*Murder*, c. 17, 126–7.
47. *Murder*, 120 n. 1.
48. *De multro*, c. 20, 49/*Murder*, c. 20, 132–3.
49. *De multro*, c. 24, 59/*Murder*, c. 24, 143.
50. *De multro*, c. 14, 35/*Murder*, c. 14, 117.
51. *De multro*, c. 26, 63/*Murder*, c. 26, 147.
52. *De multro*, c. 27–8, 65–9/*Murder*, c. 27–8, 149–53.
53. *De multro*, c. 29, 69–71/*Murder*, c. 29, 154.
54. *De multro*, c. 41, 90–1/*Murder*, c. 41, 175.
55. Cf. Strickland, *War and Chivalry*, 153–82, 330–40.
56. *De multro*, c. 79, 131/*Murder*, c. 79, 248 and *De multro*, c. 116, 162/*Murder*, c. 116, 302–3. Cf. *De multro*, c. 4, 13/*Murder*, c. 4, 92.
57. Cf. Strickland, *War and Chivalry*, 98–125.
58. See *inter alia De multro*, c. 93, 141, c. 94, 141, c. 95, 142–53/*Murder*, c. 93, 265–6; c. 94, 266–7; c. 95, 267–70.
59. *De multro*, c. 119, 166/*Murder*, c. 119, 307.
60. *De multro*, c. 121, 168/*Murder*, c. 121, 311.
61. *De multro*, c. 58, 109–10/*Murder*, c. 58, 212–13.
62. *De multro*, c. 27, 67 and c. 28, 67/*Murder*, c. 27, 150 and c. 28, 151.

63. *De multro*, c. 31, 75/*Murder*, c. 31, 157–9.
64. Cf. Bisson, *Crisis*, 265.
65. *De multro*, c. 21, 51/*Murder*, c. 21, 135.
66. *De multro*, c. 22, 53–5/*Murder*, c. 22, 137–40.
67. *De multro*, c. 33, 77–9/*Murder*, c. 3, 160–1.
68. *De multro*, c. 43, 92–3/*Murder*, c. 43, 178–9.
69. *De multro*, c. 55, 104/*Murder*, c. 55, 203–4.
70. *De multro*, c. 55, 105/*Murder*, c. 55, 204–6 and 203 n. 8.
71. *De multro*, c. 66, 118–19/*Murder*, c. 66, 227–30.
72. *Murder*, 203 n. 8; Nicholas, *Medieval Flanders*, 64–6.
73. *De multro*, c. 93, 141/*Murder*, c. 93, 265–6.
74. *De multro*, c. 88, 138/*Murder*, c. 88, 260.
75. *De multro*, c. 94, 141/*Murder*, c. 94, 266–7.
76. *De multro*, c. 95, 142/*Murder*, c. 95, 267.
77. See esp. *De multro*, c. 95, 142–3/*Murder*, c. 95, 267–71.
78. Here I must disagree with Bisson, *Crisis*, 262 that the Brugers were uniformly aggrieved by the count's murder.
79. *De multro*, c. 36, 83/*Murder*, c. 36, 165.
80. *De multro*, c. 45, 95/*Murder*, c. 45, 182.
81. *De multro*, c. 75, 128/*Murder*, c. 75, 244.
82. *De multro*, c. 45, 95/*Murder*, c. 45, 182.
83. *De multro*, c. 45, 96/*Murder*, c. 45, 184.
84. See *De multro*, c. 45, 95–6 and c. 113, 158/*Murder*, c. 45, 182–5 and c. 13, 295–6.
85. *De multro*, c. 113, 158/*Murder*, c. 113, 295–6.
86. *De multro*, c. 1 and c. 2, 7/*Murder*, c. 1, 84 and c. 2, 84–5.
87. *De multro*, c. 2, 63/*Murder*, c. 26, 147.
88. *De multro*, c. 54, 103/*Murder*, c. 54, 200.
89. *De multro*, c. 89, 139/*Murder*, c. 89, 262.
90. *De multro*, c. 69, 122, c. 70, 122–3, c. 71, 125–6, c. 75, 127–8/*Murder*, c. 69, 237, c. 70, 237–8, c. 71, 238–40, and c. 75, 243.
91. *De multro*, c. 116, 163 and c. 121, 168–9/*Murder*, c. 116, 303–4 and c. 121, 310–12.
92. Bisson, *Crisis*, 142–3; cf. Geoffrey Koziol, "Baldwin VII of Flanders and the Toll of Saint-Vaast (1111): Judgment as Ritual", in Brown and Górecki, eds., *Conflict*, 151–61.
93. Koziol, *Begging Pardon and Favor*, 139, 143 n. 23, 150–1, 155, 168.
94. Cf. ibid., 109, 218–19; Vollrath, "Probleme um die Landfrieden", 26.

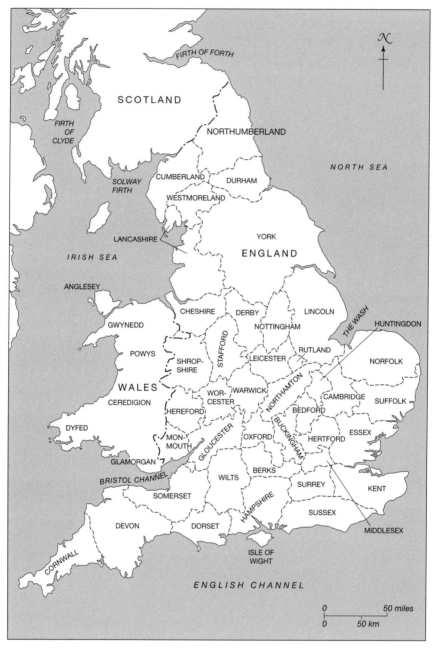

**Map 6**  The English counties (From R.V. Turner, *King John* (Longman, 1994))

## chapter seven

# VIOLENCE AND THE LAW IN ENGLAND

Another symptom of the economic, social, and political transformations that we explored in the previous chapter was the development
of the so-called "learned law", that is, written, codified, and rationally
organized bodies of norms that were studied and taught in law schools
by legal scholars and that came to possess their own logic, rules, and
vocabulary.[1] In the course of the later eleventh and twelfth centuries,
princes from kings downward, as well as lesser lords, found themselves
facing an increasingly complex and monetarized economy. With the new
opportunities for wealth came a need for more sophisticated and consistent regulation of things such as sales, loans, and contracts – a need
also felt by merchants. Competition for power likewise fueled a demand
for law, as princes, seeking to justify and regulate their positions vis à vis
their magnates and townsmen, looked for legal authorities to justify and
regulate their rights and powers.

At just this historical moment a legal voice from the Roman past began
to speak to these needs. By no coincidence, in the later eleventh century
manuscripts of parts of the sixth-century Roman emperor Justinian's *Corpus
Iuris Civilis*, or "Body of Civil Law", began to surface in Italy.[2] The *Corpus
Iuris Civilis* had been brought to Italy in late antiquity. However, in the
early Middle Ages its constituent texts had languished forgotten in
monastery and church archives, until conditions changed in ways that made
them useful again. As the *Corpus Iuris Civilis* was gradually resurrected
and copied, people looking for useful legal principles and procedures found
themselves confronted by a massive and highly articulated body of legal
texts that stemmed from a vanished and alien society, but that nevertheless appeared to address the needs of their own time. The Justinianic
*Corpus* appealed not only to notaries and advocates but also to rulers,
because – assuming as it did an all-powerful emperor with authority over
both secular and ecclesiastical affairs – it provided a legal basis for their
claims to authority that came clothed in the aura of imperial Rome.

By the turn of the twelfth century law students were congregating above all in Bologna to study Justinian with masters. They learned how to reinterpret parts of the *Corpus* so that they spoke to contemporary conditions and concerns. They were helped along by commentaries written by the great doctors of law in and around the text of the *Corpus* itself – the so-called "glosses" that led to their authors being called the "glossators". From Bologna and other early law schools, law students then fanned out across Europe, finding ready employment for their technical legal training at courts or schools and bringing the terminology and logic of the re-interpreted Roman law with them.

A similar development took place in the sphere of canon law.[3] Although there had been efforts to produce useful collections of canon law as early as the Carolingian period (our acquaintance Bishop Burchard of Worms had produced an important one during the first decades of the eleventh century), the canons were in general too widely scattered, incoherently collected, and internally contradictory to meet the legal demands of a Church that, like the secular polities in which it was embedded, was evolving along with its economic and political environment. The need for a rational Church law was made especially acute by the great surge in the ambitions and power of the Roman papacy that began in the later eleventh century, and that in the course of the twelfth transformed the western Church into a hierarchically organized, bureaucratic, and centralized institution focused on Rome.

As a consequence, and spurred by the example of Roman law, Church lawyers began producing better organized and internally consistent collections of canon law. The first great milestone in this process was reached by an Italian monk named Gratian in 1140. Gratian's *Concord of Discordant Canons* (or *Decretum*, as it came to be called from its assembly of papal decretals) was not intended at first to be any more than a private legal handbook. But Gratian's comprehensive effort to systematize and rationally order the canons and to iron out their contradictions proved to be so useful that the *Decretum* quickly became the standard canon law text of the age.

The boundaries between what we think of as "Church" and "State" were still so fluid in this period that law students found it useful to study both Roman and canon law. Armed with their glossed texts and commentaries on Justinian, and the soon equally profuse glosses and commentaries on Gratian and his successors, these students, qualified *in utroque iure* ("in both laws"), took positions as bureaucrats and advisors throughout Europe in both secular and ecclesiastical courts. By the middle of the thirteenth century, some lawyers were treating Roman and canon law together as a *ius commune*, that is, as a "common law" providing a normative frame of reference for all who lived in western Christendom.

Law in Europe was thus beginning to have an existence of its own as an academic discipline for the first time since the end of Roman rule in the West. Those trained in law thought increasingly in terms of the law's own logic and language, whether or not it coincided with the norms according to which the people around them processed and acted on their world. And what the learned lawyers said and did influenced the norms and practice of violence, in different ways in different places.

In this chapter, we will look at the impact of laws and judicial systems on the norms and practice of violence not on the continent, but rather in England. England in the twelfth and thirteenth centuries saw the birth of a homegrown common law whose midwives were the early kings of the house of Anjou, otherwise known as the Angevins. This royal law, and the judicial institutions that went with it, reflected familiar neo-Carolingian impulses on the part of kings to turn their duty to maintain order on God's behalf into wide-ranging claims to regulate violence. The ways that these impulses found their concrete expression in Angevin England were influenced by the example, language, and logic of the two continental learned laws. By the thirteenth century, the English *ius commune* was on its way to becoming a third learned law with its own specialist judiciary and legal scholarship.

Equally important, however – and the main reason I have chosen to focus on England here – is what happened when royal initiatives ran into the far older norms of violence followed by most of the English population. Recent scholarship on the early English common law has shown with exemplary clarity how legal innovations promoted by kings presented ordinary men and women with new challenges and opportunities, and how the choices made by these men and women in response shaped how royal law itself developed. This scholarship enables us, therefore, to see three threads cross, namely royal ambitions, the legal culture of the continental law schools, and the ancient norms of personal violence, and watch as their meeting transformed English social practice, the English kingship, and English law.

## The Past of English Law

It is a commonplace among scholars of English history that England enjoyed a precocious tradition of strong royal authority reaching back deep into the Anglo-Saxon past. Royal claims to power surged especially from the reign of Alfred the Great of Wessex (r. c. 885–99), whose successful defense of his own kingdom against the Danes and the counter-offensives that followed set the stage for the eventual creation of a unified English kingship.[4] Nevertheless, even the strongest of the Anglo-Saxon kings could do no more than influence, rather than control, a culture that clung tightly to the personal right to violence.[5] The kings justified their intervention in violent conflicts along Carolingian-style lines, that is, by presenting themselves as God's representatives who were responsible for the proper order of the Christian society entrusted to their care.[6] Their efforts differed from those of Charlemagne, however, in that they did not try to banish violent self-help completely, but rather to regulate it and make themselves important to it.

Royal claims to regulate violence were broadcast by the law codes issued in the names of successive kings.[7] The laws of Alfred, for example, extended the king's protection to certain sanctuary sites, especially churches and monasteries; they also regulated church sanctuary rights (literally the churches' "peace" or *frið*) by mandating how long sanctuary-seekers could remain safe from attack.[8] Violent offenses against the king himself were to be met with the death penalty; offenses against royal officials or against royal protection brought punitive fines (*wite*) much like the old Carolingian *bannum*.[9] Enmities not involving the king were to be settled if at all possible without violence. A man with a grievance had to give his opponent a chance to surrender before attacking. Should he lack the power to compel his opponent's surrender, he was to appeal for help to the local ealdorman, or, should the ealdorman refuse aid, to the king himself. Only if his opponent refused to surrender and give up his weapons could he fight.[10] The laws of Edmund I (r. 939–46) gave royal sanction to the kindred that refused to support a killer from among its own ranks.[11] As long as the slayer's kin refrained from helping the slayer in any way, they were to be immune from attack by the victim's relatives; the killer had to face the violence (*faeþe*) of his victim's kin alone. Should a member of the victim's kin nevertheless take vengeance on someone other than the actual slayer, he would incur the enmity of the king himself and his friends. Edmund's laws also encouraged non-violent settlements. Before a slayer could come to the royal court, he had to pay compensation and undergo ecclesiastical penance.[12] Once a slayer had pledged to pay wergeld, and given a surety, the settlement process came under the king's *mund* or personal protection.[13] In other words, any act of violence taking place after that point would be treated as an offense against the king himself.

It is in the laws of King Aethelred (r. 978–1016), that we first see explicit mention of so-called "bootless" (*bótléas*) offenses, that is, wrongs that were so serious that they could not be made good by compensation (*bót* = good or remedy).[14] These wrongs brought death. The guilty could be slain by anyone, not just kings or their officials, but only the king could remit the death penalty for bootless offenses. Aethelred made bootless a breach of the king's protection (*grið*) extended to a person or a religious institution, as well as homicides committed in churches.[15] In the latter case, he declared in 1014, all friends of God became the enemies of the slayer, unless he managed to reach such an important sanctuary that the king was persuaded to spare his life for the sanctuary's sake. Under the Danish king of the English Cnut (r. 1016–35),[16] the list of bootless offenses was extended to include assaults upon houses, arson, treachery to one's lord, manifest theft, and clearly evident murder (*æbere morð*).[17] *Morð* was different from homicide (*mannslege*).[18] It denoted a slaying so heinous that it could not be compensated, and especially one that involved betrayal or treachery. It thus meant something slightly different than the Frankish *morther*, which the Malberg glosses to the Salic Law used to denote a secret or hidden killing. *Morð* was bootless well before Cnut had it made so in writing.[19]

In their specific arenas, these bootless cases took wrongs and made them injuries to king and God. They were, therefore, similar to the cases that had fallen under the old Carolingian *bannum*. But by claiming special rights over only a small subset of cases, the Anglo-Saxon kings implicitly recognized and legitimated the right to seek violent redress for wrongs that fell outside of their purview. They integrated themselves into customary responses to wrong by regulating them and by making themselves important factors in them. At the same time as they were reshaping these customary practices, however, they were participating in and legitimizing the wider culture of conflict of which they were a part.

The relationship between royal authority and the local practice of violence began to change after the Norman conquest of England in 1066, but only slowly. With the conquest came an almost complete displacement of the old English aristocracy in favor of William's Norman supporters.[20] The culture of violence that these Norman magnates brought with them did not differ appreciably from that of the natives; they prosecuted many of their disputes with violence just as they had on the continent.[21] Nevertheless, the conquest does provide us with one example of a shift in how a particular kind of violence was understood. As noted above, *morð* to the Anglo-Saxons had meant a particularly heinous and especially a treacherous killing. To the Franks, whose culture the Normans absorbed, *morther* had meant a secret or hidden killing, i.e., one for which the killer had tried to avoid responsibility. After the Norman Conquest, the idea of murder in England changed accordingly. William instituted, or more probably revived, what came to be called the *murdrum* fine. The new king declared that the men who had come with him were under his personal peace and protection. Should one of them be killed, and the slayer's lord could not produce the guilty party, then the lord himself had to pay the fine. Should the lord's property not suffice, then the entire population of the village or hundred in which the killing had taken place had to pay.[22] Bruce O'Brien has argued that the fine was most likely originally levied by Cnut to protect his Danes, who were under his personal peace (*grið*). An attack on the king's men was by definition treachery, and therefore qualified as *morð* (though for political reasons, Cnut mandated a steep fine rather than death). When William revived the fine, he may have understood it in the same way.[23] Nevertheless, the *murdrum* fine came to be understood in line with the Norman/Frankish understanding of murder. A twelfth-century Latin translation of the passage from Cnut's laws noted above renders *morð* as *mortificatura*, with the explanation, "namely, a secret killing" (*scilicet clancula occisio*).[24] In the later part of the century, Richard FitzNigel, in his famous dialogue on the workings of the royal exchequer, defined *murdrum* as "the concealed death of a man at the hands of an unknown slayer"; the *murdrum* fine, he says, was originally levied for the hidden or secret slaying of a Norman.[25]

An important step in the transformation of English legal culture came with the accession of William the Conqueror's son Henry I to the English throne in 1100. Henry (r. 1100–35) did not exactly come to power in a peaceful fashion. He usurped the rights of his eldest brother Robert, and as a result he had to fight for his throne. Once in power, he had to establish his authority over his subjects. He took an ideological tack similar to that taken by Count Charles the Good of Flanders at roughly the same time; he based his claims to authority on his royal responsibility to keep the peace. In a charter issued after his coronation, Henry declared his intent to establish his firm peace throughout the kingdom and proclaimed himself as the guarantor of the freedom and rights of the Church (while at the same time offering incentives for support by lifting what he called "bad customs" and pardoning *murdra* fines incurred before he had ascended the throne).[26] The "peace" he proclaimed embraced the ancient grants of peace and protection (*mund, frið,* or *grið*) that had been given or guaranteed by Henry's Anglo-Saxon predecessors. At the same time, it evoked the more general protection of the Church, its rights, and the defenseless associated with the continental Peace and Truce councils, in which Henry's father William had participated and which Henry himself as duke of Normandy continued to sponsor in a way similar to other continental princes.[27]

The so-called Laws of Henry I (*Leges Henrici Primi*) highlight the king's role in upholding and regulating the peace. Written between 1114 and 1118, most likely by an Anglo-Norman cleric with experience in royal justice, this text is not a compilation of Henry I's statutes, but rather a royalist legal treatise designed to link Anglo-Norman authority with the Anglo-Saxon royal past.[28] As part of his mission, its author notes acts of violence subject to the king's jurisdiction; these resemble the bootless offenses of Henry's Anglo-Saxon predecessors. They include breach) of the king's personal peace or protection, offenses against the king's person or household (such as homicide or injury), offenses against royal authority or dignity (such as insult to the king), and various serious offenses against persons or property (such as housebreaking or robbery).[29] In other respects, however, the author of the *Leges Henrici Primi* presents the king as a regulator of violent vengeance, not as its sole purveyor. In many cases outside the king's concern he still recognizes the right of aggrieved parties to act on their own.[30]

Henry I had to work with an ancient and complex landscape of judicial institutions.[31] Courts for the regional districts known as shires (treated by the Normans as equivalent to the county) sat atop judicial gatherings for local districts: the hundred courts or Danish *wapentakes*.[32] Alongside these, and frequently penetrating their jurisdictions, were the lords' or seigneurial courts. These courts stemmed from the long-standing rights wielded by lords (including some churches and monasteries) over their households and unfree dependants. Depending on the energy and ambition of individual lords, their reach could be extended to cover all offenses committed on a lord's land, or over all of a lord's dependants. A lord's judicial authority could also be supplemented in individual cases by specific ancient rights of jurisdiction, such as "infangthief", i.e., the right to try and punish a thief caught within a lord's possessions. In addition, a separate system of ecclesiastical courts was developing, as it was throughout Europe, as part and parcel of the great Gregorian reform of the Church that had begun in the middle of the eleventh century. Emerging in England after the Norman conquest, these Church courts were formally distinct from the secular courts; they had their own procedures and their own personnel. They had jurisdiction over all clerics, but also over laypeople in matters in which ecclesiastics thought they had an interest, such as marriage, legitimacy of children, or some cases of lay sin. Despite their formal separation, however, the ecclesiastical courts were intimately connected to the wider world of conflict in which they were embedded. Disputes frequently moved between secular and ecclesiastical courts as people weighed their options and cast their claims to get them into the most advantageous court, as secular and ecclesiastical officials cooperated with each other in cases in which they both had an interest, etc.

It is no contradiction to find such a diverse system of courts alongside a social practice still conducive to violent vengeance. The appeal to a lord's court for redress of a wrong is only a formalization of an appeal to one's lord for help; making an appeal to a hundred or shire court is but a formalization of the appeal for help to one's kin and neighbors. As we have seen repeatedly on the continent, resort to courts could form one stage in lengthy dispute processes that also included more informal appeals, negotiation, and direct violent action.[33] In England, the sheer variety of court options may in fact have encouraged English men and women to use them as they sought the forum that would be most useful for their purposes and sympathetic to their interests.[34]

The courts described above could on occasion be supplemented or superseded by courts attended or summoned by royal representatives, especially for serious cases such as those described by the *Leges Henrici Primi*. On the whole, however, English courts in the Anglo-Norman period were dominated by and operated generally in the interests of the locally powerful. Everyone involved in them still acted according to an undifferentiated idea of wrong; neither plaintiffs, victims, nor judges made any distinction between what we would call "civil" and "criminal", or "public" and "private" matters. The king was a factor insofar as he had laid claim to jurisdiction over certain kinds of cases; in these cases, therefore, he or his officials figured among those powerful people to whom disputants could appeal for help and thus draw into the dispute.

As English men and women chose what paths to follow to gain redress for their grievances, they made their choices based on their aims, their resources, the size and resources of the support-group they were able to muster, and the risks they were willing to take.[35] In private or in public, they (or those recording their cases in writing) shaped their accusations and appeals in a flexible language that nevertheless provided the seeds for a more precise legal vocabulary. The Latin term *iniuria*, or injury, covered virtually all wrongs. The Latin word *crimen* (Old French *crime* or *crimne*) was also used.[36] Its semantic field was, however, much more flexible and extensive than that of the modern word crime. *Crimen* was not restricted to any particular category of acts; if it leaned in a particular direction it was towards the idea of sin.[37] Trespass and felony also appear as terms for wrong. They are at this point virtually indistinguishable. The Old French *trespass* simply denoted transgression, as in crossing some sort of line; it covered any offense, wrong, or sin. The Old French *felonie* was also used for wickedness, villainy, or sin. It did, however, have a particular connotation of treachery or disloyalty, which would shape how it developed.[38]

## *The Angevin Reforms*

All of the behaviors, tactics, resources, and words described above formed the materials out of which the English common law and its particular attitudes towards violence developed. The catalyst was provided once again by particular changes in context, namely the civil war in England that followed the death of Henry I. Henry had designated his daughter Matilda, widow of the German Emperor Henry V, heir to the English throne. However, when Henry died in 1135 Matilda was pushed aside by Stephen of Blois, a grandson of William the Conqueror in the female line. Stephen reigned peacefully for a few years, but by 1139 he had alienated enough people that Matilda could launch a revolt against him. The resulting war raged for over a decade. Finally, in 1153, King Stephen agreed to a treaty, according to which he retained his throne but designated as his heir the young Henry, son of Matilda and her second husband Geoffrey Plantagenet, Count of Anjou. Henry ascended the throne as Henry II the following year.[39]

The civil war left Henry II with a number of serious headaches. Stephen and Matilda had had to bargain for support in men and castles from an aristocracy that was on the whole motivated less by loyalty and idealism and more by the thought of wringing whatever advantage they could out of the situation. As a consequence, royal authority and prestige had dwindled. Moreover, land titles throughout England had fallen into confusion as each side confiscated land from the supporters of the other and distributed it among its own followers. Magnates from barons downward had taken advantage of royal weakness to assert whatever direct control they did not already enjoy over local institutions, especially the courts. Unwilling to trust the courts and having no reliable king to whom they could appeal, people involved in disputes turned more frequently to direct action, that is, violence, to assert or protect their claims to property. Many people at the level of knight and below also took advantage of the situation to rob and plunder simply because no one could or would stop them.[40]

When Henry II became king, therefore, he had to assert his own authority, and the authority of the kingship, in an unstable political landscape dominated by independent-minded magnates who had firm control of local courts. His opportunity lay in the vast sea of unresolved disputes. There was a ready market for royal authority among that segment of the population that had grievances and could see no recourse in local courts. Henry therefore offered justice. He did not try to replace or override the local courts, however. Instead, he made himself available as an alternative through his judicial representatives.

Hints of Henry's tactics are visible in a document issued at a council held at Clarendon in 1164, the so-called Constitutions of Clarendon.[41] The Constitutions were designed to set limits on the independence of clergymen and church courts, an independence that had developed under the pressure of papal reforms and had only grown during the power vacuum of the civil war. The interesting articles for our purposes are six and nine. The first deals with the case of laymen who were suspected of an offense subject to a church court but who were too powerful for individuals to accuse; the second handles the case that a layperson and a cleric were disputing over property that the cleric wanted treated as free church property (free alms) but that the layperson argued was under the authority of a lay lord (lay fee). The two clauses ordered panels of "twelve lawful men" from the neighborhood, in the first case to accuse the suspect and in the second to decide the status of the land. In article nine the decision of the panel was to be rendered in the presence of the king's chief justice. The Constitutions of Clarendon thus empowered panels of people not directly involved in a dispute to intervene in that dispute under the king's watchful eye.

Two years later, Henry issued the so-called Assize of Clarendon.[42] "By the counsel of all his barons", the king ordained that "for the preservation of peace and the enforcement of justice", twelve "of the more lawful men" of every hundred, and four from each village, should be put on oath to tell whether there was anyone in their hundred or village who had been accused or was publicly known as a "robber or murderer (*murdrator*) or thief", or whether anyone was known to have received robbers or murderers or thieves, since Henry took the throne. The panels were to be interrogated by royal justices and sheriffs. Anyone whom the panel accused was to be seized and forced to clear himself if he could by the ordeal of water. Jurisdiction over all those who could not clear themselves was reserved for the king and his justices. No one was to prevent sheriffs from convening these panels of inquiry, or from going wherever they wished to seize accused persons. Nor were the sheriffs to be prevented from taking accused persons who had not been able to clear themselves and producing them at the courts of itinerant royal justices when the justices arrived in their areas.[43]

It is to this set of decrees that students of the English common law trace the origins of the grand jury, that is, a group of local men empowered and ordered by the king to indict, or present (hence the noun: presentment), serious wrongdoers without anyone having to step forward themselves and make an appeal. The specific wrongs concerned were theft, robbery, and murder (i.e., a secret killing); Henry classified these cases as belonging to him alone. This opened an important door. There were lots of notorious wrongdoers around. Many of them were far too powerful for those they had wronged to make an appeal against them, especially in the local courts that they were likely to be able to control or at least influence. The Assize of Clarendon made it possible for the less powerful to feed accusations to royal justices without having to make themselves known to their powerful local oppressors.[44] Henry promptly backed up his words with deeds. Between 1168 and 1170 itinerant justices – that is, justices in "eyre" holding their "eyre" courts (from the Latin *in itinere* = on a journey) – fanned out across the kingdom.[45]

This robust assertion of royal authority may well have helped provoke the rebellion against Henry II that coalesced around his son Henry "the young king" and that lasted from 1173 to 1174.[46] Not only did the Assize of Clarendon strike at the heart of entrenched local interests; nobles of a more idealistic bent may have wanted to fight what looked like an attempt to undermine the ancient right of an accused to face off against his or her accuser.[47] Henry II emerged from the rebellion the victor. From then on he was in a virtually unassailable position in England. Two years later, he renewed and sharpened the provisions of the Assize of Clarendon with the Assize of Northampton (1176).[48] This assize extended the list of offenses reserved for the royal justices to include arson, as well as counterfeiting or forgery. Equally interesting is the fact that these offenses were now being called "felonies", most likely because by committing them, offenders had offended against – and were therefore being disloyal to – the king.[49] That same year, Henry II appointed eighteen judges to travel in six judicial circuits. From then on, the justices in eyre were a permanent feature of the English judicial landscape, although the number and the duration of their circuits was uneven.

It is worth asking why Henry II did not meet with more resistance to all this, and why anyone bothered to pay attention to his decrees. It certainly helped that after the rebellion of 1173–4, Henry looked like the winning horse, and that he was able to issue his decrees with the participation and consent of the greatest barons of the realm both lay and ecclesiastical. It is also possible that since he introduced his changes gradually, their ultimate scope was hard for potential opponents to see in advance. Some local magnates may have decided that Henry's assizes served their interests; while presentment, juries, and the eyre courts may have harmed them as local lords, the new institutions and procedures may well have helped them deal with their own lords.[50]

The most plausible explanation for the lack of resistance to Henry's reforms, however, is the fact that local magnates found them easy to undermine and to manipulate.[51] Henry's sheriffs could convene their grand juries, but they could not separate them from their local environments.

Local lords were perfectly able to control who served on the panels, that is, to determine who were counted among the "more lawful men" of the hundred or village. The locally powerful were also well able to pressure local juries to indict their enemies and look away from their own offenses. Grand juries therefore "probably picked mostly on the defenseless and the enemies of the rich and powerful".[52] Already after the first eyre courts of 1166, Henry had to order a judicial commission, the Inquest of Sheriffs, to investigate whether indictments had been either lodged or suppressed for motives, such as fear or hatred, friendship, or direct payment, that could reflect undue outside influence on the juries.[53]

Even when they were not being influenced by the locally powerful, local grand juries (and occasionally even royal justices) sometimes ignored the king's norms and followed those of the local community.[54] According to a record from an eyre court held in Lincoln in 1202, one Alan Hayward captured Thomas fitzLefwin on the road and took him to his house. There Thomas was robbed and beaten so badly that a bone was broken in his arm. Next, Alan held Thomas down while his wife Emma cut off one of Thomas's testicles and a friend cut off the other. The battered and mutilated Thomas was then taken back to the road where he had been captured and left there in full public view.[55] No one contested the facts of this affair. When the case came before the Lincoln eyre court, the justices were able to confirm the story, to the point of visiting Alan Hayward's house and finding a knife and testicle bowl. Nevertheless, they threw out Thomas's appeal and even fined him, while declaring Alan quit of all charges. Apparently Thomas had done something – perhaps, given the form of his mutilation, something sexual to a member of Alan's household – that prompted the entire local community and the eyre justices to decide that he had gotten what he deserved, and that the violent and patently symbolic response by Alan and his wife had been justified.

### Violence and the Common Law

If Henry II and his advisors did not succeed in imposing a downward royal justice on what were becoming known as felonies in the way that they had intended, their efforts nevertheless had a profound and probably unintended impact on the local practice of violence. Simply by existing, the grand juries and the eyre courts changed people's disputing strategies. People involved in conflict with each other found that they could use royal norms and institutions to achieve the very old end of taking vengeance for wrong.

For time out of mind, if one had been unable to handle an opponent alone, one had appealed for help to those in one's support group, i.e., kin, friends, lord, the local church or monastery, etc. The king too had figured among the possible sources of aid, if one could get to him and convince him that his interests were involved. The grand juries and the ⎫ eyre courts dramatically widened and regularized people's access to the king. One just had to get one's case heard at an eyre court rather than at the local shire or hundred court. If one's opponent had committed an offense that would automatically fall under the purview of an eyre court (and if one could count on the grand jury to actually testify to this effect) then there was no problem. If not, however, that is, if one's ⎬ case fell within the broader range of minor injuries, quarrels, insults, or petty theft that remained a matter for local authorities and that were still covered by the term "trespass" (or if one could not count on the grand jury to indict one's opponent), one had to get it into the eyre court by spinning or enhancing it somehow so that it became a matter for the king's justice. In other words, one had to come up with an appeal of felony. Hence the development, for example, of the charge that one's opponent had acted *vi et armis*, that is, with force and arms; this accusation turned an offense into a breach of the king's peace, regardless of whether it was on its face a felony or a trespass and regardless of whether it had really happened that way or not. If one saw trouble coming in advance, one could also get a special, specific grant of the king's peace, in the form of a writ from a royal official such as a justice or sheriff. Such a writ automatically turned an attack on its bearer into a felony.[56]

In other words, people found that they could use the courts to get at their enemies under the cover of royal justice, in a variety of ways and for a variety of purposes. A classic example from the early thirteenth century is that of one Thomas of Eldersfield. This affair, which Paul Hyams has discussed at length, is described in the Life of St. Wulfstan, bishop of Worcester, written by a Worcester monk in the 1230s. The law case at the heart of the story is also recorded on a royal plea roll.[57] Thomas was the son of a minor freeholder who, in search of the patronage and employment necessary to gain a freehold of his own, ended up in the household of Geoffrey Fitz Peter, chief justiciar of England. Thomas worked hard, and within a few years had saved the money he needed to settle down at Eldersfield in Worcestershire. Thomas must have been a handsome young man, because he caught the attention of the wife of the lord of nearby Northway manor. An affair soon developed that lasted for two years, until a priest to whom Thomas confessed told him to break off the affair and do penance.

Thomas complied, but the lady of Northway was undeterred; she repeatedly tried to restart the affair. When her husband died, she proposed marriage. Although the match would have given Thomas a considerable leg up the social and economic ladder, he refused. The adage about hell, fury, and a scorned woman then became for him a bitter reality. The lady of Northway's love turned to hatred, a hatred which she nursed until she found another man to marry. Her new husband, George, learned about the affair and came to share (for his own reasons, no doubt) his wife's hatred. But he too bided his time. Meanwhile, the couple interacted with Thomas as if nothing were wrong.

On Whitsunday (Pentecost Sunday) of 1217, George and Thomas got drunk together at a tavern that lay across a river from Eldersfield, in neighboring Gloucestershire. On their way home, alcohol overcame George's inhibitions, and his hatred of Thomas erupted. Without warning, he clubbed Thomas on the head with his heavy stick. Thomas, in good Christian fashion, refused at first to retaliate. He told George that he would consider the attack a product of the ale, but that he would resist if George attacked him again. George hit him again. Thomas pulled out a hatchet and faked a thrust at his assailant. Unfortunately, his control was not good; he struck George on the shoulder hard enough to draw some blood.

George promptly ran off, crying out that Thomas had drawn his innocent blood in violation of the king's peace. Reaching his house, he proceeded to raise the hue and cry.[58] When his neighbors had gathered, George claimed that Thomas had broken into his house bent on theft, and that George had received his wound trying to defend it. This, as Hyams notes, "augmented the allegation from simple wounding to the more serious crime of burglary". The story, backed as it was by George's standing and prestige as lord of Northway, was believed.

For his part, Thomas realized what was happening and fled across the shire border to his home in Eldersfield. George was nevertheless able to have him repeatedly arrested; each time Thomas had to call on the influence of the courtiers at his old employer the justiciar's household to get free. In the meantime, George launched an appeal in his shire court. Since the charge was breach of the king's peace, the case waited until the next eyre court convened in Gloucestershire, in this case, four years.

In June of 1221, the eyre court took up George's appeal. It is clear at this point what George was trying to do. His appeal, were it to go through to completion, would go to a judicial duel followed by hanging – and George was athletic and a skilled fighter. Should he win, his own kin would carry out the punishment. The threat of such an outcome might provoke Thomas to settle, but at great cost. Once a case had come before an eyre court, settling out of court brought a fine payable to the king, and Thomas's resources, already reduced by repeatedly having to get himself out of jail, could only have been strained further by having to compensate George. This is very old disputing behavior: the threat of violence and extreme community pressure brought to bear, with either violence or a settlement the outcome. George was simply trying to achieve his ends through the mechanisms and with the authority of the royal court.

Once before the eyre justices, George dropped his charge of burglary but persisted in his claim of wounding in violation of the king's peace. He tried to claim, however, that he was incapable of fighting a duel because he had been maimed by the wound Thomas had given him four years earlier. Had his claim been accepted, Thomas might have been forced to defend himself by undergoing the ordeal of hot iron. The judges were not naïve, however; they refused George's claim. They then gave Thomas his opportunity to deny George's charges, which he did. But at this point George's public relations campaign paid off; the jury, drawn from the locality and certainly acquaintances of the Lord and Lady of Northway, judged Thomas guilty. In other words, they declared that George's appeal was valid.[59] The judges accordingly ordered a judicial duel.

The pair met for their duel in early August. Thomas, conscious of his ultimate guilt in getting involved with the lady of Northway to begin with, begged St. Wulfstan for aid (says the monk of Worcester) and placed his trust in God and the virgin Mary, but to little apparent avail. George threw him to the ground and so injured his right eye that he had to admit defeat. Instead of sentencing Thomas to hang, however, the eyre justices – following a common practice – "mixed mercy with judgment" and sentenced him to castration and blinding.[60] The punishment was carried out, with savage pleasure, by George's kin, in front of a substantial crowd. It is at this point that we learn why this story is told to us in such loving detail in a saint's life. On the point of death from his wounds, according to the monk of Worcester, Thomas continued to pray for help. In response, he received a vision of the Virgin followed by St. Wulfstan. He then recovered his sight and had his testicles restored (though they were smaller than before).

A case recorded in two different collections of miracles attributed to St. Thomas Becket likewise shows someone using legal procedures to take vengeance, this time with the connivance of a local official.[61] Written shortly after the events it purports to describe, the story concerns a peasant named Ailward, who in the early 1170s was owed a penny by his neighbor, who would not pay. The story adds the odd but legally important detail that Ailward was baptized on Whitsunday eve, which according to local belief made him immune both to fire and to sinking in water. By definition, then, he would always pass the ordeal of fire but fail the ordeal of water.[62] One feast day in a tavern, Ailward needed money to buy beer. He therefore asked his neighbor to pay half of the debt, saying that he could pay the other half later. The neighbor refused, claiming a lack of money. The angry Ailward declared his intent to take revenge, got drunk (with what funds the story does not say), and went to his neighbor's house. There he took, as security for the unpaid debt, some of his neighbor's property, including the padlock from the door and a whetstone. Witnessing the break-in, some of the neighbor's children told their father, who rushed off in pursuit of Ailward. Catching up with him, the neighbor wrested the whetstone from Ailward and launched it at his head, "thus breaking the whetstone on his head and his head with the whetstone". The neighbor then cut the prostrate Ailward's arm with a knife, and dragged him back to his house "as a thief, robber, and burglar".[63]

A crowd gathered, including the local reeve (an official who worked for the local lord). The reeve suggested that they make the theft look more serious by adding more property to it. The wounded Ailward and the augmented stash were then taken to the sheriff. Ailward was held in custody until he could be taken to the next meeting of the royal judges. There Ailward denied being a thief, saying he had only taken enough property to serve as security for the unpaid debt. He asked either to fight a duel with his accuser or undergo the ordeal of fire. The reeve, however (who had apparently been bribed for this purpose), pushed for Ailward to undergo the ordeal of water. The judges agreed, and, sure enough, Ailward's baptism date made a difference; he failed. Ailward was taken away "to the place of execution". There, before a crowd, he had his eyes put out and his testicles cut off; his neighbor himself took part in the mutilation. But, as in the above story, a saint intervened; Ailward's devotion to St. Thomas restored both his sight and his testicles.

A case from 1202, recorded in the plea rolls of Lincolnshire, tells of enmity within a kindred over inheritance being processed in part through the courts.[64] A certain John charged his cousin Andrew with going to the house of John's father Thorold, throwing Thorold and his household out of the house, and treating Thorold so badly that he became ill and died. John also claimed that Andrew had robbed Thorold of four swords, four hatchets, two bows, and fifteen arrows, as well as cloth and all documents pertaining to his inheritance. Andrew denied the charges. He declared instead that Thorold was his uncle and that Thorold was the son of a priest. Thorold's land should, therefore, have come to him (i.e., Andrew). When Thorold began to die, Andrew entered the house that was to come to him without any force whatever.[65] Andrew paid money "to the lord king" (i.e., to the court) to have the case considered more quickly. In addition, he purchased an inquisition "concerning hatred and spite" (*per odium et attiam* [sic]). This kind of investigation (more commonly referred to as the inquisition *de odio et athia*) shows again that the king and his advisors knew full well how some people were using the eyre courts; it was aimed at finding out whether the charge had been brought not for just cause but rather out of hatred or spite.[66] In other words, Andrew wanted the court to determine whether John had brought the case not because it was justified on its face, but because he wanted to hurt Andrew. Finally, Andrew bought a license to reach an agreement out of court. The dispute must indeed have been settled out of court, because the record ends only with the laconic note that both parties had paid the fine to settle.

This case provides us with a couple of interesting bits of information. First, it shows in the list of items purportedly taken from Thorold's house just what kind of arsenal an Englishman at the dawn of the thirteenth century could have. Second, if one believes John, then Andrew employed the threat of the investigation *de odio et athia*, which might not have gone John's way, to pressure John into settling his claim. If one believes Andrew, it shows John handling a bitter grievance with his cousin over inheritance rights by turning his story into something that a royal court would take up. He might have hoped to win and therefore take physical vengeance on Andrew under cover of the court judgment, or he might have hoped to use the threat of judgment to force Andrew to the bargaining table. No matter whom we believe, however, this dispute again shows old impulses being clothed in the forms, procedures, and authority of a royal court.

As the above example indicates, when one resorted to a royal court instead of to violence or the threat of violence, one made the court and its rules resources that one could use for attack, but that one's opponent could also use for defense. Another case recorded in 1202 has a man displaying a virtuoso knowledge of how to do the latter. The case began with a killing; the subdeacon William son of Adam had at some point killed the cousin of William of Nettleham.[67] For this he was deposed from his subdeaconate. A brawl then broke out in Bicker Market, between Adam's sons on the one hand, and on the other William of Nettleham and one Hugh of Wigtoft, who must have been a friend or relative of William of Nettleham. The Nettleham/Wigtoft party came out ahead; William of Nettleham killed the ex-subdeacon William; Hugh of Wigtoft wounded the latter's brother Alan. Weakened and apparently unwilling to resort to further direct action, the Adam clan struck back at their opponents through the courts. Adam himself appealed William of

Nettleham for the death of his son William, on the grounds of a breach of the king's peace. He asked, however, that his son Alan carry out the proof (either through ordeal or duel) because he himself was too old. His son Alan appealed Hugh of Wigtoft on the same grounds but also included a charge of robbery.

Had Adam and Alan succeeded with their appeal, they would have won the right to kill or mutilate their opponents, or at least the chance of pressuring them into a good settlement. William of Nettleham, however, cleverly protected himself on procedural grounds. He pointed out that Alan could not offer proof on his father Adam's behalf because Alan had not taken the required preliminary step of himself appealing William of Nettleham in the local shire court. Alan's legitimate appeal was against Hugh of Wigtoft, and it was still unresolved. He admitted that Adam's lord had launched Adam's appeal in the shire court as was proper, and that the lord had told the court that Alan would take over the appeal should Adam's age prevent him. However, Alan himself had not been present. The justices sided with William of Nettleham; Adam had excused himself from the appeal on account of his age, and Alan had no standing in the case. In response, Alan settled his appeal with Hugh of Wigtoft and agreed to pay the fine for a settlement,[68] then appealed William of Nettleham directly for his brother's death. William of Nettleham again denied the charges on procedural grounds; he had been released from Adam's original appeal in the matter, and Alan himself had not appealed him on this case at the shire court. Alan's dispute had been with Hugh of Wigtoft and Alan had voluntarily allowed the judges to release Hugh. At this point the judges threw up their hands; the case was remanded to the royal court at Westminster.[69]

The threat alone of royal justice could serve as an effective pressure device. Anyone committing an act that an opponent could turn into a matter subject to royal jurisdiction risked an appeal or an indictment by a local jury, followed by hanging or (if the eyre justices were merciful) mutilation. It is no surprise then that people accused of such a wrong, even if the charges were hyped or trumped up, often fled. If they did not flee, the threat of violent punishment that lay at the end of an eyre process prompted many to settle. A witness to this phenomenon is provided by the increasing numbers of "licenses to agree" purchased by disputants from the 1180s onwards; as we have seen above, these licenses allowed disputants to settle out of court, in exchange, of course, for a fee.[70] Out-of-court settlements in Angevin England incorporated the same kind of public, symbolic display and careful balancing of honor and face with substance that we have seen elsewhere.[71] A man facing a kindred angry over the death of one of its members paid for masses for the dead person's soul in exchange for the dropping of charges. Perpetrators were sent off on pilgrimage to get them away from the victim's party and to allow that party the satisfaction of seeing their enemy do public penance. Men accused of homicide underwent public submissions that allowed their enemies the satisfaction of declaring their right to vengeance even though in this instance they did not take it. And, as always, sums of money or pieces of property changed hands, or were given to third parties such as monasteries, as a public display of compensation and satisfaction for wrong. Such acts were couched in language declaring that an enmity had been turned into a positive friendship. Among the knightly class, at least, public submission and the creation (or restoration) of friendship was often expressed in the ritual of homage, where a party with a grievance received formal homage from his opponent or opponents. This seems not to have been done to create formal ties of lordship and vassalage, but rather to advertise in a ritual fashion the former opponents' intent to act henceforward as friends should to their friends.[72] In short, the ancient dance of vengeance with settlement continued, with the royal courts now one of the tools available to help bring about settlement.

The picture offered in the preceding pages is not one in which royal authority over select acts of violence was imposed from above. The eyre courts instead channeled and regulated pre-existing impulses and mechanisms for dealing with wrong.[73] Because of the incentives they offered and the pressures they created, power flowed not from the center to the localities but rather from the localities to the center, as people of all social ranges found the new institutions useful for carrying out old aims.[74] However, recognizing the legitimacy of the royal decrees regulating violence, and of the royal system for enforcing those decrees, put new constraints on people's actions. Anyone tempted to take direct, violent vengeance on an enemy outside of the courts risked an appeal or presentment for homicide followed by hanging or mutilation if the jury and judges did not see things his way. Direct killing became, in a reversal of older attitudes, not a matter for publicity but rather for stealth and secrecy.[75] Open vengeance was taken through court sanctioned execution or mutilation before a crowd. In other words, the old norms of violent vengeance in Angevin England coexisted with and took advantage of the norms projected by Henry II, in which the king's duty to provide peace to his subjects gave him exclusive jurisdiction over violent felonies. The creative use of royal norms and institutions offered those bent on vengeance the opportunity to take revenge with impunity, or at least at reduced risk. But doing so legitimized the royal system, and gradually strengthened its claim that violent vengeance was a matter for the king alone.

## *The Common Law and the Learned Law*

The manifold ways that people accepted and used the distinction between what was not the king's business and what was allowed learned lawyers at court to work out a legal category of offenses that were separate and qualitatively different from other wrongs and whose redress belonged to the king alone. Some of the men surrounding King Henry II in England and his successors had training in school law, and their training shaped the language and procedures of the royal courts.[76] A direct symptom is the formalization and classification of legal procedures and concepts. For example, the inquisition *de odio et athia* reflected the learned law principle that royal justice should not be used to avenge personal grievances. We have already noted the way that felony was coming by the later twelfth century to mean violations of the king's peace, or wrongs that touched closely the royal interest. Felony eventually came to stand in contrast to trespass, which remained to cover all actionable wrongs falling outside the king's purview.[77] Even in these cases, however, an accusation that a trespass was carried out in breach of the king's peace, or by force and arms (*vi et armis*), could turn it into a matter for the royal judges. Ultimately, the lawyers would create from this the separate appeal of trespass to cover matters that fell under the king's purview but that did not constitute felonies.[78] The meaning of the word "crime" began to change in a similar fashion. As noted above, the Roman term *crimen* had served earlier as simply one term of many to describe a wrong. By the end of the twelfth century it was beginning to be used to refer to those particularly serious offenses in which the king had an interest.[79]

At the same time, English law began to be written down in a form that likewise reflected the influence of the law schools. Sometime around 1188, a text was penned titled *Treatise on the Laws and Customs of the Kingdom of England*. The text is commonly attributed to King Henry II's justiciar Ranulf de Glanvill, but its true authorship is still debated.[80] Glanvill reflects the learning of the law schools not so much in the actual substance of what it says about law and procedure, but rather in the way its legal arguments are organized and in some of the words that it uses.[81] The text also reflects the way that law was serving the interests of ambitious rulers; in particular, it advances the rights of the king at the expense of Henry II's *bête noire*, the law of the Roman Church. Glanvill found a ready market; within a few decades of its creation, copies were in the hands of royal justices who used it to help them administer what was already being called an English Common Law on a par with the Roman/canon *ius commune*.

Sometime in the early to mid thirteenth century, Glanvill was followed by the royal judge Henry of Bracton's *On the Laws and Customs of England*.[82] Bracton tried even more so than Glanvill to arrange rationally all of English law. His legal training is clearly visible in the way that he tried to understand English law in terms of the principles and analytical categories of the continental *ius commune*.[83] These principles included the distinction between public and private law and the distinction between civil and criminal offenses. The learned law distinctions could be – and were – made to map onto the homegrown distinctions between offenses that were matters for the king and offenses in which the king had no interest. The increasingly technical use of the term crime to denote especially serious offenses in which the king had an interest eventually led to a distinction being made between crime and trespass, or – to use another Old French term for injury or wrong – between crime and tort.[84] The distinction was firmly entrenched in English jurisprudence by the time of Bracton; for Bracton a crime by definition was a breach of the general peace as opposed to a wrong inflicted on a specific party.

## Conclusions

As royal advisors worked to further their masters' interests and as legal thinkers and judges applied their law school training to the rules that resulted, a language was created in England whereby royal justice became public justice. This language resulted from the reasoned working out, under the influence of the continental learned laws, of the ideals implicit in the neo-Carolingian vision of rulership advanced by Henry II at his coronation. The result was a feedback loop in which royal institutions and academic ideas on the one hand and local disputing strategies on the other symbiotically affected each other.

What the king said, and the institutions he created, mattered. Everyone acknowledged his right to make law and to do justice. Henry II tried to do so by setting up mechanisms through which power could flow downward from the court to localities that were still under the control of the men who had profited from the war between Stephen and Matilda. He got away with it not just because he had ideological legitimacy behind him. For all of Henry II's best efforts, power did not flow from the court to the localities; it flowed rather from the localities to the court. People caught up in disputes with each other, who were used to thinking in terms of old norms of wrong and vengeance, found that they could factor the juries and eyre courts into their strategies.[85] They could take vengeance for or redress wrongs by getting the courts to do so for them, or by using judicial procedures to pressure opponents into settlements. The eyre courts also made it easier for those who were locally weak to gain the king as an ally against those who were strong; the eyres at a stroke brought the king to the localities. Ordinary English men and women were, in other words, still doing the same old things for the same reason, just with the addition of some new tools.

But recognizing the legitimacy of the royal courts and participating in their procedures and rules imposed new constraints on people's actions. A change in the institutional context for violence provoked a gradual shift in the norms surrounding violence, though the underlying drive to take violent vengeance remained the same. Getting the king to carry out one's violent vengeance led to behavior coalescing around the norm that only the king could carry out vengeance, at least in the case of a select but ever growing list of serious wrongs that included homicide, violent robbery or assault, etc. For offenses that fell outside this list, victims either spun their charges to make them matters for the king's attention – including by charging violence when there may well have been none involved – or turned to actions for trespass that led ultimately towards the civil suit for damages. As a consequence, direct violent action was delegitimized, and in most cases became a matter for secrecy and stealth[86] – something that would have been anathema to the old Anglo-Saxons for whom, like the Franks, publicity had been an essential part of using violence to redress a wrong.

## Notes

1. For the following survey see Landau, "The Development of Law"; Susan Reynolds, "Medieval Law", and Magnus Ryan, "Rulers and Justice, 1200–1500", in *The Medieval World*, eds. Peter Linehan and Janet. L. Nelson (London: Routledge, 2001), 485–502 and 503–17; Stein, *Roman Law*, 43–57.
2. Stein, *Roman Law*, 43–4.
3. See Brundage, *Medieval Canon Law*, 5–69.
4. An excellent and readable survey of this period in English history: Richard A. Fletcher, *Bloodfeud: Murder and Revenge in Anglo-Saxon England* (Oxford: Oxford University Press, 2003), 13–57.
5. John Hudson, "Faide, vengeance et violence en Angleterre (c. 900–1200)", in Barthélemy *et al.*, eds., *La Vengeance*, 71–98, and Paul Hyams, "Feud and the State in Late Anglo-Saxon England", *The Journal of British Studies* 40, no. 1 (2001): 1–43. Hyams in particular argues against the "maximalist" view of Anglo-Saxon kingship offered by Patrick Wormald, "Giving God and King their Due: Conflict and its Regulation in the Early English State", in idem, *Legal Culture in the Early Medieval West: Law as Text, Image and Experience* (London: The Hambledon Press, 1999), 333–57, and by James

Campbell, "The Late Anglo-Saxon State: A Maximum View", *Proceedings of the British Academy* 87 (1995): 39–65.

6. See, for example, the prologue to the Laws of Ine (r. 688–94): Felix Liebermann, ed. and trans., *Die Gesetze der Angelsachsen*, 3 vols. (Halle: Niemeyer, 1903–16), vol. 1, 88–9, translated into English in Dorothy Whitelock, ed. *English Historical Documents*, vol. I, c. 500–1042 (London: Eyre Methuen, 1979), 399; the prologue to the second group of laws of Edmund I (r. 939–46): *Gesetze*, 186–7/Whitelock, 428.

7. The essential point of departure for the study of Anglo-Saxon law: Patrick Wormald, *The Making of English Law: King Alfred to the Twelfth Century*. Vol. 1. *Legislation and its Limits* (Oxford: Blackwell, 1999). See also Hudson, "Faide", 352–61; Hyams, *Rancor*, 71–110.

8. Alfred 2 and 5: *Gesetze*, 48–53/Whitelock, 409–10.

9. Alfred 2.1 and 38: *Gesetze*, 48–9/Whitelock, 409 and *Gesetze*, 70–3/Whitelock, 414.

10. Alfred 42: *Gesetze*, 74–7/Whitelock, 415. See Hudson, "Faide", 352–3; Hyams, *Rancor*, 80 and "Feud and the State", 11–13; Wormald, "Giving God and King their Due", 336–7.

11. II Edmund 1: *Gesetze*, 186–9/Whitelock, 428. See Hudson, "Faide", 355, 357–8; Hyams, *Rancor*, 82–4 and "Feud and the State", 14–17; cf. Wormald, "Giving God and King their Due", 337–8.

12. II Edmund 4; two very different interpretations of this provision are offered by Hyams, *Rancor*, 83 and Wormald, *Making of English Law*, 312.

13. II Edmund 7: *Gesetze*, 188–91/Whitelock, 428–9.

14. Bosworth and Toller, s.v. *bót*; Hyams, "Feud and the State", 10–11, 17–18.

15. III Atr 1: *Gesetze*, 228/Whitelock, 439–40; VIII Atr. 1.1: *Gesetze*, 263/Whitelock, 448–9; Hyams, *Rancor*, 84–5.

16. M. K. Lawson, *Cnut: The Danes in England in the Early Eleventh Century* (London: Longman, 1993).

17. II Cn 64: *Gesetze*, 352–3/Whitelock, 464.

18. Bosworth and Toller, s.v. *morð, mannslege*.

19. Bruce R. O'Brien, "From Morðor to Murdrum: The Preconquest Origin and Norman Revival of the Murder Fine", *Speculum* 71, no. 2 (1996): 321–57, @342–7.

20. Hugh M. Thomas, *The Norman Conquest: England after William the Conqueror* (Lanham, MD: Rowman and Littlefield, 2008).

21. Hyams, *Rancor*, 111–12; Hudson, *Formation*, 14–15 and "Faide", 364–7.

22. *Willelmi I. articuli X*, nr. 3, *Gesetze*, 487, translated into English as "William I: Ten (Attributed) Articles", nr. 3, in Carl Stephenson and Frederick George Marcham, eds., *Sources of English Constitutional History* (New York: Harper & Row, 1937), online at **http://www.constitution.org/sech/sech_.htm**, 36; Hudson, *Formation*, 62–3; Hyams, *Rancor*, 115.

23. O'Brien, "From Morðor to Murdrum", 349–50.

24. *Consiliatio Cnuti* 64: *Gesetze*, 353; Wormald, *Making of English Law*, 254–5, 350–1, 405–6.

25. Richard FitzNigel, *Dialogus de Scaccario: The Course of the Exchequer*, ed. and trans. Charles Johnson, 2nd edn (Oxford: Clarendon Press, 1983), 52–3;

Bruce R. O'Brien, *God's Peace and King's Peace: The Laws of Edward the Confessor* (Philadelphia: University of Pensylvania Press, 1999), 77–80, and "From Morðor to Murdrum", 322, 327–9.

26. Original: William Stubbs, *Select Charters and Other Illustrations of English Constitutional History from the Earliest Times to the Reign of Edward the First*, 9th edn (Oxford: Clarendon Press, 1913, reprint 1962), 117–19; English translation: Stephenson and Marcham, *Sources*, 46.

27. Hudson, *Formation*, 82–3; O'Brien, *God's Peace and King's Peace*, 63–84.

28. Editions: L.J. Downer, ed., *Leges Henrici Primi* (Oxford: Clarendon Press, 1972); *Gesetze*, 547–611. See Richard L. Keyser, "'Agreement Supersedes Law, and Love Judgment': Legal Flexibility and Amicable Settlement in Early-Twelfth-Century England", *Law and History Review* (forthcoming 2010); Hyams, *Rancor*, 137; Hudson, *Formation*, 249–50.

29. *Leges Henrici Primi* c. 10, 108–9; Hudson, *Formation*, 29–30.

30. Hyams, *Rancor*, 137–45.

31. Hudson, *Formation*, 24–51; O'Brien, *God's Peace and King's Peace*, 98–102.

32. OED online, s.v. *wapentake*.

33. Hyams, *Rancor*, 115–16.

34. Hudson, *Formation*, 50–1.

35. Hyams, *Rancor*, 174.

36. OED online, s.v. "crime".

37. Hudson, *Formation*, 56–7.

38. OED online, s.v. "felony"; Hudson, *Formation*, 161.

39. Marjorie Chibnall, "England and Normandy, 1042–1137", in NCMH IV/2, ed. David Luscombe and Jonathan Riley-Smith, 191–216 @209–10; Thomas K. Keefe, "England and the Angevin Dominions, 1137–1204", ibid., 549–80 @549–64.

40. Hudson, *Formation*, 119–22.

41. Stubbs, 161–7/*Sources*, 73; Hudson, *Formation*, 128–34; Hyams, *Rancor*, 158–66.

42. Stubbs, 167–73/*Sources*, 76; Hyams, *Rancor*, 164–8; Hudson, *Formation*, 131.

43. See esp. 1, 2, 5, 9, 11.

44. Hyams, *Rancor*, 164–8; Hudson, *Formation*, 131.

45. OED online, s.v. "eyre".

46. Hudson, *Formation*, 132.

47. Hyams, *Rancor*, 163.

48. Stubbs, 178–81/*Sources*, 80.

49. Hudson, *Formation*, 132, 162.

50. Hudson, *Formation*, 155–6.

51. Hyams, *Rancor*, 168–71, 184–6.

52. Ibid., 170.

53. Ibid., 163, 184–5.

54. Ibid., 185 and n. 116.

55. FitzLefwin v. Hayward in Hyams, *Rancor*, Appendix, 280; Linc., nr. 773, 133.

56. Hyams, *Rancor*, 196–8.

57. Paul Hyams, "The Strange Case of Thomas of Eldersfield", *History Today* 36:6 (June 1986): 9–15; *The Vita Wulfstani of William of Malmesbury*, ed. R.R. Darlington (London: Camden Society, 1928), 168–75; F.W. Maitland, ed., *Pleas of the Crown for the County of Gloucester, 1221* (London: Macmillan & Co., 1884), no. 87, 21–2. Both texts are translated into English at the Internet Medieval Sourcebook, **http://www.fordham.edu/halsall/source/wulftrans.html.**

58. That is, to summon his neighbors to help him catch a wrongdoer whom he had witnessed committing an offense: OED online, s.v. "hue and cry".

59. Hyams, "Eldersfield", 11.

60. Ibid., 12.

61. R.C. van Caenegem, ed., *English Lawsuits from William I to Richard I*, 2 vols. (London: Seldon Society, 1990–1), 2, nr. 471A and 471B, 507–14; Hudson, *Formation*, 159–60.

62. LDM, s.v. "Gottesurteil"; Robert Bartlett, *Trial by Fire and Water: The Medieval Judicial Ordeal* (Oxford: Clarendon Press, 1986).

63. Van Caenegem, *Lawsuits*, 2, nr. 471B, 510.

64. Linc. nr. 594, 105–6; Hudson, *Formation*, 171.

65. Andrew may have misunderstood the rules governing succession to children of priests. Such children were by definition illegitimate; they could not, therefore, leave property to anyone besides a direct heir. In Thorold's case, this would have been John, not Andrew. Andrew appears to have thought that Thorold's illegitimacy excluded John and therefore made him the heir. Otherwise, it is hard to understand why he brought up Thorold's status. See Stenton's notes to this case, Linc., 106.

66. Hudson, "Faide", 365 and n. 108; Hyams, *Rancor*, 175–83.

67. Linc. 931, 931a, 931b, 154–5.

68. Linc. 931b: they both placed themselves in mercy, i.e., agreed to pay the fine, which suggests a bilateral agreement.

69. Cf. also Linc. 931b, where Adam's son Thomas withdrew his appeal against the brothers of Hugh of Wigtoft.

70. Hudson, *Formation*, 134.

71. Hyams, *Rancor*, 199–202.

72. Ibid., 202–6.

73. Hudson, *Formation*, 22, 139, 175, 184.

74. Hyams, *Rancor*, 249–50 notes that some people in Angevin England reacted to judicial executions as if they were matters requiring violent vengeance, thus demonstrating how thoroughly they had integrated royal justice into older attitudes towards violence.

75. Ibid., 265.

76. Ibid., 221; Stein, *Roman Law*, 56, 63–4; Reynolds, "Medieval Law", 491.

77. Hyams, *Rancor*, 220 and n. 11.

78. Hudson, *Formation*, 164–5.

79. Hyams, *Rancor*, 221.

80. Ranulf de Glanville, *The Treatise on the Laws and Customs of the Realm of England Commonly Called Glanvill*, ed. and trans. G.D.G. Hall (Oxford: Clarendon Press, 1993).

81. Hyams, *Rancor*, 221–2; Hudson, *Formation*, 149–55. Hudson, 155 notes an extant copy of Glanville that has written in the margin in red the terms *distinctio, quaestio*, and *solutio*, indicating that its copyist was thinking in terms of the analytical categories of the law schools.
82. Henry de Bracton, *On the Laws and Customs of England*, trans. Samuel E. Thorne (Cambridge: Belknap Press, 1968).
83. Stein, *Roman Law*, 64.
84. Paul Hyams, "Nastiness and Wrong, Rancor and Reconciliation", and Charles Donahue Jr., "The Emergence of the Crime-Tort Distinction in England", in Brown and Górecki, *Conflict*, 195–228; Hyams, *Rancor*, 218–22.
85. Hudson, "Faide", 380.
86. Hudson, *Formation*, 207.

*PART IV*

# A MONOPOLY ON VIOLENCE?

**Map 7** Germany in the thirteenth century (From D. Abulafia, *Frederick II: A Medieval Emperor* (Penguin, 1988) p. xvi)

*chapter eight*

# A SAXON MIRROR

It was in the Empire[1] that the tactic of using sworn peaces to legitimate royal and princely control of violence developed the furthest. Peace and truce councils had been held east of the Rhine as well as west from the eleventh century onwards.[2] Their political character in the east was boosted by the struggle for supremacy between the German emperors and the Roman popes that broke out in the 1070s. As Germany's political landscape fragmented in response to the conflict, and different interest groups formed to take advantage of the struggle for their own purposes, some of these groups resorted to sworn peaces to unify themselves and regulate the relationships of their members with each other. In response to these local and regional peaces, the Emperor Henry IV and the princes of the Empire in 1103 swore a peace that Henry declared to be valid throughout his realm and that was to last for four years. This was the first time that such a peace had been extended to cover the entire Empire. Henry IV's peace of 1103 therefore stands at the head of the list of what scholars have come to call the *Reichslandfrieden* or "Imperial Land-Peaces".[3]

The term "Land-Peace" or Landfriede is a modern scholarly label; it tends to create the impression of an institution when in fact these sworn peaces were mostly ad hoc.[4] This is not to say, however, that the German kings and emperors did not use them as an instrument of royal power. The Empire was vast and still expanding on its eastern frontiers. No king or emperor could directly control more than a part of it, particularly in the face of powerful dukes and other lords with their own claims to rule in particular areas of the whole. The emperors, therefore, promoted communities of interest. Building on the traditional claim that they were responsible for God's peace and order, the Hohenstaufen emperors Frederick I (r. 1152–90, emperor from 1155) and Frederick II (r. 1215–50, emperor from 1220) in particular crafted peace oaths that formalized cooperation between the emperor and regional lords in the interests of both. The princes of the Empire gathered and swore an oath to uphold the peaces that the emperors proclaimed; the princes then returned to their localities and had their people swear the same oaths. Regional and local princes and lords upheld the terms of the peaces on the emperor's behalf, which strengthened their own local jurisdiction and legitimated their own local power.[5]

The Landfrieden for the most part defined peace largely as had the early peace councils, that is, as protection from violence for certain locations, such as churches and major roads, and for certain classes of people, especially clergy, women, merchants, and Jews. They did not, as a whole, attempt to ban personal violence outright. In a Landfriede of 1152, Frederick I did try; he declared that anyone who killed (*occiderit*) another would be subject to the death penalty.[6] He apparently met with substantial resistance, however; his later Landfrieden limit and regulate the personal resort to violence rather than banning it. In contrast to the early peace council acts, the Landfrieden emphasize violent punishment for breaches of the peace, punishments that could include death or mutilation.[7] This punishment was not left to the victim or to his or her relatives, but rather to the authorities behind the peace, that is, the king/emperor and his judicial representatives.

Frederick I's Rhine-Frankish Landfriede of 1179 nicely illustrates the above points. It also makes it easy to see how these sworn peaces were gradually changing into what we might call legislation. The text itself looks less like the acts of a peace council and more like a Carolingian capitulary.[8] It has Frederick, by the grace of God emperor and Augustus, presiding over a judicial assembly. The emperor declares that, compelled by the responsibilities of his office, he must arrange for peace throughout his empire and strengthen that peace with the authority of his office. He then explicitly bases his actions on Carolingian precedent; he proclaims that he is renewing a peace supposedly issued by Charlemagne himself. The peace was to remain in force for two years from the coming Easter. What "peace" meant is embodied in the list of decrees that follows. Among other things, certain classes of people and places were to have peace every day, namely villagers, villages, monks, women, merchants, mills, Jews belonging to the royal household, hunters, and those who drove hunted animals (though the text exempts those who set nets and traps; in a flash of royal irritation, it says that these should under no circumstances and at any time have peace). Plows, mills, and villages were to serve as sanctuaries. Anyone fleeing from an enemy who reached one of these places was to have peace; if caught in an open field, however, his pursuer could capture him. No one could pursue an enemy save on Mondays, Tuesdays, and Wednesdays. Someone caught red-handed committing a homicide (*homicidium*) in breach of the terms of this peace was to receive the death penalty; wounding someone in breach of the peace cost the malefactor a hand. Enforcement was to be overseen by judges. A person caught by his enemy in an open field was to be taken by his captor to a judge. Plundering required not only compensation to the victim but also a payment to the judge. A peace-breaker brought before a judge could appear in company with no more than twenty-nine men armed with no more than a sword each. Judges could summon armed peasants to pursue someone who had breached the peace. The judges answered ultimately to the emperor; if someone refused a summons to a court made three times within fourteen days, the judge could order him outlawed, but he had to report the situation to the emperor in person and get his blessing. Listed at the end are the "princes, nobles, and excellent men" who were party to the peace; they are presented not as participants in an oath but rather as witnesses to the "ordination and confirmation of this peace".

In the course of the twelfth and thirteenth centuries, Landfrieden were repeatedly issued, some valid for the empire as a whole and others regional or local in scope. The latter in particular provided a basis for order in areas of splintered or contested authority, or gave shape to arrangements of mutual interest among lords.[9] All were issued for limited periods of time, save for one that will be discussed in detail below: the Imperial Landfriede of Mainz issued by Frederick II in 1235.[10] Along the way, the Landfrieden began to take on a legal cast. The texts of many were picked up and spread by scholars copying and glossing Roman law because they corresponded to how these scholars understood an emperor's role in lawmaking, i.e., by decree. As consequence, they were disconnected from their particular contexts and given a new kind of legal validity, namely validation by legal exegesis. It was not just inclusion in works on Roman law that provided such validity. The text of Barbarossa's Landfriede of 1152, for example, survives because it was copied into early versions of the *Libri feudorum*, a systematic compilation of the law of fiefs.[11]

The scholarship remains divided on just what the Landfrieden represent. Were they in fact legal texts aimed at supporting and spreading the authority of judicial institutions?[12] Or were they rather ad hoc decrees aimed at addressing particular political circumstances? Do we look to them as the source of the claim by territorial or central governments in the east to a monopoly on the legitimate use of force?[13] Did they have any practical impact or effect? If so, how were they enforced?[14]

Similar questions apply to another legal phenomenon that developed in the same period, in response to economic development and the growing complexities of medieval life: written texts of vernacular legal custom, or custumals.[15] The Empire too had its towns and cities. As elsewhere, they were products of and participated in a more complicated economic world, with manufacture and commerce taking place with greater intensity and over a wider area than in earlier centuries. More widely ranging economic activity and concomitant political development fueled a demand for legal consistency. Because of the Empire's size, the resulting process of rationalizing, organizing, and recording legal traditions took place not at a central but rather at a regional level. This process did not stem directly from the law schools. Nevertheless, it was strongly affected by their culture, and by the example of both Roman and canon law. The writers of the custumals followed directly in the footsteps of Gratian and were responding to similar imperatives.[16]

First among these vernacular legal texts was a compilation of Saxon legal custom, the *Sachsenspiegel* (literally the "Saxon mirror").[17] Its earliest version stems from the years between 1225 and 1235 and from an area that we have already visited in company with Thietmar of Merseburg, that is, around Magdeburg. Its author was one Eike von Repgow.[18] Eike's status and antecedents are still debated. His family seems to have originally belonged to the free aristocracy; it is possible, however, and perhaps likely, that at some point they voluntarily entered the ranks of the so-called noble unfree or ministerials, that is, people who were technically unfree but set apart by their military or administrative service to a lord.[19] Nevertheless, even if Eike were a ministerial, by his own testimony he and his family had retained a specific privilege of their former freedom, namely their ability to serve as judges or *Schöffen*;[20] that is, they were *Schöffenbarfreie*.[21] Magdeburg in this period was particularly well known for its college of *Schöffen*, which served as a resource of learning and legal opinion for judges caught in difficult cases. Eike's parents owned a house in Magdeburg; it is possible, therefore, that Eike himself acquired his knowledge of law there.

Eike wrote his first version of the *Sachsenspiegel* in Latin. At the urging of Count Hoyer of Falkenstein, who was the lay advocate for the great abbey at Quedlinburg, he then produced a version in the local dialect of German. It is this version that survives, and that became the basis for all later versions of the *Sachsenspiegel*. According to his rhymed preface to the text, Eike compiled it in order to collect and preserve inherited legal rules and make them available to everyone.[22] He also incorporated the traditions of the Landfrieden; he drew directly on the Saxon Landfriede of Frederick II's son Henry (VII), very probably on the same Henry's *Treuga Henrici* of 1224, and possibly on other Landfrieden texts as well.[23]

Eike also had a broader purpose that he expressed in his choice of title. As one modern translator of the text has noted, he wanted to teach those with an interest in the law about legal virtues, much as a by then very old genre, the so-called "mirrors of princes", sought to do for rulers.[24] Accordingly, this "mirror of the Saxons" is not entirely neutral or objective; Eike tried on occasion to influence the legal world he was describing. For example, he went out of his way to highlight the judicial privileges of the *Schöffenbarfreie*, and to separate them from the ranks of the normal ministerials. This suggests that he feared an influx of lower-status ministerials into the judicial apparatus.[25]

Like Gratian a century before him, Eike originally intended his collection for private use. Like Gratian's *Decretum*, however, his *Sachsenspiegel* was met with open arms and soon spread widely. By 1235 it was being read and referred to by members of the colleges of *Schöffen* in Halle and Magdeburg.[26] From there, it spread throughout Saxony, and then throughout Germany. The *Sachsenspiegel* survives today in over three hundred manuscripts and one hundred fragments; there were probably very many more.[27] By the first half of the fourteenth century it began to be glossed, and thus to be treated as an authoritative legal text which required expert commentary like the *Decretum* or the *Corpus Iuris Civilis*. The glosses aimed not only to explain its provisions but to reconcile them with the provisions of Roman and canon law.[28]

Along the way, the *Sachsenspiegel* developed and grew branches. Eike himself revised and added new provisions to his original; later copyists did the same to make the text reflect their particular conditions and needs. The text was also reorganized into two sections. The first, in three books, dealt with regional law (*Landrecht*); the second, in one book, with the law of fiefs (*Lehnrecht*). The *Sachsenspiegel* also spawned offspring, among them the High German *Deutschenspiegel*, and another High German translation that specifically applied to Swabia, the *Schwabenspiegel*.[29]

In this chapter we will look at the norms of violence projected by the *Sachsenspiegel* as it appears in one particular manuscript. This manuscript moreover directly connects the phenomenon represented by the *Sachsenspiegel* with that of the Landfrieden; the *Sachsenspiegel* text is preceded by that of the Imperial Landfriede issued by Frederick II in Mainz in 1235. Now known as the Wolfenbüttel *Sachsenspiegel*, the manuscript was penned in upper Saxony in the third quarter of the fourteenth century.[30] It is one of a group of four illustrated *Sachsenspiegel* manuscripts (the so-called *codices picturati* or *Bilderhandschriften* of the *Sachsenspiegel*) that derive from a now lost exemplar probably copied in the last decade of the thirteenth century.[31] The recension of the *Sachsenspiegel* that it offers includes a number of additions to Eike's original and was most likely compiled before 1270.[32] The manuscript has the additional attraction of being beautifully illustrated. Its illuminations serve as a sort of pictorial gloss on the text, elucidating visually the passages they accompany.[33]

The Wolfenbüttel *Sachsenspiegel* thus captures a continuum of time: from the years between 1225 and 1235 when its component texts were first written to the third quarter of the fourteenth century when it was produced. Along the way, the *Sachsenspiegel* text it contains was rearranged and augmented, and the Imperial Landfriede of Mainz placed alongside it. The result freezes what was at the time of its final compilation a living legal text. As is true of any normative text and especially of "mirrors" such as the *Sachsenspiegel*, the statements it contains, the legal world it describes, and the normative culture that it reflects were idealized, on occasion flagrantly so. Nevertheless, the contents of the Wolfenbüttel manuscript must have connected with and been relevant and important to the real experiences of those who referred to it; it is otherwise difficult to explain not only why this manuscript was copied out but also why so many other copies of both the *Sachsenspiegel* and the 1235 Imperial Landfriede were produced. The manuscript must, therefore, in some way reflect its users' understanding of their political and legal world, even if it may not always accurately describe people's actual behavior in concrete situations.

The Wolfenbüttel manuscript projects a thoroughly Carolingian image of law and justice. Both law and justice originated with God; they were channeled through the king/emperor and manifested on the ground through a system of courts that could wield violence to punish wrong and enforce their decisions. Embedded within the manuscript, however, is evidence for how some people in Saxony who were not legal scholars or jurists thought about violence, courts and law, why and how they resorted to violence, and what the imperatives were that drove them to do so. This evidence is sometimes at odds with the ideology that the manuscript tries to project.

### Imperial Peace

The manuscript opens on f. 1r with the text of the Imperial Landfriede of Mainz from 1235. It is accompanied by an image of an emperor, enthroned with his orb and staff.[34] **[Plate 1]** The text is, however, disconnected from any context; it projects as institutional and timelessly legal something that was originally neither. This Landfriede was promulgated by Frederick II in the wake of a rebellion in Germany led by his son Henry (VII) in 1234. Predictably, it devotes a great deal of attention to rebellions by sons against their fathers. It is also unprecedented in its length and in the subjects it covered. It was an imposing statement of

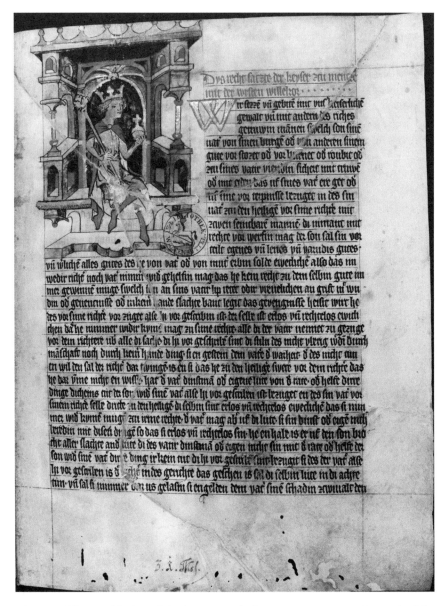

**Plate 1**  The Wolfenbüttel Sachsenspiegel, f. 1r: an emperor enthroned with orb and staff (http://www.sachsenspiegel-online.de). © Herzog August Bibliothek Wolfenbüttel

imperial authority that aimed at restoring stability and order to a troubled empire.[35] The Wolfenbüttel text, however, says nothing about Frederick II, or about the year 1235; it opens simply by saying, "The Emperor promulgated this law at Mainz with the agreement of the princes."

Frederick himself is thus genericized into a symbol of an eternal emperor.[36] Moreover, the text does not call itself a peace, but rather "this law" (*dis recht*). It has thus lost its original character as a sworn peace, becoming instead part of a transcendent and timeless "right".

As the text of the Landfriede unfolds, the emperor appears as the source of judicial authority. His authority operates on the ground through princes and judges who hold their judicial authority from him. Princes in turn enforce the work of judges who hold courts from them (*di von en gerichte haben*).[37] Judges are empowered to wield violence in pursuit of justice. They can raze town walls, burn towns, and destroy houses, with the power of the emperor at their back if necessary.[38] They also collect punitive fines (*was iclichem richter gewettit wirt*).[39] The text envisions a special judge for the imperial court (*hofe richtere*). He is to judge cases brought to the court, save for those concerning princes or other high-ranking persons when the penalty for the offense concerned is death, or when the case concerns legal rights, inheritances, fiefs, or some "other important matter" (*andir hoe sache*). These cases are reserved to the emperor himself.[40]

The text is clearly out to reinforce the authority of these judicial institutions and personnel, and to limit violent self-help in disputes. It opens with the case that a son wields violence against his father; the rebellious son loses among other things all of his property and legal rights.[41] It then continues with what looks like a general prohibition on private revenge: "this law is concerned with preventing anyone from taking revenge himself" (*das sich nimant selbe reche*).[42] Something similar is implied in a later section titled "Concerning fighting" (*Dis is von dem orlouge*). When two parties are engaged in hostilities, when one or both of the parties has a protective escort, and when one party attacks the other's men and harms them, the aggressor (if convicted) is to be treated as a highway robber.[43]

On further examination, however, it emerges that the text aims not to ban violent self-help outright but rather to regulate and limit it. No one may exact revenge for damage suffered, it says, before he has brought his complaint to a judge and follows the judicial process (*clage*) through to its end, unless the dispute has reached the point where he must defend his life and property with arms. Someone who does take revenge on another must repay twice the damage he did in the process; he remains uncompensated for any damage he sustained, and he may make no further claims for compensation. However, someone with a grievance who does bring charges to a judge but is refused a hearing (*wirt im nicht gerichtet*) may publicly declare his intent to resort to violence (*sinen viendin widersagin*).[44] Even then, however, he must follow certain rules; he has to declare hostilities in daylight and wait for four days before doing his enemy any harm.[45] The text thus recognizes (albeit within a tight set of limits) a man's fundamental right to prosecute grievances personally and violently. It distinguishes legitimate from illegitimate acts of violence; only the latter count as breaches of the peace.[46]

The image of peace and the range of imperial authority over violence presented here echo those of the earlier Peace and Truce of God pacts. The text seeks to protect churches and ecclesiastical property from violence (i.e., damage by robbery, arson, or seizure of property) carried out in response to some wrong done by their advocates or to injure their advocates.[47] People travelling on "proper highways" (*di rechten lantstrasen*) are not to be ejected by force.[48] The text also claims for the emperor a right to protect country people (*lantlute*); if a lord wishes to build additions to his town or castle, he may not use the property of the country people, only his own or that of his own men.[49] "Peace" itself is, as before, a multivalent term that can be used in several specific ways. For example, the four days that must pass before a legitimate violent conflict can begin are called peace (*vride*).[50] A personal peace between two people sealed by a handshake is called a "hand-peace" (*hantvride*); breaking such a peace brings outlawry. Should a hand-peace be broken by homicide (*mit totslage den vride breche*) the resultant outlawry can only end in death.[51]

All the while that it is regulating violence, this text of the Mainz Landfriede suggests that there was plenty of violence to regulate. The text assumes, for example, that court judges faced pressure, including threats of violence, from those with an interest in their judgments; judges were to swear that they would not, "for reason of love, pain, pleading, or fear", judge other than according to what was right.[52] So too ecclesiastical officials; people in towns and villages were not to oppose the commands of bishops, archpriests, or local priests with force (*gewalt*).[53] The passage noted above about damage to ecclesiastical property similarly assumes that people might attack, plunder, or burn churches or monasteries in order to harm their lay advocates, or to seek restitution for something that their advocates had done.

The Wolfenbüttel manuscript thus takes what was originally a limited sworn peace produced under very specific circumstances and turns it into a general statement of the emperor's law. As it is presented, this law clearly aimed at reinforcing the authority of imperial judicial institutions and at reining in violent self-help. It depicts the emperor, however, as working to channel and regulate the impulse to violence, not shut it down. The text does not ban violent self-help entirely; it in fact recognizes violent self-help as the right of someone with a grievance who can find redress in no other fashion. It simply seeks to constrain this right by mandating that disputants resort to the imperial judiciary first, a judiciary that can itself wield violence on behalf of justice.

## *The* Sachsenspiegel

At the end of the Imperial Landfriede of Mainz, on ff. 3v and 4r, is appended a brief passage describing the lineages of the princes of Saxony. Then comes, starting on f. 4v, a table of contents for the *Sachsenspiegel*, along with (divided somewhat awkwardly between f. 7r and f. 8r) a topical index.[54] This index was presumably designed to provide users with a quick way to find subjects in which they would be interested. Neither violence itself – the likely words would have been *gewalt* ("force") or *urlouge* ("fighting") – nor peace (*vride*) are listed; apparently the manuscript's compiler(s) did not expect users to be interested in either as categories *per se*. The index lists only specific manifestations of violence: rape (*von der not* – revealed in the clauses listed to mean sexual violation), trial by battle (*von deme kamphe*), robbery (*roup*), and theft (*dube*).

After two blank pages, the text of the *Sachsenspiegel* itself begins. As with all normative texts, it is seductive; it entices us to see its provisions as a systematic representation of reality. Just how problematic it is to do so, however, is highlighted by a clause that deals with lifting outlawry. A person who has been outlawed by the emperor for a year and a day and who has then had his legal rights withdrawn may have his outlawry lifted to the point that his life is safe. He may not regain his legal rights, however, "unless he fights a joust before the emperor's retinue and prevails over a foreign king". The manuscript reinforces this point with a picture of two knights jousting before another mounted figure wearing a crown.[55] [**Plate 2**] While not impossible, it seems very unlikely that such a scenario ever took place.[56] We are not, therefore, dealing with a literal representation of actual legal procedures. Instead, what we have before us is a text that communicates basic assumptions about how the legal world works, about the problems that might arise, and about the values that should underlie their solution. In this particular case the message would seem to be: "it should be very, very hard for someone outlawed by the emperor to regain his legal rights".

According to two prologues that open the text, the source of law is God, and it is from God that those given the task of judging derive their authority.[57] Law was made necessary by the sin of Adam. It was transmitted to mankind through the prophets and other spiritual people, as well as through the emperors Constantine and Charlemagne. This message is reinforced by an illustration, in the left-hand margin of

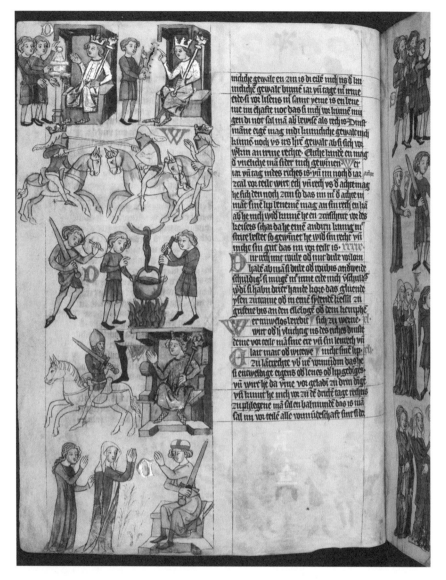

**Plate 2** The Wolfenbüttel Sachsenspiegel, f. 19v, second image from top: a man outlawed by the emperor jousts with a foreign king (http://www. sachsenspiegel-online.de). © Herzog August Bibliothck Wolfenbüttel

f. 9v. The illustration depicts the author of the text, accompanied by the Holy Spirit in the form of a dove, kneeling in front of Constantine and Charlemagne. Just below this group is Christ handing the sword of justice to a king, followed by the creation of Adam, and Adam and Eve with the serpent. **[Plate 3]** The text's author is not given a name,

**Plate 3** The Wolfenbüttel Sachsenspiegel, f. 9v, top to bottom: the author of the Sachsenspiegel kneels before Constantine and Charlemagne, Christ hands the sword of justice to a king, the creation of Adam, Adam and Eve with the serpent (http://www.sachsenspiegel-online.de). © Herzog August Bibliothek Wolfenbüttel

however; the manuscript in fact makes no mention at all of Eike von Repgow. As with the Imperial Landfriede of Mainz, therefore, we are left with the impression that what follows is a timeless, divine law that has been channeled through imperial authority.[58]

This message notwithstanding, the text does not claim to record the totality of the law. A passage early in Book I refers to a larger body of Saxon customary law; it notes that the Saxons had retained their old law as long as it did not conflict with the law of Christianity or with correct faith.[59] Somewhat later in the same book, the text acknowledges the personal laws of people other than Saxons, at least by pointing out where they do not apply; immigrants inheriting land in Saxony are to do so according to Saxon territorial law (*noch des landes rechte*), not according to their personal law, whether it be Bavarian, Swabian, or Franconian.[60]

The *Sachsenspiegel* covers a spectrum of social groups. Prominent at the beginning are those of knightly birth (*von ritters art*), that is, the armed aristocracy.[61] As the text unfolds, we meet a far broader range of people, categorized according to their legal, economic, or professional status. In a list of wergeld amounts, for example, we meet everyone from kings, princes, and the *Schöffenbar*, through sharecroppers (*birgelden*), tenants (*pfleghaften or lantsesin*), day laborers (*tageworchten*), children of priests (*phaffenkindere*) and the illegitimate (*di unelich geborn sind*), to the lowest of the low: bondsmen (*all, di sich zu eigen geben*), minstrels (*spillute*), professional champions (*kemphin* – that is, people who made their living fighting judicial duels for others), and people who had lost or had diminished legal rights (*unelicher lute, unechte lute*).[62]

The members of this society are thoroughly armed. The text repeatedly refers to lords and their armed retainers, to knights, and to castles.[63] Knights are characterized as much by their martial activities as by their social, political, or economic status. Prominent among the property a knight leaves behind at his death, for example, is his military equipment. His widow must hand over to his heirs all of the equipment he had at his death, including his sword, his best charger or riding horse, his best coat of mail, his tent, and his field gear (that is, a cot, pillow, linen sheet, tablecloth, two washbasins, and a towel).[64] Below the level of knights, people who live in villages as well as in towns and castles are assumed to have swords; all who are old enough to wield them (with the exception of priests, women, sacristans, and stockherders) are required to respond to the hue and cry (*gerufte*).[65]

Correspondingly, the text has a great deal to say about violence. Much of the violence it describes is carried out by people other than the representatives of constituted authority and is therefore illegitimate. Saxons beat each other and get into brawls. They injure and kill each other. They also wound with insults, that is, with "fighting words" (*mit kemphlichen Worten*, i.e., words so serious that they bring on a fight or challenge).[66] This latter point is made in a clause that entered the *Sachsenspiegel* text tradition in the third quarter of the thirteenth century. If Eike von Repgow had originally failed to mention violence by insult, it was nevertheless an important enough feature of thirteenth-century Saxon life that someone later felt compelled to do so.[67]

The text also deals with violence between lords and vassals and violence within kindreds. Lords sometimes kill their men and men their lords. In the latter case, says the text, the man forfeits his life, his reputation, and the property he received from his lord. The same penalties apply to a lord who kills his man, because the offense prevents the overlord of the property from giving the perpetrator's property to his children. Members of kindreds fight with each other over property. Some people in particular use violence in order to speed up the inheritance process. Such is implied by the statement that should someone seize the property of another by force so that the possessor dies, he loses all rights to possess the property even if it would normally have fallen to him on the possessor's death. Similarly, should a man with expectations to property kill his father, his brother, his kinsman, or someone belonging to the property for which he is waiting, he loses his rights to the property, unless he killed in self-defense or unwittingly.[68]

Violence emanating from castles gets a great deal of attention. Here the term "castle" (*burg*) seems to include both stand-alone forts and fortified towns.[69] The text assumes that people stage armed raids from castles and take refuge in castles, and that castle inhabitants might be complicit in acts of violence. A lengthy passage at the end of Book II, for example, regulates the case that peace breakers (*vridebrechere*) have found refuge in a castle and that the castle's inhabitants, faced with a judge's summons to hand over the malefactors, have refused. In this case, the castle itself is treated as a legal entity; the castle and all of its habitants are to be outlawed. Should someone wish to accuse a castle of robbery, i.e., charge that an act of robbery had originated from within the castle, then the castle's lord or one of its citizens must clear the castle with an oath on relics. But if someone wants to prosecute the castle with a trial by combat then the castle's lord or its citizens must defend their innocence (i.e., fight) against their peers **[Plate 4]**. If someone complains that someone else had attacked him from the castle, then the castle's lord has to bring the accused forward so that he can either make restitution for the damages or clear the castle of the charges. Whenever people ride from a castle, cause harm, and do not return within three days and nights, and stolen goods are not found in or near the castle,

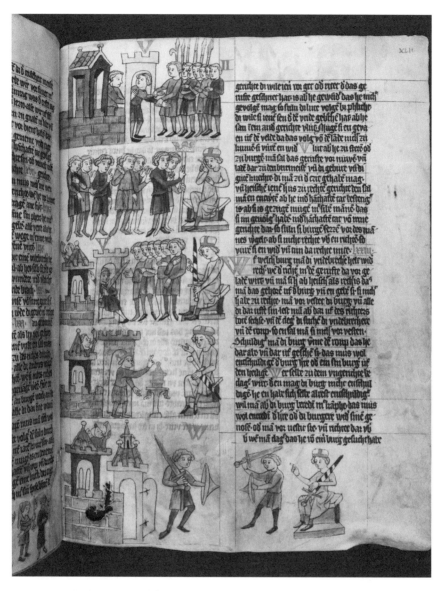

**Plate 4** The Wolfenbüttel Sachsenspiegel, f. 42r, bottom two images: an accusation of robbery against a castle leads to an oath on relics or trial by combat (http://www.sachsenspiegel-online.de). © Herzog August Bibliothek Wolfenbüttel

then the castle is innocent; but should the robber return, and stolen goods appear there or nearby, then the castle is responsible for the deed.[70]

Illicit violence is controlled, says the text, through an articulated set of judicial institutions, headed by judicial officeholders with defined spheres of activity. Counts (*Grafen*) hold courts (*des greven ding*) every eighteen weeks under the king's authority and protection (*undir kuniges banne*), as well as at other times when necessary; the *Schöffen* are required to attend. Magistrates (*Schultheissen*) appointed by the count also hold courts (*des schultheizen dinc* [sic]). Courts have officers (*vronebote*)[71] who are chosen from among the king's tenants. Local districts, or gaus, have their own judges (*gougreven*) who hold courts every six weeks. Each advocate or *Vogt* (*voit*) of an ecclesiastical institution must also hold a court. Leaders of villages (*burmeister*) are required to raise the hue and cry when necessary and to bring charges against, among others, people who inflict bloody wounds on another or who draw a sword with intent to harm. Alongside this secular judicial system are ecclesiastical courts headed by bishops, cathedral provosts (*tumprobiste*), and archpriests. Every Christian is required to attend the ecclesiastical courts in the bishopric where he resides three times per year; the *schöffenbar* must attend the bishop's court, royal tenants the cathedral provost's court, and all other tenants the archpriest's court.[72]

The courts operate within a normative framework provided by the emperor's peace. This is made clear in a lengthy passage in Book II, beginning "Now hear about the old peace (*vride*) that the imperial power confirmed with the agreement of the respected princes (*guten knechte*) of the land", that corresponds very closely to the *Treuga Heinrici* issued by Henry (VII) in 1224.[73] This passage combines the imperatives of both the Peace and the Truce of God councils. Priests and religious, girls and women, and Jews are to have peace (i.e., freedom from injury) in their persons and property at all times. The same applies to churches and churchyards, villages within their own ditches and fences, plows, mills, and the king's highway. Holy days and Thursday through Sunday of every week (following the calendar of Christ's execution and resurrection) are peace days. On those days, only those caught red-handed in an offense or imperial outlaws may be attacked. Like the version of the Imperial Landfriede of Mainz at the beginning of the manuscript, this section of the *Sachsenspiegel* leaves out anything that suggests that the original peace texts on which Eike had drawn were issued for limited periods of time. Everything is part of a decontextualized, eternal imperial peace.

This normative framework is sometimes called "peace law" (*vrides rechte*). For example, someone who wants to charge a dead or wounded man with a breach of the peace and fails to prove his charge is himself to be judged *noch vrides rechte*; so too are those who act violently towards those with diminished legal capacity.[74] Nevertheless, peace is at the same time a multivalent word whose meaning can extend beyond the terms of the imperial peace to peaces between individuals or groups or to peaces covering particular places. The term "sworn peace" (*geswornen vride*) describes a peace sworn between individuals; such peaces are sometimes imposed by a court. No one may carry a weapon other than a sword during a sworn peace, save in the imperial service or to tournaments, on pain of imperial outlawry.[75] To violate a peace one swore oneself is to risk one's neck (*is get im an den hals*) – i.e., to face execution.[76] Castles and princes have their own intrinsic peaces. "It is said", we read early in Book III, "that castles and princes need no peace" because castles have fortifications and princes lead armed men. "But this is not so", at least in the case of princes; anyone who pledges peace to the princes and is bound in loyalty to it will be judged if he violates it.[77]

"Right" and "wrong" in the *Sachsenspiegel* are similarly multivalent. For "wrong" the text consistently uses *unrecht* (or the noun *ungerichte*); right is rendered as *recht*. In modern German, *recht* is often translated as "law". At the time this manuscript was penned, however, it could mean anything from law to justice, right, rectitude, or righteousness, depending on the context. The possible translations for *unrecht* can range from illegal, unjust, or wrong to vice or wickedness.[78] *Unrecht* therefore encompasses different flavors of wrong. The most pronounced difference distinguishes those wrongs that merit compensation and those that trigger violent punishment. The text projects clearly the idea that there are some wrongs that constituted authority has the right as well as the duty to avenge. These wrongs are listed in a lengthy section of Book II, that begins "Now hear of the offenses (*ungerichte*) and the judgments (*gerichte*) that apply."[79] Thieves are to be hanged, unless the theft concerned amounts to less than three shillings in value, in which case the thief is to be flogged and have his hair cut off. Those who murder (*alle mordere* – as opposed to simple killing or *totslag*; see below), murderous arsonists (*mortburnere*), those who forcibly take a plow or something from a mill or a church or a churchyard, traitors, and all those who abuse power delegated to them, are to be broken on the wheel. Beating or kidnapping, robbery, regular arson, rape, and adultery bring beheading. Those who keep property acquired through theft or robbery are to receive the same penalty as the original thieves or robbers. Christian men or women who practice magic or mix potions are to be burned [**Plate 5**].

Murder and homicide are clearly distinguished. Murder (*mord*) still appears to mean a secret as opposed to an open killing. The *Treuga Heinrici* of 1224, on which Eike drew, says so explicitly: "anyone who kills another in secret, which is called *mord*, shall be punished on the wheel."[80] The *Sachsenspiegel* text itself implies the same when it declares that if a man is murdered (*gemordit*) in a field and the perpetrator remains unknown, the man who buries the body in a field or in the village is

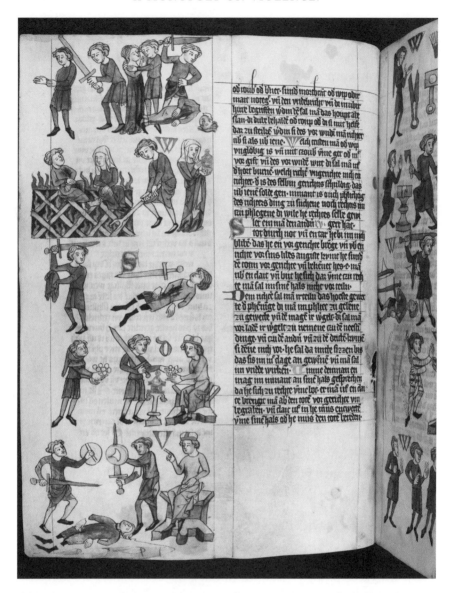

**Plate 5** The Wolfenbüttel Sachsenspiegel, f. 29v, top two images: men guilty of assault, kidnapping, robbery, rape, or adultery are beheaded; a Christian man and women guilty of practicing magic or mixing potions are burned (http://www.sachsenspiegel-online.de). © Herzog August Bibliothek Wolfenbüttel

safe from accusations of wrong as long as he does so with the knowledge of neighbors, that is, publicly.[81]

The text thus, if not in terminology then certainly in effect, creates a
practical distinction between what we might call civil and criminal wrongs.
The latter are judged and punished by courts that draw their authority
from the emperor. The distinction between those wrongs that merit
imperial attention and those that do not is reflected in the jurisdictions
of the various courts; these are divided based on whether or not an offense,
and therefore the possible penalty, involved bloodshed. Only the courts
of the king, a count, or a *Schultheiss* could preside over cases whose penalties involved death or mutilation.[82] The text does recognize that one did
not have to shed blood to kill or seriously injure. If one person blud-
geons another so that wounded places swell up, or beats him black and
blue, and if the injured party brings charges in time to prove it as a recent
crime (*in der vrischen tat*), the accused should appear to answer them.
Should he fail to do so, or to make proper compensation, he is to be
outlawed. For, as the text observes, "a man can even kill or permanently
disable another without breaking the skin, be it by beating, shoving
or punching, throwing, or in many other ways". A man so injured may
challenge the alleged perpetrator to a judicial duel; if convicted, the
perpetrator loses his life, or forfeits his hand, or is outlawed [**Plate 6**].[83]
The same applies, as noted above, to serious insults. As this example
suggests, a central procedure for determining guilt or innocence in such
cases is the trial by combat. The text carefully details the procedures for
launching one. An aggrieved party has to bring formal charges that the
offender had violated the peace against him either on the king's road or
in a village and describe the offense. Among other things, if the plaintiff were to accuse his opponent of wounding him and using force against
him, he had to show a wound or scar.[84]

For their part, the representatives of constituted authority are to be held
accountable for their performance, and they can be punished violently
for derelictions of their duties. Those who abuse delegated authority are
also to be broken on the wheel. Judges who fail to sentence a person
for an offense draw the same penalty as the offender. Court officers who
have had fines assessed against them for failure to perform their duties
are to be lashed.[85]

The *Sachsenspiegel* does contain lists of wergelds and compensation penalties for injuries. Though the lists are nowhere near as detailed and specific
as those we saw in the *Pactus Legis Salicae*, they do indicate that the
culture of compensation for violent injury was still alive. It is difficult to
say precisely when and under what circumstances corporal punishment
leaves off and compensation applies.[86] The text does not allow us to say

**Plate 6** The Wolfenbüttel Sachsenspiegel, f. 27r, top two images: a man is bludgeoned and brings charges before a judge; third image from top: a man is killed or crippled with a club and stones, i.e., without breaking the skin (http://www.sachsenspiegel-online.de). © Herzog August Bibliothek Wolfenbüttel

simply that offenses against the imperial peace merit punishment while all others require compensation. It appears instead that the two responses to wrong operate in tandem. A man who can prove that he killed in self-defense may not be condemned to death, but he must still pay the victim's wergeld to his family.[87] A person who kills or injures another through negligence similarly keeps his life while paying the appropriate wergeld.[88] Children may not be condemned to death no matter what they do; if a child kills or injures someone, his guardian is responsible for paying compensation.[89] These clauses suggest that under normal circumstances, i.e., circumstances not covered by these exceptions, someone who kills or injures another must both suffer punishment and pay compensation to his victim's kin.[90] Wergeld also serves as a stand-in for someone's value when he fails to appear at a court. For example, in a case requiring capital punishment, if a person who gives surety that he will bring the defendant to court fails to do so, he must pay the amount of the defendant's wergeld to the plaintiff.[91]

Wergeld is graduated according to social categories. Princes, lords, and the *Schöffenbar* are classed for this purpose as equals.[92] Those at the bottom end of the scale receive only symbolic compensation. Minstrels and bondsmen are to be compensated by "the shadow of a man", champions and their children by "the reflection of a shield against the sun". Compensation for injuries and wounds (i.e., injuries to the mouth, nose, eyes, tongue, ears, sexual organs, hands, or feet) is set at half of the victim's wergeld. Fingers and toes are an exception; these are compensated each at one-tenth of the victim's wergeld. If a victim receives many injuries in the course of a single violent act, he is nevertheless to be compensated with one half of his wergeld, as long as he does not die. Only people who are crippled to begin with must be paid for each injury separately. Here too we are told that words injure; calling someone a liar also requires compensation.

So far we have focused on illegitimate violence. The text of the Wolfenbüttel *Sachsenspiegel* does, however, cast some acts of violence as legitimate. As noted above, self-defense makes violence acceptable, though the perpetrator must still pay wergeld to the victim's kin and a fine to the judge.[93] Violence is also legitimate when it helps enforce the emperor's peace. One may attack someone who has been caught red-handed in the act of theft, robbery, "or some other deed", as long as one can then prove the victim's guilt with an oath by seven witnesses.[94] One may likewise kill or wound someone caught in the act of breaking the peace, or in flight from such an act, as long as one can attest to the fact with six oath-helpers.[95] These clauses reveal that publicity is crucial to the legitimacy of a violent act; one has to have witnesses. Similarly with self-defense; charges of rape, or claims that a killing took place in the course of self-defense, have to be validated with the hue and cry to ensure that the offense is evident.[96]

The Wolfenbüttel *Sachsenspiegel* thus recognizes as legitimate not only violence carried out by the representatives of constituted authority to punish breaches of the emperor's peace, but also violence carried out by others that supports that peace, or in self-defense. Alongside what it recognizes as legitimate violence, however, the text implicitly exposes other kinds of violence, driven by norms that compete with those represented by the courts. These norms are old and familiar. A clause in Book III takes aim at the impulse to match violence with violence. If someone seizes a castle belonging to another and holds it by force, while the legitimate possessor refrains from the use of force (*al di wile he ir ungewaldig is*), no one may charge the castle with anything that would cause it to be razed. In other words, if the victim reacts to the forcible seizure of his castle in kind and launches a *guerra*, he loses legal protection for his castle.[97] Such a statement only makes sense in a world in which at least some people who had their castles seized responded with violence. Courts themselves could get swamped by anger and the desire for vengeance. According to a clause in Book III, if one man challenges another to a judicial duel and the court decides to postpone the matter until the next day, both parties must pledge peace; if one party breaks this sworn peace, then he must pay compensation before a legitimate duel can take place.[98] The text thus recognizes the possibility that tempers could flare and that the parties could decide not to wait for court sanction to fight the matter out. In order to lessen the likelihood that something like this would happen, a separate clause declares that someone charged with an offense could not bring more than thirty men to the court with him, and that these men could carry no weapons save for swords.[99]

If someone helped an injured person reach his village, and the injured man died on the way, the good Samaritan apparently risked vengeance at the hands of the injured person's relatives. Such is implied by a section of Book III declaring that a person in this situation should incur no difficulties and that the heirs of the dead man should pay any expenses he had incurred if they could not be covered by the property the dead man had on him.[100] Barroom brawls too were evidently a problem; the owner of a hostel was declared to be not liable if one of his guests killed (*slet . . . tot*) another without cause, nor were the peasants (*di gebure* – i.e., those gathered at the hostel, or perhaps those from the neighborhood) if they were unable to catch the malefactor.[101]

The text also recognizes the fear of hot vengeance when it notes that if someone kills another in self defense (*Slet ein man den andern tot durch not*) and cannot remain with the dead man in order to bring him before a court because he fears for his life, he may come to court without the corpse. If he does this and admits what happened before anyone else charges him, and offers to do his duty, he may not be condemned to death. He still must pay compensation to the family of the dead man and a fine to the judge; however, if the family does not appear to claim the wergeld, he may keep it and will remain henceforth immune from charges in the matter.[102] One could imagine that this clause rests on stories such as the following: one man, driven by a grievance or by enmity, attacks another, but his victim kills him in self-defense. The survivor flees the scene out of fear that the dead man's kin would seek vengeance, but goes directly to a court and publicizes what had happened. The dead man's kin, perhaps afraid that their dead kinsman's reasons for launching the attack in the first place, or even his right to resort to violence at all, would not be judged legitimate, fail to show up at the court and voluntarily give up their claim to compensation.

Sometimes Saxons sought to take vengeance on their enemies by assaulting their servants. Whoever beats, seizes, or robs a man's servant (*eins mannes knecht*) solely because of wrongdoing by the servant's master, says the text, must pay compensation to both, unless he is prepared to swear on relics that he did it neither to insult or to harm the master. The clause goes on to specify the meaning of "insult" and "harm". "Insult" means to beat the servant because of the master's wrongdoing; "harm" means beating the servant to prevent him doing work for his master.[103]

Not only does the *Sachsenspiegel* react against the norms that would lead to acts of personal violence; it also reveals that people in its world could and did try to use constituted judicial authority and its institutions in ways driven by those same norms. The evidence for this consists of prohibitions. Some people, for example, apparently tried to cloak attacks in a veil of legitimacy by engaging a professional champion to carry them out; the text prohibits hiring a champion to prosecute someone (i.e., force someone to fight a judicial duel) who had not been charged with anything.[104] Other people must have been known to manufacture or hype charges of breaching the peace in order to legitimate an assault, charges that if pressed they could not or did not want to support in court. Another of the later thirteenth-century additions to Eike's original states that if someone wounded or killed another and then tried to justify the attack by claiming that the victim had violated the peace, he had to press the prosecution through to its end or suffer the penalty for the same offense.[105] Similar tactics are addressed with the requirement that anyone who charges another with a serious offense be held in custody unless he is able to offer security that he will attend the court hearing,[106] and with the prohibition on raising the hue and cry without then following through and pressing charges.[107] One could not force another to pursue a court case that one did not oneself initiate before a judge; in other words, it was not acceptable either to force someone else to act as your proxy in a judicial attack on your opponents or to take advantage of a wrong committed against someone else for your own purposes.[108] People apparently tried to spring judicial duels on their opponents by surprise; a clause in Book II requires that a man caught unaware by a challenge to trial by combat, who knows nothing about the charges against him, have time to prepare if he requests it.[109] Someone who wounds or beats another without killing or permanently injuring him does not have to answer to the victim's heir if the victim dies after a year has passed, unless the heir had pressed charges before the year had elapsed; this statute of limitations evidently seeks to prevent people from opportunistically using a death to get at someone by charging him with an old assault.[110]

All of these clauses speak to a great awareness in the world outside the *Sachsenspiegel* of the laws and of the judicial system, and of how they might be used to advantage to pursue personal grievances, including with violence, under cover of judicial legitimacy. As we saw in Angevin England, here too the law mattered, not only for its own sake, but also because it affected the strategies and tactics that people employed to achieve their ends.

## Conclusions

I have argued throughout this chapter that the texts contained in the Wolfenbüttel manuscript project an image of the normative world in thirteenth- and early fourteenth-century Saxony as it was imagined or understood by Eike von Repgow, by the people who copied and updated Eike's *Sachsenspiegel*, and by those who copied it out into the manuscript together with the Imperial Land Peace of Mainz. I have left open the question of whether anyone else paid attention to them and, if so, who, why, and to what degree. Tackling these questions requires drawing on different kinds of sources. A great deal of the necessary work has been done, and has produced the following picture of how our texts might have interacted with the real world.

Courts and judicial officials like those described in the *Sachsenspiegel* are attested in other sources.[111] Nevertheless, concrete references to the *Sachsenspiegel* in judicial records, or in the testimony about legal custom given by knowledgeable local men (the so-called *Weistümer*),[112] are few and far between, surprisingly so given how many such texts survive.[113] It is apparent that whatever else it may have been, the *Sachsenspiegel* was not understood by contemporaries as a collection of laws to be applied literally and consistently in practice. The specific references to the *Sachsenspiegel* that do survive stem mostly from legal opinions, such as those rendered by *Schöffen*, or in records of cases that were settled by arbitration rather than judgment, from the fourteenth and fifteenth centuries. These references indicate that in this period it was learned jurists who used the *Sachsenspiegel*. When they gave their opinions, these jurists often cited the text chapter and verse, along with equally specific citations to Roman and to canon law. For them, it seems, the *Sachsenspiegel* had attained the same stature as a source of legal principle as these far older learned legal texts.[114]

The manuscript tradition of the *Sachsenspiegel* points in a similar direction. The most common commissioners or owners of *Sachsenspiegel* manuscripts in the thirteenth through the fifteenth centuries were colleges of *Schöffen* in the cities, such as those of Magdeburg and Halle, urban ecclesiastical institutions such as the Franciscan house in Magdeburg, and legal scholars such as Johann von Buch, who around 1325 compiled the first set of glosses on the text.[115] An important exception is provided by the Oldenburg illuminated *Sachsenspiegel*, which by its own testimony was commissioned by Count Johann von Oldenburg to educate his own knights in the law.[116]

Similar conclusions apply to the extant texts of the Landfrieden. It is difficult to find records of cases that state unequivocally that a particular clause of a particular Landfriede had been applied in a particular case (though a handful of examples do exist).[117] There are, however, a number of records in which people refer to oaths taken to uphold peace and justice in the land, or legitimate their position in a dispute with reference to such oaths, and in which what happened follows the general requirements laid down in one or the other Landfrieden. It appears, therefore, that the Landfrieden were providing – or reflecting – a framework of norms governing violence, peace, and the judicial process that was available to be drawn on.[118]

As combined into the Wolfenbüttel manuscript, the texts of the Mainz Imperial Landfriede of 1235 and of the *Sachsenspiegel* project an image of an order stemming from God that was maintained by the authority of the emperor. Violence wielded by the emperor and his representatives served to uphold that order, whose normative contours were provided by the emperor's peace as well as by the legal traditions governing individual peaces or peaces sworn in specific contexts. God's order was also supported by other members of society, who were charged with wielding violence if necessary against peace breakers.

Yet familiar norms, that saw violence as a means to assert or defend claims and to take vengeance for wrong, are still visible. These norms competed visibly with those asserted by our legal texts. Many people in thirteenth- and fourteenth-century Saxony still believed that they were entitled to use violence on their own behalf, to assert their perceived rights and redress perceived wrongs. If necessary or helpful, they might use or manipulate the institutions and practices of imperial judicial power to do so.

The continued existence and viability of the norms associated with the personal right to violence is not only visible in the efforts made by the *Sachsenspiegel* to suppress them, but also in the composition of the Wolfenbüttel manuscript itself. Eike von Repgow himself did not believe that violence wielded outside of the framework of the imperial peace could be legitimate; his original *Sachsenspiegel* text in no way acknowledges a fundamental personal right to violence, even hedged about with restrictions, in the way that other texts we have examined do. In the *Sachsenspiegel* the emperor's peace reigns supreme; it provides a normative framework that organizes and regulates judicial institutions designed to enforce the peace, and that organizes the rest of society to do so as well. The old norms and impulses to violence are visible but in a negative image; Eike clearly thought they should be suppressed. This attitude is preserved in the later recension of the *Sachsenspiegel* used in the Wolfenbüttel manuscript. None of the innovations in this manuscript tradition recognizes a fundamental right to wield violence in pursuit of one's rights or to redress grievances. They do expand our knowledge of the sorts of things jurists thought that people might have tried to do, but again in a negative fashion.

However, the compilers and users of the Wolfenbüttel manuscript itself thought about their world differently than did Eike von Repgow and those who added to his text. The Wolfenbüttel manuscript opens with the text of the Mainz Imperial Landfriede of 1235. As noted above, this text of the Landfriede also projects an image of a timeless, imperial peace. Nevertheless, like most other Landfrieden texts it recognizes the fundamental right of an individual to resort to violence on his own behalf. The legal scholars, *Schöffen*, and others who resorted to this manuscript and to the other manuscripts put together in the same way must have recognized that this right, however hedged about with limits and hurdles, still formed part of their legal culture. In their mind, the emperor's peace could coexist with a man's personal right to violence.

## Notes

1. Hanna Vollrath, "The Western Empire under the Salians", and Benjamin Arnold, "The Western Empire, 1127–97", in NCMH IV/2, 38–71 and

384–421; Michael Toch, "Germany and Flanders: Welfs, Hohenstaufen, and Habsburgs", in NCMH V, ed. David Abulafia, 375–404; Peter Herde and Ivan Hlaváček, "The Empire", in NCMH VI, 515–69.

2. LDM, s.v. "Landfrieden"; Arno Buschmann, and Elmar Wadle, eds., *Landfrieden: Anspruch und Wirklichkeit* (Paderborn: Schöning, 2002); Elmar Wadle, *Landfrieden, Strafe, Recht: Zwölf Studien zum Mittelalter* (Berlin: Duncker & Humblot, 2001).

3. Benjamin Arnold, *Princes and Territories in Medieval Germany* (Cambridge: Cambridge University Press, 1991), 6, 21–2, 44; Elmar Wadle, "Heinrich IV. und die deutsche Friedensbewegung", in *Landfrieden, Strafe, Recht*, 41–74; Reinhold Kaiser, "Selbsthilfe und Gewaltmonopol: Königliche Friedenswahrung in Deutschland und Frankreich im Mittelalter", *Frühmittelalterliche Studien* 17 (1983): 56–72 @67–8.

4. LDM, s.v. "Landfrieden"; Elmar Wadle, "Zur Delegitimierung der Fehde durch die mittelalterliche Friedensbewegung", in *Landfrieden, Strafe, Recht*, 103–22 @119 n. 37.

5. Arnold, *Princes and Territories*, 43, 64–5, 69, 93, 118.

6. "Der Landfriede König Friedrichs I. (1152, Juli/August) – de pace tenenda", in *Quellen zur Deutschen Verfassungs-, Wirtschafts- und Sozialgeschichte bis 1250*, ed. Lorenz Weinrich (Darmstadt: Wissenschaftliche Buchgesellschaft, 1977), 214–23, @nr. 1, 216–17.

7. Elmar Wadle, "Die peinliche Strafe als Instrument des Friedens", and "Die Entstehung der öffentlichen Strafe", in *Landfrieden, Strafe, Recht*, 197–218 and 219–41; Arno Buschmann, "Landfriede und Landfriedensordnung im Hoch- und Spätmittelalter: Zur Struktur des mittelalterlichen Landfriedensrechtes", in Buschmann and Wadle, *Landfrieden*, 95–121 @106–7.

8. "Rheinfränkischer Landfriede. 1179. Februar 18", in Weinrich, *Quellen*, 290–7.

9. Arnold, *Princes and Territories*, 44; Michael Vollmuth-Lindenthal, "Die Erzbischöfe von Magdeburg in Landfrieden des 14. Jahrhunderts", in Buschmann and Wadle, *Landfrieden*, 213–30 @216.

10. Arno Buschmann, "Landfriede und Landfriedensordnung", 95–121 @102.

11. Elmar Wadle, "Frühe deutsche Landfrieden", in *Landfrieden, Strafe, Recht*, 75–102 @92, 97, 100–2.

12. Pro: Buschmann, "Landfriede und Landfriedensordnung"; contra: Vollrath, "Probleme um die Landfrieden".

13. Vollmuth-Lindenthal, "Erzbischöfe von Magdeburg", 215, citing Dietmar Willoweit, *Deutsche Verfassungsgeschichte vom Frankenreich bis zur Teilung Deutschlands: ein Studienbuch* (Munich: Beck, 1997), 79–80.

14. Vollrath, "Probleme um die Landfrieden", 26–8 and "Die deutschen königlichen Landfrieden und die Rechtssprechung", in *La Giustizia nell'alto Medioevo* (secoli IX–XI), Settimane di Studio del Centro Italiano di Studi sull'alto Medioevo 44/1 (Spoleto: Presso la Sede del Centro, 1997), 591–630; Elmar Wadle, "Landfriedensrecht in der Praxis", in Buschmann and Wadle, *Landfrieden*, 73–94.

15. LDM, s.v. "Coutume, Coutumier" and "Rechtsbücher".
16. Landau, "The Development of Law", 115, 141–2; Arnold, *Princes and Territories*, 171–4.
17. Karl August Eckhardt, ed., *Sachsenspiegel. Landrecht, Lehnrecht.*, MGH Fontes iuris Germanici antiqui, n.s., vol. 1 pts. 1 and 2 (Göttingen: Muster-Schmidt, 1973); Hiram Kümper, *Sachsenspiegel: Eine Bibliographie – mit einer Einleitung zu Überlieferung, Wirkung und Forschung* (Nordhausen: Verlag Traugott Bautz, 2004); K. Kroeschell, "Rechtsaufzeichnung und Rechtswirklichkeit: das Beispiel des Sachsenspiegel", in *Recht und Schrift im Mittelalter*, ed. P. Classen (Sigmaringen: Thorbecke, 1977), 349–80.
18. Kroeschell, "Rechtsaufzeichnung", 351–4.
19. LDM, s.v. "Ministerialität, Ministerialen"; Benjamin Arnold, *German Knighthood, 1050–1300* (Oxford: Clarendon Press, 1985).
20. LDM, s.v. "Schöffe, -ngericht, -nbank".
21. Kümper, *Sachsenspiegel*, 19–20; Kroeschell, "Rechtsaufzeichnung", 353–4.
22. Maria Dobozy, "Introduction" to *A Saxon Mirror: A Sachsenspiegel of the Fourteenth Century*, trans. Maria Dobozy (Philadelphia: University of Pennsylvania Press, 1999), 1–40 @3.
23. Kümper, *Sachsenspiegel*, 6–7.
24. Dobozy, "Introduction", 7–9; LDM, s.v. "Fürstenspiegel".
25. Kroeschell, "Rechtsaufzeichnung", 359–61.
26. Ibid., 367–80.
27. Kümper, *Sachsenspiegel*, 8–9.
28. Ibid., 12; Dieter Pötschke, "Die Glossen zum Sachsenspiegel", in *Alles was Recht war: Rechtsliteratur und literarisches Recht. Festschrift für Ruth Schmidt-Wiegand zum 70. Geburtstag*, ed. Hans Höffinghof *et al.* (Essen: Item Verlag, 1996), 161–78.
29. Kümper, *Sachsenspiegel*, 8–13; Dobozy, "Introduction", 28–33.
30. The Wolfenbüttel *Sachsenspiegel*, Herzog August Bibliothek Wolfenbüttel, Cod. Guelf. 3.1 Aug. 2°: *Sachsenspiegel-online*, ed. Björn Dittrich, **http://www.sachsenspiegel-online.de/cms/**. English translation of the Wolfenbüttel text: Dobozy, *Saxon Mirror*.
31. Kümper, *Sachsenspiegel*, 13–17; Ruth Schmidt-Wiegand, "Die Wolfenbütteler Bilderhandschrift im Kreis der Codices Picturati des Sachsenspiegels", in *Die Wolfenbütteler Bilderhandschrift des Sachsenspiegels: Aufsätze und Untersuchungen. Kommentarband zur Faksimile-Ausgabe*, ed. Ruth Schmidt-Wiegand (Berlin: Akademie Verlag, 1993), 1–25 and esp. 6.
32. Kümper, *Sachsenspiegel*, 11.
33. Brigitte Janz, " 'Wir sezzen unde gebiten . . .': Der Mainzer Reichslandfrieden in den Bilderhandschriften des Sachsenspiegels", *Beiträge zur Geschichte der deutschen Sprache und Literatur* 112 (1990): 242–66 @263–6.
34. Cod. Guelf., f. 1r.
35. Janz, "Wir sezzen unde gebiten", 256–7; Arnold, *Princes and Territories*, 209. Cf. Wadle, "Praxis", 75 n. 5.
36. Janz, "Wir sezzen unde gebiten", 259. The text does preserve a reference to Frederick II's father Henry VI, but simply refers to him as *keiser Heinrich*: Cod. Guelf., f. 2r, r/Dobozy, 45.

37. Cod. Guelf., f. 2v, l/Dobozy, 46.
38. Cod. Guelf., ff. 2v, r–3r, l/Dobozy, 47.
39. Ibid.
40. Ibid. Dobozy translates *andir hoe sache* more literally as "other valuable thing".
41. Cod. Guelf, f. 1r/Dobozy, 43.
42. Cod. Guelf, f. 1r, l/Dobozy, 44.
43. Cod. Guelf, f. 2r, l/Dobozy, 45. MHW, s.v. *urlouge*, translates the word as "war" or "fight". Dobozy translates it as "feud".
44. Cod. Guelf, f. 1v, r/Dobozy, 44; MHW, s.v. *widersagen*. Dobozy translates *widersagin* [sic] as "declaring a feud".
45. Cod. Guelf, f. 1v, r; Dobozy, 44.
46. Buschmann, "Landfriede und Landesordnung", 111; Wadle, "Delegitimierung der Fehde", 116, 121.
47. Cod. Guelf, f. 3v, l/Dobozy, 48.
48. Cod. Guelf, f. 2r, l/Dobozy, 45.
49. Cod. Guelf, f. 2r, r/Dobozy, 45.
50. Cod. Guelf, f. 1v, r/Dobozy, 44.
51. Cod. Guelf, f. 2r, r/Dobozy, 45–6.
52. Cod. Guelf, f. 3r, l/Dobozy, 47.
53. Cod. Guelf, f. 3v, l/Dobozy, 48. Dobozy translates *der lute pristere* as lay priests; it might be better translated as "the people's priests".
54. Cod. Guelf, f. 7r, l and f. 8, r/Dobozy, 65.
55. I/38, Cod. Guelf, f. 19v/Dobozy, 80.
56. Cf. Vollmuth-Lindenthal, "Erzbischöfe von Magdeburg", 218; Kroeschell, "Rechtsaufzeichnung", *passim*.
57. Cod. Guelf, f. 9v/Dobozy, 67.
58. Janz, "Wir sezzen unde gebiten", 261; Dietlinde Munzel-Everling, "Sachsenspiegel, Kaiserrecht, König Karls Recht? Überschrift und Prolog des kleinen Kaiserrechtes als Beispiel der Textentwicklung", in *Alles was Recht war: Rechtsliteratur und literarisches Recht*, ed. Hans Höffinghof *et al.* (Essen: Item Verlag, 1996), 97–111 @97.
59. I/18, Cod. Guelf, f. 15r/Dobozy, 74.
60. I/30, Cod. Guelf, f. 18r/Dobozy, 78. See also III/73, Cod. Guelf, f. 55r/Dobozy, 135 on the law of the Wends.
61. For example I/20, Cod. Guelf, f. 15r/Dobozy, 75.
62. III/45–6, Cod. Guelf, ff. 47v–48r; the passage is numbered III/46–7 in Dobozy, 126–7. See also I/38, Cod. Guelf, f. 19r/Dobozy, 80.
63. See inter alia II/72, Cod. Guelf, f. 42r–42v, numbered II/73 in Dobozy, 114–15; III/8, Cod. Guelf, ff. 43v–44r/Dobozy, 118; III/66 and 67, Cod. Guelf, f. 53r–53v/Dobozy, 133–4.
64. I/22, Cod. Guelf, f. 16r–16v/Dobozy, 76. See also I/10, 19, 22, 23, 24, 28, Cod. Guelf, ff. 13r–18r, Dobozy, 72–8.
65. II/71, Cod. Guelf, ff. 41v–42r/Dobozy, 113–14. See also II/72, Cod. Guelf, f. 42r–42v, numbered II/73 in Dobozy, 114–15.
66. I/68, Cod. Guelf, f. 27r/Dobozy, 90.
67. Kümper, *Sachsenspiegel*, 11 n. 33, with reference to Eckhardt, ed., *Sachsenspiegel*, 128.

68. III/84, Cod. Guelf, f. 56r/Dobozy, 138. The beginning of this section is missing from the Wolfenbüttel manuscript; Dobozy has taken it from the virtually identical text of the Dresden manuscript.

69. Cf. Werner Peters and Friedrich Scheele, "Glossar der Rechtswörter", in Schmidt-Wiegand, *Die Wolfenbütteler Bilderhandschrift*, 249–325 @257, s.v. *burg*.

70. II/72, Cod. Guelf, f. 42r–42v, given as II/73 in Dobozy, 114–15.

71. Rendered by Dobozy as "bailiff"; see the glossary to Dobozy, 182.

72. I/2, Cod. Guelf, f. 10r–10v/Dobozy, 68. See Dobozy, "Introduction", 17–20 and Dobozy's glossary to Dobozy, 181–200.

73. II/66, Cod. Guelf, f. 41r–41v/Dobozy, 112–13. Dobozy translates *knechte* more literally as "servants". See also Kroeschell, "Rechtsaufzeichnung", 363–4.

74. I/69, Cod. Guelf, f. 27r/Dobozy, 90; III/46, Cod. Guelf, f. 48r–48v, given in Dobozy as III/47, 127.

75. II/71, Cod. Guelf, f. 41v/Dobozy, 113.

76. III/9, Cod. Guelf, f. 44r/Dobozy, 119.

77. III/8, Cod. Guelf, ff. 43v–44r/Dobozy, 118.

78. Dobozy, "Introduction", 10.

79. II/13, Cod. Guelf, f. 29r–29v, given as II/14 in Dobozy, 96–7.

80. Weinrich, ed., *Quellen*, 396–403 @c. 9, 398–9. The same text expands the definition of *mord* to include a dishonorable attack: ibid., c. 11, 398–9.

81. III/91, Cod. Guelf, f. 57v/Dobozy, 140.

82. Dobozy, "Introduction", 17–18.

83. I/68, Cod. Guelf, f. 27r/Dobozy, 89–90.

84. I/63, Cod. Guelf, ff. 24v–26r/Dobozy, 87–8.

85. II/13, Cod. Guelf, f. 29r, numbered II/14 in Dobozy, 97; II/16, Cod. Guelf, f. 30r, numbered as II/17 in Dobozy, 98.

86. Dobozy, "Introduction", 21–3.

87. II/14, Cod. Guelf, f. 29v; given as II/15 in Dobozy, 97.

88. II/36, Cod. Guelf, f. 35r/Dobozy, 104.

89. II/65, Cod. Guelf, f. 41r/Dobozy, 112.

90. Cf. *Lex familae Wormatiensis ecclesiae*, c. 30, c. 30, 643–4, in which an alleged killer who had passed an ordeal would still have to pay the victim's wergeld, but would have peace from the victim's kin.

91. III/9, Cod. Guelf, f. 44r/Dobozy, 118–19. See also I/65, Cod. Guelf, f. 26v/Dobozy, 89.

92. III/45, Cod. Guelf, ff. 47v–48r, numbered III/46 in Dobozy, 126–7. See also II/16, Cod. Guelf, f. 30r, numbered II/17 in Dobozy, 98.

93. II/14, Cod. Guelf, f. 29v, numbered II/15 in Dobozy, 97.

94. I/64, Cod. Guelf, f. 26r/Dobozy, 88–9.

95. II/69, Cod. Guelf, f. 41v/Dobozy, 113; Dobozy translates *vridebrechere* as "lawbreaker".

96. II/64, Cod. Guelf, f. 40v/Dobozy, 112.

97. III/67, Cod. Guelf, f. 53v/Dobozy, 133.

98. III/36, from the Dresden manuscript: Dobozy, 123.

99. II/67, Cod. Guelf, f. 41v/Dobozy, 113.

100. III/91, Cod. Guelf, f. 57v/Dobozy, 140.

101. III/92, Cod. Guelf, ff. 57v–58r/Dobozy, 140–1.

102. II/14, Cod. Guelf, f. 29v, numbered II/15 in Dobozy, 97.

103. II/32, Cod. Guelf, ff. 33v–34r/Dobozy, 103.

104. I/49, Cod. Guelf, f. 21r/Dobozy, 82. Kümper, *Sachsenspiegel*, 11 n. 33, lists this among the novellas. However, Eckhardt, *Sachsenspiegel*, 107, who numbers this passage I/48.3, does not present it as a novella.

105. I/50, Cod. Guelf, f. 21r/Dobozy, 82. See Kümper, *Sachsenspiegel*, 11 n. 33, with reference to the Eckhardt, *Sachsenspiegel*, I/50.1, 108.

106. I/61, Cod. Guelf, f. 24r/Dobozy, 86. Dobozy translates *ungerichte* here as "violent crime"; I see no reason to specify violence.

107. I/62, Cod. Guelf, f. 24r/Dobozy, 86.

108. Ibid.

109. II/3, from the Dresden manuscript: Dobozy, 94.

110. III/32, from the Dresden manuscript: Dobozy, 122.

111. Kroeschell, "Rechtsaufzeichnungen", 362–3.

112. LDM, s.v. "Weistum".

113. See ibid., 372–3 for a single specific use of the *Sachsenspiegel* in a judicial charter; a cleric challenges the validity of the *Sachsenspiegel* in an inheritance case.

114. Vollmuth-Lindenthal, "Die Erzbischöfe von Magdeburg", 218; Kroeschell, "Rechtsaufzeichnung", 367–80.

115. See the literature given in n. 28 above.

116. Kümper, *Sachsenspiegel*, 14–15.

117. Wadle, "Praxis", 85.

118. Ibid., 86–7 and passim; Vollrath, "Probleme um die Landfrieden", 14.

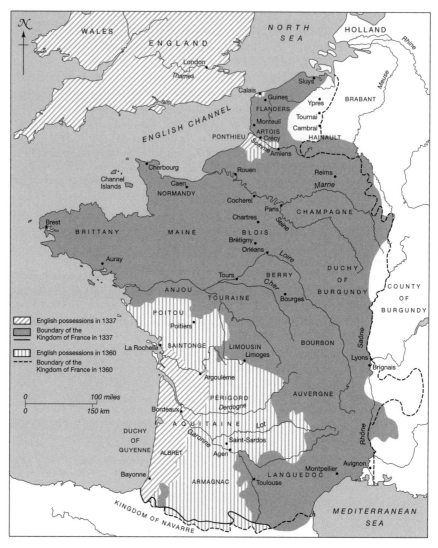

**Map 8** France in the first stages of the Hundred Years War (From
B.H. Rosenwein, *A Short History of the Middle Ages* (Broadview, 2004)
p. 293)

## chapter nine

# VIOLENCE AND WAR
# IN FRANCE

As the twelfth century progressed, the kingdom of France also developed royal mechanisms for regulating violence, if somewhat more slowly and in a different context than in England or Germany. As elsewhere, the way that they developed depended on how France itself developed, and on the particular circumstances in which individual kings operated. By the end of the thirteenth century, the landscape of power had been dramatically rearranged in favor of the French kings, and their influence was felt throughout their kingdom, north as well as south. They were also beginning to claim a monopoly on the legitimate use of violence. Among the symptoms of this claim were not only royal efforts to regulate and even ban violent self-help, but also a conceptual distinction that has so far been only sporadically visible, namely between royal and therefore legitimate war and the personal and therefore illegitimate use of force in private disputes.

Nevertheless, French aristocrats clung tightly to norms that legitimated their right to use violence in their own causes, whether or not there was a war on. They voiced their attitudes and assumptions about violence in the language of knighthood, or chivalry. This language expressed the self-image and values of a warrior aristocratic society that was not simply French but rather European; its members felt that they belonged to the same club regardless of in whose service or in what cause they fought. Since the club identified itself with violence, the ways that it used violence separated it from other social groups.

In the middle of the fourteenth century, in the early stages of what came to be called the Hundred Years War between France and England, disastrous military defeats hamstrung the French kings. As a consequence, their norms of violence temporarily lost ground, and violence convulsed their kingdom. Prominent among the purveyors of this violence were knights, but the knights were not alone. Mercenaries and soldiers of fortune, some from among the aristocracy but also some from the towns, sought to further their interests through violence. So too did townsmen acting as collectives and groups of peasants from the countryside. Members of each group fought for their own reasons. In some cases, it is easy to identify the norms according to which they acted, or to which they appealed to legitimate their actions; in others, it is difficult if not impossible. What is important, however, is that – in contrast to what we saw in the same areas in the eleventh century – the norms of violence associated with kings remained strong and widely held. Many people, from a variety of interest groups, regarded non-royal violence as a symptom of disorder, and looked to the kings to restore proper order.

Our witness to this period in French history, Jean Froissart, found himself caught between competing ideas of order. Characterized by one scholar as the first of the great war reporters,[1] Froissart sought to immortalize great deeds of arms and chivalry performed in the great conflict between France and England that took up most of his lifetime. His allegiance to the culture of chivalry, however, sometimes put him in a difficult spot when it came to reconciling the violent behavior of some of its adherents to the definition of order demanded by other elements of society.

### Kings, War, and Chivalry

The Capetian kings benefited from the same economic developments that propelled forward other princes such as the counts of Flanders. They also, however, enjoyed some advantages that proved in the long run to be important.[2] First, they possessed a remarkable ability to reproduce reliably. From Hugh Capet (r. 987–96) to Philip IV (r. 1285–1314), every Capetian produced a male heir. This dynastic continuity promoted institutional continuity, by which each king built on the financial and administrative measures of his predecessors. Limited at first to a domain that for most of the twelfth century remained rooted in the lands between and surrounding Paris and Orléans, the Capetians were forced to make the most of what they had. Successive kings managed their lands and finances carefully, with the help of officials drawn from their courts and estates, and exploited the rich agricultural resources and trade routes that their domain offered. As a consequence, when in the late twelfth century they began to expand their domain, through marriage, inheritance, and outright conquest, they had a practiced administrative network in place that they could simply extend outwards.

Second, the Capetians were kings. This meant that they were anointed, and through that anointment they could claim to be God's representatives on earth. The Capetians vigorously projected the neo-Carolingian image that as kings they had a special responsibility to protect the Church and the weak and to offer their subjects justice. By the middle of the twelfth century, they were translating that responsibility into claims to power through peace councils.[3] At a council held in Soissons in 1155, for example, Louis VII ordered all men in the royal domain to refrain for ten years from attacking churches and their possessions, farmers and their animals, merchants, and all people seeking justice.[4] Philip II Augustus (r. 1180–1223) tried to mandate a forty-day cooling off period before disputants could launch a *guerra*.[5]

Philip II's grandson Louis IX (r. 1226–70) went several steps farther.[6] He revived his grandfather's forty-day cooling off period. He forbade all violent conflict (*guerrae omnes*) in the kingdom, as well as arson, the disturbance of carts, and violence against farmers (though scholars do not agree on how widely this declaration was intended to apply or whether it was enforced).[7] Louis also established a permanent royal court of appeal in Paris that became known as the Parlement.[8] His personal involvement in dispensing justice produced the famous description, penned by his friend the Sire de Joinville, of the king sitting underneath an oak tree, with his court gathered around him, listening to cases brought by all comers.[9] These and other steps (such as sending out investigators to the localities to check on the behavior of his officials, in a way reminiscent of the Carolingian *missi*) earned Louis, and ultimately the French crown, a huge reservoir of popular good will and associated it for generations with the idea of good justice. The crown's image was only enhanced by Louis's canonization as St. Louis in 1297.[10]

Ideology and reputation, however, and even the king's personal involvement, could only go so far in making royal claims to police and regulate violence effective throughout the Capetians' expanding domain (which by the end of the thirteenth century extended to the Mediterranean). More important was the fact that, as in England, people found these claims useful. The market for royal authority stemmed in part from the diversity of legal customs that characterized medieval France. As they absorbed new territories into the royal domain, the Capetians left local and regional legal customs alone. When customs came into conflict, therefore, or when litigants in search of more favorable legal conditions wanted to bypass them, the royal courts became the places that people went for help.[11] More significant, however, were the consequences of Europe's general economic development. As more people made their living from commerce, more people had an interest in a definition of order that allowed kings to regulate violence. What the aristocracy, with its traditions of violent self-help, thought was the right and proper order of the world appeared to people with an economic interest in the absence of violence as disorder. Peasants of course had long seen a great deal of magnate behavior as disorder, but had only in isolated circumstances been able to make their own idea of order stick, and usually then (though not always) with the help of their lords (including monasteries and saints). The urban and commercial classes of the thirteenth century had a great deal more clout. It was in their interests to cooperate with a king in promoting his idea of order by resorting to his courts. In short, a new civilization was forming in France, a civilization whose needs were different from those of the civilization that had preceded it.[12]

Effective royal justice promoted the idea that warfare was a uniquely royal affair. We have of course already seen hints of a distinction between royal violence and everyone else's, as, for example, in the final clause of the peace oath offered by Bishop Warin of Beauvais to King Robert the Pious, which lifted all of the oath's injunctions in the case of a royal *werra*.[13] Having the Peace of God in France become the Peace of the King only reinforced the proposition that the king's violence was more equal than others'. But an important factor strengthening the distinction between royal war and private violence was the existence of effective royal courts. The resort to violence by an individual or collective had always been justified by a grievance, that is, by the denial of subjectively perceived rights or an affront to subjectively perceived honor. As in England so too in France: if one sought justice from royal courts, one legitimized the courts' claims to regulate violence and delegitimized violent self-help. As the thirteenth century progressed, canon and civil lawyers began to argue accordingly that only a war declared on the authority of a sovereign prince was legitimate.[14]

The view that war belonged to the king had to contend with tradition, however. And according to tradition, the noble inherited his right to make war along with his status. The long process that we saw underway in Galbert of Bruges' *Murder of Charles the Good*, in which knighthood and nobility were becoming synonymous, was by the thirteenth century essentially complete.[15] Knighthood was defined by violence. Its culture crossed all borders of kingdom, principality, and personal allegiance within Latin Christendom. Despite the best efforts of clerical reformers, knights in general did not feel that they could only fight in causes of which the Church approved, or against those whom the Church deemed legitimate targets, such as pagans, heretics, or infidels. Even Galbert's saintly Count Charles the Good had gone to tournaments.[16] Many if not most knights viewed their profession as a Christian calling in its own right, and they believed that God approved of knightly prowess. Countless works of chivalric literature and history (and the lines between the two are often blurred) attest to divine support for chivalric violence, wielded to display prowess and win honor and profit, "in causes any knight would consider right".[17]

Knights by this point also had their own law, namely the "law of arms". This law consisted of formalized traditions about what was legitimate behavior and what was not. It was not restricted to particular territories; it applied to all who followed the profession of arms, no matter where they lived or who they happened to be fighting for at a given moment. In theory, the law of arms had roots in Roman and canon law as well as in custom. In reality, however, it lived in the memory of its practitioners. Its lawyers were the heralds, that is, members of a professional order whose job it was to follow who did what, keep records of deeds done at tournaments and battles, to identify dead nobles on the battlefield, and to serve as neutral emissaries between parties in conflict. Heralds also provided guidance about what was lawful and proper when knights disputed over matters such as the right to fight judicial duels, rights to ransom, treatment of prisoners, justifiable tactics, lines of command and loyalty, etc.[18]

Knights did not easily accept the laws of kings and their legal advisors. The monk Matthew Paris, in his *Chronica majora*, notes in his entry for 1247 that according to members of the French nobility, the kingdom had been won not by the learned written law (*ius scriptum*), nor through the arrogance of clerics, but by the sweat of war (*per sudores bellicos*).[19] Richard Kaeuper has documented the manifold ways in which chivalric literature strongly resisted royal jurisdiction over serious matters of justice, and even more strongly resisted royal claims to a monopoly over licit violence. A recurrent theme in such literature also urged kings not to rely for guidance on lowborn advisors and lawyers but rather on people of the right blood and experience – and therefore with the right ideas about violence.[20]

Nevertheless, claims by French kings to regulate violence continued to expand. They reached a high point under the St. Louis's grandson, Philip IV "the Fair" (r. 1285–1314). In a series of judgments and ordinances, Philip declared that his wars took precedence over all others. He forbade magnates to pursue their *guerrae* while he was fighting his own; nor were they to participate in judicial duels and tournaments when he was at war. If parties were already engaged in a *guerra* when the king went to war, they were to make a truce for a year.[21] In 1303, Philip went a step farther and issued a decree echoing those of Charlemagne from five hundred years before. To fulfill his divine mandate to protect the people committed to him by God, he declared, he forbade wars (*guerrae, bella*), homicides, arson, and attacks on farmers and plowmen, of whatever station, in any part of his kingdom.[22]

As Justine Firnhaber-Baker has shown, however, there were significant differences between the language Philip the Fair used to justify his position and that of his predecessors.[23] The semantic field of the word "peace" (*pax*) in Philip's documents, Firnhaber-Baker notes, is narrower and less sacral. It does not appear to encompass right order in the world and between the world and God as it had in the past; instead, it is used in phrases such as "disturbers of the peace" (*turbatores pacis*) and even "peace and quiet" (*pax et quies*) in ways suggesting that it means a simple absence of violence.[24] Philip's ordinances also present themselves as motivated less by the threat of God's vengeance for mankind's sins and more by the common good and welfare of his realm. The ordinance of 1311 that forbade all wars even described non-royal warfare as a "danger to the common-weal" (*in periculum reipublicae*).[25] Nevertheless, Philip cast himself as obligated to protect the public good from non-royal violence because he had been given this task by God. In an ordinance of 1304, for example, he declared that people ought not to take vengeance into their own hands but rather defer to kings and princes, who had been "divinely deputized" (*divinitus deputati*) to handle grievances.[26]

This line of argument departs from that followed by French kings ever since the eleventh century in that it disconnects the king's peace from the traditions of the sworn peace developed by the Peace of God movement and refined into the Landfrieden in Germany. Earlier kings up to and including Philip's immediate predecessors had co-opted and built on the language and mechanisms of the Peace of God by summoning peace councils and by relying on oaths, ecclesiastical sanctions, and agreement among participants for enforcement. Even after Louis IX stopped acting in conjunction with church councils and began to proclaim peaces on his own authority as king, he continued to reflect the traditions of the peace movement by focusing his attention on the helpless (such as farmers and their property) and by treating heresy as a breach of the peace.[27] While novel in their immediate context, however, the ordinances of Philip IV reconnected with an even older tradition of royal peacemaking: that of Charlemagne. The king was ordained directly by God, by virtue of his kingship, to uphold the peace of his realm.

But Philip IV had inherited a difficult position. The expansion of the Capetian domain had by the end of the thirteenth century reached a maximum; the costs of maintaining an expanding bureaucracy as well as a paid army were outstripping royal revenues. As a consequence, Philip was constantly hungry for money. His demands provoked such intense and organized resistance from the nobility in the years 1314–15 in particular that his son Louis X (r. 1314–16) was forced, among other things, to recognize once more nobles' rights to hold tournaments, fight judicial duels, and engage in their own wars.[28]

In 1328, the direct Capetian line came to an end with the death of Philip IV's youngest son Charles IV. The French kingship continued in the person of Philip VI (r. 1328–50), son of Philip IV's brother Charles, Count of Valois.[29] By accepting Philip of Valois as king, the French nobility bypassed a person with a potentially stronger claim to the French throne, namely King Edward III of England (r. 1327–77), son of Philip IV's daughter Isabella. This step touched off a war. The underlying causes of the war were complex. The French and English crowns had lived in tension for decades over the remaining English possessions on the continent in Gascony. Moreover, they continued to vie for control of Flanders, on which England depended for its lucrative wool trade. Edward III's claim to the French throne was simply a lit match. When in 1337 Philip VI tried to take Gascony from England by force, Edward put the match to the powder, not only to preserve his continental holdings but also to take the crown that he thought was his by right.

## Jean Froissart

The great chronicler of the Hundred Years War,[30] Jean Froissart, was an infant when the fighting started.[31] Froissart came from town stock; he was born, probably in 1337, in Valenciennes, now in northeastern France but then within the territory of the Counts of Hainault.[32] His family were most likely money-lenders. Froissart himself, however, gravitated towards the court and life as a clerk and poet. By 1361 he had left Hainault for England, where he entered the service of Edward III's queen, Philippa of Hainault. It is in Philippa's service that he took on the role of court chronicler and historian.

Froissart's *modus operandi* was simple. He talked to people who had taken part in great events, and he traveled; he made a point of getting himself attached to important missions or military campaigns. He crossed the English Channel repeatedly, returning to his homeland, traveling in France whenever a truce between the warring powers permitted it, and making it as far as Italy in the train of a royal marriage. Wars also took him as far north as Scotland. When his patroness Queen Philippa died in 1369, Froissart remained on the continent and entered the service of a sequence of great lords. It was apparently for one of them, Count Robert of Namur in Flanders, that he began writing (or, more likely, assembling out of pre-existing notes and pieces) his great chronicle of the wars between France and England. His effort would eventually cover the period up through 1400.

Despite his bourgeois origins, Froissart adopted the worldview of his patrons and of the aristocrats with whom he associated. His *Chronicles of England, France, Spain, and the Adjoining Countries* were intended to record their great deeds of arms and chivalry. When it came to deeds performed before he had come on the scene, Froissart borrowed from or adapted the work of others, particularly the knight Jean Le Bel, also from Hainault, on whose account of the early part of the war he relied heavily. Otherwise, Froissart traveled, inquired, and listened. Froissart's interest did not depend on allegiance. His ultimate loyalty lay with those who followed the profession of arms. As a result, he developed an international reputation among the members of that class, who eagerly sought him out to have their adventures recorded for posterity.

By his own testimony, Froissart did his best to get good information from reliable sources, and he was himself often present at events he reported. Nevertheless, as a factual source, Froissart sometimes falls short, even very short; modern historians have made something of an industry out of pointing out places where he got it wrong. Yet Froissart was quite good at picking up what rumor and conventional wisdom thought had happened, and at capturing the moral judgments people around him were making about events, even if his particulars were out of place. It is precisely in this regard that Froissart is interesting for our purposes. Froissart sculpted his narratives in terms of his own ideas of the admirable and the despicable and his assumptions about the possible. He shared his assumptions and norms with his audience and patrons. But he moved in a world in which assumptions and norms were in conflict. The ancient attitudes towards violence of the military aristocracy were often at odds with the attitudes of kings. Other people saw violence in general not as a chance to gain glory and honor but as a painful disruption of order. At several points, Froissart struggles visibly with these contradictions, and it appears from his text that he was not the only one. The conflict among norms is made more visible by crisis. During the first part of the Hundred Years War, the kingdom of France was devastated. All of the power and authority over violence carefully garnered by generations of French kings seemed at times to have evaporated. At such moments, different norms of violence, which previously might have seemed submerged or on the defensive, re-emerged to compete with the norms of royal power.

### Violence and Knights

Very early in Book I of the *Chronicles*, Froissart tells us that a formal state of war made a difference in how people behaved. In the fall of 1337,

Edward III of England renounced his homage to Philip VI of France and declared war. As events took their course, a fleet under the command of Sir Hugh Kieret, carrying a large group of Norman and Genoese fighting men, waited for news. Only when Sir Hugh and his companions heard that war had opened did they set sail for England. On a Sunday morning, they entered Southampton harbor, landed, and "pillaged and looted [the town] completely". They killed many people, raped women and girls ("which was a deplorable thing", says Froissart), loaded their ships with plunder, and sailed back to Normandy. There they shared out their booty.[33]

As the war proper begins, Froissart tells us of English armies repeatedly besieging towns in Normandy or in Aquitaine, or moving across the countryside dragging wagonloads of plundered goods behind them while being pursued by (usually much larger) French armies. Twice in Book I (which covers the period up to 1377) the English and the French meet in great battles: the battle of Crécy in 1346, and the battle of Poitiers in 1356. Both are disasters for the French. Froissart's accounts of this fighting – which up to about 1360/61 are based on those of Jean Le Bel – reveal that knights had their own rules and allegiances, and that these rules and allegiances transcended all political division. The normative culture of knighthood is clearly visible in his account of the English assault on the Norman town of Caen in July of 1346.[34] Inside the town was a small force under the command of the Constable of France (Raoul II de Brienne, Count of Eu) and the lord of Tancarville (Jean de Melun). Against the Constable's better judgment, the townspeople of Caen insisted on meeting the English in open battle. When they caught sight of their enemy approaching, however, they panicked and fled in disorder back to the town, forcing the Constable, the lord of Tancarville, and their men to do the same. Some of the French knights and squires (the latter being men entitled by blood to be knights but who had not yet, either through youth or lack of desire, gone through their formal dubbing)[35] managed to reach the safety of Caen castle. The Constable and the lord of Tancarville did not; they were forced to take refuge inside a gate-tower. They looked on in horror as English soldiers killed without mercy. The Constable and the lord of Tancarville feared that if they were caught they too would be killed out of hand by men who "did not know who they were". To their relief, they caught sight of a one-eyed English knight named Sir Thomas Holland with five or six other knights. They recognized him because they had campaigned together, crusading in Granada and Prussia and on other expeditions "in the way in which knights do meet each other". They called out to Sir Thomas, who, once he recognized them, happily made them and the twenty-five or so knights with them his prisoners. Sir Thomas was delighted not only because he had been able to save the lives of his fellow knights, "but also because their capture meant an excellent day's work and a fine haul of valuable prisoners" worth a considerable ransom in gold.

Knights, in other words, could be counted on to play by the rules of capture and ransom, which tended to keep all of the members of the chivalric club alive and provided them with the chance of a nice income. Sir Thomas went on to demonstrate that at least in Froissart's view, good knights also tried to keep their subordinates from committing atrocities, even against the non-noble. "He was able that day", says Froissart, "to prevent many cruel and horrible acts which would otherwise have been committed, thus giving proof of his kind and noble heart. Several gallant English knights who were with him also prevented a number of evil deeds and rescued many a pretty townswoman and many a nun from rape."[36] This chivalric view of violence emerges in mirror image a bit later, in Froissart's comments about the aftermath of the Battle of Crécy. After the battle, pillagers and irregulars from among the English army, "Welsh and Cornishmen with their long knives", went out on to the field among the French fallen. These men did not follow the same rules as the nobility; "when they found any in difficulty, whether they were counts, barons, knights, or squires, they killed them without mercy". This was a great misfortune, says Froissart. For his part, King Edward III seems to have been more concerned about the loss of income; according to Froissart, he was furious that none of the French nobles had been taken for ransom.[37]

On several occasions, Froissart refers to the "law of arms". This is something that good knights followed regardless of their allegiance. Froissart refers to it particularly in situations involving prisoners and ransom. During the English sack of Limoges in 1370, for example, the Duke of Lancaster found himself in hand-to-hand combat with the French knight Sir Jean de Villemur, who was "a fine knight, strong and of superb physique". Next to them, the Earl of Cambridge fought against Sir Hugues de la Roche, and the Earl of Pembroke against Roger de Beaufort. The fighting continued for some time, and offered such a display of skill that when the English commander, Edward III's son Edward (a.k.a. "the Black Prince"), happened by, he halted. Though the Black Prince was quite ill, he had himself rolled up in his wheeled litter and watched the fighting "with keen interest". Eventually the French knights decided that they had had enough. They stopped fighting simultaneously and said, "Sirs, we are yours, you have beaten us. Treat us according to the law of arms." The Duke of Lancaster replied to de Villemur, "By God, Sir Jean, we would never dream of doing anything else. We accept you as our prisoners."[38]

The law of arms helps Froissart separate good knights from the less good. Particular embodiments of the latter are the Germans; Froissart seems to display what in later centuries would be a typically French antipathy for their trans-Rhenish neighbors. Late in Book III, while narrating an English campaign in Scotland, Froissart indulges himself in a general sermon about the fighting qualities of the English and the Scots. Among his points: when the English and the Scots surrender to each other "according to the law of arms", they do not press too hard for money and treat their prisoners chivalrously. The Germans do not. It would be better, in fact, for someone to be captured by pagans or Saracens rather than by the Germans. The latter were known to constrain gentlefolk in harsh confinements beyond all reason, with chains, fetters, and other prison instruments, "by means of which they injure or weaken a man's limbs to extort more money". "To tell the truth," Froissart ends, "the Germans are in many ways outside all reasonable laws and it is surprising that others will associate with them or allow them to practice arms beside them."[39]

Froissart presents the law of arms as a formalized subset of more generally chivalric behavior. His account of a tournament held at Saint-Ingelvert in 1390 provides a stream of examples. During a three-year truce between the French and the English, three French knights set up shop near Calais and invited all comers to meet them in an amicable test of arms. A large number of English knights answered the call. One of these, Sir Godfrey Seton, challenged the Frenchman Sir Regnault de Roye. The knights made two passes at each other without doing any damage. On the third pass, Sir Godfrey hit Sir Regnault on the helmet without harming him. Sir Regnault, however, struck such a powerful blow with his lance on Sir Godfrey's shield – "for he was one of the strongest and toughest jousters in France at that time and also he was truly in love with a gay and beautiful young lady" – that his lance went through the shield and broke off in Sir Godfrey's arm. Froissart notes that although Sir Regnault had wounded the other knight, "not a single abusive remark was made to him, for such are the hazards of arms".[40] A contrast is provided by Herr Hans, a Bohemian knight in the service of the queen of England whose name – and Froissart's treatment of him – suggests that he was German. Herr Hans lined up against the French knight Boucicaut. In their first pass the two knights missed each other with their lances. Herr Hans, however, "dealt a foul blow which was strongly condemned"; as he passed Boucicaut he struck the Frenchman's helm with a sideways thrust before riding on. The assembled English knights recognized instantly that the French could by rights confiscate Herr Hans's horse and armor for the "improper thrust", but after some discussion the French graciously declined to avoid offending the Bohemian's English employers. Herr Hans begged to be allowed to joust one more time. He found a willing opponent in the above-named Sir Regnault de Roye, who hit him so hard that he "lifted him right out of the saddle and sent him flying to the ground with such force that they thought he was killed". The English, says Froissart, were delighted at this turn of events, because of the unchivalrous way that Herr Hans had fought in his first joust.[41]

## Homicide, Vengeance, and Settlement

Underneath the talk of war, and of chivalry and the law of arms, Froissart mentions some rather familiar looking violence, that is, homicides and *guerrae*. This violence does not seem to have depended on whether there was a war on. For example, in his brief discussion of the Black Death that struck Europe beginning in 1347, Froissart tells us of the flagellants who in 1349 emerged from Germany and traveled from town to town. These penitents scourged themselves with whips made of knotted leather and small iron spikes until the blood flowed, in order to persuade God to end the plague. While describing with evident disapproval their impact on a gullible populace, Froissart admits that the flagellants were able to settle what had been intractable and violent conflicts. "Many reconciliations were achieved through the penitents as they went about, for instance, over killings (*morts d'hommes*) which had taken place and about which it had been impossible to reach an accord; but by means of the penitents peace was made."[42] A similar bit of information appears in Froissart's description of the battle of Poitiers in 1356. As the French disaster was becoming complete, says Froissart, hordes of English soldiers crowded around King John II of France. They each sought to be the one to capture the king, not only for the glory but also to claim a share in the surely massive ransom that would follow. As King John looked about for someone of rank to whom he could honorably surrender, a knight from St. Omer named Denis de Morbecque pressed forward. He explained to the king that he had been with the English for the last five years because he had been banished from France in his youth for participating in a *guerra* and for killing a man.[43] The relieved French king promptly surrendered to him. De Morbecque's case not only reveals violent *guerrae* to have been alive and well; it also indicates that, at least in 1351, they were being controlled and punished by royal justice.

In other parts of the *Chronicles*, Froissart tells us that the sensitivity to insult or injury and the impulse to vengeance were pervasive. Moreover, he has people responding to these imperatives in a way perfectly consonant with what we have seen in earlier periods. During a truce before the battle of Poitiers, while the English and French armies were impatiently waiting out a last-ditch effort by the Cardinal of Périgord to negotiate a settlement, a knight from each side rode out to scout the dispositions of the other. The English knight, Sir John Chandos, crossed paths with his French counterpart, Sir Jean de Clermont, and the pair exchanged insults, for they (says Froissart) were "young and in love". The particular problem was that the two knights were both wearing, on their left arms, an emblem of a lady in blue surrounded by a sunbeam. They argued over who had the better right to wear it. "If there were not a truce between us," declared de Clermont, "I would show you here and now that you have no right to wear it." "Ha!" declared Chandos in return; "tomorrow morning [i.e., when the battle was to start] you will find me more than ready to prove by force of arms that it belongs to me as much as to you."[44]

Froissart has vengeance motivating violent behavior in situations that we might expect to be governed by politics. Early in Book II, he narrates the start of the Great Schism in the Roman papacy, which began in 1378 and pitted one claimant to the See of St. Peter, Clement VII, against another, Urban VI.[45] He tells us that a "very gallant knight from Brittany", Sir Silvester Bude, with two thousand Bretons had taken up a position near Rome in support of Clement, who would soon move to Avignon. Bude took possession of the great Castel de Sant'Angelo so that he could better coerce and harass the Romans, who supported Urban. But the Romans banded together with a group of Germans and forced the Bretons to withdraw. Bude, says Froissart, was enraged; he "considered how he could get his revenge on the Romans". When he learned that the leading men of the city were meeting in council on the Capitol, Bude gathered a force. He made his way into the city and arrived on the scene just as the councilors were leaving the council chamber. The Bretons lowered their lances and charged, killing a great number. The next morning, the Romans (who were, it seems, equally bent on revenge) carried out what Froissart calls "a very barbarous act". In an echo of the ethic against harming the uninvolved, he says that the Romans hunted down "the poor clerics who were staying in Rome and had had nothing to do with the attack on the Capitol". They killed and wounded, says Froissart, over three hundred of the clerics, paying especially merciless attention to those from Brittany.[46]

Froissart lets his own assumptions about vengeance shine through when he needs to get inside the head of one of his subjects, especially when he does not have his facts straight. A particularly telling example comes towards the end of Book III, when he is narrating the first power struggle in 1387–8 between the young King Richard II of England (r. 1377–99) and his uncles.[47] In a narrative rife with errors of fact, he tells us that one of Richard's supporters, a knight named Sir Simon Burley, was accused of various crimes and beheaded as a traitor outside of the Tower of London while the king was away. Shortly afterwards, another of Richard's knights, Sir Robert Tresilian, was caught spying on the Duke of Gloucester and likewise executed. After a few more of his supporters were beheaded, Richard II was forced by his uncles – who were now firmly in command – to go through a ceremony that made him look as if he were still in charge.[48] Froissart comments: "However, if [Richard] had had the upper hand of them, he would not have done so, but would have exacted vengeance for the execution of Sir Simon Burley and his other knights who had been taken from him and put to death undeservedly . . ."[49]

Finally, Froissart assumes what we have seen throughout this journey, namely that God himself took violent vengeance for injury or affront. An English squire went to a village and began to plunder it just as a priest was chanting mass in the village church. The unnamed squire entered the church, went up to the altar, and seized the chalice in which the priest was about to consecrate the communion wine; he was so rough about it that some of the wine spilled on the ground. When the priest protested, the squire hit him a backhanded blow with his gauntlet with such force that the priest's blood spurted onto the altar. The troop then left the village, with the squire carrying the chalice as well as the communion plate and cloth. According to Froissart, what happened next "was a true example of God's anger and vengeance and a warning to all other pillagers". The squire's horse and the squire with it began to whirl madly in the fields, raising such an outcry that no one dared approach them. At length, the squire and his horse fell in a heap with their necks broken and turned instantly to dust and ashes.[50]

One of Froissart's vengeance stories provides a small but interesting new wrinkle. We have seen before that a crucial step towards legitimating violent vengeance was making public the grievance behind it. Just how one went about making a grievance public, however, could change over time. In the wake of the French disaster at Poitiers, the provost of the merchants of Paris, Étienne Marcel, led a revolt in favor of King Charles of Navarre, son of a daughter of Louis X.[51] To protect the city from the forces of the dauphin Charles (son of John II and later Charles V) and his regent the Duke of Normandy, Marcel hired English and Navarrese mercenaries. These promptly alienated the citizens, and a brawl erupted in which more than sixty of the mercenaries were killed. To propitiate the Parisians, "who were clamoring to kill" the mercenaries, Marcel imprisoned 150 of them, but then let them go under the cover of darkness.

The mercenaries gathered at St. Denis, where Charles of Navarre was based. There "they decided to avenge their comrades and the treatment inflicted on themselves". To declare publicly their grievance and intent, the mercenaries sent a formal declaration of war to the Parisians (*envoyèrent tantòt défier ceux de Paris*). Then they roved around outside the city "killing and hacking to pieces" any of the inhabitants who dared to venture out.[52] This story tells us two things. First, a declaration of war carried out in proper form lent legitimacy to the killing spree that followed. Second, for the mercenaries at least, legitimate war did not belong only to kings.

### The Towns and the Peasants

As the above stories about the citizens of Rome and Paris indicate, the towns and cities of Froissart's world – like those of Galbert of Bruges' Flanders – were purveyors of violence in their own right. Froissart mentions townsmen under arms quite frequently throughout his work. The citizens of walled towns defended themselves (or tried to) against attack. Townsmen hired themselves out as mercenaries to others. Towns also, however, sometimes fought on their own behalf. These represented for Froissart a threat to the established aristocratic order. Froissart's attention was particularly drawn by the towns of Flanders. In the late 1330s, as tension between the English and the French kings mounted, Flanders found itself caught in the middle. The counts of Flanders were allies of the French kings. But some of the townsmen of Flanders, especially those of Ghent, Bruges, and Ypres, feared that war would disrupt the vital wool trade on which Flanders' economy depended. Between 1338 and 1382, they formed, under the leadership of Ghent, leagues of Flemish towns in opposition to the counts.[53] In 1382, the Ghenter Philip van Artevelde launched a revolt against Count Louis II. Froissart devotes a great deal of Book II to this revolt, and, as usual, he interprets it for us.

Froissart respected bravery and fine deeds of arms no matter who carried them out. His depiction of van Artevelde and his Flemish townsmen in battle is at times quite sympathetic. However, he shows where his true sympathies lay in his account of a battle that took place at Rooscbeke in 1382. There the French king (by this point Charles VI) and a French army, together with the count, met and crushed van Artevelde's forces. The French victory at Roosebeke, says Froissart, "was greatly to the honor and advantage of all Christendom and of all the gentry and nobility – for if the villeins had achieved their purpose, unexampled ravages and atrocities would have been committed by the commons in rebellion everywhere against the nobly born . . ."[54]

Nowhere does Froissart's prejudice against the commons come out more strongly than in his account in Book I of the great peasant rebellion known as the Jacquerie (from a derisive nickname given to French peasants: Jacques Bonhomme or "Jack Goodman") that broke out in 1358.[55] Key to Froissart's depiction of the peasant rebels are his descriptions of how they wielded violence. Their violence is the very embodiment of evil; it stands in sharp contrast to the noble violence wielded by the members of the aristocracy. As chaos spread through France in the wake of the battle of Poitiers, some of the men from the country towns of the Beauvais region came together.[56] At first they numbered less than a hundred, and they had – Froissart asserts – no leaders. One of them got up and declared that the nobility of France was disgracing and betraying the realm, and that it would be a good thing if they were all destroyed. The assembled responded, "He's right! He's right! Shame on any man who saves the gentry from being wiped out." They then went, armed with only pikes and knives, to the house of a knight who lived nearby. They broke in and killed the knight, his lady, and his children, and burned the house down. Next they went to another knight's castle "and did much worse"; they tied the knight to a post and made him watch while they raped his daughter and pregnant wife, then killed them and all of his other children before cruelly putting him to death and burning and razing the castle.

As the uprising spread, the swelling band of peasants did more of the same to knights' castles and great houses, forcing the gentry to flee. "Without leaders and without arms", they "pillaged and burned everything and violated and killed all the ladies and girls without mercy, like mad dogs". For Froissart, the peasants' violence was "worse than anything that ever took place between Christians and Saracens. Never did men commit such vile deeds. They were such that no living creature ought to see, or even imagine or think of, and the men who committed the most were admired and had the highest places among them. I could never bring myself to write down the horrible and shameful things which they did to the ladies." This last comment notwithstanding, he then tells us how the peasants roasted a knight on a spit, gang-raped his wife, then tried to force the wife and her children to eat from the knight's flesh.[57]

Froissart stresses the peasants' cruelty to women and their disorganization. He only briefly mentions, or glosses over, evidence that they were in fact not entirely leaderless (i.e., the comment above that the men who committed the worst atrocities had the highest places among them, and a brief note somewhat later that they had a "king" whom they had chosen from among their ranks).[58] To Froissart, the peasants represent disorder. They are the antithesis of the knights who eventually gathered to rescue the group of noble ladies trapped at Meaux.[59] The knights were led by the Count of Foix and the Captal de Buch. They formed up in the marketplace "in warlike order" and were ready armed. Opening the gates of the market, they faced off against the thousands of peasants, who were "small and dark and very poorly armed". The knights and their men-at-arms mowed the villeins "down in heaps and slaughtered them like cattle . . . for none of the villeins attempted to take up any sort of fighting order". That the norms of violence changed when "inside" fought "outside" can hardly find starker expression. The knights did not have to treat their enemies according to the law of arms. The peasants were not human; their behavior, as well as their appearance, betrayed them as animals.

### The Free Companies

Events, however, sometimes forced Froissart to describe a world in which the lines between legitimate and illegitimate violence were not so clear. This world was that of the so-called free companies. The free companies comprised aristocrats and their followers who had come to depend for their livelihoods on service in someone's army during a legitimately declared war.[60] When a truce came, they lost their jobs and could not think of (or did not want to think of) anything else to do besides go into business for themselves.[61] When talking about these men, Froissart wrestles with contradiction. He wants to praise fine behavior and deeds of arms by members of his chosen class, but the men he is describing were often performing outside of the bounds of legitimacy as defined by the kings, and sometimes in direct conflict with it.[62]

The free companies first emerged in the aftermath of the French disaster at Poitiers in 1356. Froissart at first casts them in a negative light.[63] He tells us that Sir Regnault de Cervole, nicknamed "the Archpriest", took command of a company of men-at-arms assembled from many countries. "These men found that their pay had ceased with the capture of King John and could see no way of making a living in France." The Archpriest took them south to Provence, captured a number of fortified towns and castles, and plundered the entire country as far as Avignon.[64] Another such company, which ranged the country between the Seine and the Loire in groups of twenty to forty, was led by a Welshman named Ruffin who had himself made a knight and who "became so powerful and rich that his wealth was uncountable".[65] A similar group, led by Sir Robert Knollys and composed of English and Navarrese "pillagers and plunderers", went into operation along the coast of Normandy. Knollys "had a large number of mercenaries at his command and paid them so well that they followed him eagerly".[66]

Froissart soon runs into trouble, however. After noting that "the kingdom of France was plundered and pillaged in every direction, so that it became impossible to ride anywhere without being attacked", he turns to one Sir Eustace d'Aubrecicourt.[67] He tells us that Sir Eustace, the virtual master of Champagne, could muster from 700 to 1000 fighting men at a day's notice; he and his men made almost daily raids in every direction. But then Froissart slips into the language of chivalry: "This Sir Eustace performed many fine feats of arms and no one could stand up to him, for he was young and deeply in love and full of enterprise." He won himself great wealth through ransoms, through sales of towns and castles, through money paid to redeem estates and houses that he had seized, and through the sale of safe-conducts through his territory. Sir Eustace was spurred on by love; he was in love with a "young lady of high breeding and she with him". The lady in question was the daughter of a count and a niece of the queen of England. She had fallen for Sir Eustace because of "his great exploits as a knight". She sent him horses, love-letters, and other tokens of affection, "by which the knight was inspired to still greater feats of bravery and accomplished such deeds that everyone talked of him".

Froissart is visibly juggling two different pictures of Sir Eustace here. On the one hand we have one of those adventurers who were plundering and pillaging the kingdom of France in every direction and who were extorting money from those whom (or whose property) they had captured. On the other we have the gallant knight Sir Eustace, who daily performed fine feats of arms and was spurred on by the love of his lady. Froissart lets his chivalric sensibilities win out. In the end, fine feats of arms are their own justification, especially when performed in the service of love. Though Froissart does not mention it, it may have helped that Sir Eustace was likewise a Hainaulter.[68]

The contradictions embodied by the free companies are perfectly captured in Froissart's account of his conversations with a Gascon squire, the Bascot de Mauléon, or "Bastard of Mauléon".[69] Froissart encountered the Bascot on a trip south in 1388 to visit the court of the Count of Foix. He describes the Bascot as a man of about fifty-five, "with the air of a bold and experienced soldier". One evening after supper, says Froissart, he, the Bascot, and others were sitting around the fire in their hostel in Orthez, waiting for a summons to attend the count. Through the good offices of the Bascot's cousin, Froissart got the Bascot talking about his life and experiences.[70]

Born Gascon, the Bascot's allegiance lay with the king of England.[71] He had fought on the English side at Poitiers, then, with nothing else to do, had gone campaigning in Prussia with the Count of Foix and the Captal de Buch. He had, therefore, been present at Meaux when their force rescued the ladies trapped there by the Jacquerie. After that, he had served under the Captal de Buch with the King of Navarre, who, although there was at that point a truce between the kings of France and England, was fighting the Regent of France for his own purposes.[72] The Bascot went with the Captal's forces into Picardy, where, by his own account, "we became masters of the farmlands and the rivers and we and our friends won a great deal of wealth".[73] When the truce between France and England ended, the King of Navarre and the Regent made peace, so the Bascot went with the Captal de Buch to rejoin the King of England, who had just launched a major campaign and laid siege to Rheims.

When the kings of England and France concluded another peace at Chartres,[74] it was under the condition that all "fighting men and companions-in-arms" had to clear out of the castles and forts that they held. Forced out of their strongholds, "large numbers of poor companions trained in war came out and collected together". Some of their leaders held a conference to decide what to do, for "though the kings had made peace, they had to live somehow".[75] They decided to go to Burgundy and set up in business for themselves. The Bascot signed on as a captain. His fellow captains came from all over the map; they included English, Gascons, Spaniards, Navarrese, Germans, and Scots. Altogether they fielded more than 12,000 men in Burgundy and along the Loire.[76]

The Bascot talked with evident pride about the skills of his companions. "And I tell you," he said,

> that in that assembly there were three or four thousand really fine soldiers, as trained and skilled in war as any man could be, wonderful men at planning a battle and seizing the advantage, at scaling and assaulting towns and castles, as expert and experienced as you could ask for . . .[77]

Their skills paid off at a battle at Brignais, "when we thrashed the Constable of France and the Count of Forez with a good two thousand lances of knights and squires".[78] The Bascot and his companions followed the rules of capture and ransom, which is hardly surprising since the point of their activities was to make money. All of them grew rich from prisoners and from the towns and fortresses they captured. The crowning moment, declared the Bascot, came after they captured Pont-Saint-Espirit, a Provençal town not far from Avignon, "for then they made war on the Pope and the Cardinals and really made them squeal". The pope only extricated himself by brokering an agreement that sent several of the leading captains and most of the companions off to fight in Italy.[79]

But the Bascot, along with many other captains, decided to stay put. He boasted of the towns and castles they still held and bragged, "we held the whole country to ransom. They couldn't get rid of us, either by paying us good money or otherwise".[80]

The Bascot also talked at length about Sir Jean Aimery, an English knight and "the greatest captain we had".[81] He casts Sir Jean's actions as motivated by simple calculations of profit and loss; in contrast to the activities of knightly warlords in the same region in the eleventh century, it is hard to discern here any personal claim, grievance, or desire for revenge driving the English knight's actions. While marauding along the banks of the Loire, Sir Jean fell into an ambush laid by the lords of Rougemont and Voudenay and by men of the Archpriest.[82] He was captured, and had to pay a cash ransom of 30,000 francs to regain his freedom. Sir Jean was furious, and swore that he would not return to his castle until he regained what he had lost. He gathered a large number of followers, then asked other captains (including the Bascot) if they wanted to go out on a raid with him. He wanted, he said, to strike at the "Sancerre boys", that is, the Count of Sancerre and his two brothers. If the companions could capture the Sancerre brothers and their garrison inside their castle, "we should recover our losses and be sitting on top of the whole country".[83] As Froissart describes things, Sir Jean was apparently not concerned with taking revenge on the men who had captured and humiliated him. Instead, he aimed to recover his financial losses and restore his standing and position of power in the region by hitting a good and available target (to no avail – the Sancerre brothers learned of his plans and laid an ambush. Sir Jean was defeated and later died of his wounds).

The Bascot related other incidents that further expose his attitudes towards violence (or the attitudes towards violence that Froissart is projecting through him). As he described the towns and castles he and his men had seized and plundered, and the safe-conducts people had to get from them if they wanted to venture out into the country, he revealed that legitimacy conferred by constituted authority did matter, and that the companions reached for it when they could – or when they found it useful – to justify what they were doing. He noted that the Archpriest decided for a time to be "a loyal Frenchman" and had taken official command in the city of Nevers, though according to the Bascot he had to work through his friendships and connections with the companions to get anything done. After narrating a particular string of his own exploits, the Bascot let drop that he and his men "were carrying on that particular war with the knowledge of the King of Navarre, and in his name".[84]

The newly minted French king Charles V (r. 1364–80) was trying to rein in the companies, in part by paying them off. At one point, Froissart has the Bascot relate how, at a particularly low point in his career, he and his men went looking for a town to capture so that they could recover their fortunes.[85] They settled on the town and castle of Thurie. They captured the town easily by having a few of their number dress as women and sneak up to the gates with the townswomen who had gone out in the morning to fetch water; once there they seized the gates and held them until their companions arrived. The castle, bragged the Bascot, "has since brought me in, through plunder, protection-money, and various strokes of luck which I've had, one hundred thousand francs". But now, he sighed, he did not know what to do. He had been negotiating with the Count of Armagnac and the Dauphin of Auvergne, who had been given powers by the king to buy towns and fortresses from free companions, as well as from anyone who was fighting or had fought in the King of England's name. Several other captains had already given up theirs, but the Bascot had not yet decided whether or not he should give up his.

On at least one occasion, French efforts against the companions provided a useful weapon for someone out to avenge himself on a former comrade. One of the leading captains of companions, Louis Roubaut,[86] had a companion and brother-in-arms named Limosin. Louis Roubaut also had a very beautiful mistress, whom he entrusted to Limosin's care when he had to travel. Limosin took his duties very seriously; he "looked after the good lady so well that he got all he wanted from her".[87] That is, he did until Louis found out about the affair. Louis's friendship for Limosin was replaced with such hatred that, "so as to shame him more". Louis had Limosin stripped to his underwear and flogged through the town.[88] A trumpet was sounded ahead of him, and at each crossroads his misdeed was proclaimed. Then he was banished from the town as a traitor, with only a tunic on his back. A humiliated Limosin promptly declared his intent to "get his revenge when he could".[89] He went to the town and castle of a baron whom he had served as a boy, and whose lands he had assiduously avoided in his prosperous days as a freeboot-ing plunderer. He managed to reach his lord and told his story. The lord agreed to let him stay, as long as he promised to be a "good and loyal Frenchman"; he also made Limosin make his peace with everyone in the area whom he had harmed.[90] When Limosin "could ride again as an hon-orable man", he was given a horse and armor, and taken to see the seneschal of Velay at Le Puy.[91] There he was interrogated closely about Louis Roubaut and his travel habits and freely told all he knew. Spies were sent out and a place for an ambush identified; Louis was success-fully captured. Confronting the captive, Limosin reproached him for having treated him so badly because of his mistress. "If you had done the same thing to me", he said, "I should never have minded, for two companions-in-arms, such as we were then, could surely, at a pinch, have overlooked a woman."[92] Shortly afterwards all of Roubaut's garrisons surrendered in exchange for their lives. News of Louis Roubaut's capture was sent to the king, who was delighted. Soon after, Louis was sentenced and beheaded.[93]

### The Aristocracy, the Law, the Kings, and the Courts

If Froissart valorizes, or allows the Bascot de Mauléon to valorize, deeds of arms for their own sake, he nevertheless freely admits the suffering and hardship that they caused. He is also aware that the idea of the king's responsibility to maintain order was still out there, and that the king and those loyal to him (or those who had decided for whatever reasons to act as if they were loyal to him) were struggling to uphold it in a very difficult situation. Elsewhere in his *Chronicles*, he tells us that he himself regarded royal justice as essential to order. When narrating the gradual disintegration of the government of King Richard II of England in 1399,[94] he says that the absence of functioning royal courts led directly to a chaos in England very similar to that produced by the free companies in France. Richard had closed the courts in England, "to the dismay of honest men who asked only for tranquility and fair dealing, with the payment of their honest debts". These honest men then began to be attacked by people who "roamed the country in troops and gangs". Merchants feared to ride out on their business for fear of being robbed, and did not know where to turn for protection or justice. Farmers were plundered of their grain and livestock. People complained of King Richard's idleness and contrasted the sorry state of affairs with the reign of "good King Edward of happy memory".[95]

A very odd story, in contrast, presents us with at least one aristocrat who had absolutely no use for courts. The story itself is not about courts. Instead, it is about how the Count of Foix came to know about future events in advance.[96] Nevertheless, the anecdote assumes an aristocrat who preferred to base his property rights on the threat of violence rather than on the law. While Froissart was visiting the count's castle in search of material in 1388, a squire told him about the count's uncanny ability and swore that his story was absolutely true. An eager Froissart pressed him for details. His informant hesitated, but then finally pulled Froissart into an angle of the wall of the castle chapel and told the following story.

Some twenty years previously, there was in the region an influential noble named Raymond, who was lord of Corresse. Raymond was entangled in a dispute with a cleric from Catalonia over the rights to the tithes from the church of Corresse. The case was heard before the papal court in Avignon. The cleric was "very learned in canon law", and claimed to have an indisputable right to the tithes. He proved his case, and Pope Urban V himself delivered the verdict rejecting Raymond's claim. Armed with documents showing the pope's decision, the cleric took possession of the tithe rights. But Raymond had no use for the learned law, and he refused to recognize that it had any power over him. As far as he was concerned, the tithes from the church were part of his estate, and his claim to them depended on his sword arm, not on some documents. Indignantly he confronted the cleric, saying, "do you think I am going to give up my inheritance because of your papers? I doubt if you will be so bold as to make off with things that are mine, for if you do you will be risking your life. Now go and look somewhere else for a benefice. You are not going to get anything from my estate, and once for all I'm telling you to keep off."[97]

The cleric was frightened of Raymond, who was known as a violent man. Just before leaving, however, he told Raymond, "Sir, by force and not by right you are depriving me of the rights of my church, and in all conscience you are acting very wrongly. I am not as strong as you are in this country, but I would like you to know that as soon as I can I shall send you a champion who will frighten you more than I do."[98] Shortly thereafter, like the young man who attacked the monks of Conques in a similar situation in the *Miracles* of St. Foy, Raymond had to confront a supernatural power – though this particular supernatural power would not have met with the Church's approval. The cleric's champion turned out to be an invisible spirit named Orton, who threatened to leave Raymond no peace until he honored the cleric's rights. Raymond, however, persuaded the spirit to leave the cleric and come to work for him. Orton began telling Raymond everything that he saw in his travels, and, since he obviously traveled much faster than people, it was as if Raymond knew about events in advance. And it was Raymond who passed this information on to the Count of Foix.

Unlike Raymond, some other members of the French aristocracy found law and courts – at least royal law and royal courts – to be useful because they legitimated their own violence and protected them from the violence of others. One such case, which Froissart narrates at length and which spanned the years 1386 and 1387, ended up producing a spectacular judicial combat following a decision by the High Court, or Parlement of Paris.[99] The principals were a knight named Sir Jean de Carrouges and a squire by the name of Jacques Le Gris. Both men belonged to the household of Count Pierre d'Alençon. Froissart telegraphs his attitudes right away by noting that Le Gris was a squire of humble birth whom fortune had cast upwards until he became the count's favorite. This is one of Froissart's principal moral concerns in the *Chronicles*. When the lowborn rose above their station and unduly influenced the great, evil resulted. Good rulers kept men of quality around them and did not allow themselves to fall under the sway of men like Le Gris.[100]

Sir Jean de Carrouges went on an expedition overseas to help in his advancement. He left his wife, a good and sensible woman, alone with her servants in her castle. "Through a strange, perverse temptation", the devil entered into Jacques Le Gris and caused him to become obsessed with Sir Jean's wife. Planning carefully, Le Gris allowed himself to be seen early in the morning at the count's castle, then rode quickly to Sir Jean's castle. He was openly admitted because he was trusted. Greeted by Sir Jean's wife as a friend, he raped her, then threatened to expose her to public shame if she revealed what had happened. He then rode quickly back to the count's castle, to all appearances having never left.

When Sir Jean returned from his expedition, his wife told him what had happened. At first he refused to believe her. Finally, however, his doubts gave way, and he said to his wife, "if the thing happened as you say, I forgive you; but the squire shall die for it in some way to be decided by my friends and yours."[101] Having decided on vengeance, Sir Jean rallied his support group; he wrote letters to his wife's closest friends and to his own asking them to come to his castle. When they were all assembled, he told them his wife's story. The assembled urged him to go to Count Pierre, the lord of both Sir Jean and Le Gris, and tell him what had happened. Le Gris was, however, a favorite of the count, who accordingly refused to believe Sir Jean. The count instead set a date for Le Gris, Sir Jean, and Sir Jean's wife to appear before him. When Sir Jean and his wife (who was accompanied by members of her family) formally accused Le Gris before the count, Le Gris fell back on his alibi; he had been seen at the count's court. Count Pierre decided that Sir Jean's wife must have dreamed the whole thing, ordered the charge to be dropped, and forbade any questions to be raised about it again.

Sir Jean "had great courage and believed his wife"; he refused to obey the count's ruling. He did not, however, take direct action. He chose instead to bypass his lord and appeal Le Gris before the Parlement in Paris. The case ended up staying before the court for a year and a half. Froissart explains that the two parties "could not be reconciled because the knight believed absolutely in his wife's account and because the case had become so notorious that he felt bound to pursue it to the end". In other words, under normal circumstances the court would have served, as courts had in previous ages, as a forum for negotiation and mediation rather than for adjudication. In this case, the efforts to bring about a settlement lasted a very long time. But taking the case to the court was a wise move on Sir Jean's part, because according to Froissart the court protected him. His lord Count Pierre was so infuriated by Sir Jean's stubbornness "that there were many times when he would have had him killed, but for the fact that they had already gone to court".[102]

Finally the court ruled that since the lady could not prove her charge against Le Gris, the matter should be settled by a judicial combat. The combat was set for the first Monday of 1387. Word of the judgment reached King Charles VI (r. 1380–1422), who was with his barons waiting to embark on a planned invasion of England.[103] The king asked that the duel be postponed until he could get to Paris to watch it. When the combat finally took place, it was on a glittering stage. Vast crowds of people surrounded the lists, which were set up in St. Catherine's square, behind the Temple. The king, his uncles, and other lords sat in large stands that had been built on one side of the lists. The two champions, Sir Jean and Le Gris, came on to the field armed from head to toe, and sat down, accompanied by their seconds. Before the duel began, Sir Jean went over to his wife, who was dressed in black and sitting in a carriage. "Lady," he said, "on your evidence I am about to hazard my life in combat with Jacques Le Gris. You know if my cause is just and true." "My lord," replied the lady, "it is so. You can fight confidently. The cause is just." "In God's hands be it then," said her husband; he kissed his wife, made the sign of the cross, and entered the lists.[104] Sir Jean's wife prayed to God and the Virgin. She was, says Froissart, justifiably anxious; if her husband lost, the sentence was that he be hanged and that she be burnt without appeal.

Froissart gives us a lengthy, blow-by-blow account of the battle, which started on horseback and ended on foot. Though wounded, Sir Jean managed in the end to knock Le Gris down and thrust his sword through his body, killing him on the spot. With this the case ended. Le Gris's body was handed over to the executioner, who hanged it. King Charles gave Sir Jean a thousand francs and made him a member of his chamber with a pension of 200 francs per year.

In this, the last known case in which the Parlement of Paris ordered a judicial combat,[105] we see the same sort of blending of old and new that we saw in Angevin England. Sir Jean had a grievance, and an ample support group willing to back him up. He was not strong enough, however, to take on his opponent and his lord, who backed his opponent, directly. He therefore skillfully used the Parlement, and the publicity attached to it, both to protect himself against his lord's anger and, eventually, to take violent vengeance on his opponent with the sanction of the king's authority.

## Conclusions

The society that Froissart projects for us was still plainly medieval in its attitudes towards violence. Members of all social groups felt entitled to, and did, use violence to further or defend their interests. People took violent vengeance for insult or injury, and relied for help on support groups built of kin, friends, and followers. Some violent conflicts were so intractable that, like some we have seen in earlier chapters, they could only be settled by a transcendent religious experience. Over all ruled a God who himself used violence to achieve his ends and to avenge injuries and affronts.

The aristocracy whose deeds Froissart chronicled lived to fight. Whether a knight were English, Scottish, French, Flemish, Navarrese, Bohemian, or (here Froissart would probably give only a grudging "even") German, his reputation rested ultimately on his prowess. At the same time, Froissart's knights at least pretended to follow norms that carefully regulated their violence. Some of these norms were covered by the term "law of arms". Others were encompassed by the looser rubric "chivalrous". According to Froissart, these norms separated knights from other purveyors of violence, and they distinguished good knights from bad ones (and from German ones). Knights whenever possible captured rather than killed each other. Good knights fought fairly, treated their prisoners well, and charged only reasonable ransoms. Chivalric norms did not, however, apply to those outside the ranks of the nobility, nor does Froissart think they should have. Violent members of the commons, whether they were townspeople or peasants, represented a threat to the proper order of society. They did not use violence for the right reasons and in the right ways and were therefore not entitled to the respect that (good) knights accorded each other. In the most extreme case, the peasants of the Jacquerie were violent as animals were violent; aristocrats were therefore entitled to kill them as they would animals. In Froissart's mind, violence served to demarcate social divisions as well as to enforce them.

Yet Froissart's knights were not that different from their predecessors in earlier ages. Knights fought in *guerrae*. They fought to display their prowess, to gain power, and to make money. They fought to take revenge for insults to themselves or their ladies, and to assert or protect what they thought were their rights. That fourteenth-century knights assumed they had the right to do so is visible not just in Froissart's *Chronicles*, but also in the writings of a knight who was widely regarded as the best of the breed. Sir Geoffroy de Charny died at Poitiers in 1356, near to King John II, defending the French royal standard or *oriflamme* from the English.[106] Before his death, de Charny wrote a manual of chivalry, the *Livre de Chevalerie*.[107] Among the pearls of wisdom he offered the followers of his profession, which he regarded as "the most dangerous for both soul and body",[108] are overt statements about a knight's right and duty to be violent on his own initiative. An exemplary knight had first to fight when his lord called him to take part in a war, as long as that war was begun in the proper manner and in due form. But he also had to fight to defend his kin against attempts to disinherit them or seize their estate. He had to do the same for defenseless maidens or widows or orphans. Moreover, one could "wage war and embark on battles on one's own account to defend one's land and inheritance" when it could not be defended in any other way. Finally, one had to fight to protect the rights of the Church.[109] Bad knights, in de Charny's view, waged war without a good reason. They seized people without good cause and robbed and stole from them, or wounded and killed them. They attacked people without a proper challenge and without any wrongdoing on the part of those attacked. Finally, they robbed churches.[110] This string of negatives implies, of course, a set of positives. There were good reasons for a knight to wage war; there were good causes to seize people and take their goods, or harm or kill them. If someone had done wrong and one challenged them properly, it was licit to attack him.

De Charny's assertion that knights had the right and duty to defend the defenseless, particularly women, widows, orphans, and the Church, suggests that chivalric theory had adopted some of the ancient ideology of kingship. This makes perfect sense, given the efforts of, for example, the early peace councils to make knights swear to do just that.[111] De Charny accompanies this claim, however, with an older one: knights were entitled to fight to defend their own property and interests and those of their kin. The way that he puts this, and his counter-image of the bad knight, creates the impression that his world was full of bad men, motivated by greed, who used violence to do injustice. What Froissart tells us about violence in the French countryside, particularly after the battle of Poitiers, certainly tells us that there were men like that out there. But we have seen repeatedly that medieval ideas of justice were highly subjective. Behind at least some of de Charny's bad men must have lain many a knight who was convinced that he too was wielding violence in defense of his own rights, interest, and honor.

Although de Charny stresses that knights had to be loyal to kings, there is little in his text suggesting that kings could regulate knightly violence, or override their right to use arms on their own in what they considered to be just causes. His idea of war is broad and all embracing; whether it was large scale or small, it simply had to be begun in the proper form. Froissart, in contrast, given that his text is history on a European scale rather than a didactic treatise, cannot avoid telling us of kings who could declare when violence was legitimate and when it was not. When a king declared a war, all manner of typical knightly behavior – plundering, pillaging, capturing, ransoming, killing, and raping – became *ipso facto* legitimate (though if we are to believe Froissart's vignette about Sir Thomas Holland at the sack of Caen, the dictates of chivalry sometimes softened the latter even in wartime). The aristocracy continued to do what the aristocracy had always done, but there were now limits. When there was a war on, all was licit. When there was not, a killing could lead to a royal judgment and exile.

The strength of the norms of royally sponsored order in Froissart's world is paradoxically most evident at their moment of greatest weakness in the aftermath of Poitiers. The free companies gathered soldiers from all regions of Europe and from all walks of life who, deprived of the ability to make a living fighting for kings, set up shop on their own. A significant number of these soldiers, and most of their leaders, were members of the international warrior aristocracy, that is, knights and squires (one apparent exception being the Welshman Ruffin, who nevertheless, according to Froissart, felt it necessary to have himself made a knight). These knights and squires did what knights ever since the tenth century had done; they purveyed their skill at violence into wealth and power, at least temporarily. But now there was a difference. Froissart, though seduced by the rascally charm of a Bascot de Mauléon or the chivalric romance of a Sir Eustace d'Aubrecicourt, nevertheless writes of plundering and pillaging, of entire regions whose inhabitants were afraid to stir beyond their castle or town walls, of fields laid waste and commerce disrupted. He openly describes protection rackets and extortion. That the so-called Secretary to Chivalry[112] could even do so (as opposed to the churchmen who had long been happy to describe knightly violence in these terms) reveals that he was living in a changed world. The antidote to what appeared to him and therefore perforce even to his audience as disorder was the gradual resurrection of royal authority. The "French", that is, the aristocrats who had decided to remain or become "loyal Frenchmen" and thus followers of the French king, slowly defeated the companions in battle or bought them off. Even the companions themselves, according to Froissart, betrayed a need for the legitimacy that kings conferred in their preference for fighting under someone's banner, be it the king of the English, the king of Navarre, or the king of France.

As the French kings Charles V and then Charles VI managed to revive the position of the French crown, royal claims to regulate violence attracted the cooperation of those who could use them, as they had before the war with England had broken out. A somewhat sordid example is that of Limosin, who used royal efforts to suppress the free companies to take his vengeance on Louis Roubaut. More spectacular is the case of Sir Jean de Carrouges, who managed to use an appeal to the Parlement of Paris both to take violent vengeance on his opponent and to protect himself from his angry lord. The private urge to violence was well on its way towards being co-opted by the institutions of public justice.

## Notes

1. G. Brereton, "Introduction" to Froissart, *Chronicles*, 9–29 @9.
2. Constance B. Bouchard, "The Kingdom of the Franks to 1108", and John W. Baldwin, "The Kingdom of the Franks from Louis VI to Philip II: Crown and Government", both in NCMH IV/2, 120–53 and 510–29; William C. Jordan, "The Capetians from the Death of Philip II to Philip IV", NCMH V, 279–313; Michael Jones, "France: The Last Capetians and Early Valois Kings", NCMH VI, 388–421.
3. Justine Firnhaber-Baker, "From God's Peace to the King's Order: Late Medieval Limitations on Non-Royal Warfare", *Essays in Medieval Studies* 23 (2006): 19–30; Kaiser, "Selbsthilfe und Gewaltmonopol", 64–71; T.N. Bisson, "The Organized Peace in Southern France and Catalonia, c. 1140–c. 1233", *The American Historical Review* 82 no. 2 (April 1977): 290–311.
4. *Recueil des historiens des Gaules et de la France*, vol. 14, ed. Michel-Jean-Joseph Brial (Paris: Victor Palmé, 1877), 387–8.
5. Kaiser, "Selbsthilfe und Gewaltmonopol", 70.
6. Kaeuper, *Chivalry and Violence*, 100–1 and *War, Justice, and Public Order: England and France in the Later Middle Ages* (Oxford: Clarendon Press, 1988), 231–5; Firnhaber-Baker, "God's Peace", 20–1.
7. *Ordonnances des roys de France de la troisième race*, 21 vols. (Paris: Imprimerie royale, 1723–1849), I, ed. Eusèbe Jacob de Laurière, 84; Kaueper, *War, Justice, and Public Order*, as above.
8. Jean Dunbabin, "The Political World of France, c. 1200–c. 1336", in *France in the Later Middle Ages*, ed. D. Potter (Oxford: Oxford University Press, 2002), 23–46 @35–7.
9. *The Memoirs of the Lord of Joinville: A New English Version*, trans. Ethel Wedgwood (New York: E.P. Dutton and Co., 1906), available at the University of Virginia Electronic Text Center, **http://etext.lib.virginia. edu/toc/modeng/public/WedLord.html**, Part 1, 21.
10. Dunbabin, "The Political World", 44.
11. Ibid., 35–6.
12. Kaeuper, *Chivalry and Violence*, 19–29.
13. See Chapter 4 above @n. 72.
14. Maurice Keen, *The Laws of War in the Late Middle Ages* (London: Routledge, 1965), 2, 68–76.

15. C.B. Bouchard, *"Strong of Body, Brave and Noble": Chivalry and Society in Medieval France* (Ithaca, NY: Cornell University Press, 1998), esp. 1–27; Keen, *Chivalry*, 28, 143–61.

16. See Chapter 6 above @nn. 23–4.

17. Kaeuper, *Chivalry and Violence*, 87. See also ibid., 47–8; Keen, *Chivalry*, 43–63; Strickland, *War and Chivalry*, 57–68.

18. Keen, *Laws of War*, 19–52; Strickland, *War and Chivalry*, 31–54. On heralds in particular see Keen, *Chivalry*, 125–42.

19. Matthew Paris, *Chronica Majora*, ed. H.R. Luard (London: Longman, 1872–83), IV, 593.

20. Kaeuper, *Chivalry and Violence*, 105–6.

21. *Ordonnances*, 328–9; Kaeuper, *Chivalry and Violence*, 101–2.

22. *Ordonnances*, 390.

23. Firnhaber-Baker, "God's Peace", 21–3.

24. *Ordonnances*, 390 and 492–3.

25. *Ordonnances*, 493.

26. *Ordonnances*, 390.

27. Firnhaber-Baker, "God's Peace", 20–1.

28. *Ordonnances*, 559; Kaeuper, *War, Justice, and Public Order*, 235–47.

29. Jones, "The Last Capetians and Early Valois Kings"; François Autrand, "France under Charles V and Charles VI", NCHM VI, 422–41; Robert J. Knecht, *The Valois: Kings of France, 1328–1589* (London: Hambledon, 2004).

30. Anne Curry, "France and the Hundred Years War, 1337–1453", in Potter, ed., *France in the Later Middle Ages*, 90–116; John A. Wagner, *Encyclopedia of the Hundred Years War* (Westport: Greenwood Press, 2006); L.J. Andrew Villalon and Donald J. Kagay, eds. *The Hundred Years War: A Wider Focus* (Leiden: Brill, 2005); Jonathan Sumption, *The Hundred Years War*, 2 vols. (Phildalephia: University Press, 1991–9).

31. *Les Chroniques de sire Jean Froissart qui traitent des merveilleuses emprises, nobles aventures et faits d'armes advenus en son temps en France, Angleterre, Bretaigne, Bourgogne, Escosse, Espaigne, Portingal et ès autres parties*, ed. J.A.C. Buchon, 3 vols. Abridged English translation based on Buchon's edition: Froissart, *Chronicles*, All quotations will be taken from *Chronicles* unless otherwise noted.

32. Brereton, "Introduction" to *Chronicles*; D. Wages, "Froissart, Jean", in C.J. Drees, ed., *The Late Medieval Age of Crisis and Renewal, 1300–1500: A Biographical Dictionary* (Westport: Greenwood Press, 2001), 169–71; D. Maddox and S. Sturm-Maddox, eds., *Froissart Across the Genres* (Gainesville: University Press of Florida, 1998); P.F. Ainsworth, *Jean Froissart and the Fabric of History* (Oxford: Clarendon Press, 1990); J.J.N. Palmer, ed., *Froissart: Historian* (Woodbridge, Suffolk: Boydell Press, 1981).

33. *Chroniques*, vol. 1, I, 1, c. LXXX, 72–3/*Chronicles*, 60–1.

34. *Chroniques*, vol. 1, I, 1, c. CCLXXI–CCLXXII, 223–5/*Chronicles*, 73–5; Sumption, *Hundred Years War*, I, 507–11.

35. Keen, *Chivalry*, 144–5.

36. *Chroniques*, vol. 1, I, 1, c. CCLXXII, 225/*Chronicles*, 75.
37. *Chroniques*, vol. 1, I, 1, c. CCXCIII, 241/*Chronicles*, 93.
38. *Chroniques*, vol. 1, I, 2, c. CCCXVI, 620/*Chronicles*, 179.
39. *Chroniques*, vol. 2, III, c. CXXIII, 731/*Chronicles*, 345–6.
40. *Chroniques*, vol. 3, IV, c. XII, 46–7/*Chronicles*, 376–7.
41. *Chroniques*, vol. 3, IV, c. XII, 54/*Chronicles*, 378–9.
42. *Chroniques*, vol. 1, I, 2, c. V, 289/*Chronicles*, 111.
43. *Chroniques*, vol. 1, I, 2, c. XLIV, 356/*Chronicles*, 140–1. Brereton translates *par guerre d'amis et d'un homicide qu'il avoit fait* to say "after killing a man in a family feud".
44. *Chroniques*, vol. 1, I, 2, c. XXXIII, 344/*Chronicles*, 131–2.
45. H. Kaminsky, "The Great Schism", in NCMH VI, 674–96.
46. *Chroniques*, vol. 2, II, c. XLVIII, 59, XLIX, 61/*Chronicles*, 206, 208–9.
47. Caroline M. Barron, "The Reign of Richard II", in NCMH VI, 297–333, esp. 311–16.
48. i.e., go through having his vassals formally renew their oaths to him.
49. *Chroniques*, vol. 2, III, c. LXXIV–LXXXI, 613–27/*Chronicles*, 319–27. See *Chronicles*, 327 n. 1 and Barron, as above n. 47, re Froissart's errors of fact.
50. *Chroniques*, vol. 1, I, 2, c. XCVII, 408/*Chronicles*, 162–3.
51. Michael Jones, "The Crown and the Provinces in the Fourteenth Century", in Potter, *France in the Later Middle Ages*, 61–89 @85–6; Sumption, *Hundred Years War*, II, 250–350.
52. *Chroniques*, vol. 1, I, 2, c. LXXI, 380–1/*Chronicles*, 156–7.
53. Nicholas, *Medieval Flanders*, 217–24, 228–30.
54. *Chroniques*, vol. 2, II, c. CXCVIII, 252/*Chronicles*, 249–50.
55. Pierre Charbonnier, "Society and the Economy: Crisis and its Aftermath", in Potter, *France in the Later Middle Ages*, 117–29 @124–5; Sumption, *Hundred Years War*, II, 327–36.
56. *Chroniques*, vol. 1, I, 2, c. LXV, 375/*Chronicles*, 151.
57. *Chroniques*, vol. 1, I, 2, c. LXV, 376/*Chronicles*, 151–2.
58. *Chroniques*, vol. 1, I, 2, c. LXV, 376/*Chronicles*, 152.
59. *Chroniques*, vol. 1, I, 2, c. LXVIII, 378/*Chronicles*, 153–5.
60. K. Fowler, *Medieval Mercenaries*. Vol. 1. *The Great Companies* (Oxford: Blackwell, 2001).
61. Sumption, *Hundred Years War*, II, 351–404.
62. Cf. Keen, *Chivalry*, 228–33.
63. *Chroniques*, vol. 1, I, 2, c. LX–LXI, 373/*Chronicles*, 148–9.
64. Sumption, *Hundred Years War*, II, 360–5.
65. Ibid., 288.
66. Ibid., 286 and 379–85.
67. *Chroniques*, vol. 1, I, 2, c. XCI, 410/*Chronicles*, 161–2. Sumption, *Hundred Years War*, II, 406–10.
68. Sumption, *Hundred Years War*, II, 406.
69. *Chroniques*, vol. 2, III, c. XV–XVII, 406–14/*Chronicles*, 280–94; Sumption, *Hundred Years War*, II, 38. R. de Gorog, *Lexique Français Moderne – Ancien Français* (Athens, GA: University of Georgia Press, 1973), s.v. *bascot*.

70. Fowler, *Medieval Mercenaries*, 14 and n. 53 notes that he was unable to find any record of the Bascot in archival sources; he suggests that the Bascot might have been a fictional character created by Froissart to enable him to tell stories of the companies himself.
71. *Chroniques*, vol. 2, III, XVI, 410/*Chronicles*, 288.
72. Cf. Jones, "Crown and Provinces", 80–3; Sumption, *Hundred Years War*, II, 365–73, 418–21.
73. *Chroniques*, vol. 2, III, c. XV, 407/*Chronicles*, 281.
74. The Treaty of Brétigny, May 1360: Sumption, *Hundred Years War*, II, 445–8.
75. *Chroniques*, vol. 2, III, c. XV, 407/*Chronicles*, 282.
76. Cf. Sumption, *Hundred Years War*, II, 460–5.
77. *Chroniques*, vol. 2, III, c. XV, 407/*Chronicles*, 282.
78. Ibid.; cf. Sumption, *Hundred Years War*, II, 477–9.
79. *Chroniques*, vol. 2, III, c. XV, 407/*Chronicles*, 282–3; Sumption, *Hundred Years War*, II, 466–8.
80. *Chroniques*, vol. 2, III, c. XV, 408/*Chronicles*, 283.
81. *Chroniques*, vol. 2, III, c. XVI, 408/*Chronicles*, 284. Sumption, *Hundred Years War*, II, 475, 478, 485.
82. *Chroniques*, vol. 2, III, c. XVI, 408–10/*Chronicles*, 284–7.
83. *Chroniques*, vol. 2, III, c. XVI, 409/*Chronicles*, 285.
84. *Chroniques*, vol. 2, III, c. XV, 408/*Chronicles*, 283–4.
85. *Chroniques*, vol. 2, III, c. XVI, 410–11/*Chronicles*, 289–90.
86. *Chroniques*, vol. 2, III, c. XVII, 411–13/*Chronicles*, 290–3; Sumption, *Hundred Years War*, II, 485–8, 521, 531.
87. *Chroniques*, vol. 2, III, c. XVII, 412/*Chronicles*, 291.
88. *Chroniques*, vol. 2, III, c. XVII, 412/*Chronicles*, 291–2.
89. *Chroniques*, vol. 2, III, c. XVII, 412/*Chronicles*, 292.
90. *Chroniques*, vol. 2, III, c. XVII, 412/*Chronicles*, 292–3.
91. *Chroniques*, vol. 2, III, c. XVII, 412/*Chronicles*, 293.
92. *Chroniques*, vol. 2, III, c. XVII, 413/*Chronicles*, 293.
93. Cf. Sumption, *Hundred Years War*, II, 531.
94. Barron, "Reign of Richard II", 325–33.
95. *Chroniques*, vol. 3, IV, c. LXX, 338–9/*Chronicles*, 441–2.
96. *Chroniques*, vol. 2, III, c. XXII, 434–8/*Chronicles*, 295–9.
97. *Chroniques*, vol. 2, III, c. XXII, 435/*Chronicles*, 297.
98. Ibid.
99. *Chroniques*, vol. 2, III, c. XLIX, 534–8/*Chronicles*, 309–15.
100. Ainsworth, *Jean Froissart*, 100, 105; cf. Kaeuper, *Chivalry and Violence*, 105.
101. *Chroniques*, vol. 2, III, c. XLIX, 535/*Chronicles*, 311.
102. *Chroniques*, vol. 2, III, c. XLIX, 536/*Chronicles*, 313.
103. Knecht, *The Valois*, 42–3.
104. *Chroniques*, vol. 2, III, c. XLIX, 536/*Chronicles*, 313–14.
105. *Chronicles*, 315 n. 1; E. Jager, *The Last Duel: A True Story of Crime, Scandal, and Trial by Combat in Medieval France* (New York: Broadway, 2004).
106. Sumption, *Hundred Years War*, II, 237–8, 247.

107. Geoffroi de Charny, *A Knight's Own Book of Chivalry*, trans. E. Kennedy (Philadelphia: University of Pennsylvania Press, 2005).
108. Ibid., 91.
109. Ibid., 89–90.
110. Ibid., 96.
111. Cf. Chapter 4 above @nn. 65–72; Kaeuper, *Chivalry and Violence*, 71.
112. Ainsworth, *Jean Froissart, inter alia* 31 and 77.

## chapter ten

# CONCLUSION: COMPETING NORMS, AND THE LEGACY OF MEDIEVAL VIOLENCE

O ur journey has taken us through a Middle Ages that from a modern perspective looks very dangerous. For much if not most of the period, a person's right to wield violence on his own behalf and in his own interests was assumed. Not only was violence, when used by the right person for the right reasons, acceptable and even laudable; in some circumstances to avoid or renounce violence was wrong and even outrageous. In such situations the consequences for avoiding violence were collective as well as personal. If one failed to uphold one's reputation for strength and courage, or to adequately protect the property and honor of one's kin, friends, or followers, one risked shame, isolation, and victimization by others; if one were head of a group or of a polity, that group or polity might collapse. As a consequence, violence was not kept discreetly out of sight. Instead, when it was used in the right cause in the right way, it was advertised and its grisly consequences openly displayed (or written about). It was eagerly watched by crowds of men, women, and children; its perpetrators were celebrated through the streets of a town. When violence overstepped its bounds and threatened the interests of the uninvolved or of the broader community, the parties involved were pressured into non-violent settlement. Nevertheless, compensation amounts were negotiated, and settlements publicly enacted, in ways that made sure honor was publicly satisfied and the ability and willingness to use violence acknowledged.

Christianity was interpreted by many medieval people in a way consonant with these norms. Christian bishops and monks were either violent themselves, or they celebrated violence carried out on their behalf by others. Christian saints both alive and dead used violence to defend themselves, their honor, and their followers, and to attack the enemies of God. So too kings and other rulers: they often appear to have thought about and participated in violence in the same ways as everyone else.

Most of our evidence for this picture has come from observing the behavior and reading the words of those most visible in our sources, namely, members of the aristocracy. We have, however, seen flickers of light, and sometimes more than that, cast on attitudes towards violence held by common people both free and unfree living in the countryside and in the towns. Members of the commons show up most often as victims of violence wielded by their betters. Medieval aristocrats drew clear lines between themselves and everyone else. They would do violent things, or tolerate violent things being done, to those outside the pale that they would never tolerate being done to their social equals. As aristocrats fought with each other, they would kill and rob peasants, and plunder and lay waste to their property, in order to hurt their opponents economically and politically.[1] When peasants or townsmen rose up to assert their own rights and interests, aristocrats killed them without mercy, unless they needed their support or shared interests with them.

Nonetheless, many if not most common people thought about violence in ways similar to their masters. Not all peasants were passive victims; they could at times be active agents. Some peasants liked their lords and fought to protect them. Others fought with each other, for similar reasons as their lords if not with similar weapons, and shared with their masters ideas about violence, rights, and honor. The same holds true for townsfolk; it is townsfolk responding to the same norms of violence as their lords, or generalizing those norms to themselves as collectives, that underlay much of their behavior in the Flanders of Galbert of Bruges.

At the same time, however, alternative norms of violence were always present to a greater or lesser degree. The norms according to which violence was judged were constantly contested; whether or not our sources depict violence as legitimate depends on the perspectives, interests, and power of the parties involved and of those doing the writing or reporting. Normative frameworks clashed as people in conflict appealed for support; writers sought to advance one set of norms and suppress others, as they sought to seize and hold the normative high ground for themselves or for the people they were writing about. Even when one particular set of norms appears to dominate the sources from a given time and region, there are almost always voices advocating others, either in writing from the margins or tacitly in their behavior.

A book of this nature, of course, is forced to be selective. Choosing to highlight particular regions within medieval Europe at particular moments in time has meant leaving out other places and times. It would have been rewarding, for example, to look in more detail at violence and political order in Gaul in the fourth and fifth centuries, in the

Merovingian kingdoms in the seventh and eighth, or in Bavaria in the twelfth.[2] It would have added an entire new dimension to our story to extend our gaze southwards, into the medieval societies of Italy, Spain, and other parts of the Mediterranean world.[3]

Nevertheless, we have looked at enough parts of medieval Europe to hazard a narrative about how the norms and practice of medieval violence developed over time. Attitudes towards violence in the Middle Ages were not static. Norms of violence rose and fell, went latent, and then reappeared in a fashion that depended on changes in constellations of power and especially in the number of powerful interest groups. Norms that appear to dominate in a particular time and place lost ground when newly powerful groups emerged whose interests were better served by different norms. If these groups were powerful enough and circumstances were right, as they were for Charlemagne and his allies and for the towns of early twelfth-century Flanders, they could force other groups within society to modify their norms or accept new ones. Norms also changed when people found that a new (or newly assertive) central authority with its own norms could help them achieve their aims, whether or not their aims and those of the central authority were the same. In such a case, as we saw in Angevin England, we see people acting according to an old set of norms taking advantage of new institutions to achieve old goals, while in the process legitimating the new institutions and the norms according to which they operated.

Norms all but vanished when a society changed in such a way that they ceased to have any meaning. In central and southern France in the eleventh century, it made little sense for most people to invoke norms of public authority and the restrictions on private violence that came with them. There was simply no one on the scene with enough power relative to other political actors either to attract or compel obedience to those norms; power, advancement, self-protection, and even survival depended on mastering, invoking, and acting according to the norms associated with loyalty, honor, vengeance, a subjective view of proper order, and the personal right to violence. When society changed again, however, latent norms could emerge to dominate once more. The interests of the French king and those of the French commons dovetailed in the course of the twelfth and thirteenth centuries in a way that aided the revival of royal norms. In the mid-fourteenth century, French royal authority was incapacitated, leaving large numbers of heavily armed men to act according either to the old norms of personal violence (as colored by the culture of chivalry) or the naked dictates of profit and loss. The interests of the broader mass of French society, however, helped central authority to reimpose its norms relatively quickly – though members of the old warrior aristocracy still clung tightly to their ancient rights to wield violence on their own behalf.

A thread connecting the chapters in this book has been the idea that rulers had the right to regulate the violence of others, and ultimately to claim a monopoly on the legitimate use of force. This idea was almost invisible in sixth-century Gaul. In the sources we examined, the early Merovingian kings appear as larger and more powerful versions of a basic unit of political action: the warleader with his armed following. The kings participated completely in a culture that respected the personal right to violence, as long as that violence did not spill out of control and affect the innocent or uninvolved, or the interests of other powerful people. By virtue of being among the most powerful human players in the political game – which meant having more resources with which to reward followers and thus having bigger armed followings with which they could fight on a larger scale and project power over longer distances – kings could in effect extend or contract the sphere of legitimate violence in particular contexts by extending or withdrawing their protection over people or places. Nevertheless, there was little qualitative difference between the norms according to which they wielded violence and those followed by others.

Sixth-century Gaul was also, however, a world in which God and His saints were real and present, and played an active role in human affairs. God wielded violence to avenge injuries and affronts, to assert or protect His rights, and to advance His own interests and those of His followers. Simply by acting, God made violence legitimate, or made it clear that someone else's violence was illegitimate. And when He saw fit, He could act through even the most ruthlessly violent kings, such as Clovis.

As the early Middle Ages progressed, God and king became inextricably joined. God's interests became the king's interests and vice versa. A king's ability to extend or retract his protection became a tool in his arsenal for carrying out his duties as God's representative to promote God's order. As a consequence, kings could generalize their protection. They could not only extend their protection over their own friends and followers and withdraw it from their enemies; they could do the same for the friends, followers, and enemies of God. Charlemagne, with unprecedented power and prestige at his back, thus claimed to extend his protection over entire classes of God's favorites. Acting *in loco dei* and for the salvation of his people, Charlemagne also claimed the right to take vengeance on God's enemies and to delegitimize all violence but his own or that which worked in his interests and thus in the interests of divine order. Nevertheless, the old norms of personal violence persisted.

They leap quickly back into view in the sources when the landscape of power began to change, and fewer people found themselves induced or compelled to buy into the norms Charlemagne had projected.

The image of kingship that Charlemagne had projected, with its claims to a right and duty to regulate violence, remained part of what in German would be called the European *Kulturgut*, or cultural patrimony. In the west Frankish kingdom of the eleventh century, Charlemagne's norms were invoked from the sidelines by the theorist Bishop Gerard I of Cambrai, who had his own interests in invoking them. The Peace of God councils likewise broadcast what was essentially a Carolingian vision of right order, though they assumed and tolerated a great deal of the habitual violence that was central to the political culture of the west Frankish aristocracy. East of the Rhine, the Ottonian emperors directly cast themselves, or were cast by loyal writers such as Thietmar of Merseburg, in Charlemagne's mold as God's agents responsible for protecting God's favorites and maintaining God's order. As Thietmar himself revealed, however, the limitations of their own power and the power of their competitors constrained the Ottonians to act according to the culture of violence in which they were embedded. In the west, when economic and/or political conditions and personal ability made it possible for lords to coerce or attract the cooperation of larger numbers of their fellow aristocrats over wider areas, they too reached for neo-Carolingian norms to legitimate their power, either directly or by co-opting the peace movement.

It is no accident that neo-Carolingian norms of violence re-emerge more strongly in the sources of the later eleventh but especially the twelfth and thirteenth centuries. This is the period in which economic developments, at different rates in different times and places, were making more resources available and thus transforming the landscape of power throughout Europe. These changes allowed towns and cities as collectives to join the ranks of the powerful. They also allowed successful warleader princes – such as the Capetians – to attract or coerce more followers, to pay more officials, and thus to extend their power. The same phenomena in Germany produced the cities, the more complex societies, and the urban jurists and judges whose needs for systematic and consistent access to law were addressed by the manuscripts of the *Sachsenspiegel* and other legal texts like it. As the interests of the urban classes in Flanders and in France ultimately aligned with those of kings, so too did they in Germany, hence the emphasis in the Wolfenbüttel manuscript of the *Sachsenspiegel* on the emperor as the conduit for God's law and God's punishment, and on the right of the emperor and his judicial officials to regulate the violence of others.

Nevertheless, royal norms of violence remained contested. Everywhere we turn we see older norms protecting the right of the individual or the group (whether bound by kinship or by oath) to wield violence either latently present or being actively advanced. By the fourteenth century this right as maintained by the warrior aristocracy had become formalized, and to an extent codified, in reaction to the learned laws and the laws of the kings. This aristocracy continued to believe that because the commons did not play entirely by its rules, its rules did not apply to the commons. When armies from Flemish towns took to the field in the fourteenth century and were defeated, Jean Froissart could rejoice that his nobility had crushed a threat to the proper order of things, as he did when they crushed the Jacquerie.

The competition between what would become known as "private" and "public" or "state" violence was by no means complete by the end of the Middle Ages; it persisted throughout the late medieval, early modern, and modern periods. The competition ebbed and flowed in different times and places; the victory of state norms was by no means progressive or even assured. The aristocracy's assumption of its right to wield violence on its own behalf in particular died hard; it continues to be visible, for example, in the practice of *Fehde* in Germany, in the Italian vendetta, and in the culture of the duel.[4] Nor did the commons always respect central authority's claim to a monopoly on violence. Peasants fought amongst themselves in similar ways and for similar reasons as their social betters. Mobs wielded violence against prisoners, suspected witches and sorcerers, religious opponents, or members of minority groups; violence could explode in the course of popular rituals such as the carnival.[5] Words of course also continued to serve as weapons. In an early modern world characterized by the vastly expanded production and distribution of written texts through printing, vicarious verbal violence of the kind we have seen in some of our medieval texts could only expand in its scope and potential viciousness.[6] The norms of private violence also continued to work through the medium of public judicial institutions themselves; one could always exploit the norms and interests of public authority in order to achieve private ends. This process, by which the impulse to private violence was channeled through central authority, had a great deal to do with the latter's ultimate victory.[7]

Attitudes towards violence that look medieval remain visible in the modern West. What has changed are the prevailing standards of legitimacy.[8] For much of the Middle Ages, people of all social classes assumed the right to wield violence, on their own behalf or on behalf of those with whom they were connected, in circumstances that had a lot to do with their own subjective worldview. Some people still do this, but they are now generally regarded as deviant, psychopathic, or criminal.[9] Two people, one medieval and one modern, might well both respond violently to a perceived injury or wrong, or denied claim of right. The actions of the former would have been judged, assessed, and described according to contemporary standards of legitimacy; if his actions met those standards they would have been accepted. The actions of the latter would almost never be accepted, least of all by those who work for the state, unless they were carried out in an insular community whose members shared his values and were in a position to ignore the state. Such sub-cultures of violence, in which different norms of violence apply than do within the dominant culture, have been identified in frontier areas of the American West in the nineteenth century and in parts of the United States in the nineteenth and twentieth centuries. Their deviance from the dominant culture has been captured with such labels as "vigilante justice", "lynch mobs", or "mountain feuds".[10] Similar behavior is visible when normally law-abiding communities, whether expressed in the form of juries or not, judge an act of violence positively in defiance of the state's laws and authority. In such cases, the members of the community evidently feel that the victim had gotten what he deserved.[11]

Sub-cultures of this kind are not, of course, unique to North America; one need look only at mafias in Sicily and elsewhere. These too seem often to follow norms that respect a personal right to violence in defense of rights and honor, and to avenge injury or insult, that look similar to those that held sway in much of the Middle Ages – at least within the sub-culture itself. And they are sometimes supported by people under their sway, people who for whatever reason distrust the motives, perceived corruption, or instability of central authority, prefer the protection and stability offered by their mafia protectors, and are willing to accept the coercion and rules that are part of the package. The difference lies in the context of such sub-cultures, and especially in their attitudes and behavior towards the dominant culture; from the perspective of constituted order, and of those who depend on or are invested in it, they are plainly corrosive.[12]

Perhaps the most visible legacy of medieval violence, however, is the state with its claim to a quasi-monopoly on the legitimate use of force. If the economic/social/political context, and the array of interest groups capable of wielding power, helped select which normative framework was promoted by whom from among those available and thus which came to predominate, then the future lay with that promoted by Charlemagne. Europe developed in such a way that kings and other rulers became interested in asserting claims to monopolize violence, claims that were based on their duty to act on God's behalf to uphold God's peace.

As contexts changed, other groups in particular times and places found it in their interest to support these claims. Over time, the norms of public order have become the dominant framework for understanding and evaluating violence in modern European and post-European societies.

As a result, it is those norms that are often applied to view and to judge violence in the Middle Ages. It may well be a testament to Charlemagne's success in imprinting his idea of order on the collective European and post-European consciousness that so much of the scholarship on medieval violence evaluates it not on its own terms, but rather on whether or not it shows a given society succeeding or failing according to the Carolingian model. As we have seen throughout this book, "success" and "order" depend a great deal on who is looking at them and from what perspective. It is the recognition that there are other models of order from our own, and other ways of understanding violence – even if we do not like them and would not like to live according to them – that makes it possible to understand behavior that to us might at first seem wrong or incomprehensible.

## Notes

1. Cf. Strickland, *War and Chivalry*, 176–81, 258–90.
2. See *inter alia* Drake, ed., *Violence in Late Antiquity*; Fouracre, "Conflict, Power and Legitimation" and "Attitudes Towards Violence"; Fouracre and Gerberding, *Late Merovingian France*; Patrick J. Geary and John B. Freed, "Literacy and Violence in Twelfth-Century Bavaria: The 'Murder Letter' of Count Siboto IV", *Viator* 25 (1994): 116–29.
3. See *inter alia* Garcia Moreno, "Legitimate and Illegitimate Violence in Visigothic Law", T.S. Brown, "Urban Violence in Early Medieval Italy: The Cases of Rome and Ravenna", and R. Balzaretti, "'These are things that men do, not women': The Social Regulation of Female Violence in Langobard Italy", in Halsall, *Violence and Society*, 46–59, 76–89, 175–92; Bisson, *Tormented Voices* and *Crisis*; David Nirenberg, *Communities of Violence: Persecution of Minorities in the Middle Ages* (Princeton: Princeton University Press, 1996).
4. See *inter alia* Brunner, *Land and Lordship*; Buschmann, "Landfriede und Landfriedensordnung"; Rolf Sprandel, "Legitimation und Delegitimation handgreiflicher Gewaltanwendung in Chroniken des spätmittelalterlichen Deutschlands", in Mensching, *Gewalt und ihre Legitimation*, 184–203; Hillay Zmora, *State and Nobility in Early Modern Germany: The Knightly Feud in Franconia, 1440–1567* (Cambridge: Cambridge University Press, 2003); A. Patschovsky, "Fehde in Recht: eine Problemskizze", in *Reich und Recht im Zeitalter der Reformation: Festschrift für Horst Rabe*, ed. Christine Roll (Frankfurt: Peter Lang, 1996), 145–78; Stuart Carroll, *Blood and Violence in Early Modern France* (Oxford: Oxford University Press, 2006); E. Muir, *Mad Blood Stirring: Vendetta in Renaissance Italy* (Baltimore: Johns Hopkins

University Press, 1998); Keith M. Brown, *Bloodfeud in Scotland, 1573–1625: Violence, Justice, and Politics in an Early Modern Society* (Edinburgh: J. Donald, 1986); Kagay and Villalon, *The Final Argument*.

5. See *inter alia* Christine Reinle, *Bauernfehden: Studien zur Fehdeführung Nichtadliger im spätmittelalterlichen Römisch-Deutschen Reich, besonders in den Bayerischen Herzogtümern* (Stuttgart: Franz Steiner, 2003); R.B. Shoemaker, *The London Mob: Violence and Disorder in Eighteenth-Century England* (London: Hambledon, 2004); Muir, *Mad Blood Stirring*; Natalie Zemon Davis, "The Reasons of Misrule" and "The Rites of Violence", in *Society and Culture in Early Modern France* (Stanford: Stanford University Press, 1975), 97–123 and 152–87.

6. Eming and Jarzebowski, *Blutige Worte*. Cf. Muir, *Mad Blood Stirring*, xxv–xxvi and 174–5 on vendetta in sixteenth-century Italy being carried out in part by means of pamphlets.

7. For example, J.A. Sharpe, "'Such Disagreement Betwyx Neighbors': Litigation and Human Relations in Early Modern England", in Bossy, ed., *Disputes and Settlements*, 167–87; Jenny Wormald, "The Blood Feud in Early Modern Scotland", in Bossy, ed., *Disputes and Settlements*, 101–44.

8. Cf. William Ian Miller, *Eye for an Eye* (Cambridge: Cambridge University Press, 2006).

9. A search of the Internet in July of 2009 turned up the following examples: (1) a 39-year-old man in Hamburg, Germany, was convicted of having killed his girlfriend. No sooner had the verdict been rendered than a 57-year-old man who claimed to be a friend of the victim leaped the barrier separating the spectators' gallery from the court and stabbed the convicted man to death with a long kitchen knife. "Tödliche Rache vor Gericht", *Berliner Zeitung*, Textarchiv, 15 September 1994, **https://www.berlinonline.de/ berliner-zeitung/archiv/.bin/dump.fcgi/1994/0915/vermischtes/ 0072/index.html**. (2) in Birmingham crown court, three men were jailed for life for the execution of a 55-year-old man and his 51-year-old wife. The trio had killed the couple in retaliation for a killing committed earlier by their son. "Life for revenge killing gangsters", *The Daily Mail, Mailonline*, 30 June 2006, **http://www.dailymail.co.uk/news/article- 393284/Life-revenge-killing-gangsters.html**.

10. Cf. James W. Clark, "Without Fear or Shame: Lynching, Capital Punishment and the Subculture of Violence in the American South", *British Journal of Political Science* 29, no. 2 (1998): 269–89; in his use of the term "subculture" Clark follows M.W. Wolfgang and F. Ferracuti, *The Subculture of Violence: Towards an Integrated Theory in Criminology* (London: Tavistock, 1967), esp. 140–1, 272–84; John Ed Pearce, *Days of Darkness: The Feuds of Eastern Kentucky* (Lexington, KY: University Press of Kentucky, 1994). See also the examples from both the United States and the United Kingdom cited in the OED, s.v. "vigilante".

11. See, for example, the 2007 case in which Joe Horn of Pasadena, Texas, shot and killed two men who were burglarizing his neighbor's home, despite a request from an emergency dispatcher to refrain and wait for the police to arrive. A grand jury later refused to indict Horn for the killings: Wikipedia

contributors, "Joe Horn shooting controversy", *Wikipedia, The Free Encyclopedia*, **http://en.wikipedia.org/w/index.php?title=Joe_Horn_shooting_controversy&oldid=304585605** (accessed July 28, 2009).

12. See *inter alia* Henner Hess, *Mafia: Ursprung, Macht und Mythos* (Freiburg: Herder, 1993), translated into English by Ewald Osers as *Mafia and Mafiosi: Origin, Power, Myth* (New York: New York University Press, 1998); Raimondo Catanzaro, *Il delitto come impresa: storia sociale della mafia* (Padova, Liviana: 1988), translated into English by Raymond Rosenthal as *Men of Respect: A Social History of the Sicilian Mafia* (New York: Free Press, 1992).

# BIBLIOGRAPHY

## Manuscripts

Herzog August Bibliothek Wolfenbüttel. *Sachsenspiegel-online*. Online facsimile edition of Cod. Guelf. 3.1 Aug. 2°. Edited by Björn Dittrich. **http://www. sachsenspiegel-online.de/cms.**

## Primary Sources and Source Collections

Ademar of Chabannes. *Ademari historiarum libri III*, edited by D.G. Waitz, MGH SS IV, 106–48. Hanover: Hahn, 1841.

Alcuin. *Vita Willibrordi, archiepiscopi Traiectensis auctore Alcuino*. Edited by Wilhelm Levison. MGH SSRM 7, 81–141. Hanover: Hahn, 1920.

———. "The Life of Saint Willibrord." In *Soldiers of Christ: Saints and Saint's Lives from Late Antiquity and the Early Middle Ages*, edited by Thomas F.X. Noble and Thomas Head, 189–211. University Park: Penn State Press, 1995.

Attenborough, F.L., ed. *The Laws of the Earliest English Kings*. New York: Russell & Russell, 1963.

Bethmann, L.C., ed. *Gesta episcoporum Camaracensium*, MGH SS 7, 402–89. Hanover: Hahn, 1846.

Beyerle, Franz and Buchner, Rudolf, eds. *Lex Ribuaria*. MGH LL nat. Germ. 3, 2. Hanover: Hahn, 1954.

Bitterauf, Theodor, ed. *Die Traditionen des Hochstifts Freising*. 2 vols. Aalen: Scientia Verlag, 1967, reprint of the original edition, Munich, 1905.

Boretius, Alfred, ed. *Capitularia regum Francorum I*. MGH Legum Sectio II. Hanover: Hahn, 1883.

——— and Krause, Victor, eds. *Capitularia regum Francorum II*. MGH Legum Sectio II. Hanover: Hahn, 1890.

Bracton, Henry de. *On the Laws and Customs of England*. Translated by Samuel E. Thorne. Cambridge: Belknap Press, 1968.

Brial, Michel-Jean-Joseph, ed. *Recueil des historiens des Gaules et de la France*, vol. 14. Paris: Victor Palmé, 1877.

Burchard of Worms. "Lex Familae Wormatiensis Ecclesiae." In MGH Legum Sectio IV, Const. 1, edited by Ludwig Weiland, 639–44. Hanover: Hahn, 1893.

Charny, Geoffroi de. *A Knight's Own Book of Chivalry*. Translated by E. Kennedy. Philadelphia: University of Pennsylvania Press, 2005.

Dobozy, Maria, trans. *A Saxon Mirror: A Sachsenspiegel of the Fourteenth Century*. Philadelphia: University of Pennsylvania Press, 1999.

Downer, L.J., ed. *Leges Henrici Primi.* Oxford: Clarendon Press, 1972.

Dümmler, E., ed. *Epistolae Karolini Aevi II–III.* MGH Epist. 4–5. Berlin: Weidmann, 1895.

Dutton, Paul Edward, ed. *Carolingian Civilization: A Reader.* Peterborough, Ontario: Broadview Press, 1993.

———, ed. *Charlemagne's Courtier: The Complete Einhard.* Peterborough, Ontario: Broadview Press, 1998.

Eckhart, Karl August, ed. *Pactus Legis Salicae.* MGH LL nat. Germ. 4, 1. Hanover: Hahn, 1962.

———, ed. *Sachsenspiegel. Landrecht, Lehnrecht.* MGH Fontes iuris Germanici antiqui, Nova series, 1, parts 1 and 2. Göttingen: Muster-Schmidt, 1973.

Einhard. *Translatio et miracula SS. Marcellini et Petri auctore Einhardo.* Edited by G. Waitz. MGH SS 15, 1, 238–64. Hanover: Hahn, 1887.

———. "The Translation and Miracles of the Blessed Martyrs, Marcellinus and Peter." In *Charlemagne's Courtier: The Complete Einhard,* edited and translated by Paul Dutton, 69–130. Peterborough, Ontario: Broadview Press, 1998.

FitzNigel, Richard. *Dialogus de Scaccario. The Course of the Exchequer.* Edited and translated by Charles Johnson. 2nd edition. Oxford: Clarendon Press, 1983.

Fouracre, Paul and Gerberding, Richard, eds. *Late Merovingian France: History and Hagiography, 640–720.* Manchester: Manchester University Press, 1996.

Froissart, Jean. *Chronicles.* Translated by Geoffrey Brereton. New York: Penguin Books, 1968.

———. *Les Chroniques de sire Jean Froissart qui traitent des merveilleuses emprises, nobles aventures et faits d'armes advenus en son temps en France, Angleterre, Bretaigne, Bourgogne, Escosse, Espaigne, Portingal et ès autres parties.* Edited by J.A.C. Buchon. 3 vols. Paris: Société du Panthéon Littéraire, 1838–40.

Galbert of Bruges. *Galbertus notarius Brugensis de multro, traditione, et occisione gloriosi Karoli comitis Flandriarum.* Edited by Jeff Rider. Turnhout: Brepols, 1994.

———. *The Murder of Charles the Good.* Translated by James Bruce Ross. Toronto: University of Toronto Press, 1982.

Glanville, Ranulf de. *The Treatise on the Laws and Customs of the Realm of England Commonly Called Glanvill.* Edited and translated by G.D.G. Hall. Oxford: Clarendon Press, 1993.

Gregory of Tours. *Zehn Bücher Geschichten: Auf Grund der Übersetzung W. Giesebrechts neubearbeitet von Rudolf Buchner.* 2 vols. Darmstadt: Wissenschaftliche Buchgesellschaft, 1967–70.

———. *The History of the Franks.* Translated by Lewis Thorpe. New York: Penguin Books, 1974.

Halsall, Paul, ed. *The Internet Medieval Sourcebook.* **http://www.fordham.edu/halsall/sbook.html**.

Hübner, Rudolf. *Gerichtsurkunden der fränkischen Zeit.* Aalen: Scientia Verlag, 1971, reprint of the original, Weimar, 1891–3.

Jean, Sire de Joinville. *The Memoirs of the Lord of Joinville: A New English Version*. Translated by Ethel Wedgwood. New York: E.P. Dutton and Co., 1906.

Jonas of Bobbio. "Life of St. Columbanus." In *Monks, Bishops and Pagans: Christian Culture in Gaul and Italy, 500–700*. Edited by Edward Peters, translated by William C. McDermott. Philadelphia: University of Pennsylvania Press, 1975.

———. *Vita Columbani abbatis discipulorumque eius libri duo auctore Iona*. Edited by Bruno Krusch, MGH SSRM 4, 64–108. Hanover: Hahn, 1902.

Krusch, Bruno, ed. *Vita Sanctae Balthildis*. MGH SSRM 2, 475–508. Hanover: Hahn, 1888.

Laurière, Eusèbe Jacob de, ed. *Ordonnances des roys de France de la troisième race*, vol. 1. Farnborough: Gregg Press, 1967, reprint of the original, Paris, 1723.

*The Laws of the Salian Franks*. Translated by Katherine Fischer Drew. Philadelphia: University of Pennsylvania Press, 1991.

Letaldus of Micy. "Delatio corporis s. Juniani ad synodem Karoffensem." *Patrologia Latina*. Edited by Jacques-Paul Migne. 221 vols. 137: 823–6. Paris: Migne, 1844–64.

Liebermann, Felix, ed. and trans. *Die Gesetze der Angelsachsen*, 3 vols. Halle: Niemeyer, 1903–16.

Maitland, F.W., ed. *Pleas of the Crown for the County of Gloucester, 1221*. London: Macmillan & Co., 1884.

Mansi, Joannes Dominicus *et al.*, eds. *Sacrorum conciliorum nova et amplissima collectio*, 53 vols. Paris: H. Welter, 1900–27.

Martindale, J. ed. "Conventum inter Guillelmum aquitanorum comes et Hugonem chiliarchum." *English Historical Review* 84 (1969): 528–48.

Matthew Paris. *Chronica Majora*. Edited by H.R. Luard. London: Longman, 1872–83.

Noble, Thomas F.X. and Head, Thomas, eds. *Soldiers of Christ: Saints and Saint's Lives from Late Antiquity and the Early Middle Ages*. University Park: Penn State Press, 1995.

Pognon, Edmond, ed. and trans. *L'an mille. Oeuvres de Liutprand, Raoul Glaber, Adémar de Chabannes, Adalberon, Helgaud*. Paris: Gallimard, 1947.

*Readings in Medieval History*. Edited by Patrick J. Geary. 3rd edition. Peterborough, Ontario: Broadview Press, 2003.

Richard, A., ed. *Chartes et documents pour servir a l'histoire de l'abbaye de Saint-Maixent*. Vol. 1. Poitiers: Oudin, 1887.

Rio, Alice, trans. "The Formulary of Marculf." In *The Formularies of Angers and Marculf: Two Merovingian Legal Handbooks*, 103–244. Liverpool: Liverpool University Press, 2008.

Rivers, Theodore John, trans. *Laws of the Salian and Ripuarian Franks*. New York: AMS Press, 1986.

Robertini, Luca, ed. *Liber Miraculorum Sancte Fidis*. Spoleto: Centro Italiano di studi sull'alto medioevo, 1994.

Rodulf Glaber. *Rodulfi Glabri Historiarum libri quinque = The Five Books of the Histories.* Edited and translated by John France. Oxford: Clarendon Press, 1989.

Rosenwein, Barbara H., ed. *Reading the Middle Ages: Sources from Europe, Byzantium, and the Islamic World.* Peterborough, Ontario: Broadview Press, 2006.

Sayers, Dorothy L., trans. *The Song of Roland.* New York: Penguin Classics, 1957.

Schwind, Ernst von, ed. *Leges Baiwariorum.* MGH LL nat. Germ. 5, 2. Hanover: Hahn, 1926.

Sheingorn, Pamela, trans. *The Book of Sainte Foy.* Philadelphia: University of Pennsylvania Press, 1995.

Stenton, Doris M., ed. *The Earliest Lincolnshire Assize Rolls, A.D. 1202–1209.* Lincoln: Lincoln Record Society, 1926.

Stephenson, Carl and Marcham, Frederick George, eds. *Sources of English Constitutional History.* New York: Harper & Row, 1937.

Stubbs, William, ed. *Select Charters and Other Illustrations of English Constitutional History from the Earliest Times to the Reign of Edward the First.* 9th revised edition. Oxford: Clarendon Press, 1913.

Thietmar of Merseburg. *Chronicon.* Edited by Rudolf Buchner. Darmstadt: Wissenschaftliche Buchgesellschaft, 1957.

———. *Ottonian Germany: The Chronicon of Thietmar of Merseburg.* Translated by David A. Warner. Manchester: Manchester University Press, 2001.

Van Caenegem, R.C., ed. *English Lawsuits from William I to Richard I.* London: Selden Society, 1990–1.

Weinrich, Lorenz, ed. *Quellen zur Deutschen Verfassungs-, Wirtschafts- und Sozialgeschichte bis 1250.* Darmstadt: Wissenschaftliche Buchgesellschaft, 1977.

Whitelock, Dorothy, trans. *English Historical Documents.* Vol. I, c. 500–1042. 2nd edition. London: Eyre Methuen, 1979.

Widukind of Corvey. *Rerum gestarum Saxonicarum libri tres = Die Sachsengeschichte des Widukind von Korvei.* In *Quellen zur Geschichte der sächsischen Kaiserzeit. Widukinds Sachsengeschichte, Adalberts Fortsetzung der Chronik Reginos, Liudprands Werke,* edited by A. Bauer and R. Rau, 1–183. Darmstadt: Wissenschaftliche Buchgesellschaft, 1971.

William of Malmesbury. *The Vita Wulfstani of William of Malmesbury,* edited by R.R. Darlington, 168–75. London: Camden Society, 1928.

Wipo of Burgundy. "The Deeds of Conrad II." In *Imperial Lives and Letters of the Eleventh Century,* edited by Robert L. Benson, translated by Theodore E. Mommsen and Karl F. Morrison, 52–100. New York: Columbia University Press, 2000, reprint of the original, 1962.

Zeumer, Karl, ed. *Formulae Merowingici et Karolini aevi.* MGH LL 5. Hanover: Hahn, 1886.

## Secondary Sources

Ainsworth, Peter F. *Jean Froissart and the Fabric of History.* Oxford: Clarendon Press, 1990.

Airlie, Stuart, Cubitt, Catherine, Garrison, Mary, Larrington, Carolyne and Rosenwein, Barbara H. "The History of Emotions: A Debate." *Early Medieval Europe* 10, no. 2 (2001): 225–6.

Alfonso, Isabel, Kennedy, Hugh and Escalona, Julio, eds. *Building Legitimacy. Political Discourses and Forms of Legitimacy in Medieval Societies.* Leiden: Brill, 2004.

Almond, Andrea. "LA Police Investigate Arrest in Which Suspect Hit with Flashlight after Apparent Surrender." *Associated Press*, 24 June 2004.

Althoff, Gerd. *Family, Friends and Followers: Political and Social Bonds in Medieval Europe.* Translated by Christopher Carroll. Cambridge: Cambridge University Press, 2004.

———. *Die Macht der Rituale: Symbolik und Herrschaft im Mittelalter.* Darmstadt: Primus Verlag, 2003.

———. *Die Ottonen: Königsherrschaft ohne Staat.* Stuttgart: Kohlhammer, 2000.

———. "Schranken der Gewalt. Wie Gewalttätig war das 'finstere Mittelalter'?" In *Der Krieg im Mittelalter und in der frühen Neuzeit: Gründe, Begründungen, Bilder, Bräuche, Recht.* Edited by Horst Brunner. Wiesbaden: Reichert Verlag, 1999.

———. *Spielregeln in der Politik im Mittelalter. Kommunikation in Frieden und Fehde.* Darmstadt: Wissenschaftliche Buchgesellschaft, 1997.

———. *Verwandte, Freunde und Getreue: zum politischen Stellenwert der Gruppenbindungen im frühen Mittelalter.* Darmstadt: Wissenschaftliche Buchgesellschaft, 1990.

——— and Keller, Hagen. *Heinrich I. und Otto der Große. Neubeginn und karolingisches Erbe.* 2nd edition Göttingen: Muster-Schmidt, 1994.

Arnold, Benjamin. *German Knighthood, 1050–1300.* Oxford: Clarendon Press, 1985.

———. *Princes and Territories in Medieval Germany.* Cambridge: Cambridge University Press, 1991.

———. *Power and Property in Medieval Germany: Economic and Social Change c. 900–1300.* Oxford: Oxford University Press, 2004.

Barclay, Gordon, Tavares, Cynthia *et al.* "International Comparisons of Criminal Justice Statistics 2001." *Home Office Statistical Bulletin*, 24 October 2003. **http://rds.homeoffice.gov.uk/rds/pdfs2/hosb1203.pdf**.

Barthélemy, Dominique. *L'an mil et la paix de Dieu: la France chrétienne et féodale, 980–1060.* Paris, Fayard, 1999.

———. *La mutation de l'an mil, a-t-elle eu lieu?: servage et chevalerie dans la France des Xe et XIe siècles.* Paris: Fayard, 1997.

———. *The Serf, the Knight, and the Historian.* Translated by Graham Robert Edwards. Ithaca, NY: Cornell University Press, 2009.

——— and White, Stephen D. "Debate: The 'Feudal Revolution'. Comment 1, Comment 2." *Past and Present* 152 (1996): 196–223.

———, Bougard, François and Le Jan, Régine, eds. *La Vengeance, 400–1200.* Rome: École Française de Rome, 2006.

Bartlett, Robert. *Trial by Fire and Water: The Medieval Judicial Ordeal.* Oxford: Clarendon Press, 1986.

Bisson, Thomas N. *The Crisis of the Twelfth Century: Power, Lordship, and the Origins of European Government*. Princeton: Princeton University Press, 2009.

———. "The 'Feudal Revolution'." *Past and Present* 142 (1994): 6–42.

———. "The Organized Peace in Southern France and Catalonia, c. 1140–c. 1233." *The American Historical Review* 82, no. 2 (1977): 290–311.

———. *Tormented Voices: Power, Crisis and Humanity in Rural Catalonia*. Cambridge, MA: Harvard University Press, 1998.

Black-Michaud, Jacob. *Cohesive Force: Feud in the Mediterranean and the Middle East*. London, 1975.

Bloch, Marc. *Feudal Society*. Translated by L.A. Manyon. London: Routledge and Kegan Paul, 1961.

Bossy, J., ed. *Disputes and Settlements: Law and Human Relations in the West*. Cambridge: Cambridge University Press, 1983.

Bouchard, Constance B. *"Strong of Body, Brave and Noble": Chivalry and Society in Medieval France*. Ithaca, NY: Cornell University Press, 1998.

Braun, Manuel and Herberichs, Cornelia, eds. *Gewalt im Mittelalter: Realitäten, Imaginationen*. Munich: Fink, 2005.

Brown, Keith M. *Bloodfeud in Scotland, 1573–1625: Violence, Justice, and Politics in an Early Modern Society*. Edinburgh: J. Donald, 1986.

Brown, Warren C. "Die Karolingischen Formelsammlungen – warum existieren sie?" In *Die Privaturkunden der Karolingerzeit*, edited by Peter Erhardt, Karl Heidecker, and Bernhard Zeller, 95–101. Dietikon-Zürich: Urs Graf Verlag, 2009.

———. *Unjust Seizure: Conflict, Interest and Authority in an Early Medieval Society*. Ithaca, NY: Cornell University Press, 2001.

———. "The Use of Norms in Disputes in Early Medieval Bavaria." *Viator* 30 (1999): 15–40.

——— and Górecki, Piotr, eds. *Conflict in Medieval Europe*. Aldershot: Ashgate, 2003.

Brundage, James A. *Medieval Canon Law*. London: Longman, 1995.

Brunner, Heinrich. *Deutsche Rechtsgeschichte*. 2nd edition. Vol. 1. Munich: Duncker & Humblot, 1906–28.

Brunner, Otto. *Land and Lordship: Structures of Governance in Medieval Austria*. Translated by Howard Kaminsky and James Van Horn Melton. Philadelphia: University of Pennsylvania Press, 1992. Translation of the German 4th revised edition, Vienna, 1959.

Buc, Philippe. *The Dangers of Ritual: Between Early Medieval Texts and Social Scientific Theory*. Princeton: Princeton University Press, 2001.

———. "The Monster and the Critics: A Ritual Reply." *Early Medieval Europe* 15, no. 4 (2007): 441–52.

Buck, Thomas M. *Admonitio und Praedicatio. Zur religiös-pastoralen Dimension von Kapitularien und kapitulariennahen Texten (507–814)*. Frankfurt: Peter Lang, 1997.

Bullough, Vern L. and Brundage, James A., eds. *Handbook of Medieval Sexuality*. New York: Garland, 2000.

Buschmann, Arno and Wadle, Elmar, eds. *Landfrieden: Anspruch und Wirklichkeit*. Paderborn: Schöning, 2002.

Byock, Jesse L. *Feud in the Icelandic Saga*. Berkeley: University of California Press, 1982.

Campbell, James. "The Late Anglo-Saxon State: A Maximum View." *Proceedings of the British Academy* 87 (1995): 39–65.

Carroll, Stuart. *Blood and Violence in Early Modern France*. Oxford: Oxford University Press, 2006.

———. "The Peace in the Feud in Sixteenth- and Seventeenth-Century France." *Past and Present* 178 (2003): 74–115.

Catanzaro, Raimondo. *Men of Respect: A Social History of the Sicilian Mafia*. Translated by Raymond Rosenthal. New York: Free Press, 1992.

Clarke, H.B. and Brennan, Mary, eds. *Columbanus and Merovingian Monasticism*. Oxford: B.A.R., 1981.

Clarke, James W. "Without Fear or Shame: Lynching, Capital Punishment and the Subculture of Violence in the American South." *British Journal of Political Science* 29, no. 2 (1998): 269–89.

Classen, Albrecht, ed. *Violence in Medieval Courtly Literature: A Casebook*. New York: Routledge, 2004.

Colson, Elizabeth. *Tradition and Contract: The Problem of Order*. Chicago: Aldine Publishing Company, 1974.

Crowder, George. Review of *Justice, Law, and Violence*, edited by James B. Brady and Newton Garver; *Violence, Terrorism, and Justice*, edited by R.G. Frey and Christoper W. Morris. *The American Political Science Review* 86, no. 4 (1992): 1035–6.

Davies, Wendy and Fouracre, Paul, eds. *The Settlement of Disputes in Early Medieval Europe*. Cambridge: Cambridge University Press, 1986.

Davis, Natalie Zemon. *Society and Culture in Early Modern France*. Stanford: Stanford University Press, 1975.

Dean, Trevor. *Crime in Medieval Europe*. London: Longman, 2001.

DeVries, Kelly. *Medieval Military Technology*. Peterborough, Ontario: Broadview Press, 1992.

Drake, H.A., ed. *Violence in Late Antiquity: Perceptions and Practices*. Aldershot: Ashgate, 2006.

Duby, Georges. *A History of French Civilization*. Translated by James Blakely Atkinson. New York: Random House, 1964.

———. "Laiety and the Peace of God." In *The Chivalrous Society*, 123–33. Berkeley and Los Angeles: University of California Press, 1977.

———. "Les laics et la paix de Dieu." In *I laici nella "societas christiani" dei secoli xi e xii*. Milan: Vita e pensiero, 1968.

———. *Les trois ordres: ou, l'imaginaire du féodalisme*. Paris: Gallimard, 1978.

———. *The Three Orders: Feudal Society Imagined*. Translated by Arthur Goldhammer. Chicago: University of Chicago Press, 1980.

Dunbabin, Jean. *France in the Making, 843–1180*. 2nd edition. Oxford: Oxford University Press, 2000.

Ember, Carol R. and Ember, Melvin. "War, Socialization, and Interpersonal Violence: A Cross-Cultural Study." *Journal of Conflict Resolution* 38 no. 4 (1994): 620–46.

Eming, Jutta and Jarzebowski, Claudia, eds. *Blutige Worte: internationales und interdisziplinäres Kolloquium zum Verhältnis von Sprache und Gewalt in Mittelalter und früher Neuzeit.* Göttingen: Vandenhoeck & Ruprecht, 2008.

Ensminger, Jean and Knight, Jack. "Changing Social Norms: Common Property, Bridewealth, and Clan Exogamy." *Current Anthropology* 38, no. 1 (1997): 1–24.

Epstein, Steven A. *An Economic and Social History of Later Medieval Europe, 1000–1500.* Cambridge: Cambridge University Press, 2009.

Fichtenau, Heinrich. *Das Karolingische Imperium. Soziale und geistige Problematik eines Grossreiches.* Zürich: Fretz & Wasmuth, 1949.

Firnhaber-Baker, Justine. "From God's Peace to the King's Order: Late Medieval Limitations on Non-Royal Warfare." *Essays in Medieval Studies* 23 (2006): 19–30.

Fletcher, Richard A. *Bloodfeud: Murder and Revenge in Anglo-Saxon England.* Oxford: Oxford University Press, 2003.

Foucault, Michel. *Madness and Civilization: A History of Insanity in the Age of Reason.* Translated by Richard Howard. New York: Pantheon Books, 1965.

Fouracre, Paul. *The Age of Charles Martel.* London: Longman, 2000.

Fowler, Kenneth. *Medieval Mercenaries.* Vol. I. *The Great Companies.* Oxford: Blackwell Publishers, 2001.

Fox, James Allen and Zawitz, Marianne W. "Homicide Trends in the United States." *Bureau of Justice Statistics.* **http://bjs.ojp.usdoj.gov/content/homicide/homtrnd.cfm**.

Frend, W.H.C. *The Early Church.* Minneapolis: Fortress Press, 1982.

Fried, Johannes, ed. *Träger und Instrumentarien des Friedens im hohen und späten Mittelalter.* Sigmaringen: Jan Thorbecke, 1996.

Fryde, Natalie and Reitz, Dirk, eds. *Bischofsmord im Mittelalter.* Göttingen: Vandenhoeck & Ruprecht, 2003.

Ganshof, F.L. *The Carolingians and the Frankish Monarchy.* Translated by Janet Sondheimer. London: Longman, 1971.

———. "Charlemagne et l'usage de l'écrit en matière administrative." *Le Moyen Age* 57 (1951): 1–25.

———. *Feudalism.* Translated by Philip Grierson. 3rd edition. Toronto: University of Toronto Press, 1996.

———. *Frankish Institutions under Charlemagne.* Translated by Bryce and Mary Lyon. Providence: Brown University Press, 1968.

———. *Qu'est-ce que la féodalité?* Brussels: Office de Publicité, 1947.

———. *Was waren die Kapitularien?* Weimar: H. Böhlaus Nachfolger, 1961.

Geary, Patrick J. *Before France and Germany: The Creation and Transformation of the Merovingian World.* Oxford: Oxford University Press, 1988.

———. *Furta Sacra: Theft of Relics in the Central Middle Ages.* 2nd edition. Princeton: Princeton University Press, 1990.

—— and Freed, John B. "Literacy and Violence in Twelfth-Century Bavaria: The 'Murder Letter' of Count Siboto IV." *Viator* 25 (1994): 116–29.

Given, James B. *Society and Homicide in Thirteenth Century England.* Stanford: Stanford University Press, 1977.

Glazer, Andrew. "LAPD Critics Decry May 1 Melee as Latest Example of 'Warrior' Cop." *The Associated Press*, 12 May 2007.

Gluckman, Max. *Custom and Conflict in Africa.* Oxford: Blackwell, 1959.

——. "The Peace in the Feud." *Past and Present* 7 (1955): 1–14.

Godman, Peter and Collins, Roger, eds. *Charlemagne's Heir: New Perspectives on the Reign of Louis the Pious (814–840).* Oxford: Clarendon Press, 1990.

Goffart, Walter A. *The Narrators of Barbarian History (A.D. 550–800): Jordanes, Gregory of Tours, Bede, and Paul the Deacon.* Princeton: Princeton University Press, 1988.

Graus, František. *Volk, Herrscher und Heiliger im Reich der Merowinger. Studien zur Hagiographie der Merowingerzeit.* Prague: Nakladatelství Československé akademie věd, 1965.

Grierson, Philip and Blackburn, Mark. *Medieval European Coinage.* Cambridge: Cambridge University Press, 1986.

Halsall, Guy. Review of *Anger's Past: The Social Uses of an Emotion in the Middle Ages,* edited by Barbara H. Rosenwein. *Early Medieval Europe* 10, no. 2 (2001): 301–3.

——. *Warfare and Society in the Barbarian West.* London: Routledge, 2003.

——, ed. *Violence and Society in the Early Medieval West.* Woodbridge, Suffolk: The Boydell Press, 1998.

Halsall, Paul, ed. "Feudalism?" Internet Medieval Sourcebook: **http://www. fordham.edu/halsall/sbook1i.html#Feudalism.**

Head, Thomas. "The Development of the Peace of God in Aquitaine (970–1005)." *Speculum* 74, no. 3 (1999): 656–86.

——. "Hagiography." *Online Reference Book for Medieval Studies.* **http:// www.the-orb.net/encyclop/religion/hagiography/hagindex.html.**

—— and Landes, Richard, eds. *The Peace of God: Social Violence and Religious Response in France around the Year 1000.* Ithaca, NY: Cornell University Press, 1992.

Heinzelmann, Martin. *Gregor von Tours (538–594): "Zehn Bücher Geschichte": Historiographie und Gesellschaftskonzept im 6. Jahrhundert.* Darmstadt: Wissenschaftliche Buchgesellschaft, 1994.

——. *Gregory of Tours: History and Society in the Sixth Century.* Translated by Christopher Carroll. Cambridge: Cambridge University Press, 2001.

Hess, Henner. *Mafia and Mafiosi: Origin, Power, Myth.* Translated by Ewald Osers. New York: New York University Press, 1998.

Hill, John M. *The Cultural World in Beowulf.* Toronto: University of Toronto Press, 1995.

Höffinghof, Hans *et al.,* eds. *Alles was Recht war: Rechtsliteratur und Literarisches Recht. Festschrift für Ruth Schmidt-Wiegand zum 70. Geburtstag.* Essen: Item Verlag, 1996.

Hoffman, Hartmut. *Gottesfriede und Treuga Dei.* Stuttgart: Hiersemann, 1964.

Hudson, John. *The Formation of the English Common Law: Law and Society in England from the Norman Conquest to Magna Carta.* London: Longman, 1996.

Huizinga, Johan. *The Waning of the Middle Ages: A Study of the Forms of Life, Thought and Art in France and the Netherlands in the XIVth and XVth Centuries.* Translated by F. Hopman. Garden City, NY: Doubleday and Company, 1924.

Hyams, Paul. "Feud and the State in Late Anglo-Saxon England." *The Journal of British Studies* 40, no. 1 (2001): 1–43.

———. *Rancor and Reconciliation in Medieval England.* Ithaca, NY: Cornell University Press, 1993.

Jager, Eric. *The Last Duel: A True Story of Crime, Scandal, and Trial by Combat in Medieval France.* New York: Broadway, 2004.

Jansen, E. *et al.* "Paleoclimate." In *Climate Change 2007: The Physical Science Basis. Contribution of Working Group I to the Fourth Assessment Report of the Intergovernmental Panel on Climate Change* (Cambridge: Cambridge University Press, 2007), edited by S. Solomon *et al.* Online at **http://www.ipcc.ch/pdf/assessment-report/ar4/wg1/ar4-wg1-chapter6.pdf.**

Janz, Brigitte. "'Wir sezzen unde gebiten . . .'. Der Mainzer Reichslandfrieden in den Bilderhandschriften des Sachsenspiegels." *Beiträge zur Geschichte der deutschen Sprache und Literatur* 112 (1990): 242–66.

Kaeuper, Richard W. *Chivalry and Violence in Medieval Europe.* Oxford: Oxford University Press, 1999.

———. *Violence in Medieval Society.* Woodbridge, Suffolk: Boydell, 2000.

———. *War, Justice, and Public Order: England and France in the Later Middle Ages.* Oxford: Clarendon Press, 1988.

Kagay, Donald J. and Villalon, L.J. Andrew, eds. *The Final Argument: The Imprint of Violence on Society in Medieval and Early Modern Europe.* Woodbridge, Suffolk: The Boydell Press, 1998.

Kaiser, Reinhold. "Selbsthilfe und Gewaltmonopol. Königliche Friedenswahrung in Deutschland und Frankreich im Mittelalter." *Frühmittelalterliche Studien* 17 (1983): 56–72.

Keen, Maurice. *Chivalry.* New Haven: Yale University Press, 1984.

———. *The Laws of War in the Late Middle Ages.* London: Routledge, 1965.

Keyser, Richard L. "'Agreement Supersedes Law, and Love Judgment': Legal Flexibility and Amicable Settlement in Early-Twelfth-Century England." *Law and History Review* (forthcoming 2010).

Knecht, Robert J. *The Valois: Kings of France, 1328–1589.* London: Hambledon, 2004.

Koziol, Geoffrey. *Begging Pardon and Favor: Ritual and Political Order in Early Medieval France.* Ithaca, NY: Cornell University Press, 1992.

———. "The Dangers of Polemic: Is Ritual Still an Interesting Topic of Historical Study?" *Early Medieval Europe* 11, no. 4 (2002): 367–88.

Kroeschell, K. "Rechtsaufzeichnung und Rechtswirklichkeit: Das Beispiel des Sachsenspiegel." In *Recht und Schrift im Mittelalter,* edited by Peter Classen, 349–80. Sigmaringen: Thorbecke, 1977.

Kümper, Hiram. *Sachsenspiegel. Eine Bibliographie – mit einer Einleitung zu Überlieferung, Wirkung und Forschung.* Nordhausen: Verlag Traugott Bautz, 2004.

Kurrild-Kiltgaard, Peter and Tinggaard Svendsen, Gert. "Rational Bandits: Plunder, Public Goods, and the Vikings." *Public Choice* 117 (2003): 255–72.

Landes, Richard. *Relics, Apocalypse, and the Deceits of History: Ademar of Chabannes (989–1034).* Cambridge, MA: Harvard University Press, 1995.

Lapidge, Michael, ed. *Columbanus: Studies on the Latin Writings.* Woodbridge, Suffolk: Boydell Press, 1997.

Lawson, M.K. *Cnut: The Danes in England in the Early Eleventh Century.* London: Longman, 1993.

Leyser, Karl J. *Rule and Conflict in an Early Medieval Society: Ottonian Saxony.* London: Edward Arnold Ltd., 1979.

Linehan, Peter and Nelson, Janet L., eds. *The Medieval World.* London: Routledge, 2001.

Löwe, Heinz, ed. *Die Iren und Europa im früheren Mittelalter.* Stuttgart: Klett-Cotta, 1982.

MacCormick, Neil. *Institutions of Law: An Essay in Legal Theory.* Oxford: Oxford University Press, 2007.

Maddox, D. and Sturm-Maddox, S., eds. *Froissart Across the Genres.* Gainesville: University Press of Florida, 1998.

Martindale, Jane. *Status, Authority and Regional Power: Aquitaine and France, 9th to 12th Centuries.* Aldershot: Ashgate, 1997.

McCormick, Michael. *Eternal Victory: Triumphal Rulership in Late Antiquity, Byzantium, and the Early Medieval West.* Cambridge: Cambridge University Press, 1986.

———. *Origins of the European Economy: Communications and Commerce A.D. 300–900.* Cambridge: Cambridge University Press, 2001.

McGlynn, Sean. "Violence and the Law in Medieval England." *History Today,* April 2008: 53–9.

McKitterick, Rosamond. *The Carolingians and the Written Word.* Cambridge: Cambridge University Press, 1989.

———. *Charlemagne: The Formation of a European Identity.* Cambridge: Cambridge University Press, 2008.

———. *The Frankish Kingdoms under the Carolingians, 751–987.* London: Longman, 1983.

———. *History and Memory in the Carolingian World.* Cambridge: Cambridge University Press, 2004.

——— et al., eds., *The New Cambridge Medieval History.* 7 vols. Cambridge: Cambridge University Press, 1995–2005.

Mensching, Günther, ed. *Gewalt und ihre Legitimation im Mittelalter.* Würzburg: Königshausen & Neumann, 2003.

Meyerson, Mark D. et al., eds. *"A Great Effusion of Blood?": Interpreting Medieval Violence.* Toronto: University of Toronto Press, 2004.

Miller, William Ian. *Bloodtaking and Peacemaking: Feud, Law, and Society in Saga Iceland.* Chicago and London: University of Chicago Press, 1990.

————. *Eye for an Eye*. Cambridge: Cambridge University Press, 2006.

————. "Getting a Fix on Violence." In *Humiliation and Other Essays on Honor, Social Discomfort, and Violence*. Ithaca, NY: Cornell University Press, 1993.

Mitchell, Kathleen and Wood, Ian, eds. *The World of Gregory of Tours*. Leiden: Brill, 2002.

Mordek, Hubert. *Bibliotheca capitularium regum Francorum manuscripta. Überlieferung und Traditionszusammenhang der fränkischen Herrschererlasse*. Munich: Monumenta Germania Historica, 1995.

Muir, Edward. *Mad Blood Stirring: Vendetta in Renaissance Italy*. Baltimore: Johns Hopkins University Press, 1998.

Nelson, Janet. "Ninth-Century Knighthood: The Evidence of Nithard." In *Studies in Medieval History: Presented to R. Allen Brown*, edited by C. Harper-Bill, C. Holdsworth, and J. Nelson, 235–66. Woodbridge, Suffolk: Boydell and Brewer, 1989.

Nicholas, David. *Medieval Flanders*. London: Longman, 1992.

Nirenberg, David. *Communities of Violence: Persecution of Minorities in the Middle Ages*. Princeton: Princeton University Press, 1996.

O'Brien, Bruce R. "From Morðor to Murdrum: The Preconquest Origin and Norman Revival of the Murder Fine." *Speculum* 71, no. 2 (1996): 321–57.

————. *God's Peace and King's Peace: The Laws of Edward the Confessor*. Philadelphia: University of Pennsylvania Press, 1999.

Olson, Mancur. "Dictatorship, Democracy, and Development." *The American Political Science Review* 87, no. 3 (1993): 567–76.

Palmer, J.J.N., ed. *Froissart: Historian*. Woodbridge, Suffolk: The Boydell Press, 1981.

Patschovsky, A. "Fehde in Recht: eine Problemskizze." In *Reich und Recht im Zeitalter der Reformation*, edited by Christine Roll, 145–78. Frankfurt: Peter Lang, 1996.

Pearce, John, ed. *Days of Darkness: The Feuds of Eastern Kentucky*. Lexington: University Press of Kentucky, 1994.

Pfister, Christian. *Etudes sur le règne de Robert le Pieux (996–1031)*. Paris: F. Vieweg, 1885.

Poly, Jean-Pierre and Bournazel, Eric. *The Feudal Transformation, 900–1200*. Translated by Caroline Higgitt. New York: Holmes and Meyer, 1991.

————. *La mutation féodale: Xe–Xiie siècle*. 3rd edition. Paris: Nouvelle Clio, 2004.

Potter, David, ed. *France in the Later Middle Ages*. Oxford: Oxford University Press, 2002.

Prinz, Friedrich. *Frühes Mönchtum im Frankenreich. Kultur und Gesellschaft in Gallien, den Rheinlanden und Bayern am Beispiel der monastischen Entwicklung (4. bis 8. Jahrhundert)*. Vienna: Oldenbourg, 1965.

Reinle, Christine. *Bauernfehden. Studien zur Fehdeführung Nichtadliger im spätmittelalterlichen Römisch-Deutschen Reich, besonders in den Bayerischen Herzogtümern*. Stuttgart: Franz Steiner, 2003.

Renna, Thomas. "The Idea of Peace in the West, 500–1150." *Journal of Medieval History* 6 (1980): 143–67.

Reuter, Timothy. *Germany in the Early Middle Ages, c. 800–1056.* London: Longman, 1991.

———, Wickham, Chris and Bisson, Thomas N. "Debate: The Feudal Revolution. Comment 3, Comment 4, Reply." *Past and Present* 155 (1997): 177–225.

Reynolds, Susan. *Fiefs and Vassals: The Medieval Evidence Reinterpreted.* Oxford and New York: Oxford University Press, 1994.

Riché, Pierre. *Les Carolingiens: une famille qui fit l'Europe.* Paris: Hachette Littératures, 1983.

———. *The Carolingians: A Family Who Forged Europe.* Translated by Michael Idomir Allen. Philadelphia: University of Pennsylvania Press, 1993.

Rider, Jeff. *God's Scribe: The Historiographical Art of Galbert of Bruges.* Washington, DC: The Catholic University of America Press, 2001.

Rio, Alice. *Legal Practice and the Written Word in the Early Middle Ages: Frankish Formulae, c. 500–1000.* Cambridge: Cambridge University Press, 2009.

Rosenwein, Barbara H. *Emotional Communities in the Early Middle Ages.* Ithaca, NY: Cornell University Press, 2006.

———. *Negotiating Space: Power, Restraint, and Privileges of Immunity in Early Medieval Europe.* Ithaca, NY: Cornell University Press, 1999.

———, ed. *Anger's Past: The Social Uses of an Emotion in the Middle Ages.* Ithaca, NY: Cornell University Press, 1998.

Schmidt-Wiegand, Ruth, ed. *Die Wolfenbütteler Bilderhandschrift des Sachsenspiegels: Aufsätze und Untersuchungen. Kommentarband zur Faksimile-Ausgabe.* Berlin: Akademie Verlag, 1993.

Shoemaker, R.B. *The London Mob: Violence and Disorder in Eighteenth-Century England.* London: Hambledon, 2004.

Stancliffe, Clare. "Jonas's *Life of Columbanus and His Disciples.*" In *Studies in Irish Hagiography: Saints and Scholars,* edited by John Carey *et al.,* 189–220. Dublin: Four Courts Press, 2001.

Stein, Peter. *Roman Law in European History.* Cambridge: Cambridge University Press, 1999.

Stockstill, Mason. "Officer May Have Feared Man Beaten During LAPD Arrest Was Armed." *The Associated Press,* 26 June 2004.

Strickland, Matthew. *War and Chivalry: The Conduct and Perception of War in England and Normandy, 1066–1217.* Cambridge: Cambridge University Press, 1996.

Sumption, Jonathan. *The Hundred Years War.* Vol. I. *Trial By Battle.* Philadelphia: University of Pennsylvania Press, 1991.

———. *The Hundred Years War.* Vol. II. *Trial By Fire.* Philadelphia: University of Pennsylvania Press, 1999.

Thomas, Hugh M. *The Norman Conquest: England after William the Conqueror.* Lanham, MD: Rowman and Littlefield, 2008.

Van Caenegem, R.C. "Galbert of Bruges on Serfdom, Prosecution of Crime, and Constitutionalism." In *Law, Custom, and the Social Fabric in Medieval*

*Europe: Essays in Honor of Bryce Lyon*, edited by Bernard S. Bachrach and David Nicholas, 89–112. Kalamazoo: Medieval Institute Publications, 1990.

Van Dam, Raymond. *Saints and their Miracles in Late Antique Gaul*. Princeton: Princeton University Press, 1993.

Villalon, L.J. Andrew, and Kagay, Donald J., eds. *The Hundred Years War: A Wider Focus*, History of Warfare 25. Leiden: Brill, 2005.

Vollrath, Hanna. "Die deutschen königlichen Landfrieden und die Rechts-sprechung." *La giustizia nell'alto Medioevo (secoli IX–XI)*, Settimane di studio del Centro Italiano di studi sull'alto medioevo 44, no. 1 (1997): 591–630.

Wadle, Elmar. "Frühe deutsche Landfrieden." In *Überlieferung und Geltung normativer Texte des frühen und hohen Mittelalters*, edited by Hubert Mordek, 71–92. Sigmaringen: Thorbecke, 1986.

———. *Landfrieden, Strafe, Recht: Zwölf Studien zum Mittelalter*. Berlin: Duncker & Humblot, 2001.

Wages, Dan. "Jean Froissart." In *The Late Medieval Age of Crisis and Renewal, 1300–1500: A Biographical Dictionary*, edited by Clayton J. Drees, 169–71. Westport, CT: Greenwood Press, 2001.

Wagner, John A. *Encyclopedia of the Hundred Years War*. Westport, CT: Greenwood Press, 2006.

Wallace-Hadrill, J.M. *The Frankish Church*. Oxford: Oxford University Press 1983.

———. *The Long-Haired Kings, and Other Studies in Frankish History*. London: Methuen & Co., 1962.

Wallach, L. *Alcuin and Charlemagne: Studies in Carolingian History and Literature*. New York: Johnson Reprint Corporation, 1968.

Weinfurter, Stefan, ed. *Die Salier und das Reich*. Sigmaringen: J. Thorbecke, 1991.

White, Stephen D. "Feuding and Peace-Making in the Touraine around the Year 1000." *Traditio* 42 (1986): 195–263.

———. "From Peace to Power: The Study of Disputes in Medieval France." In *Medieval Transformations: Texts, Power, and Gifts in Context*, edited by Esther Cohen and Mayke B. de Jong, 203–18. Leiden: Brill, 2001.

———. "Politics of Fidelity: Hugh of Lusignan and William of Aquitaine." In *Georges Duby: L'écriture de l'histoire*, edited by Claudie Duhamel-Amado and Guy Lobrichon, 223–30. Brussels: De Boeck, 1996.

Woll, Ingrid. *Untersuchungen zu Überlieferung und Eigenart der merowingischen Kapitularien*. Frankfurt: Peter Lang, 1997.

Wood, Ian. *The Merovingian Kingdoms 450–751*. London and New York: Longman, 1994.

———. "The *Vita Columbani* and Merovingian Hagiography." *Peritia* 1 (1982): 63–80.

Wormald, Patrick. "Giving God and King their Due: Conflict and its Regulation in the Early English State." In *Legal Culture in the Early Medieval West: Law as Text, Image and Experience*, 333–57. London: The Hambledon Press, 1999.

———. "Lex Scripta and Verbum Regis: Legislation and Germanic Kingship, from Euric to Cnut." In *Early Medieval Kingship*, edited by P.H. Sawyer and Ian N. Wood, 105–38. Leeds: University of Leeds, 1977.

———. *The Making of English Law: King Alfred to the Twelfth Century*. Vol. 1. *Legislation and its Limits*. Oxford: Blackwell, 1999.

Zmora, H. *State and Nobility in Early Modern Germany: The Knightly Feud in Franconia, 1440–1567*. Cambridge: Cambridge Unversity Press, 2003.

# INDEX

Louis IX, king of France 260
Louis X, king of France 260, 268

MacCormick, Neil 9
magnates
  of early Capetian France 99–100
    violence of 107
  and English civil war 203
  Erembalds as 174–8
  forbidden to pursue war 259
  Frankish 37–8
  power of 151–2
  and rituals 135
Maingot of Metulus 107
Saint Maixent, monastery 106–8
  Albuin (1040) 108
  Hugh VI of Lusignan (1079) 107
  Mascelinus 107–8
  and Peace of God 124
  Walter (1041) 106–7
*mallus* 53–4, 55, 77, 85
  *see also* courts (judicial)
Marcel, Étienne 268
Saint Mary, abbey of Noyers 108
Mascelinus: monasteries, violence and
  107–8
Mathilda, abbess of Quedlinburg
  143–4
Matilda, queen of England 203
Medieval violence 3
  differences with modern violence
    5–6
Merovingians
  attacks on monasteries 45–6
  capitularies of 58–61
  deposed 69
Michael, Bishop of Regensburg 143
Miller, W.I. 7, 20
monasteries
  attacks by Merovingians 45–6
  in early Capetian France
    abbots, monks, as peacemakers 111
    attacks on 100–1, 125
    and Peace of God 116, 123–4
    violence and 106–10, 111–16

*mordritum, morð, morther, murdrator*
  *see* killings: murder
murder *see* killings
*murdrum* fine 199–200

non-violent settlement *see* ritual
    settlements, settlements
normative framework, normative
    culture *see* norms
norms
  defined 9
    explicit 9–10
    implicit 9
    and law 10, 47, 195–7
    and rules 10
  of violence 8–10, 12–13, 17–19,
      288–94
    Carolingian 71, 291–2, 294–5
      in capitularies 58
      of Charlemagne 78
      in early Capetian France 122,
        126–7
      in Flanders 187–9
      in Germany 228
      of honor and vengeance 82
    change in 18–20, 126, 271,
        290–1
    contested 139, 150, 176–7, 206,
        247–8, 262, 289, 293
    in England 197
      royal and local 206, 213,
        215–16
    in Flanders 167, 171, 184, 187–8
      Galbert of Bruges 172–4,
        175–7, 178, 185, 186–7
    in France
      early Capetian 103, 126
        peace councils 124, 127
      Froissart, Jean 262
      and knights 255, 263, 271, 280
      mercenaries, townsmen, peasants
        256
      royal 255–6, 282
    in Germany 246–8
      Thietmar of Merseburg 155–6